THE 16TH
MISSISSIPPI INFANTRY

Flag of the Sixteenth Mississippi Infantry Regiment, Army of Northern Virginia. Handwritten in the upper quadrant is the inscription, "Through God we shall do valiantly for He is that shall tread on our enemies." Photo courtesy of Norman B. Gillis, Jr.

To Grady Tollison, Jr -

With warmest regards,

Robert Evans (signature)

THE 16TH MISSISSIPPI INFANTRY

☆ *Civil War Letters and Reminiscences* ☆

Compiled and Edited by Robert G. Evans

University Press of Mississippi / *Jackson*

www.upress.state.ms.us

Copyright © 2002 by University Press of Mississippi
All rights reserved
Manufactured in the United States of America

10 09 08 07 06 05 04   4 3 2
♾

Library of Congress Cataloging-in-Publication Data

The 16th Mississippi Infantry : Civil War letters and reminiscences / compiled and edited by
Robert G. Evans.
    p. cm.
Includes bibliographical references (p.) and index.
    ISBN 1-57806-486-4 (cloth : alk. paper)
1. Confederate States of America. Army. Mississippi Infantry Regiment, 16th.   2.
Mississippi—History—Civil War, 1861–1865—Personal narratives.   3. United
States—History—Civil War, 1861–1865—Personal narratives, Confederate.   4.
Mississippi—History—Civil War, 1861–1865—Regional histories.   5. United
States—History—Civil War, 1861–1865—Regimental histories.   6.
Soldiers—Mississippi—Correspondence. 7. Soldiers—Mississippi—Diaries. 8.
Soldiers—Mississippi—Biography. I. Title: Sixteenth Mississippi Infantry. II. Evans, Robert G.,
1949– .

E568.5 16th .A23 2002
973.7′462—dc21   2002001737

British Library Cataloging-in-Publication Data available

For Bret, Bethany, Zachary, and Dylan
—so they will know

CONTENTS

Chapter 21
". . . Fort Gregg will never be surrendered"

Chapter 22
". . . the loss of all—save honor"

PREFACE

In this book, the men of the Sixteenth Mississippi Infantry, Army of Northern Virginia, tell their story of their war in their words. And who could tell it better? In their writings, the reader finds flesh and blood men. Men who worry about their families back home; men who get cold and hungry; and men who feel forgotten when family members don't write.

Eyewitness accounts made contemporaneous with the events are the preferred vehicles for relating the Sixteenth's story, and these have been relied on wherever available. As expected, such documents are not always existent. To move the story forward then, it was necessary to resort to other sources, though these sources are a type of eyewitness accounts. Four such sources deserve mention. In *A Historical Sketch of the Quitman Guards, Company E, Sixteenth Mississippi Regiment, Harris' Brigade, by One of the Quitman Guards*, the anonymous author (probably one of the Conerlys) claims to report the company's history, in part from memory, some twenty years after the war. Matters related to the Sixteenth Mississippi while under the command of Brigadier General Nathaniel H. Harris were extracted from the general's book *Movements of the Confederate Army in Virginia and the part taken by the Nineteenth Mississippi Regiment: from the Diary of General Nathaniel H. Harris*, published in 1901. Selections appear from *The Veteran's Story* which relates in the first-person the war-time experiences of Ransom Jones Lightsey of Company F, as told to his daughter. A handful of first-person recollections of Sixteenth members from the book *Reminiscences of the Boys in Gray* (which purport to be eyewitness accounts from Confederate veterans collected by Mamie Yeary) also appear. Though not primary sources, their value here lies in their principal purpose, filling gaps between primary source entries.

Editing has been kept to a minimum. Words have been inserted when inadvertently omitted by the writer and when apparent and necessary for clarity. Such additions are enclosed in brackets. Nothing has been added, however, that would change the tenor, character, or content of any writing, and no "creative non-fiction" strategies have been employed. The words are all theirs, except the introductory paragraphs that precede each chapter. Irrelevant, repetitious, or illegible portions of letters have been deleted and marked by ellipses.

Contradictions and inconsistencies in the entries are the result of the writers' perspectives or interpretations. The reader is left to resolve such seeming contradictions. Endnotes containing substantive information are liberally included. Unless otherwise stated, soldiers mentioned in endnotes are members of the Sixteenth Mississippi.

Three of the four mid-Mississippi counties I serve as circuit court judge sent companies to the Sixteenth Mississippi Infantry Regiment, and my great-grandfather and nine of his brothers and cousins served in Company H. For these reasons, I hold an affinity for the Sixteenth and its men, yet no attempt has been made to glorify them. For better or worse, they are my people. My people by blood and by place. They tell their truth—as defined by their time—in their terms.

Likewise, I have not judged them, nor should they be judged by present-day (though long overdue) sensibilities. They are men from a different time and a different world, and their writings let us visit it. At times, they perform brave, noble, and heroic acts. At times, they commit prejudiced, insensitive, and ugly acts. At all times, then, they are much like we are.

Acknowledgments

This project could not have been completed without the invaluable assistance of the following friends:

Mrs. Robert H. (Martha) Albritton, (great-granddaughter of William Harris Hardy) Jacksonville, Florida

Yvonne Arnold, Archives Specialist, McCain Library and Archives, University of Southern Mississippi

Victor Bailey, Mississippi Department of Archives and History

Stennis L. J. Boykin, Panama City, Florida

Bret Boyles, Alexandria, Virginia

Robert A. Calvert, Texas A & M University

Will D. Campbell, Mt. Juliet, Tennessee

John M. Coski, Historian, The Museum of the Confederacy, Richmond, Virginia

Mrs. Betty Currie, Floyd Robinson Memorial Library, Raleigh, Mississippi

Mary Paula Pitts Evans, my wife and best friend, for her forbearance and support

Ralph L. Elder, Assistant Director, Center for American History, University of Texas at Austin

John Few, *The Smith County Reformer* (for his excellent work on the photos), Raleigh, Mississippi

Clayton and Earl Faggert, Heidelberg, Mississippi

Patricia M. Finley, Mendenhall, Mississippi (God bless her tired eyes)

Donald Firsching, Reference Archivist, Center for American History, University of Texas at Austin

Colonel William Frazier Furr, Montgomery, Alabama

Craig Gill, Editor-in-Chief, University Press of Mississippi

Honorable Norman B. Gillis, Jr. (great-grandson of Fletcher Drake Lewis), McComb, Mississippi

Sheriff Tom R. Green, Louin, Mississippi

Michael Hennen, Special Projects Officer IV, Mississippi Department of Archives and History

Mrs. Judy Herrington, Magee, Mississippi

H. Grady Howell, Jr., Madison, Mississippi

Ted Lighsey, Laurel, Mississippi

Honorable J. Larry Lee, Jackson, Mississippi

John South Lewis (grandson of Captain John South Lewis), Woodville, Mississippi

Mrs. Edwin K. (Margie) Myrick (great-granddaughter of William Harris Hardy), Memphis, Tennessee

Courtney Page, Special Collections, Howard-Tilton Memorial Library, Tulane University

Mrs. Denise Pitts, Morgan City, Louisiana

Honorable Crymes G.Pittman, Jackson, Mississippi

William H. Richter, Center for American History, Reference Archivist, University of Texas at Austin

Honorable R. Jackson Rogers, Morton, Mississippi

Jeffrey S. Rogers, Graphic Records Curator, Mississippi Department of Archives and History

Honorable Thomas E. Royals, Jackson, Mississippi

Richard A. Schrader, Archivist, Wilson Library, University of North Carolina at Chapel Hill

Bill Simmons, Research Assistant, Texas State Library and Archives Commission

Mrs. Glenn (Karen) Taylor (relative of Hugh Carroll Dickson), Terry, Mississippi

Mrs. William C. (Sallie) Trotter, Jr., Greenville, Mississippi

Honorable Eugene C. Tullos, Raleigh, Mississippi

Dr. Bobs Tusa, Archivist, McCain Library and Archives, University of Southern Mississippi

Sarah Walters (great-granddaughter of Ransom Jones Lightsey), Meridian, Mississippi

Paul Walker, Louin, Mississippi
Michael Weinstein, National Park Service, Sharpsburg, Maryland
Bruun Whitehead, Alexandria, Virginia
James Whitehead, Fayetteville, Arkansas
Terrence J. Winschel, National Park Service, Vicksburg, Mississippi

—Robert G. Evans

INTRODUCTION

In 1861, war came to the South, bringing dreams of glory to Mississippi's men and boys. They enlisted by the thousands. Before the war's end, some eighty-two thousand Mississippians would "see the elephant," and their dreams would become nightmares.[1]

Some enlisted in answer to glory's call and others to defend what they saw as an unconstitutional assault on their property rights and their right to live free in a country of their own making. Since the "property" was slaves, planters rightly saw the assault as synonymous with abolition. Additionally, the federal government, controlled by Northern business, placed high tariffs on European goods, then allowed Northern businesses to raise the cost of their goods to match. The North lined its pockets, the South felt, with unjustifiable increased profits at Southern expense. Even though most of these tariffs were repealed prior to Lincoln's election, the damage was done: the South was offended and concluded that the North was trying to destroy the "Southern way of life." Northern attitudes, exhibited in the wake of John Brown's bloody attempt to provoke a slave uprising at Harper's Ferry in October, 1859, entrenched the Southern view.[2]

Despite the fact that only about one-third of the Confederate soldiers came from slave-holding families and could afford little in the way of mercantile goods, whether European or American, yeoman farmers and their sons bought into the notion that the "Southern way of life" was the target of a life-threatening attack. This "way of life," however, was substantially different for the planter than it was for the farmer who worked his own few acres. In fact, a day in the life of a yeoman farmer more resembled that of a field slave than that of a planter. Within a year of the war's first fire, some concluded that it was a "rich man's war and a poor man's fight."[3]

Most Confederate soldiers felt they were fighting for freedom, the second such war fought on American soil. (As irony would have it, it would be just that.) Just as the Founding Fathers and patriots had seceded from the oppressive rule of Great Britain in 1776 and fought for their right of self-government, ". . . so the Southern patriots of 1861 seceded from the tyrannical Yankee empire."[4] They were engaged in a revolution, not a rebellion. As Union soldiers moved onto Southern soil, the Confederate soldier fought for more primal reasons: defense of home and family, the most powerful motivations known.[5]

Recruits were anxious to fight, fearing a quick Union surrender would end the war before they had a chance to show their mettle against the Yanks. As they were soon to admit, that was the least of their worries. The average recruit in the Sixteenth Mississippi Infantry came from a largely rural society, made up of non-slaveholding families living in the "Piney Woods" of South Mississippi. What this recruit lacked in polish, he made up for in sturdiness. More likely than not, he was young and unmarried. His independence and individuality inclined him to an irresponsibility that tried his officers' patience during inactive times. Leaving home light-hearted and confident of quick victory, he grew homesick and war-sick, especially as friends died from disease or wounds and both food and clothing rations grew inadequate.[6]

The Sixteenth Mississippi was an average Confederate unit, made up of ordinary Southern men. But they were ordinary men caught up in extraordinary circumstances, and what they underwent in the war was far from average. They were the only Mississippi regiment to serve as "foot cavalry" with Stonewall Jackson in the famous Shenandoah Valley Campaign of 1862, then fought with him in the Seven Days' Battles near Richmond. After helping capture Harper's Ferry, they marched all night to fight in the "Bloody Lane" of Antietam in September, 1862; were at Fredericksburg in December, 1862; Chancellorsville and Gettysburg in 1863; The Wilderness and in the "Bloody Angle" at Spotsylvania in 1864; defended Fort Gregg on April 2, 1865, and were with General Lee at Appomattox.

These battles are most often thought of in vague terms of tens of thousands of soldiers, moving *en masse* according to the tactics of their generals. The letters and writings of the men, however, are reminders that those who filled the ranks were blood flesh and individuals—individuals who shared the frailties common to all humans. Wars are about ideas—political and religious; battles are about men. The trials and hardships the Sixteenth Mississippi infantrymen endured in and out of battle would seem melodramatic were they not all too real. According to John Berryman Crawford, they went through ". . . enough to kill a mud turtle."[7] Certainly, many of their trials seemed beyond the limits of human endurance, few modern men or women could survive them. Each fought for his own reason, but looking beyond the ideologies and motives to the spirit, the grit of the men must be admired. Finding the odds virtually always against them in numbers, equipment and supplies, they persevered and, in a sense, their spirits prevailed. Remember them for their pluck and valor and because they leave the best of their blood and spirit as a legacy.[8]

THE WRITERS

☆ **Samuel E. Baker, Company D (Adams Light Guard #2), Captain, Major, Colonel**

Thirty-one year-old Samuel Baker was a bookkeeper and pharmacist in Natchez, Mississippi when the war began. Considered a good tactician, disciplinarian, and among the best of the regiment's captains, he was elected major in the spring of 1862 when the Sixteenth Mississippi was reorganized. Baker was promoted to colonel when Carnot Posey became brigadier general in December, 1862.[1]

☆ **Buxton Reives Conerly, Company E (Quitman Guards), Private**

Conerly was born February 5, 1848 (or 1847), near Holmesville, Mississippi, the son of Owen Conerly and Ann Louise Stephens Conerly. He joined the Sixteenth Mississippi in December, 1863 at Orange Court House, Virginia. He is a possible author of the anonymous work *A Historical Sketch of the Quitman Guards, Company E, Sixteenth Mississippi Regiment, Harris' Brigade, by One of the Quitman Guards*.[2]

☆ **Luke Ward Conerly, Company E (Quitman Guards), Private, Sergeant**

The older brother of Buxton Reives Conerly, Luke Ward Conerly was born February 3, 1841. He is also a possible author of the Quitman Guards history.[3]

☆ **John Berryman (J. B.) Crawford, Company F (Jasper Grays), Private**

A farmer from Jasper County, Mississippi, Crawford was conscripted into Confederate service at Enterprise, Mississippi, on January 13, 1863, and reported to the Sixteenth Mississippi on March 18th of that year. He wrote to his wife, Martha and their children, Frances, Laura, Thomas (Tomy), and Josephine.[4]

☆ **Hugh Carroll Dickson, Company C (Crystal Springs Southern Rights), Private**

Hugh Carroll Dickson was born January 29, 1842. His father (Joseph J. Dickson) was a colonel of the Abbeville Dragoons, a South Carolina state militia unit, when he moved his family to a farm near Utica, Mississippi, in 1859. Hugh Carroll enlisted in the Crystal Springs Southern Rights and wrote to his father, mother (Rachael Liddell Dickson) and brother (James L. "Jimmie" Dickson).[5]

Photo courtesy of Mrs. Glenn (Karen B.) Taylor, relative of Dickson.

☆ **Winfield Scott Featherston, Captain, Colonel, Brigadier General**

The youngest of seven children, Winfield Scott Featherston was born in Rutherford County, Tennessee, August 8, 1820. A lawyer, he fought in the Creek Indian War and was elected to Congress in 1847, a seat which he held until his defeat in 1851. He moved to Holly Springs, Mississippi in 1857, where he practiced law until Mississippi's governor sent him to Kentucky as a commissioner to organize the secession movement.

When the war broke out, he captained a volunteer company and was elected colonel of the Seventeenth Mississippi Infantry Regiment while at Corinth. He was appointed brigadier general on March 6, 1862. In the fighting around Richmond in 1862, he led Feather-ston's "Mississippi Brigade," which included the Six-teenth Mississippi, until he transferred to Mississippi in 1863.[6]

Photo courtesy of Mississippi Department of Archives and History and H. Grady Howell, Jr.

☆ Abram Morrell Feltus, Company K (Wilkinson Rifles), Captain, Lieutenant Colonel

Feltus was born in Woodville, Mississippi on Octo-ber 6, 1833, and graduated from the University of Pennsylvania in 1854. He enlisted in the Wilkinson Rifles and was elected its captain after it became Com-pany K of the Sixteenth Mississippi in June, 1861. On December 20, 1862, he was promoted to lieutenant colonel. His friends called him "Dode."[7]

☆ William Harris Hardy, Company H (Smith County Defenders), Captain

Born in Collirene, Lowndes County, Alabama, on February 12, 1837, Hardy was the son of Robert Wil-liam Hardy and wife, Temperance L. Toney Hardy. After establishing Sylvarena School near Raleigh, Smith County, Mississippi, Hardy began practicing law in Raleigh in 1858 and on October 10, 1860, married seventeen-year old Sallie Ann Johnson of Brandon, Mississippi, the daughter of Ellen Weaver Johnson and step-daughter of Thomas H. Johnson.

When Mississippi seceded in January, 1861, Hardy raised a militia company of eighty men, the first in the county to volunteer, calling them "The Smith County Defenders." They became Company H of the Six-teenth Mississippi Infantry.

Hardy's letters are to his wife at their home in Raleigh, Mississippi. At the time Hardy left for service, Sallie was expecting their first child.[8]

Photo compliments of Mrs. Martha Albritton (great-granddaughter of Hardy), Dr. Bobs Tusa and Yvonne Arnold, Archivists, McCain Library and Archives, University of Southern Mississippi.

☆ Nathaniel Harrison Harris, Captain, Lieutenant Colonel, Colonel, Brigadier General

Harris was born in Natchez on August 22, 1834. He received a law degree from the University of Louisiana (now Tulane) and moved to Vicksburg. There, he and his older brother practiced law under the firm name Harris and Harris until May of 1861, when Harris and his state militia company (the Warren Rifles) were mustered into Confederate service. The company would become Company C of the Nineteenth Mississippi Infantry Regiment, with Harris as its captain. Rising through the ranks, Harris eventually became brigadier general of the "Mississippi Brigade," consisting of the Twelfth, Sixteenth, Nineteenth, and Forty-Eighth Mississippi Regiments.[9]

General Harris' reminiscences concerning the Sixteenth Mississippi are extracted from the general's book *Movements of the Confederate Army in Virginia and the part taken by the Nineteenth Mississippi Regiment: From the Diary of General Nathaniel H. Harris.*

Photo courtesy of Mississippi Department of Archives and History.

☆ Jesse Ruebel Kirkland, Captain and Regimental Commissary

From Brandon, Mississippi, Kirkland, originally assigned to the Fourteenth Mississippi Infantry, became the commissary officer for the Sixteenth Mississippi following its organization in Corinth in June 1861. He wrote to Lucinda, his pregnant wife whom he often addressed as "Ma" or "Lucy," and to his brother,

Joseph, showing great concern for his children, Fannie, Joseph, Oscar David, Arsine, and Obed.[10]

Photo courtesy of Mississippi Department of Archives and History.

☆ James Johnson Kirkpatrick, Company C (Crystal Springs Southern Rights), Private, First Sergeant

James Johnson Kirkpatrick, born March 7, 1839, in Indiana County, Pennsylvania, was the son of Presbyterian minister John H. Kirkpatrick and his wife, Jane S. McKee. After graduating Washington and Jefferson College, he joined his older brother to study law in Independence, Missouri, in the fall of 1859, but quickly abandoned his studies. January 1860 found him near Crystal Springs in Copiah County, Mississippi, teaching at a private school. Well educated and religious, Kirkpatrick read both Latin and Greek. He was described as having "a boyish complexion, dark curly hair, sparkling eyes, and an engaging smile." At age twenty-one, the war broke out, and he joined the "Crystal Springs Southern Rights." Kirkpatrick's dry wit is reflected in the diary he kept throughout most of the war.[11]

Photo courtesy of U. Grant Miller Library, Washington and Jefferson College and Terrence Winschel.

☆ John South Lewis, Company K (Wilkinson Rifles), Captain

The oldest of three Lewis brothers who served in Company K of the Sixteenth Mississippi Infantry, John South Lewis was born on December 28, 1837 in Woodville, Mississippi. The brothers' father, also named John South Lewis (1780–1848), served as a colonel in the Seminole War, and their mother, Nancy Thomas Bruce Lewis, met the colonel when she came from Maine to Mississippi to work as a governess.

After attending prep school in Maine, John studied

law at the University of Virginia. He is occasionally referred to as "Bud" in the letters by his brother Harry. His letters, along with Harry's, are to his mother.[12]
Photo Courtesy of John South Lewis.

☆ William Henry Harrison Lewis, Company K (Wilkinson Rifles), Third Lieutenant

Better known as "Harry," William Henry Harrison Lewis, the middle Lewis brother, was born in Woodville, Mississippi, on June 28, 1840.[13]

The third Lewis brother to serve in the Sixteenth was the youngest, Fletcher Drake Lewis, born September 10, 1844 in Woodville, Mississippi. Fletcher was a sophomore at Centenary College in Jackson, Louisiana, when the Civil War began.[14]

☆ Ransom Jones Lightsey, Company F (Jasper Grays), Private

Born near the Pleasant Hill Community of Jasper County, Mississippi, on February 10, 1838, Ransom Jones Lightsey was the fifth of seven sons born to David Lightsey and Mary Loper Lightsey. He enlisted in the Jasper Grays at Paulding, Jasper County, Mississippi on April 27, 1861, and left with them for Corinth on May 21, 1861. His reminiscences are recorded in *The Veteran's Story*.[15]
Photo courtesy of Sarah Walters.

☆ Carnot Posey, Company K (Wilkinson Rifles), Captain, Colonel, Brigadier General

Carnot Posey was born at Sligo Plantation near Woodville, Mississippi, in Wilkinson County on August 5, 1818, the son of Judge John Brooks Posey and Elizabeth Seriven Posey. In 1836, he undertook the study of law at the University of Virginia. Upon his return to Mississippi, he became the "gentleman planter" of Sligo and in 1840 married Mary Collins of

Adams County, Mississippi. Before her death in 1844, she bore him two sons, Stanhope and Jefferson. The elder, Stanhope, a captain, served as his father's assistant adjutant general, and Jefferson, a lieutenant served as aide-de-camp. Following Mary's death, Posey partnered with George M. Gordon in the practice of law.[16]

When the Mexican War began in 1846, Posey enlisted in the Wilkinson Volunteers (also known as the Woodville Volunteers) which became Company B of the First Mississippi Rifles, led by Colonel Jefferson Davis. Lieutenant Posey was cited favorably in Davis's reports of the Monterry battle and the Buena Vista battle, where Posey was wounded. His actions won the special admiration of Davis that continued throughout Davis's lifetime. Following his one year enlistment, Posey returned to Woodville and resumed law practice then was appointed United States Attorney for the Southern District of Mississippi by President James Buchanan. On February 15, 1849, Posey married Jane White of Wilkinson County, and together they had six children.[17]

Called a deeply religious man, Posey converted to Catholicism and was elected Grand Master of the Grand Lodge of Mississippi, Ancient, Free and Accepted Masons in 1854 and served for two years. When Mississippi seceded, Posey resigned his position as U. S. Attorney and was immediately appointed to the same position for the Confederate States by President Davis. He then organized the "Wilkinson Rifles" and, upon his election as captain, offered their services to the Confederate government. When the offer was accepted, the company traveled by train from New Orleans to Corinth, Mississippi.

Posey was described as being ". . . a tall, slender, and strikingly handsome man whose coal black hair and beard and piercing eyes made him conspicuous in uniform." [18]

Photo courtesy of Mississippi Department of Archives and History and H. Grady Howell, Jr.

☆ **Isaac Ridgeway Trimble, Colonel of Engineers, Brigadier General**

Isaac Ridgeway Trimble (1802–1888) was born in Pennsylvania and received appointment to the United States Military Academy from Kentucky, graduating in 1822, seventeenth in class of forty cadets. He resigned U.S. Army in 1842 to become chief engineer and general superintendent of several railroads on the east coast. In August 1861, he was appointed brigadier general in the Confederate Army and in November 1861 took command of the Seventh Brigade (consisting of the Fifteenth Alabama, Sixteenth Mississippi, Twenty-first Georgia, and Twenty-first North Carolina), which he commanded until mid-July, 1862.[19]

Trimble was described as ". . . plain in his dress, quick (and if need be, rough) in his orders, prompt in execution, almost reckless in his courage, and stubborn and unyielding in holding any position assigned him. . . ."[20]

Photo courtesy of the Library of Congress.

☆ **Jefferson J. Wilson, Company C (Crystal Springs Southern Rights), Private**

Twenty-one year-old J. J. Wilson, from Crystal Springs, Copiah County, Mississippi, wrote to his father (James E. Wilson), his brother (John N.), and his sister (Julia).[21]

☆ **Jerome Bonaparte Yates, Company C (Crystal Springs Southern Rights), Private**

Yates was born in Hinds County, Mississippi, in 1841, the son of Ignatius and Obedience Arthur Yates. He was about twenty years old when the war started and wrote to his mother and Marie, his sister.[22]

Photo courtesy of H. Grady Howell, Jr.

THE 16TH
MISSISSIPPI INFANTRY

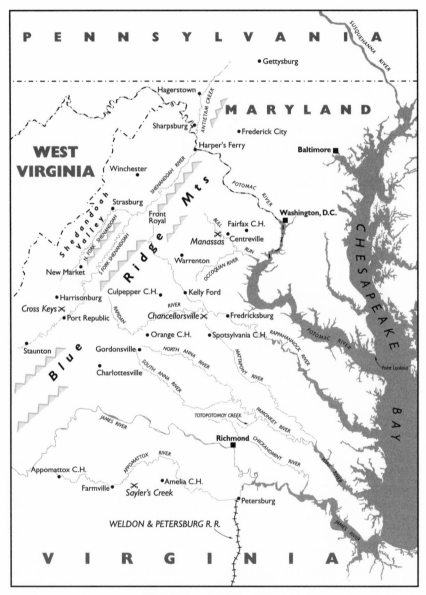

Virginia, 1861–1865

— *Chapter 1* —

"A COMMON ENTHUSIASM AND EAGERNESS FOR THE FRAY . . ."

In the spring of 1861, Mississippi Governor John J. Pettus ordered local militia units to Corinth, Mississippi for muster into the embryonic Confederate States Army. Sent off in the "pride, pomp and circumstance of glorious war," the soon-to-be-soldiers settled into the less than glorious routine and discipline of army camp life.

☆ ***James Johnson Kirkpatrick Diary***, May, 1861:

Among the many bands of volunteers who first responded to the Southern tocsin in the spring of 1861, my fortune was cast with the "Crystal Springs Southern Rights," a company made up equally of Hinds and Copiah County boys and organized at Crystal Springs, Mississippi early in April '61. Our captain was Parson J. C. Davis of Utica, Hinds County [Mississippi]. . . . He faithfully promised all that he would take care of all the boys. . . .[1]

After its organization, the company occasionally met at Crystal Springs for drill and to receive new members until the 23rd of May, '61, when we were presented with a beautiful flag by the ladies of Crystal Springs and vicinity. The occasion . . . was honored by a numerous attendance and fine dinner. The affair was terminated by a ball in the evening at which "all went merry as the marriage ball," notwithstanding during the day a dispatch had been received from Governor Pettus ordering us to rendezvous forthwith at Corinth. This was to us most welcome news. A common enthusiasm and eagerness for the fray seemed to animate all and a rivalry among different organizations who should be first in the field. . . . No one entertained a doubt of our final success. . . .[2]

We reassembled at Crystal Springs on May 25th and embarked on the New Orleans and Jackson Railroad in route for Corinth. . . . But few who were present, and had tears to shed, failed shedding some that day. The closing acts were a most fervent and appropriate prayer . . . and indiscriminate shaking hands. We then filed into the cars and rolled off. All along the way, we were greeted by the waving of handkerchiefs, hats, miniature flags and by vociferous cheering. . . .

Reached our place of rendezvous at eleven o'clock a.m. May 26th. Our new mode of life was very new to us. Sleeping on the ground with nothing but blankets was not very pleasant. We experienced that every substance at our command was harder than our heads. Pillows would have commanded good prices. We soon got wall tents, one for each mess of eight. The more industrious . . . put up arbors, made seats, tables, and cooking utensils. Haversacks, knapsacks, and canteens were duly distributed around, the later inferior in material and structure.

One serious disadvantage to us at first was not knowing how to cook properly. Our rations were varied and abundant, and after experience had given us many lessons in the culinary department, we could have feasted in luxury from what our commissary supplied us. Yet had it not been for the many boxes of "nice things" sent from home, we would have thought our fare exceedingly bad. Our rations consisted of bacon, flour, sugar, coffee, rice, beans, molasses, vinegar, soap, candles, etc.

Our camp duties at first seemed very arduous. Rising so early for roll call, doing guard duty, etc., but especially drill merited extreme dislike from all. But we were in school learning these evolutions, that "confidence in the touch of elbows," that capability of endurance, without which soldiers cannot be effective. . . .

☆ *Jerome B. Yates to Mrs. Obedience Yates:*

May 27, 1861

Dear Ma,

I've arrived safe at this place and was regular mustered into the minutia of a soldier's life. There is fifteen hundred men here. Companies are coming in every hour. I have seen everybody I ever saw before. I get along very well with the boys. There is eight in our mess, namely, Kirkpatrick, Myers, Cy, Tom, Throgmorton, Mimms, and Bolls. . . . I never expected to see as many men together as I have seen here. Of a night, it looks like it is five thousand lights. . . .[3]

You can see men doing everything imaginable, some playing the fiddle, some dancing, playing cards, fighting chickens, doing everything. Joe liked to of cut a man's throat. Write soon up here,

Jerome

☆ *Jerome B. Yates to Mrs. Obedience Yates:*
Corinth, Mess Number 6, June 2, [1861]

Dear Ma,

As today I have time, I will write you a letter as I have only written notes before. . . . There is some talk of us leaving next Wednesday but there is no telling. There is no dependence to be put in anything we hear, some seems to think there will be no fighting at all. . . .

I am getting stronger every day. In two months, I will be as fat as anybody. We got a box of provisions from Crystal Springs day before yesterday. We have done very well since that came. . . . If it was not for Mac Mimms, I do not know what we would do. He is the only one in this mess that knows anything about cooking. He does it all. We have commenced camp life in earnest now.[4]

I dreamt last night that I was at home. I was the happiest boy in the world. The other morning I waked up and heard a pack of dogs running. I thought it was Tom Murphy until I got awake. Tell me what has become of all the dogs, and tell Tom Murphy to write to me.

The rules are very strict up here. We are not allowed to go out of camp without permission from the captain. All have church today. A few of them remain to write home like myself.

The expenses of this mess for the last week was thirty-five cents apiece. We bought . . . butter, eggs, cake, and a few other articles. We have not done any washing yet. We have hired it all done. So far, we give forty cents apiece for shirts, pants. All smaller things are thrown in.

Tell Pole Yates to write, tell them all to write. Tell Tom Murphy to take good care of my dogs. Tell him I expect to get back home.

Jerome

☆ *William Harris Hardy to Sallie Johnson Hardy:*
Camp Clark, Corinth, Mississippi
June 2nd, 1861

My Dear Sallie,

This will inform you that I arrived safely at this place on yesterday with my company all in fine health and spirits, except a little diarrhea, headache, etc., caused from fatigue and the use of lime water. . . . Three deaths occurred here yesterday, one being shot accidentally, second drowned and the other died of dysentery. . . .

We will probably remain here four to six weeks when we will be sent to Union City, Tennessee, there to be prepared to meet the Army of Republicans now concentrating at Cairo.

My love to all. Be of good cheer, my dear, for I will be with you again. I will probably send Brother Tom home next week to bring our new recruits. Please have me, if you can, two checked linen shirts made to send me. Your dear husband,[5]

William Harris Hardy

☆ *J. J. Wilson to John N. Wilson:*
Camp Clark, Corinth, Mississippi, June 14th, 1861

Dear Brother,

I take the present opportunity of informing you all that I am well at present, and I hope to remain so while beyond the limits of Copiah County, and I hope that these few lines will find you all enjoying the same blessing. There is not much news a-stirring here as we are not allowed to go to town without a pass from the captain. I want you to give me the news in general, what everybody is doing and thinking about the war question, how crops are and how you are getting along with the grass, how cotton and corn looks, and when you will have ripe watermelons.

I received a box of provisions yesterday. Everything was good except the cornbread which was spoiled. If they send any more, they need not put in any cornbread as we have plenty of meal all the time. I was glad to get the peas and apples if there had been a few more.

I do not know when we will leave nor where we will go. We may stay here two weeks or maybe not more than three or four days. We cannot calculate far ahead now a-days.

There was two men to be hung in or about Corinth (taken as spies), but I do not know whether they were hung or not.

I have nothing more at present but will close hoping that you will write soon. Give my love to all. I remain, your brother,

J. J. Wilson

☆ *Jesse Ruebel Kirkland to Lucinda Kirkland:*
Corinth, Mississippi
June 16th, 1861

My Dear Wife,
I have been very sick. The fourteenth, I was compelled to be on duty—and the sun being so very warm I was fearful of a setback, but fortunately I escaped and am now improving though weak. I am growing leaner every day but hope . . . to be as fleshy in a short time as ever. (Not quite so much so as you are at present.)[6]

Oh, Lucy, if I could see you and the children if but a half an hour. What is [it] I would not give, but tis at present impossible. It's hard, but I must grin and bear it. . . . Kiss all the children a thousand times a day for me and [tell them] that they must be good and obedient while I am away. Good night. The boy has just done bathing my feet, and I must go to bed as I am weak and tired. Good night—a thousand kisses for you. Your affectionate husband,

Jesse

☆ *James Johnson Kirkpatrick Diary*, June 17, 1861, Monday:

We made our regimental organization, and our captain being third senior, our position was right center of [the] color company and our letter "C." The regiment was numbered and styled "The Sixteenth Regiment, Mississippi Volunteers." Field officers elected were colonel, Carnot Posey, captain of Company K; lieutenant colonel, Robert Clarke, captain of Company D; major, [Thomas Jefferson] Bankston, lieutenant of Company F. Soon after, T. R. Stockdale, lieutenant of Company E, was elected to fill the vacancy occasioned by the resignation of Major Bankston.[7]

The companies forming the Sixteenth Mississippi Regiment were:

A = Summit Rifles—Captain Blincoe
B = Westville Guards—Captain Funchess

C = Crystal Springs Southern Rights—Captain Davis
D = Adams Light Guards—Captain Baker
E = Quitman Guards—Captain Matthews
F = Jasper Grays—Captain Shannon
G = Fairview Rifles—Captain Moore
H = Smith County Defenders—Captain Hardy
I = Adams Light Guards—Captain Walworth
K = Wilkinson Rifles—Captain Feltus.[8]

There was considerable sickness in Company C at Corinth. Measles and diarrhea were most annoying. The latter doubtless owing to bad water and unhealthy diet.

☆ *Harry Lewis to Mrs. Nancy Lewis:*
Camp Clark
June 26th, 1861

Dear Mother,
I sent you a letter per P. G. Feltus . . . and . . . as I feel in the mood for writing, I intend speaking a few words with you, dear Mother, through medium of pen and paper.[9]

Philip, the barber, brought our colonel his horse, and yesterday evening Colonel [Posey] mounted on his newly-bought steed and clothed in his flashing gray uniform with his tri-cornered continental hat, distinguished afar by a waving plume of red, came on parade, I suppose, for the purpose of showing off, but I think the horse is not as fine an animal as could be, nor that he is as fine a colonel as Jeff Davis was in Mexico.

Dear Mother, I told you in my last [letter] that I intended to run for third lieutenancy. Well, I did run and made an awful race of it, and you know that Gad Feltus was elected over all the candidates, and Jeff Hamilton came out second best, but I did not mind it, for I anticipated the result of the election. Bud, as you know, gained first lieutenancy, elected unanimously. . . .[10]

There are a great many sick in the regiment and numbers in our own company. The disease is the measles, and I am happy to say that all our cases are in a fair way of recovering. I do not know, dear Mother, whether I ever had them or not—have I? Considering everything, I think that your three sons are healthy, for though we at times have complained a little, still there has been no laying up for any length of time with anyone of them, a fact which can be said of but few in camp. . . .

I have no idea when we will get off, nor do I believe anyone else in the company or regiment does know, not even the colonel himself in all his *wisdom* and *foresight*. Evident it is, however, we will be off as soon as there is need for more soldiers. Our destination doubtless will be to Missouri.

I went to church Sunday, or rather to the church, for I went to two different ones and heard a part of two sermons and an exhortation. Camp is a bad place for religion it is true, but, dear Mother, it is not so bad as I expected. I try to do the best I know how, and though that is not the best in the world, still I know it is not what characterizes the actions of an evil boy. . . .

Your own son,
Harry

☆ *Jesse Ruebel Kirkland to Lucinda Kirkland:*
Corinth, Mississippi
June 27th, 1861

My Dear Wife,
. . . There is . . . a report in circulation here that we will certainly have marching orders by Saturday next. We only hope it may prove to be correct. Our destination will, I presume, be Missouri. . . .

I am getting as fat as I was a year ago but awfully sunburnt. I can eat more than I ever did. One o'clock, the dinner hour, seems a long time coming. If I was not so black, I would have my daguerreotype taken and sent you with all my military doings on. If you insist upon having it, I will send it. We have to wear our uniforms all the while by express order of the general—and I assure you that I have suffered from heat—almost roasted some days.

Oh, Ma, what is it I would not give to see you and the children? If it were but just an hour, but fate has willed it otherwise. If it is possible to get off you may look for me. Shall I send the picture? You will laugh at the color of it for I assure you I am as black as an Indian.

Kiss all the children for me. Tell Joseph and Fannie and Obed I will write them in the morning, tell Arsine and Jesse to kiss you for me. . . . I enclose a little letter for Oscar. Good bye, Ma. Write me. A thousand kisses to you. Your affectionate husband,

Jesse

☆ *William Harris Hardy to Sallie Johnson Hardy:*
Corinth, Mississippi
Monday, July 22nd, 1861

My Dear Sallie,

I received your favor of the 19th instant yesterday and was truly glad to hear from you and that you were well. We will undoubtedly leave here in a few days, perhaps for Tuscumbia and perhaps for Virginia. I can't tell, but we will be certain to leave for some point. . . .

Dear, be certain to save your money. I gave you nearly all I had so that should I be so unfortunate as to fall in this war, you have at least money enough to last you one year anyhow. I know that the poor widows of our state, under the probate law, stand a poor chance for support till the effects go through the court. But I do not feel that I will fall in this war. We have right on our side, and "He who tempereth the wind to the shorn lamb" will protect us. We have just received the confirmation of Beauregard's great victory at Manassas. It sent a thrill of joy and a shout throughout our camp. . . .[11]

Goodbye. May God bless and protect you. Your devoted husband,

W. H. H.

☆ *James Johnson Kirkpatrick Diary*, July 28, 1861, Sunday:

We received orders to move on 25th July. Owing to our immense quantity of luggage, we did get off until the morning of the 26th. . . . We embarked on the Memphis & Charleston Railroad not knowing our destination to a certainty, but would bet at great odds in the probability of going to Virginia. We passed through Iuka this evening . . . also through Tuscumbia, Alabama, where the ladies welcomed us en masse . . . and reached Chattanooga on the morning of the 27th. Here we changed cars, taking the train for Knoxville. . . .

☆ *Historical Sketch of the Quitman Guards:*

The regiment arrived at Cleveland, Tennessee about ten o'clock in the morning of the 28th. . . . Many citizens gathered around the cars, cheering the soldiers and calling on the officers for speeches. Captain Hardy of the Smith County Defenders responded and delivered a touching address to the assembly, after which a voice was heard calling the name of Major Stockdale, and immediately the name . . . was shouted by a thousand tongues. He arose from his position on the top of the cars and, looking around at the vast concourse of men and women and . . . said: "Fellow citizens of East Tennessee and you, too, my fellow soldiers. War is upon us—its dread tocsin has been sounded throughout the length and breath of the North American continent. In the wilds of Mississippi it has reverberated; it has re-echoed from hill to hill; nor has it sounded in vain—like knights of liberty, the sons of Mississippi have rushed from their comfortable homes to see what that alarm meant. Twas war's dread alarm. They believed their rights and their liberties would be invaded, and they have defiantly buckled on the sword; and there is not a throbbing heart in the breast of one of its hardy sons but that is resolved to do or die. You see before you, fellow citizens, specimens of these determined men." He enumerated in a brief and eloquent manner some of the causes which induced the two sections to take up arms against each other and portrayed the horrors that always follow a civil war. During his speech, the utmost stillness was preserved, and at its close a deafening applause . . . proceeded from the assembled multitude.[12]

☆ *William Harris Hardy to Sallie Johnson Hardy:*
Knoxville, Tennessee
July 28th, 1861

My Dear Sallie,
We are now amongst the Union Tories of Tennessee and have been on our guns all the time. We have with us forty thousand rounds and are ready for a fight, though we will not have one here. The people treat us very kindly here. Secession flags wave over the whole town. I spoke . . . to four thousand people at Cleveland. I was called out and got on top the cars. Major Stockdale spoke.

I left seventeen sick men at Corinth. . . . I hated to do it but could not help it. I left them all crying. The boys that are with me are well and in good spirits. Tom and Henry are well. . . .[13]

My love to all. God bless you.

W. H. Hardy

☆ *James Johnson Kirkpatrick Diary*, July 31, 1861, Wednesday:

Arrived at Lynchburg, Virginia . . . [and] went into camp near the fairground, two miles from town. . . . Much trouble in keeping the soldiers from going to town and getting drunk. Very strict guard lines kept up around the regiment and a police guard sent to town daily from each company to arrest and bring back their errant numbers. . . .

— *Chapter 2* —

"WHAT THE YANKEES DON'T KILL
WILL DIE OF DISEASE . . ."

Arriving in Virginia anxious for a fight, the men of the Sixteenth marched, camped, and waited near the Manassas battlefield. There, they first saw the real consequences of war, stood guard, and took their turn on picket duty. Enthusiasm remained high, as they organized, practiced artillery battles, and moved about as if on "a great chessboard."

In October, the Sixteenth took its first tour of picket duty, being assigned to reconnoiter and locate Union positions. As they passed General Johnston's headquarters in Fairfax Court House, he was heard to remark that they were the "finest looking men" he had seen and that they would soon "stir up a fuss." They did.[1]

☆ **J. J. Wilson to John N. Wilson:**
  Lynchburg, Virginia, August 6th, 1861

  Dear Brother,
  I take the present opportunity of dropping you a few lines to let you know that I am well at present, and I hope that these few lines may reach you all enjoying the same blessing of life. I would have sent you a letter before, but the mail was stopped for a few days on account of the abolitionists finding out what was going on, nearly all of East Tennessee being abolitionist. There is Federal volunteers being formed near Knoxville. We lay over at that place

about twenty-eight hours and met with great pleasure at that place. The ladies visited our camp and gave us three of as good a meals as I have eaten since I left. We had a jolly time of it all the way on the road except in East Tennessee where Old Uncle Abe has a good many friends. At one . . . station on the road where there was a company of "Rebels," as they call us, there was one man died in two minutes after taking a drink of whiskey. There was a great many pretty young ladies on the road seeming to sympathize with the soldiers. There was more in a little town called Tuscumbia, Alabama than I ever saw before.

I used to call Mississippi a hilly and rocky country, but when I passed through Tennessee there was some places that was nothing but rocks. I saw where they tended hills that was steeper than my hill at home and rocky accordingly. I never saw any level land after the Alabama line until we reached Virginia. We passed some mighty good land in Alabama. Corn crop promising abundant harvest. There is plenty of wheat made up here to supply the southern states. . . .

Give my love to all relations and friends. Write as soon as you get this.

J. J. Wilson

☆ *James Johnson Kirkpatrick Diary*, August 10, 1861, Saturday:

Arrived here [at Manassas] Saturday at noon. A camp site was selected for us about a mile southeast of the station. . . .

☆ *Jesse Ruebel Kirkland to Lucinda Kirkland:*
Eight o'clock at night, August 11th, 1861, Manassas Junction, Virginia

My Dear Wife,
Your kind and esteemed letter of the 31st ultimo came safely to hand and, Ma, tis useless for me to attempt to describe that feelings of pleasure it gives me to receive one of your letters. . . . I was glad to know you were all in good health and that you were in good spirits, talking as all good high minded and loving wives and mothers should. This outrageous and uncharitable war was brought upon us by Lincoln and his minions, but the Almighty Wise and Good is with us, and ere long, we will with His aid drive them from our soils and with such vengeance that they will never again dare to set foot upon our soils in a hostile way.

The wagons intended to move our regiment arrived late this evening. This looks as if they did not intend letting us remain here long. I hope not, for the nearer we approach Washington, the more anxious we are to see the enemy. In truth, our boys are more than anxious to have a chance at the enemy. Most impatient set of fellows you ever saw.

We are two miles from Bull's Run. . . . Captain Hardy and myself will visit it tomorrow if it is not raining as it is now. There are, as well as I can ascertain, thirty thousand troops on this side of the run and a great many more on the opposite. We can see thousands of soldiers in every direction while on dress parade of mornings and evenings. . . .

I saw General Johnston and his lady today. He is an ordinary sized man, about 135 pounds, about forty-nine years of age. I should think his whiskers and mustache slightly gray or white, a quick piercing eye, and every inch a soldier. His wife, ordinary size, rather good-looking, dark hair and eyes, a great talker. . . .[2]

You speak of the pepper sauce and good pickles. My dear wife, you know how I would appreciate them. If I had the former with you to make one of your stews for me tonight, I would get up in the morning well of my cold. Yes, you without the stew, to nurse me, would be the best cure. Oh, Ma, if I had millions, I would give all to be with you tonight. How silly for me to write in this strain where this is impossible, but, Ma, I cannot help it when alone at night in my tent. What else have or can I think about but you and the dear little ones?

Will write you tomorrow, Fannie next day. As usual, a thousand kisses to all. My respects to your father. Good night, my dear wife. Adieu, I go to bed to dream of you. Your affectionate husband,

Jesse R. Kirkland

☆ *James Johnson Kirkpatrick Diary*, August 12, 1861, Monday:

On Monday, August 12th, permission was granted those desiring it to visit the battlefield of Manassas. Having many others, I embraced the opportunity. . . . Leaving camp soon in the morning, we struck the battlefield near the Henry House. . . . Late in the evening, we returned to camp tired and hungry and our curiosity entirely satisfied. Its chief characteristics are a sickening, saddening spectacle of ruin and desolation. Various articles of a soldier's uniform and equipment, trees chequered by Minie balls and flawed by shot and shell. Fencing leveled as by hurricane. . . .[3]

We received our first cartridges, twenty rounds to each [man]. We were armed with muskets. Our cartridges contained a ball . . . and three buckshot. . . .

☆ *J. J. Wilson to John N. Wilson:*
Manassas, Virginia, August 15th, 1861

Dear Brother,

I take the present opportunity of dropping you a few lines to let you know that I am well at present, and I hope that this may reach you all enjoying the same blessing of life. . . .

I was out . . . on [the battlefield] Monday viewing the ground over. . . . There was about fifty dead horses in about one hundred yards square and plenty of Yankees graves, some of them with their feet out of the ground and others with hands [sticking] out. I saw where there had been fighting in a pine thicket, and all the pine was shot to pieces. Some of tops shot off and all. Every tree in the thicket had some balls in them.

We are expecting a fight every day. We are ready for them any time they wish to come.

We stayed in Lynchburg ten days. We lived fine while we were there. We could get plenty of fruit and vegetables. Up here, we cannot get a thing except a few roasting ears of corn, and then you have to steal them. I have not eaten any since I left Corinth. Corn is hardly in roasting ears yet, but the corn is fine all the way long the road and plenty of wheat for Uncle Abe to starve us on.

I have nothing more at present. Give my love to all connections and inquiring friends and the girls especially. Write as soon as you get this and . . . tell others to write. . . . I remain, your brother,

J. J. Wilson

☆ *Hugh Carroll Dickson to Joseph J. Dickson:*

Dear Pa,

I wrote yesterday and . . . have concluded to write again. . . .

I think the next place of attack . . . will be Alexandria. It will be a hard-fought battle. The Yankees fight well, there is no mistake of it. As long as we will stand off and shoot at them, they will fight well, but as soon as the command "charge bayonets" are given and the Southern boys get to sticking them, they are for getting away from there. . . .

I must close. Give my love to all the children. You and Ma write soon to your loving son,

Hugh

P. S. William is quite well and gives his love to his mother. He says he intends to fight the Yankees, but he wants to stand off and look at them fighting, and if he thinks that he will not get killed, he will fight. Write soon to your son,[4]

Hugh

☆ *J. J. Wilson to James E. Wilson:*
Manassas Junction, August 18th, 1861

Father, Dear Sir,

I take the present opportunity of dropping you a few lines to inform you that I am well at present, and I hope that these few lines may find you all enjoying the same blessing of life.

As I am wanting some clothing, I want you to send me two pair of pants, two pair flannel drawers, one gray overshirt, and two pair of socks, and send me a good pair of winter boots if you can get them, about number eight. . . .

It is very bad weather up here. It has been a raining for two or three days and still raining and cool enough to sleep under two or three blankets. Provisions is getting very short. Coffee cannot be had, candles and soap also. We get Mississippi pork, fresh beef, rice, sugar, and flour is our living. I am cooking for myself at this time with four others in my mess. . . . We are first-rate cooks. We can beat half of the Copiah [County] girls now.

Write soon. Give my love to all. I remain, your affectionate son,

J. J. Wilson

☆ *Jesse Ruebel Kirkland to Lucinda Kirkland:*
Camp Pickens, Virginia, Sunday night, August 18th, 1861

My Dear Wife,

I had this pleasure yesterday. I have nothing in the world in the way of news to communicate except the rumor is rife among the "Knowing Ones" that it will not be ten days before the greatest and hardest fought battle ever fought on the Western Continent will come off. I can only say that appearances and preparations seem to justify the predictions. We must have a battle before many days, and beyond a doubt it will be on the north side of the Potomac. (Our forces are ready and can cross at almost any point ordered.) What an army, well equipped and contending for their firesides. Ma, they are compelled and obliged to be successful. Our boys are growing impatient for the battle. . . .

Will write you as usual (every day). Oh, heavens, Ma, what would I not give to be just where they are tonight instead of sitting up all night in this dirty slow rain. But tis impossible. So good night again. God bless you, dear Lucy. Kiss all a thousand times and, Ma, write me. Your devoted husband,

the drum beats again for me—

Jesse

☆ *Jerome B. Yates to Mrs. Obedience Yates:*
Manassas Junction, Virginia, August 20th, 1861

Dear Ma,

As I have such an opportunity as I am not likely to have again, I will drop you a few lines. . . . I am in very good health and spirits. . . . Since I came up here, a letter from home is the most welcome thing a soldier can get.

I suppose you want some news about the war, but I am not in possession of any. . . . The only thing we know for certain is that we whipped the Yankees here not long since, and you know that. Of course, we hear a thousand things a day, but there is not any dependence to be put in anything we hear. I expect you all are just about as well posted as we are. A private in the army knows less than anybody. We heard that McClellan was across the Potomac with fifty thousand men advancing on us, and the next news was that he was ten miles the other side of Alexandria. So all reports turn out. . . . Some say we will be at home, others that we will spend the winter in Washington. For my part, I do not pretend to say. I had as soon believe we will be at home by winter as in Washington. We will not fight any more until the North can collect every man she can hope to muster, and then the thing will end in one big battle. . . .[5]

Tom's Negro is sick but is getting better. Some man has gave him a double barrel gun, and he says he intends to kill a few Yankees with it.

The only papers we ever see is some Richmond papers and books. Ward sends Captain Davis a bundle of news occasionally. Speaking of Captain Davis, he is doing a great deal better since he came here where he cannot get any dram. He is too good when he is tight. He lets us do as we please when he is tight, but when he gets sober he makes up for it.

You have to excuse my short letter, as I have to go to breakfast or I will not get any.

Jerome

☆ *William Harris Hardy to Sallie Johnson Hardy:*
Manassas, Virginia, August 21st, 1861

My Dear Sallie,

After a long and anxious period of one month, I received your letter of the 4th of August. . . . You may rest assured that I was proud of the unaccustomed visitor who brought tidings from my dear now more than fifteen hundred miles from me.

I have for the last five or six days been gloomy and dull. A dark and somber cloud seems to hover over my spirits and darken the bright sky and sunshine of happiness and contentment. Anything would be a relief to me, and I would hail an order to meet the enemy in deadly combat with pleasure. This sad yet desperate feeling has been produced by a combination of causes. First, this place, though it has in and around it 125,000 troops, yet it seems isolated as we see none but our own regiment scarcely and won't till we are brigaded. Hence there is a monotony about the camp that is really irksome. Second, it has rained here for ten days and the mud is shoe-mouth deep in our street. Third, I had to perform sentry in this rain and mud as Officer of the Day, being up at night and which threw me into a fever, and I am now reported on the sick list though I am up. . . .

It looks like my company will never get well. . . . You may say what you please about men who follow agricultural pursuits standing a campaign better than others, but it is all a hoax. They are the ones that are most sick. They are used to regular habits and mode of living, hence can't stand the sudden and numerous changes incident to camp life. Besides, most of my company are young indiscreet boys that have no care for their health. All these things tend to make me low-spirited, but I presume when we get a little nearer the enemy, as the prospects for an engagement brighten, these dark clouds will be dispersed.

Although your letter was gladly received, yet you didn't give me much news. What about affairs in Raleigh? . . . Write me all about these things but don't, my dear, write me about the scandals those vile hellions are circulating about me. You know that being here I can't help myself, and they only tend to make me cross and ill-humored without giving me the opportunity of avenging myself. Then everything you write let it be good. I hope to return when this war is over, and then I will set things to rights.

I am very anxious to know if you received the money I sent you . . . it was a part of my pay. I will get some more soon and will send you what I can spare. I want you to keep it, use what you want for your comfort, the balance take care of till I come back. . . . Dear, write to me every week for it is a source of great pleasure. In fact, it is the only pleasure I have. . . . Give my love to all. Goodbye. May God bless you.

W. H. H.

☆ *James Johnson Kirkpatrick Diary*, August 26, 1861, Monday:

We moved our camp to Pages Land, distant eight miles north of Manassas. The march occupied nearly a day and was very tiresome. We were not accustomed to marching. . . . At this place we are first formed into a brigade with the Fifteenth Alabama, Twenty-first North Carolina, and Twenty-first Georgia Regiments under General George B. Crittenden of Kentucky. . . .[6]

☆ *Jesse Ruebel Kirkland to Lucinda Kirkland:*
Sunday morning, August 26th, 1861, Camp Pickens near Manassas Junction

My Dear Wife,
I wrote you day before yesterday and then gave you all the news. Yesterday [two of] my friends came over to see and take dinner with me. The dinner they got, and a very good camp one it was. I had nice beef, stewed chicken and rice (well-cooked). Cold leg of mutton, tomatoes, cooked and raw roasting corn, the nicest honey and butter I have seen anywhere. . . . The truth is the army and those attached are living in this part of the state better than anyone. The reason is obvious. The country had not been ravaged by the Yankees, and the Confederacy feeds on the best bacon, beef (salt and fresh), Irish potatoes, rice, coffee, sugar, molasses, and flour just from the mill.

While writing, Ma, the sound of the drum and fife are getting very indistinct. Twelve thousand troops have left in the last twenty-four hours from this immediate locality, all going towards Alexandria. A fight must come off in the next twenty-four hours. The enemy are in full force, and the two armies for twenty-eight miles or more, up and down the Potomac . . . not more than two miles apart. Hence the collision must come and this speedily. Our troops . . . are crazy to meet them, and I tell you from my knowledge of men, you will have a good report of the Sixteenth. We are all in high spirits, and we know we will have a fight in less than forty-eight hours. . . .

Good bye, Ma. Oh, Ma, how I would love to see you and the children once more. A thousand kisses to all. Ma, good bye. God bless you a thousand kisses. Make my innocent namesake pay them. Adieu till tomorrow. Your affectionate husband,

in a hurry,
Jesse

☆ *Jesse Ruebel Kirkland to Lucinda Kirkland:*
Pages Land, Prince William County, September 1st, 1861

My Dear Wife,

Your kind and affectionate letter was received this evening . . . and Ma, you can better imagine my feelings than I can describe them, to know that our dear little babies were sick and I far away and not be able to hasten home and nurse them or at least assist and relieve you from your nightly vigils, particularly at this time. I can imagine how lonely you must be all alone, sitting by the bedside and watching the pulsations of our dear little ones. How often you wish for one that is absent. Oh, my dear Lucy, how quick should that wish be gratified if it were possible. But, Ma, it cannot be so, but let me urge you, Lucy, not to be imprudent and over-task yourself. Do trust some of the watching and nursing to some of the kind ladies you speak of, for you know in your situation the least imprudence might result in your making yourself so very ill as to be unable to give them any attention. I hope, however, the dear little ones have recovered ere this. Ma, did not Arsine's brain fever proceed from her going bareheaded? Oh, how I would like to see her tonight and hear her quarrel . . . about washing or hear her and the others talking after going to bed, which I have so often scolded them for. Would be a pleasure which I cannot promise myself for sometime.

I am still suffering from colds and cough but hope in my next [letter] to say

I am entirely well. In truth, I never was in better health aside from this trouble-some cough. . . .

All the troops in and about Manassas Junction, save a few thousand, have marched forward and tis impossible to say with any degree of accuracy their whereabouts. Everything is kept in the dark. So much so that we do not know who are in our immediate neighborhood. We are assured that our stay is a very short one, and our boys are in the highest spirits.

Good bye, Ma. Many loves to you, and the speedy recovery of our little ones shall be my prayer tonight. Your affectionate husband,

Jesse R. Kirkland

☆ *J. J. Wilson to James E. Wilson:*
Camp Beauregard near Manassas, September 3rd, 1861

Father, Dear Sir,

I received your letter on yesterday and was glad to hear that you were all enjoying good health. I am well at present, and I hope that these few lines may reach you all enjoying the same blessing of life. We have moved . . . from where we first camped out near a place called Gainesville. . . . Now we have to travel afoot and pack all of our things, which will make a fellow very tired of march-ing all day.

I am getting very tired of my living. We have nothing hardly but flour, beef, sugar, coffee, and rice. We have to drill six hours a day and then set up until nine o'clock at night for roll call and up at four in the morning and half the privileges that the Negroes have down there. We cannot leave the regiment to go anywhere without a pass, and if we are not back in time we will have to go on extra duty for twenty-four hours. I have not been on extra duty yet nor has none of the officers spoken a cross word to me yet, and I hope that they will not have to.

Give my love to all relatives and friends. . . . I remain, your son,

J. J. Wilson

☆ *William Harris Hardy to Sallie Johnson Hardy:*
Camp Beauregard, Pages Land, Virginia, September 4th, 1861

My Dear Sallie,

I just wrote to you a few days ago . . . and I know you wouldn't care if I wrote to you every day, besides I want to set you an example which I hope you will follow and that is to write two or three times a week. . . .

I had a terrible dream last night about you that made me feel very bad for a time till I realized the fact that it was a dream. I thought I returned home, and you received me cooly, and immediately afterward, I thought you got in a buggy with a young man and left in a gay and fastidious manner. And my heart became sad. I concluded to follow on and did so, and when I arrived at the party you were apparently in a fine glee, entertained by two nice-looking gentlemen. You still wouldn't notice me. My heart sunk, and the tears gushed forth from my eyes. I thought you observed me crying, and told me that I brought it all on myself and that you left me and rejoined your two favorite beaux. I became enraged and determined to settle the matter. I got my double barrel shotgun heavily loaded, and after killing both the young men, I drew a dagger and determined to terminate your life and my own with the same knife at the same time. Before executing this horrible deed, I awoke. My mind was contorted, my whole physical frame convulsed, and I almost crazy. I raised up on my cot, looked around and satisfied myself it was but a dream and, you may depend on it, I was relieved. I can't imagine why I had such a dream, unless it was from having talked with Griffith that night about how his wife had acted. Besides, I was tired and worn down, completely exhausted from a long and tedious drill. Although I *know* such a thing never will occur, and that it was a mere dream, the offspring of a heated and confused brain. Yet God forbid that I should ever dream it o'er again. . . .[7]

Take good care of yourself, my dear, for God knows you are my only source of happiness, and were it not for you I would recklessly thrust my life in the thickest of the fight regardless of consequences.

We are now drilling every day, and everything has become so monotonous that I frequently become low-spirited and gloomy and earnestly seek a change. Even a fight would be an agreeable change. . . .

May God bless you, my dear, and keep you safe til I return. Yours devotedly,

W. H. Hardy

☆ *Jesse Ruebel Kirkland to Lucinda Kirkland:*
Centreville, Virginia, September 15th, 1861, Sunday

My Dear Wife,
I have just returned and find our camp all commotion. We have orders to march in a moment's notice. Tents are now rapidly being taken down and packed, and we suppose we will have marching orders in an hour. We go

towards Alexandria, where we will doubtless have the big fight and prove as ever, victorious. . . .

Monday morning, daylight

We are already on the march for Fairfax Court House, where we will encamp tonight. The women and children have all been ordered to leave. Hence there must be a fight and that speedily. Our regiment this morning numbers nine hundred seventy-three privates and non-commissioned officers. I assure you a more gallant set of fellows are hard to find. All in high spirits, and I am confident will do some hard fighting if they get an opportunity.

My dear wife, good bye. God bless you and the dear little ones is my earnest and constant prayer. Oh, for one parting embrace this morning with all I hold dear on earth. A thousand loves to you and the babies. . . . Good bye, adieu, my dear and affectionate wife. Your affectionate husband,

Jesse R. Kirkland

☆ *James Johnson Kirkpatrick Diary*, September 16, 1861, Monday:

Broke up camp and marched through Centreville, taking the good roads toward Fairfax Court House. Cannonading in front and some excitement, supposing that an engagement was opening. But ere long, all is quiet. The cannonading was perhaps occasioned by some artillery companies practicing. At least, I could never learn any other cause for it. We reached Fairfax Court House in the evening and went into camp after a march of eight miles. . . .

☆ *James Johnson Kirkpatrick Diary*, September 18, 1861, Wednesday:

Under marching orders this morning. Formed and started back towards Centreville. Struck camp after marching three miles. A very fine situation, denominated Camp Toombs, in honor of General Toombs of Georgia, whose brigade was encamped close by. . . .[8]

☆ *J. J. Wilson to James E. Wilson:*

Camp near Centreville, September 22nd, 1861

Father,

I take the present opportunity of dropping you a few lines to let you know that I am well at present. . . . I received all of the clothes that you sent me.

. . . Clothing is mighty high up here, about three times as high as at Crystal Springs. If you can get a chance to send me some flannel drawers, I would like for you to do so, as I can not get them here, and I cannot stand it up here without, as it is getting cold up here. I was on guard last night, and I had two coats and was cold.

As for a fight, I do not know when there will be any. They may be fighting now, as I have heard some twenty guns fired since twelve o'clock and still continue to fire in the direction of Leesburg. We are about twenty-five miles from the city of Washington. . . .

The health of the regiment is tolerably healthy at this time. There is but six or eight sick in our company. I will close as I have nothing more at present. Give my love to all relatives and friends. I remain, your son until death,

J. J. Wilson

☆ *Jesse Ruebel Kirkland to Lucinda Kirkland:*
Near Camp Toombs, Virginia, Tuesday, September 25th, 1861

Dear Lucy,

I am on my horse writing on the top of my hat just having met the mail carrier. . . . I was fool enough to go to the river, strip myself, and bathe. As I was dressing, the Yankees discovered me and commenced shooting at me. Fortunately, they shot wild but, Ma, I must confess, I put my coat on in a hurry. My horse traveled some two hundred yards faster than ever before.

God bless you and the babies. I will write as soon as I get in camp. Goodbye. Your husband,

Jesse

☆ *Jesse Ruebel Kirkland to Lucinda Kirkland:*
Tuesday morning, 6 a.m., September 26th, 1861, Camp Toombs, Virginia

My Dear Lucy,

We received an order to cook three days' provisions and be ready to march to Manassas at a moment's notice. Our camp was all commotion. In a few minutes, fires were made, and every one of the men were cooking in double-quick time. We are all ready to march, only awaiting orders.

My dear wife, why is it I get no letters from home? It is all of a week since I received a line from home, notwithstanding I write almost every day, in truth, every day. Ma, I made you two remittances, one of one hundred dollars and the other of fifty dollars, which you should have received about the 20th or 22nd instant. I am anxious to hear if it went safe. I will continue to remit for I know you need money, and I have no use for it here, unless I should get sick and have to go to a private house, which I certainly shall do if I am so unfortunate. . . .

Goodbye. God bless and protect you and the babies. I kiss you and the babies adieu. Your affectionate husband,

Jesse

☆ Friday morning, September 27, 1861

My Dear Lucinda,

We are still here awaiting orders to move forward. . . . It rained all night and is still raining very hard, and though quite cold, I have on a shirt, my two heavy flannels, my uniform coat and overcoat. . . . I still feel chilly. If my decanter was not empty, I should certainly take a toddy.

Ma, I am very lonesome today. Everybody housed in their tents, and there is nothing to do while raining. I'm thinking of you and home. Dreaming, as it were, both night and day, of you and the little ones and knowing too that tis utterly impossible for me to see you. Still cannot help feeling melancholy and sad, particularly when I have not heard from you for so long a time, when at this particular time above and all this I should receive news from you regularly. For heavens sake, Ma, make someone write. . . .

God bless you and the children is my prayer. I kiss you and the children adieu. Your devoted husband,

Jesse

☆ *William Harris Hardy to Sallie Johnson Hardy:*
Camp near Fairfax Court House, Virginia, October 9th, 1861

My Dear Sallie,

I received your letter of the 29th about an hour ago and hasten to reply as we have just received orders to go forward tomorrow morning to the front, and perhaps before this reaches you, we will have engaged the enemy. They have been fighting now for two days with artillery. Its roar has been terrible. We have been sleeping on our guns ever since last Saturday, expecting every moment when the order would come for us to go forward. At last it has arrived. Our mission, though, will be that of picket duty on the outposts, which is very hazardous. I think the great day to decide the fate of this great army is near at hand. Soon we will know our fate. The Yankees are crossing in three columns at Sieversville, Long Bridge, Chain Bridge, and at Occoquan Creek. So you see, they will engage our whole front, and we will have hot work of it. Though I have not ever entertained a single doubt as to our success—Victory! Victory! will be the cry.

I do feel so sorry for my men. We are ordered to leave our tents, baggage and everything but our arms, a blanket and haversack, and half of my company haven't a coat to their names, and we are having very cold weather. Heavy frosts whiten the ground every morning, and now they have to sleep out on the ground covered with heaven's broad expanse with no coat on, wrapped in a thin blanket. What the Yankees don't kill will die of disease or return home with broken constitutions. What a pity the people of Smith County were so slow. If they had sent the clothes here by the first of October, how many glad and happy hearts would then have been in our company. I told them to begin to get ready before I left. My men are bareheaded, and God knows what I am to do. I have been relying on the government, but it seems a bad chance or at least a slow one. . . .

You would hardly know me, moustache and whiskers up so. If alive, I will visit you in December. My love to all. Good bye, my dear, take care of yourself.

W. H. Hardy

☆ *Jesse Ruebel Kirkland to Joseph Kirkland:*
Camp Toombs, Virginia, October 10th, 1861

Dear Brother,
Your kind and highly esteemed favor has just been received. . . . I have no news to communicate of interest except that our regiment has just started to Fairfax Court House, being ordered to report to General Longstreet. We will then be in six miles of the Yankee pickets and as their forces are rapidly coming over on this side of the Potomac, you may hear of a battle before this reaches you.[9]

Our regiment is said to be the healthiest in this division. One thing I do know, I am feeding nine hundred non-commissioned officers and privates and never have at any time fed more than 1,033. We have over one hundred sick and convalescent at Warrenton, many of whom will rejoin us day after tomorrow. Our boys are in the highest spirits and anxious for a fight, and my candid impression is their anxiety will soon be gratified.

I was proud to know you were all so well at home and Lucy doing so well. My health is as good as it ever was. In truth, camp life agrees with me, and I would be entirely satisfied if I could only see my family occasionally. My love to all and a thousand kisses to dear wife and babies. Your brother, in haste,

Jesse

☆ *James Johnson Kirkpatrick Diary*, October 10, 1861, Thursday:

Our regiment went on picket at Annadale and Accontick Creek. Company C on duty the first night. Dark, rainy, and disagreeable. With five others, I was on one of the infantry outposts at an old barn to the left of the pike going to Annandale. We kept ourselves well on the alert and did our duty so well that it would have been very difficult to have surprised us. Two stood duty at a time, while the others took shelter in the barn. We were somewhat excited at one time by a cow grazing in dangerous proximity. By reserving our fire, we found that our enemy was inoffensive. . . .

☆ *James Johnson Kirkpatrick Diary*, October 12, 1861, Saturday:

Company C again took the front, keeping the same picket posts as before. With a detachment of Company A and forty of our company under Major Stockdale, we made a reconnaissance in order to surprise and capture some Yankee cavalry that had been seen at Pohick Church. Not finding them here, we pushed still further on immediate guidance of our intrepid captain. After double-quicking two miles or so through the woods, we did surprise a party of the enemy at the Paget house. Fired a volley into them with some damage, at which they broke and scampered off like a flock of sheep. Pursuit was inaugurated, but our prudent major called us off—maybe wisely, too. Scarcely a shot was returned and none of us injured. Nothing else of interest marked our first picket tour. . . .

☆ *Hugh Carroll Dickson to James L. "Jimmie" Dickson:*
Camp near Centreville, Virginia, October 1861

Dear Brother,

I now take my seat to write you a few lines, thinking that you would be pleased to hear from me. I have very little news to communicate that would interest you. . . . We had to retreat from Fairfax Court House. . . . The enemy are advancing on us. They are near Fairfax, distant from here only eight miles. We are expecting an attack very soon. It is reported that three hundred of the enemy's cavalry advanced up into the town. . . .

I was on picket last week, went out on Thursday and got back in Tuesday evening. I slept very little for five nights. Had no tents to cover us. It rained on us very hard one night. The next morning after the rain was very chilly. The drum beat before daylight, and we had to bounce up and get our guns and cartridge boxes and fall into line, but no Yankees came. Our officers would not let us have no fires for fear that the Yankees would throw bomb shells into our camp. The Yankees were shooting at our pickets every chance they could get, and our pickets would return the fire. The enemy drove back our cavalry pickets about a quarter or half mile. The captain of the cavalry company . . . came down to where we were posted and . . . went to Colonel Posey who sent word to [Captain J. C.] Davis to take some of his company and drive them back. I, with thirty others of the company, volunteered my services. We went . . . and remained until daylight, but behold, the Yankees had fled precipitately. . . .

On the thirteenth . . . our company went out scouting, came across a company of Uncle Abe's children numbering seventy-five or eighty men, pitched into them, killed and wounded fifteen of them. They only fired on our company once, and then they fired while running from us. The place where our company fired on them was not more than one-fourth of a mile from their camp. . . .

The fortifications in and around Manassas are impregnable. Before the Yanks can take that place thousands of them will bite the dust. The cannons are pointing in every direction. There is no avenue by which the enemy can approach without exposing themselves to a raking fire. There is troops enough here to whip all Uncle Abe's children that will be sent against us.

At this point, I think we all get plenty to eat, get beef, flour, rice, sugar and coffee, get as much bull beef as we can eat. I have eat so much of that article that I do not think that I can face a cow when I get home.

There was fine corn crops made in this part of Virginia, but you would not believe how it has been destroyed by the soldiers and horses. War desolates any country. There is a great many houses here that have been deserted by their owners and have gone to waste. You may go to houses here and the people will look like they were frightened, have very little to say to you. The fencing has been pretty much destroyed. I do not think the people can ever get rails enough to fence in their farms. Timber is very scarce here. The country is very much worn out.

There was a Virginia girl fell in love with me the other day while on picket, Miss Mollie Summers. We were posted right at the house. The boys would go in the house and try to get milk. She would always refuse to give them any. Your brother would go around and talk to her a while and ask her for some milk. She would go off and get it but tell me not to tell the other boys. She told me that she wanted to go down to Mississippi. She is a great little girl!

Jimmie, you must excuse all mistakes and write soon. Give my love to all of the family. Reserve a large portion for yourself. Your brother,

Hugh C. Dickson

☆ *James Johnson Kirkpatrick Diary*, October 16, 1861, Wednesday:

Daylight revealed our army, which had been scattered every where between Centreville and Fairfax Court House. This was the first strategic retrograde movements of General Johnston. . . . Our army now commences digging. This perhaps may be a part of military tactics that it is necessary to learn. Our lessons are more practical than theoretical. . . .

☆ *William Harris Hardy to Sallie Johnson Hardy:*
Camp near Centreville, Wednesday, 17th October 1861

My Dear Sallie,

I received your letter of the 9th instant this evening and was glad indeed to hear from you and especially that you were in such good health. I would tonight give anything in the world to see you. . . .

We have retreated to this point . . . and the Yankees are advancing in large force from two directions. They are now at Fairfax Court House, a beautiful little village. We passed through it day before yesterday evening, and it was indeed a heart-rending scene. I could scarce keep from crying when I saw so many of the fair and lovely daughters of the Old Dominion in tears. Woman's tears to me are more powerful than the sword or cannon. . . .

I am glad you are so fat and in such good health. I weigh 165 pounds and except the dysentery which I had for three weeks, my health is very good. The health of my company is good. . . .

My love to all the family and my devoted affections and prayers for your dear self. Good-bye.

W. H. Hardy

☆ *Harry Lewis to Mrs. Nancy Lewis:*
Camp near Centreville, October 18th, 1861

Dear Mother,

Perhaps you may wonder why I have not written sooner, but I am telling the truth when I say I have not had time. We have been moving. . . . We were the guard in face of the Yankees for five days, returning on the fifth and that same night retreating here to this camp, five miles from the former.

We are about three miles from Bull Run where, if the enemy follows, we will give them battle. But no one knows the full import of this retrograde movement, and there are a thousand different interpretations of it. All we know is we, the center division, have moved back ten miles and that there are about thirty-six thousand troops around here and upwards of forty thousand back towards Manassas to support us. We are camped within ten feet of the turnpike road from Manassas, and you can form no adequate idea of the continued bustle, immense and innumerable baggage wagons, the heavy rumbling of artillery followed by long files of men pour along in a continuous stream intermingled with passing horsemen on prancing steeds. . . .

I am doing well excepting a tolerably bad cold which has fallen in love with me and seems to be gifted with the virtue of constancy. I stood the march very well with the exception of a little soreness of feet. Fletch has a sore under-lip and little cold. Bud is well. I am pleased to say to you that Posey is more popular and has improved since we were at Corinth. . . .

Doctor Holt came in camp this evening . . . anticipating a battle. But we will not have a fight before a week, I think, so Doctor Holt won't have a chance to chop our legs and arms for sometimes. The fact is, our army is maneuvering and so are the Yankees. We constitute a part of the great chessboard, and it depends upon the skill of the players, Davis and McClellan, whether we shall be victorious. It is reported that the enemy are also retreating, but I hardly think so. . . .[10]

I am glad to say Fletch has acquired no injurious and pernicious habits . . . and he has grown taller. I weigh 146 pounds, more than I ever did before. . . .

Dear Ma, I have written all I know and am quite tired of using my pen. I wish it were possible to use my tongue in a little conversation with you. So goodbye, Dear Mother. I hope to see you soon.

Your son,
Harry

— *Chapter 3* —

"WE . . . FEAR NO DANGER"

Late October found the Sixteenth waiting in fortifications near Centreville, Virginia, watching the Federal army on the opposite side of the Potomac and expecting an attack every moment. A victory at Leesburg raised the tide of Confederate confidence and optimism but little eroded chronic homesickness. Illness, an early winter (by Mississippi standards), and preparations for winter quarters offered the only relief from camp monotony.

☆ *Jesse Ruebel Kirkland to Lucinda Kirkland:*
Camp near Centreville, Virginia, October 21st, 1861

My Dear Lucy,

Ma, I am lying on my cot while I write, where I have been since the night of the 17th. I wrote Fannie I was fearful of rheumatism again but am glad to say tis only in mild form. Nothing but my left foot and knee swelled, but I tell you, dear Lucy, I have suffered intensely with my leg and foot although I had all the attention and kindness that I could desire both night and day. I have thought of and missed you all the time (no nursing like yours).

Captains Hardy, Davis, Shannon and, in truth, all the officers, as well as many of the privates, have kept my tent crowded night and day and our surgeon never more than half an hour at a time away from me, and, my dear wife, I am more than glad to tell you that I am now this morning entirely free from pain and the swelling almost gone. . . . For three nights, I had to take quite a

32

quantity of morphine to make me sleep, but, thank heaven, I am as well, you may say, as ever. . . .

Among other nurses that I had was a boy I have bought conditionally. I got him low, he is very likely, slick, black, six feet high, nineteen-years old, obedient, good boy, good cook, washes my shirts, drawers, stockings, etc., as well as I ever had them washed. . . . The conditions upon which I bought him are these. If he runs away, I pay nothing. If not, one thousand dollars. I go to see his mother, brother, two sisters eleven miles from here on the Potomac as soon as I get out, which will be tomorrow or next day. I am offered . . . these four for sixteen hundred dollars making in all twenty-two hundred dollars. . . . Ma, don't tell any one of this but Brother Joseph, for I intend buying a good many of them and don't want any interference or bidders against me, as there certainly would be if known I can buy on my own time. The owners are frightened and, in truth, I believe in some instances a little Yankeeish.

Goodbye, a thousand loves and kisses to all. Will send a name for baby soon. I kiss adieu. Your devoted husband,

                                                                                    Jesse

☆ *J. J. Wilson to John N. Wilson:*
Warrenton, Virginia, October 22nd, 1861

Dear Brother,
I take the present opportunity of dropping you a few lines to let you all know that I am in tolerable good health at this time, and I hope that these few lines may reach you all enjoying the same blessing of life. I read your letter about two weeks ago, but I had the fever and was not able to answer it. I have been away from the regiment about two weeks. I have been at the hospital down here at Warrenton, but I shall return to my regiment in three or four days.

We are expecting a large fight now. Every day our forces have fallen back to let the Yankees cross the river. Our company got into a little skirmish with a company of Yankees, and we killed seven and wounded about fifteen. There was not anybody hurt on our side.

We can get plenty of apples by paying a cent a piece for them and as for chestnuts, we can go out in the woods and pick up as many as we want in half an hour. We can get grapes of all sorts and quantities. I have missed the fruit very much while I was sick. We cannot get any watermelons nor peaches up here. I have not eat but one watermelon this year. I have had a few little knotty peaches, but a hog would hardly eat them.

I have nothing to write about, as we cannot go anywhere to hear anything. We have to stick close to our work. We are bound down ten times more than the Negroes are down there. We have to drill four times a day and most of the time in a trot at that. We have to trot for half an hour at a time before we will stop. We have fought several sham battles with our artillery, learning how to maneuver when there is cannons about.

Nothing more at present, but you must write as soon as you get this, and let me know how you are getting along. Give my best respects to all relatives and friends.

J. J. Wilson

☆ *James Johnson Kirkpatrick Diary*, October 22, 1861, Tuesday:

Tidings received of another victory of our arms at Leesburg. It seems that a heavy movement was contemplated in that direction by the Yankees and that crossing was effected. They were met . . . driven back to the river, and nearly all killed, wounded, and captured. . . . This completely checked the contemplated advance from that direction. The Federals are perhaps beginning to think that "On to Richmond" is a hard road to travel. . . .[1]

☆ *Jesse Ruebel Kirkland to Lucinda Kirkland:*
Glorious Glorious!
Camp near Centreville, Virginia, October 22nd, 1861

My Dear Wife,
. . . On the 20th instant, we heard in the evening very heavy cannonading in the direction of Leesburg. Yesterday morning we had a courier whose dispatches told of the engagement at that place and the complete rout of the infernal Hessians.

Our forces were Evans's Brigade, composed of the Thirteenth, Ninth, and Eighteenth Mississippi Regiments and one small Virginia regiment. (Mississippians commanded by Colonels Barksdale, Featherston, and Burt.) The fight commenced at two p.m. and lasted four hours. . . . Captain Singleton tells us that it was a hand to hand fight for one and one-half hours. Charge after charge was made. . . . Running, the devils would be reinforced but could not stand still, and all finally fled. Some of them say our folks do not fear either bullet or steel. Jayne was hit by a spent ball which fortunately did not hurt him. He commanded his company all the while. He had two of his men killed and several wounded. Our loss in all was seventy, Colonel Burt was severely wounded. . . .[2]

We are expecting marching orders every moment, everything is ready. They are concentrating in large numbers there. . . . We are in readiness, and you cannot imagine how eager they are to meet the Yankees, which I hope will be soon for I am confident we will send them into winter quarters. . . .

God bless you and the babies. Adieu. Your affectionate husband,

Jesse

☆ **William Harris Hardy to Sallie Johnson Hardy:**
Camp near Centreville, Virginia, November 9th, 1861

My Dear Sallie,

It has been some time since I wrote to you, and I know you are getting uneasy about me. I would have written but have been so busy here for the last ten days that I scarcely have time to write. Your last letter . . . I received a letter a week ago while out on picket. We were out five days, two and one-half of which my company stood without relief, and it rained and stormed most terribly for two days and nights. We were in it all with no tents. We had to cut logs or poles and put them together and get up on them to keep out of the water, and then it turned off cold, freezing, but thanks to our friends, we had clothes that were warm.

About the clothing, it all came safe. My coat is so small I can't wear it. You must have thought that soldiering diminished my body while it lengthened my legs, as my pants are about three inches too long and fit me like a meal bag. You sent me nothing that I can appropriate but the flannel drawers and shirts with which I am highly pleased. I gave one pair of my pants to Captain Kirkland. I wear the other pair rolled up and, of course, make a fine appearance on dress parade. But I know, my dear, you done the best you could, and hence I make no complaints. My boots I couldn't wear and immediately sold them. I wish you had sent me some overshirts—colored, for deliver me from white shirts in camp, nobody to wash them, nor iron or starch. The pickles, pepper sauce, etc., wasted out the bottles, breaking some of them. The jelly came safe.

My shoes I haven't seen as the box that was lost just came to hand this evening. I presume they are in it.

Tom's coat fits like a blanket around the neck, the collar continually contending with the cap for the supremacy over the head, but to take the company all over, I am admirably well pleased with the clothes. My men suffered intensely from cold before we got them. I gave out getting them and became disheartened so much so that I refused to go out on drill with my company for a week. It would make your heart ache almost to hear them coughing at night, but they are improving very fast now, and I have fewer sick than anytime since the first of September. One poor fellow of my company died yesterday. . . . His name was Cornelius B. Lancaster. He died of typhoid fever.[3]

You have doubtless heard of the fight at Leesburg. The Eighteenth Regiment, Mississippi, won unfading laurels in that engagement, but they did it at the loss of their gallant Colonel Burt. Poor fellow died bravely and gallantly. I think Mississippi ought to erect a monument to his memory. . . .

My dear, write me twice a week from this on. I don't know how you are getting on, nor when you will be sick. Keep me posted, as I wish to be with you if possible. I feel great anxiety about you for you are all I have to live for outside of my aged parents, and they have two besides me to care for them. The happiness which I will enjoy when I meet you again will be worth an age to me. . . . I believe you will pass the ordeal [of pregnancy] safely, but still I feel uneasy till it is passed, then you can be happy with a dear little pledge of affection to entertain you in my absence.

May God bless you. My love to all. Goodnight. Your affectionate husband,

W. H. Hardy

P. S. I have opened the box and tried my shoes. They are too short, they hurt my toes.

☆ *J. J. Wilson to James E. Wilson:*
Centreville, November 19th, 1861

Father, Dear Sir,

I take the present opportunity of dropping you a few lines to let you know that I am well at present . . . I received the box that you send me about ten days ago. The potatoes were all sound and good, but some of the turnips rotted and liked to ruined one sack of peaches. The paper and other things were safe.

It is getting very cold up here, and we will soon have to go into winter quarters. We do not know where we will go to take winter quarters. There is several of our company sick, most of them have bad colds and mumps. I had the mumps about two weeks ago, but I am well now.

Things is powerful high up here. We have to pay about four prices for anything. Butter three and four bits a pound, eggs three bits a dozen, chickens from three to five bits apiece. They are trying to get all the soldiers' money. . . .

Give my love to all. I remain, your son,

J. J. Wilson

☆ *William Harris Hardy to Sallie Johnson Hardy:*
Camp near Centreville, November 21st, 1861

My Dear Sallie,

Your long looked-for letter . . . came to hand last night, and although I wrote to you yesterday, I will write you again today as I am "Officer of the Day" and have a little leisure this evening. After having policed the camp, had the streets swept out, the tents raised and aired, dismissed my "fatigue detail" with "I'm much obliged to you, gentlemen, for the manner in which you have performed your duty," I have leisure for the balance of the evening till dark when I have to inspect the guard and see that the countersign is properly out.

I have no special news to write concerning the army. We are lying here behind our fortifications, waiting for the Yankees to attack us, which I am beginning to believe they will never do. They know full well that when they do defeat, aye, an utter rout, of their grand army will ensue. We are in hearing of their guns and have been for the last six weeks, and while out on picket, we could distinctly hear their drums, and one night I could distinctly hear their brass band from my post. Our generals expected an attack this week, and we may have it, but I think it very doubtful.

We have around us and in our midst, the constant booming of cannon, musketry, drums, fifes, brass bands, musters, dress parades, and grand reviews until they are as common as sunshine and produce but little effect upon the soldiers. In fact, it is recreation to get where you can't see a camp or a soldier. A citizen in our camps excites as much interest as a dress parade, and I fear that if our army is kept here inactive this winter, it will tend greatly to demoralize it. Even the officers are growing dissatisfied, and, in fact, several resignations have taken place already, and I expect many more this winter unless some plan of giving leave of absence be adopted. There is scarcely a company in our regiment left what have some complaints or murmurings against their officers.

The health of my company is improving rapidly. The mumps have disappeared, I believe entirely. I did not have them. The yellow jaundice then became epidemic, that is now subsiding. I think it is for the want of vegetable food. We have lived on beef and flour bread for the last four months, having one day's ration of bacon out of seven. Molasses every other week, four days' rations. . . . The whole country is devastated for miles around, and nothing but soldiers are to be seen.

I haven't seen a woman in such a long time that I would hardly know to what species of the *Genus Animalis* she belonged. I did see a mortal ugly snuff-eating Irish washerwoman holding a pair of soldier's breeches while he ran a foot race for $25. He lost the race, and when he returned, she gave him his trousers with "Oh, bad luck to the day when ye lost the race." I presume she was the Irishman's wife and acts as a laundress in the regiment.

My own health . . . is excellent. I still have a light and constant diarrhea, but it does not deplete me. In fact, I am fatter perhaps than you ever saw me. I guess I would weigh near 170 pounds. . . . As for clothing, you needn't make me another stitch till I come home. . . .

Give my love to all. Your affectionate husband,

W. H. Hardy

☆ *Jesse Ruebel Kirkland to Master Joseph Kirkland:*
Camp Centreville, Virginia, November 22nd, 1861

My Dear Son,

I am indebted to you several letters which I could not well avoid. I wrote to your sister yesterday, your mother the day before. I have nothing new to relate. One day we hear the Yankees are advancing and the next they are not, and we are at a loss to know what to believe.

My son, you cannot imagine what a source of gratification it was to me to learn from your Ma that you were studying so well and I only hope, Joseph, you will continue to do so and that we see that decided improvement and advancement there certainly will be when I come home, which will be during the holidays if I can possibly do so. You must be a good boy and always obey your mother. I was up above our camp yesterday looking at the fortifications and witnessing their target shooting with rifles and cannons, which was very rapid and accurate, shooting at the rate of five times for the minute. While on top of the works during the firing I thought often of you, Obed, and Oscar, wishing you were up there with me. However, you all would have looked on with joy and amazement, the drums, fifes sounding all around, the constant roar of the cannons, the neighing and prancing of artillery and other horses, and as far as the eye could reach in any direction, nothing but the white tents to be seen. I could but think were you there that you would never get through telling all you saw and heard.

You must write me when you can, and I will try and not be so negligent in the future. Kiss and love your dear Mother for me and all the children. Tell your Uncle Joseph I will write him in the morning, though he rarely ever writes me. Tell Obed, I will write to him. He must learn to write to me. I am very sorry to hear of his having chills. Tell him he must get well and beat you studying.

Kiss all for me. Goodbye. Your affectionate father,

Jesse R. Kirkland

☆ *Jesse Ruebel Kirkland to Lucinda Kirkland:*
Camp E. K. Smith near Centreville, Virginia, November 24th, 1861

My Dear Wife,
. . . We had a very heavy snowstorm last night, and while writing, I see outside of my tent nothing but snow. Tis bitter cold this morning. Fortunately for me, I had yesterday a detail of men (Sunday though it was, though a soldier knows no Sundays) and had me a neat rock chimney built which does finely. I never saw one draw better. . . .

This morning our division, commanded by E. Kirby Smith, all have to turn out at eleven for general review. Our brigadier general, George B. Crittenden, has been promoted to major general and left us to take command in Kentucky, where his father, John J., and brother are at the head of troops against us. Our brigadier, who made his appearance this morning, is named Trimble. . . .[4]

I have not received a letter from home in a week, have you all forgotten to write?

I hear there will be no trouble about my furlough, I only hope and pray it may prove so. Goodbye. Kiss all for me, a thousand loves to you all. I kiss you goodbye. Your affectionate husband,

Jesse R. Kirkland

☆ *William Harris Hardy to Sallie Johnson Hardy:*
Camp near Centreville, Virginia, November 26th, 1861

My Dear Sallie,

I am in receipt of your letter of the 14th and as is my custom, answer it immediately. I have nothing of interest to write you. The cry is we will fight this week, or next week, but I still hold to my opinion that we will have no general engagement here unless the Lincoln fleet should obtain some great victory on some of the Southern coast. We are anxiously awaiting the news of the results of the engagement at Pensacola. I confidently expect by tomorrow's mail to hear that Fort Pickens [Florida] is ours. If so, McClellan will perhaps attack us here to cover the loss there by a great victory here. But if he does, we'll give his vile Hessians the worst whipping they ever had. We are strongly entrenched here and now fear no danger.

It is rumored that our regiment will be put in a brigade of Mississippians and sent to Occoquan, which is south of here on the Chesapeake Bay. I hope we may, for I am heartily tired of this place. Besides, we'll have plenty of oysters there. . . .

☆ November 27th, 1861

Dear Sallie,

I couldn't finish my letter but will conclude it today as I am "Officer of the Day" again. All the captains are sick but four, and hence my time comes on pretty often. . . . It is now sleeting and snowing, the weather is miserably cold. We have to sit by the fire wrapped up all the time, and when we drill, we "double-quick" all the time to keep warm. Yet the soldiers stand it without much murmuring. We will have to go out on picket again in a day or two, and then we'll catch it. You know we are not allowed even tents on picket. We have to make shelters or bunks out of brush and build a fire in the center. If it rains, we stick up four sticks and fasten each corner of a blanket to a stick and get under that. . . .

Oh, my dear, I want to see you so much now. I would give anything to be with you from now till after your confinement. I dream of you every night of the world and am in constant suspense about you. I am so fearful that something will go wrong. I would be perfectly happy if you had safely passed the ordeal. . . .

☆ November 28th, 1861

My Dear,

. . . We have . . . been ordered to be ready to march at a minute's notice. We are expecting an attack every minute at Leesburg or Occoquan, and as we are in the reserve, we will have to go to either place if we are needed. So you needn't be surprised to hear of our being in a fight at any time. I shall leave for home in about three weeks, but you must continue to write to me regularly twice a week. I get your letters in nine days, generally, after they are written.

Goodbye, my dear. May God bless you. I send you a thousand kisses. My love to all. Your devoted husband,

W. H. Hardy

☆ *James Johnson Kirkpatrick Diary*, November 27, 1861, Wednesday:

Went on picket again. When the weather is fair, we now look forward to our picket tours, as ones of pleasure. No enemy near enough to circumscribe our foraging limits, and with more liberties than at camp, we rarely fail of having a good time. . . . Winter is near at hand, and our tents are very inadequate shelter for this cold clime. Wood has become an object—far off and bad roads to haul it over. The cold winds howling around us, like evil spirits, admonish us to prepare for "worse coming." Chimneys . . . are built to our tents, but they afford us more smoke than heat. If to furnish smoke had been the object of this erection, no amount of skill could have succeeded better. . . . Like true philosophers, we group around our smoky fire. Jests and mirth pass around, duty is cheerfully performed, although our prospects for comfort are gloomy indeed.

☆ *Jesse Ruebel Kirkland to Joseph Kirkland:*
Camp E. K. Smith, Virginia, November 28th, 1861

Dear Brother,

This is the third or fourth time I have written you in the last month. Cannot account for your silence. . . . The only news this morning is an order from headquarters to be ready at a moment's notice to march, or be ready to meet the enemy, which I assure you is all our regiment yearns for. . . . Yesterday was General McClellan's great Grand Review day. He has, tis reported, thirty-one thousand troops on this side and one hundred twenty-two ready to cross if he concludes to advance, which we hope and pray he may do.

I am urged to accept the appointment of brigade quartermaster, which I have not yet decided upon. The truth is I know every man in my regiment and am comfortable situated and cannot be benefitted much in the way of salary. The title is major instead of captain, neither of which do I care a fig, but I may change my mind and accept it.

Captain Hardy goes home in December. Should I not get off, I will send a parcel of money home. You want it there, and I have no use on earth for money here. Would have sent it by mail but was afraid of it, so many losses having occurred lately. Do write to me. I have not heard from home for two weeks. My love to all, kiss all for me, respects to inquiring friends. Your brother, in haste,

Jesse

☆ *John S. Lewis to Nancy Lewis:*
Camp E. K. Smith, near Centreville, December 7th, 1861

Dear Mother,
. . . We are getting on tolerably well here. The weather is getting rather severe in tents. The boys . . . say they can stand it if the Yankees can.

Officers and men have been expecting an advance of the enemy in great force for four or five days. If they attack us in the works, they will be badly cut up, but I don't think they will, and if they can force us to fight outside, the issue is not as certain. We have not got much over fifty thousand men and report gives them three or four times this number.

Our company was unfortunate enough to lose another man, one of the best men and soldiers we had, W. Hughes. He died . . . of typhoid.[5]
. . . I have not time to write any more, so excuse my short letter. Your son,

John Lewis

☆ *J. J. Wilson to John N. Wilson:*
Camp E. K. Smith near Centreville, December 7th, 1861

John, Dear Sir,
I take the present opportunity of dropping you a few lines to let you know that I am well at present. . . . I do not know whether we will have a fight here

or not this winter. It was reported here yesterday evening that there was eighty thousand Yankees on this side of the Potomac River advancing on us, but I do not believe it. I think that they are afraid to come here. . . .

Things is very high here. We can hardly buy anything to eat without paying twice what it is worth. . . . Whiskey is from eight to twelve dollars a barrel. I would like to have a drink of a morning but not at that price.

Give my love to all and write soon. Yours truly,

J. J. Wilson

☆ *Jesse Ruebel Kirkland to Lucinda Kirkland:*
Camp E. Kirby Smith, Virginia, December 9th, 1861

My Dear Wife,

I told you in my letter . . . that I would write again this morning but was prevented from doing so by an order from headquarters that the whole division should turn out at nine o'clock a.m. to witness two poor fellows shot. They were privates in Colonel Wheat's Battalion and belonged to Captain White's company styled the Tiger Rifles. They were court-martialed for mutiny and resisting an officer. They were taken to the place of execution in a wagon, handcuffed and strongly guarded, accompanied by a priest. Marching to within five feet of their graves, they were tied in a kneeling position to stakes planted there for that purpose then they were blindfolded and twenty-four of their own company marched up within ten paces of them when the army regulations were read in a loud and audible voice by one of General Smith's aides. Then the usual order of make ready, take aim, fire. The volley was simultaneous and their souls had taken flight. It was a sight I did not want to witness but, being on Posey's staff, was compelled to turn out. Hope never to witness another. . . .[6]

Good night. Kiss all the babies for me and tell all that are able to write to do so. My love to all and a thousand kisses to the children. I kiss you good-night. Your devoted husband,

Jesse

☆ *Hugh Carroll Dickson to Mrs. Rachael Dickson:*
Camp E. K. Smith near Centreville, Virginia, 11 December 1861

Dearest Ma,

I take my seat to respond to your welcome letter. . . . I assure you that it was perused with feelings of delight. I am not very well at present. I had a chill a day or two since, also my bowels have been running off, but they are getting better. . . .

We have had plenty of rain. It has rained every time when we were on picket. When we go out on picket, we generally remain out from three to five days, and it rains on us two days out of the five. Sometimes it commences raining after we have gone to bed tired and sleepy, and would not wake up until the water would run under us and would be half-way up our sides. We then get up, make a big fire out of logs and sit up the remainder of the night.

Notwithstanding all of the exposure that we are compelled to undergo, the health of our regiment is very good, all of them anxious for a fight, but I think they are doomed to disappointment. I do not think that there is any more chance now for a fight than there was two months since. Old McClellan, it is reported, has been ready for sometime to try his fortune, but Uncle Abe's children do not like Bull Run. They have a perfect horror of the place where so many of their cousins fell. . . . If the Yankees ever attack this place, they will be the worst whipped army that ever went anywhere. We have breastworks and fortifications all over this part of the country. The Washington Artillery practice frequently, shooting at a target a mile distant. They shoot with a great deal of accuracy. A rifle cannonball, after being discharged from the cannon, can be heard at a distance of half a mile, squalling like a cat. . . .

There was a general court-martial convened some days since. There was two of the Tiger Rifles tried and condemned to be shot for striking a sentinel while on duty. It seems that two of the Tigers went up to Centreville. While there, they found some whiskey, of which they drank too freely. In coming back, they came through a Virginia regiment and picked up something. They were ordered to put it down, which they would not do. They were arrested and put in the guard house. As soon as the Tigers heard it, these two that were condemned went over, knocked down the sentinel and took them out. They were all arrested before they could make their escape and confined. They were shot on Tuesday. Our brigade was ordered out to see them executed. I was standing in fifteen steps of them when they were shot. They seemed to be perfectly reckless in regard to their fate. I heard a man say that when they got in the wagon to go to the place of execution, one of them danced all over his coffin and said that they would show them how Louisianians could die.

Ma, you all ask me why I do not write. I have written I do not know how many letters home. I cannot see why you do not receive them. I also wrote and sent it by old Roger. The old scamp, he did not give it to you. Also, William sent one dollar by him to his Momma. I do not expect he gave that to her. I told him particularly to deliver that letter to you. I also wrote to Jimmie . . . but have never received an answer. I have thought very hard of you all for not writing oftener to me.

I received the overcoat that you sent me. I am very much pleased with it. I also received the Baroy knife that you sent me. If I ever get into a fight and am not killed, I will make more than one Yankee bite the dust with it, that is if I ever get near enough to them. It is just the thing that I want. I would not take ten dollars for it.

Excuse all mistakes. Give my best love to all of my brothers and sisters. Kiss all the children for me. Tell them all to write. You write two letters every week. . . . William sends howdy to all. Ma, you must write on the reception of this to your loving son,

Hugh

☆ *William Harris Hardy to Sallie Johnson Hardy:*
Camp near Centreville, Virginia, Saturday, December 14th, 1861

My Dear Sallie,
. . . The news that my leave of absence to go home was refused will be indeed bad news to you. But I told you all along to be prepared to receive it. I made the application today, and it was approved by the colonel, brigadier general, and major general, but disapproved by General Johnston. . . . I have, however, applied direct to President Davis, and if that fails, then I will have to wait till we get into winter quarters, which I hope will be soon.

Oh, my dear, I would give anything to be with you, and you must be patient. I will come after a while. And you say perhaps you'll have a young captain to present me when I come. Oh me, wouldn't that be a grand and *happy present*, but take care that you are not disappointed in that too, as I often told you I believe you would be. Perhaps it will be the prototype of its *mother*—aye, a second *Sallie*. It will certainly be a happy, thrice happy day to me when I lay my eyes on my firstborn. Yet I have found one thing, my dear, not to lay up too much happiness in this life in anticipation for then disappointment is more severe. It's always doubly-fanged. . . .

My love to all. Goodbye. God bless you. Your devoted husband,
You must write twice a week.

W. H. Hardy

☆ Sunday, the 16th [of] December

. . . General Trimble informed that we would go into winter quarters this week. Colonel Posey says he intends to detail me to superintend the building of the barracks. If so, I will not be made happy in taking a Christmas dinner with you. Oh, what a disappointment. But I must not complain, a soldier should never murmur at anything. Be content, my dear, I will be with you before long. Yours with much love,

W. H. Hardy

☆ *Jesse Ruebel Kirkland to Lucinda Kirkland:*
Camp E. K. Smith Virginia, December 15th, 1861

My Dear Wife,

Your kind and highly esteemed favor . . . came to hand this moment. It being night and the only opportunity I may have for several days, I hasten to reply. I say several days from the fact I am ordered to be ready at four a.m. To go where, I am unable to inform you. I notice in your letter you speak of house rent. Pay it out of the money I sent you . . . and I will send you more money by Captain Hardy or some other person on whom I can rely. I am afraid of the mail, as there has been so many losses in the last two months. Ask Brother Joseph if Virginia, Georgia, or Carolina money can be used there.

We send a detail of two hundred and fifty men in the morning to commence building winter quarters, three miles below here towards the [Manassas] Junction. It would have been well had they been ordered to do this fifteen days ago while the weather, though cold, was clear, except a few days which I wrote you was sleeting and snowing.

You speak of my coming home. I am afraid, dear Lucy, that they will not let me go. However, there is quite an excitement in camp about the recent act of Congress offering all those now in the service for twelve months, a bounty of fifty dollars, and a furlough for sixty days and transportation home and back if they will reenlist for two years. My impression now is that four-fifths of our regiment will do so. I hope so for then I could certainly go home for a little while. The Department, however, would not consent for my absence so long. . . . You know my commission is for the war, and thirty days is the longest time allowed them except in case of illness. I might perhaps get sick just before my time expired and stay longer.

My love to all and a thousand and one kisses to the dear little ones. . . . Good night, dear Lucy. Pleasant dreams to you. I kiss you. Your affectionate husband,

Jesse

☆ *Jesse Ruebel Kirkland to Lucinda Kirkland:*
Quarter past three a.m., December 17th, 1861, Camp E. Kirby Smith

My Dear Wife,

I had this pleasure yesterday morning at about this hour and then expected to leave in a few minutes. The order, however, was countermanded, which I assure you I did not regret for I had eaten the day before heartily of fish and oysters, and they did not agree with me. . . .

Tis said and believed that the Yankees are now shelling our camp at Leesburg, and that our forces have fallen back two miles to give them a chance to cross their forces in part before attacking them. Certain tis the Yankees are in force at this point with their pontoon bridges for crossing and that they also have a large force opposite Occoquan. Their object is to make the advance on both points. We, as it were, are between the two points. Would not be surprised at any moment to hear the long roll beat accompanied with an order to double-quick it to either Leesburg or the latter places. If we do have a battle, Ma, you may expect to hear of one of bloodiest battles that has been fought on the continent from the fact that we know no defeat, and McClellan knows he will be crushed and damned by the North should he fail to gain a victory, which he will as surely do as the sun rises this morning.

The health of our camp continues good, but there are a good many deaths in the division from pneumonia which, when it takes hold, does not give them long to live, from two to four days they either die or get well. Young Mr. Norwood was taken on Thursday and died on Sunday. He was as clever and good a young man as there was in the army. His death is much regretted by all. . . .[7]

Oh, Ma, how disappointed I have been in not hearing from Richmond as to my leave of absence. I thought, however, I would so arrange it as to get ahead of old General Smith. . . . Colonel Posey approved my application, so did Brigadier General Trimble, but Major General Smith vetoed it, saying no officer could leave unless very sick or disabled, unfit for service. He tells me laughingly that he has not seen his wife for seven years. He has promised, however, to grant me a furlough as soon as we go into winter quarters, which I hope will be soon.

A thousand loves to you and the dear ones. May heaven protect you. I kiss you. Your affectionate husband,

Jesse

☆ *Harry Lewis to Mrs. Nancy Lewis:*
Camp E. K. Smith, near Centreville, Virginia, December 18th, 1861

Dear Mother,
Having nothing particular to do this morning . . . I came to the conclusion that . . . it would be well to write. . . . Besides, dear Mother, I am in quandary about reenlisting for two years longer and would like to hear your opinions upon it.

You are aware, I suppose, of the terms of enlistment. To the twelve months' volunteers, which included our regiment, the following proffer has been made a part of the government: that they are to be allowed a furlough for sixty days and a bounty of fifty dollars and expenses home and back and be allowed to reorganize into companies and elect officers, after which all officers go up by promotion (except third lieutenant who may be elected by the company) if they (volunteers) will reenlist for a period of two years or for the war. These offers to the twelve-month volunteers are very liberal and a wise measure on the part of the Confederacy, for there are about fifty or eighty thousand such troops, and to take them suddenly out of the field would cause a vacuum which might prove troublesome to fill; and besides, the moral effect of such a number of troops volunteering for a longer term must have influence on the Lincoln side of the question.

Some forty of our company have signed a paper promising to reenlist upon the above conditions, and I expect others yet will. Still I have hesitated, partly because I could not see my way clearly and because Fletch has told me once or twice you might need me at home. I have always thought I would fight as long as the war lasts and . . . have nearly decided to go in for the next two years, but I thought I would . . . see what you would say before the proposition is finally laid before me. . . . If the furlough is offered before I receive a letter from you, I will accept it. Fletch says he will not go in for two years but will go home and then for the war.

Our company were out on fatigue duty yesterday building redoubts on the

Bull Run. I suppose there were from two to three hundred men at work and ten or twenty industrious men could have done as much work in the same time. . . .

Your son,
Harry

☆ *James Johnson Kirkpatrick Diary*, December 18, 1861, Wednesday:

Moved back to Manassas to build winter quarters. Went into camp one mile east of the depot. Large details immediately sent into the woods from each company to cut timber and get out boards. But the work progressed slowly on account of not having sufficient teams to haul in the timber to the site selected for the erection of our quarters. Our houses, when completed, were very comfortable. Built of round pine logs, one story high, chinked and daubed, roofed so as to be impervious to the weather with good chimneys and all the appurtenances of a regular dwelling house, primitive style. . . .

☆ *Jesse Ruebel Kirkland to Lucinda Kirkland:*
Camp near Manassas, December 23rd, 1861

My Dear Lucy,

I got here last night and had my tent put up, a fire in my stove, wood enough to last me all night, when it commenced raining and sleeting very hard, which it continued to do all night. This morning there was icicles a foot long hanging to the limbs of the trees. About six o'clock, it ceased sleeting and commenced snowing, which it is doing now rapidly. I think we will have to make rakes to rake it off our tents to keep them from breaking in under the weight.

You ask me how often we go on picket duty. You must know that we are one of the five regiments that have not been put to erecting fortifications, building bridges, making roads, etc. Hence our turn for picket duty rolls around every eight or twelve days, which the boys all hail with pleasure, for to them tis a relief from the dull monotony of camp. Aside from this, tis a change of scenery, a change of air. They all have money and can purchase, when any distance from camp, potatoes, cabbage, turnips, milk, butter, honey, etc., in abundance, which they cannot get in camp, those things all having been exhausted by the large number of troops near Centreville.

All the news I have is that Colonel Stuart started out with a hundred teams for forage on Friday last and when near Gainesville, some twenty-five miles from Centreville, he was attacked by several regiments of Lincolnites. . . . Our loss was heavy, killing and wounding eighty of them. The enemy's loss was severe but not known. Colonel Stuart is very much censured for going out with so small a force when it was well known that the enemy were in that neighborhood with a larger force.[8]

The health of our camp is not so good. Tell Brother Joseph that Alexander Murray's son died yesterday with pneumonia. He belonged to the Westville Guards (Captain Funchess).[9]

Oh, Lucy, how much would I not give to see you, if but for a day. It seems hard, but when I think there are tens of thousands in a similar situation, I should not murmur but bear it like a soldier. But I shall keep trying to get off. Ma, I must tell you goodbye again without being able to tell you when to look for me. Love and kiss all the children for me. Tell Miss Fannie I will pull her ears for not writing oftener. I kiss you goodbye. Your affectionate and devoted husband,

Jesse

☆ *Jesse Ruebel Kirkland to Lucinda Kirkland:*
Camp near Manassas, December 25th, 1861

My Dear Lucy,

After wishing you a Merry Christmas, I must offer an apology for not writing you on the 24th. . . . For the past two weeks my duties have been more arduous and complicated than since I have been in the army. It came on me, too, at a time when I was least prepared for it. . . . I was called upon to act in the double capacity of brigade and regimental commissary, sending ten wagons to Gainesville and twenty-two to Manassas, five to Thoroughfare, all the same day and my presence required at all three points to sign receipts for provisions, leaving camp at four a.m. and returning same hour next day, which compelled me to make on horseback a distance of sixty-five miles all told. . . . But I did it, fed the brigade, had a good sleep last night, a bath this morning, eat breakfast . . . and sit down to do what is my duty and a pleasure, to write you daily when I can possibly do so.

Ma, I have none of your favors to reply to, in which I was disappointed. When I returned last evening, I was almost sure I would get a letter from home but was disappointed as usual. Lucy, I fear you will conclude after a while, if not already, that I am a great hand to complain and perhaps justly so, but when you think of my loneliness, particularly at night, I hope you will forgive my impatience or pass it by. Ma, what in the world is it I would not have given to have heard what I have so often scolded about? The children in their innocent noisy way after going to bed. . . .

Goodbye. I kiss you adieu. Kiss the babies a Merry Christmas. Your affectionate and devoted husband,

Jesse

☆ *J. J. Wilson to James E. Wilson:*
Camp E. K. Smith near Manassas, December, 1861

Father, Dear Sir,

I take the present opportunity of dropping you a few lines to let you know that I am well at present. . . . Day before yesterday the box came to hand which my things were in. I got them all. The blankets will answer a very good purpose for camp. . . .

It is a very dull Christmas up here. We cannot get any whiskey to make us any eggnog. Everything is very high up here. We have to pay three prices for anything we get. . . .

There is not a prospect for a fight here. The soldiers are all going into winter quarters. We are building our quarters. . . . It will take us two weeks to finish, yet I would like to come home and spend the winter and come back in the spring so that I could get some potatoes and bacon. We have not had a pound of bacon in two months. We have eat beef so much that we have a disgust against ever seeing beef any more. I hardly ever eat it. I buy butter, and I generally have to give four bits a pound. I hope that you all have had a merry Christmas for we could not have any here. . . .

Give my love to all relations and friends. Write soon. I remain your son until death,

J. J. Wilson

— Chapter 4 —

". . . HAVE YOU ALL WINKED OUT?"

The Sixteenth waited out January and February, 1862 serving picket duty, writing home, and contemplating re-enlistment. By early March, large Federal forces threatened Alexandria and Richmond, rendering Confederate camps near Manassas Junction, including the Sixteenth Mississippi's, untenable. To shorten his defense lines and reach Richmond easier in case of Federal attack, Johnston moved his army thirty miles south to the south side of Rappahannock River. The cautious Federal pursuit allowed the Sixteenth and other regiments time to tear up the railroads.

Spring brought movement, election of officers, and a bombardment of Yankee cannons. It also brought a summons from Stonewall Jackson.[1]

☆ *Jesse Ruebel Kirkland to Lucinda Kirkland:*
Camp E. K. Smith near Manassas, Virginia, January 2nd, 1862

My Dear Lucy,
After every effort, I failed in getting . . . a leave of absence, which you know both disappointed and annoyed me. But I am not alone, there are many in the same situation. Hence I have no more reason to complain than they who are equally desirous of seeing their homes and families. . . .

On the 27th about ten o'clock, I awoke with a hard chill which continued at least two hours. I called Jim, the Negro boy, had a fire made, sent for the doctor, and I judge from what he told me today that he was alarmed. He says there is bad flu in the regiment, and it could have been that. I am sitting up writing now after the high fever that followed the chill, which did not abate at all for forty hours. Oh, how I suffered. Worlds would I have given to have seen the door of my tent opened and you stepped in. I could think only of you and home and how differently my nursing would have been, although I had every attention and kindness that could be given by the strangers. I, thank heaven, am today as well as ever. . . .

Another of Captain Hardy's company died last night. A son of old Mrs. Royals. A stout, hearty young man, always on duty. His father came to see and spend the holidays with him. He was taken the next morning and lived only four days. Died of that worst of diseases (pneumonia). His father leaves in the morning with his remains. It has nearly killed the old man.[2]

Good night. God bless and protect you and the babies is my earnest and daily prayer. Jim is here to take my boots. Good night. I kiss adieu. You affectionate and devoted husband,

Jesse

☆ **William Harris Hardy to Sallie Johnson Hardy:**
Winter Quarters near Manassas, Virginia, January 9th, 1862

My Dear Sallie,

I look anxiously every day for a letter from you and feel so disappointed when the mail comes without a letter from you. I am almost sick with cold, so is Tom, and Henry is quite sick. He has been bordering on pneumonia for several days, and I have been very uneasy about him, but his fever has gone down, and the pain in his lungs abated, and the surgeon considers him now out of danger. Pneumonia is a terrible disease in camps and proves generally fatal and in a short time, too. . . .

I finished my cabin today, and as soon as the daubing drys, I will move Henry into it. It is built of pine poles fifteen feet long and the cracks daubed with clay. The chimney is lined inside with stone. I managed to get two hundred feet of lumber to floor it. So you see, I am going to regular housekeeping, but I will lack the best ornament and greatest comforter of all, and that is yourself. I covered my cabin with rough oak boards which cost me $1.25 per hundred, nails fifteen cents per pound. I paid $2.50 for a small hatchet to cover with in place of a hammer. So you see, it has cost me a nice little sum to set up shop here. I do wish you could see me in this pine-pole cabin when I get fixed up. The floor is of rough plank laid poles which rest on the ground. An old-fashioned bedstead, one of the primitive sort, hole bored in the log and then a fork put in the ground with cross-pieces, then oak boards laid across (I tell you, this is comfortable). Then the door would remind you of the door to a horse stable, as broad as high. Then I have a fancy mantlepiece, and last but not least, I have a glass window in it. Small, only four small lights which cost me $1.25. This last I was compelled to have, as it would be as dark as Egypt inside without it.

The snow has been lying on the ground here since last Friday (six days) but melted off this evening, and the whole surface of the earth is a complete lob-lolly of red clay. It has certainly been a most terrible spell of weather and keeps me in constant trouble fearing that my men will die with pneumonia before we can get our cabins built. They all have bad colds and coughs now. We prog-ress very slowly building our cabins, as it is with great difficulty that we can get tools. . . .

I frequently spend the night upon . . . a pillow that brings no sleep, thinking of my affairs at home. God knows what the result will be. I have toiled all my life and accomplished nothing almost, yet a retrospection does no good. Hence let the past be and look carefully to the future. I make no rash promises, yet my present feelings are to move to East Mississippi. . . .

Give my love to all. Kiss the baby for me. Your devoted husband,

W. H. Hardy

☆ *Jesse Ruebel Kirkland to Lucinda Kirkland:*
Camp E. K. Smith near Manassas, Virginia, January 10th, 1862

My Dear Wife,

Your highly esteemed favor . . . was received yesterday, and I was glad to hear that you were all well. . . . We have very bad weather. It rained all day yesterday and is now raining. The mud in places, particularly on crossing the fields, is from one to ten inches deep, which will of course stop our hauling both logs and lumber. Consignments prevent our getting in winter quarters as early as anticipated, which I regret on account of the men, many of whom are suffering now with bad colds, which generally terminates in pneumonia, which is prevailing at an alarming extent. . . .

I think it probable that Captain Hardy's company, as well as Shannon, Davis, Funchess, Feltus, Baker and Walworth will all go for the war under the new act of Congress, permitting them to reorganize not only their companies but the regiment. In that event, our colonel, lieutenant colonel, and major will stand a poor chance of being reinstated. Why it is I do not know, but there seems to be a good deal of dissatisfaction. I am not satisfied myself with Colonel Posey, nor have I been from the start. I regard him (excuse me for the language) as one of the most consummate asses that ever occupied the position he does. He knows my opinion of him long since, for I gave it to him in plain language months ago in the presence of all his captains at his quarters. Then he was afraid to court-martial me. The particulars I will give you when I see you. He for months has been more than polite, inviting me, when others were not, to dine, sip eggnog, etc., all of which he would not have done (I don't think) but for his being afraid of my court-martialing him, which I can do.

Goodbye, Ma. A thousand loves to you and the children. May God bless and protect you. In haste, I kiss you adieu. Your affectionate husband,

Jesse

☆ *Jesse Ruebel Kirkland to Lucinda Kirkland*:
Camp E. K. Smith, near Manassas Virginia, January 13th, 1862

My Dear Wife,
Your two highly esteemed favors of the 3rd and 5th came to hand. . . . Having read them, I dined and sit down to answer them. As usual, I did not write this morning. My excuse is, however, a good one. I had to go out in the woods with a detail to show them where to get me some timber for building a stable for my horses. The tent that they have been staying in is so badly torn and worn that they have been suffering ever since the cold weather set in. . . .

You allude to your disappointment of the non-reality of your dream. Oh, Lucy, I wish you could have awakened and found it no dream. I could hardly sum up the number of times I kiss and talk to you and, upon awakening, find is nothing but a dream. . . . I am sure I would not only have found the steak and coffee nice, but your presence in having been prepared by you would have made it thrice appreciated by me. I hope the day is not far distant when we can realize and enjoy with the dear little ones our steak and coffee. . . .

Ma, I received enclosed in one of your letters one from Joseph, which is the second in the past few days. The first I replied to, scolding him for his miserable scrawl. Do, Ma, make him pay more attention to his writing. Tis much worse than he wrote eighteen months ago. His spelling is worse than his writing, for instance "highly," he spells "hily." Now is the time to stop him and make him do better. Miss Fannie, I presume, took offense at my criticisms and has quit writing. If so, allow me through you to apologize. I wrote to all the little fellows a few days ago, which I hope, although they can not read, will for the moment gratify and please them. Yourself and them are before me almost every hour in the day and, Ma, how very lonely I feel when bedtime comes. No one to talk to, no one to joke or tease and last but not least, no one to keep me warm. . . .

God bless and protect you and the children. Goodbye. I kiss you. Your devoted husband,

Jesse

☆ *Jesse Ruebel Kirkland to Lucinda Kirkland*:
Camp E. K. Smith near Manassas, Virginia, January 15th, 1862

My Dear Wife,

I was glad to hear you were all well. You did not mention Obed having any more chills, and I hope he has gotten rid of them. You mention my complaining of not hearing from home oftener. If you knew, Ma, how disappointed and miserable it makes me to know the mail has come in without any letters for me, you would, I think, pass over my complaining. I will, however, try and stop grumbling or scolding for fear news from home may entirely cease. I do not allude, you know, dear Lucy, to you but those very busy children of ours. I only wish Obed, Oscar, Arsine and Jessie were able to write for I am sure they would sometime during the week think of and write to me.

You speak of the fine beef you have. Let me tell you that in all my travels and looking through the markets of different cities, I have never seen anything to compare with that we have been furnished ever since we arrived in Virginia. I have often wished I could send some home.

You mention the weather as being bad. You never saw anything in that respect half as bad as we are having now. It has been sleeting and snowing for three nights and two days and after trying it all morning, has commenced raining, freezing as it runs off the fly of my tent. . . .

If the children were here, they would enjoy themselves very much catching rabbits and birds. In walking over to the brigade commissary this morning, about one-half mile, I killed three with sticks and picked up two partridges in the snow. Oh, Ma, how much I would give to have you all here this moment. You and I could sit in the tent and see all the children chasing rabbits through the fields. There is no fences or obstructions of any kind. You can see for miles. What fun and enjoyment it would be for them. . . .

Goodbye. God bless you and the babies. I kiss you,

Jesse

☆ *Jesse Ruebel Kirkland to Lucinda Kirkland*:
Monday morning, January 19th, 1862, Camp E. K. Smith near Manassas, Virginia

My Dear Lucy,

As usual, I find myself sitting at my little table to write you but . . . am in receipt of none of yours, Fannie's or Joseph's favors to reply to. . . . I was quite disappointed last night in not getting a letter from home. . . .

I was out last evening about four hours, say from half past one until nearly dark, was wet to the skin. My clothing, particularly my overcoat, was frozen stiff, my whiskers and hair full of ice, and I almost completely numbed. As soon as possible after I reached camp, I took a cold bath, dressed myself and went to bed and took a hot punch. Slept soundly and feel as well this morning as ever.

While absent yesterday my *particular friend*, Miss Innis, whom I think I mentioned or spoke of in one of my letters months ago (Miss Innis, who lives some forty miles from here), sent me . . . a fine roasted turkey, two very large loaves of beautiful bread, two large sponge cakes, one pound butter and one very large raisin and plum cake, besides any quantity of small hard (or "sec-esh") cakes, a bag of hominy, one of meal, one of turnips and white-head cabbage and . . . about one-hundred-fifty pounds of spare ribs and sausages. Ma, how I do wish you and the children were here to dine and enjoy those things with me. You must not be jealous of Miss Innis, Lucy, for her kindness and friendship for me. Were I to get sick, I should certainly go there, as I have been promised to be nursed and waited upon.

Kisses and a thousand loves to you and the babies. God bless and protect you. I kiss you.

Jesse

☆ *Hugh Carroll Dickson to Joseph L. Dickson and Rachael Liddell Dickson*:
Manassas Junction, Virginia, January 19th, 1862

Dear Ma and Pa,

It is with pleasure that I now take my seat to write you a few lines to inform you that I am quite well at present. William is not very well. He has been complaining for several days, but I hope that it will not terminate serious. He complains of his head and breast hurting him. I gave him a good dose of castor oil this morning which I think will bring him all right.

I have been looking anxiously for a letter from home for the last three weeks. What is the matter with you all? Have you forgotten me, or have you all winked out? I have written often but have not received any response. I have despaired of receiving any more letters from home. I shall hunt up correspondents that will answer my letters.

There is no war news afloat this load of poles. The Federal army has not advanced any farther than Fairfax. There they are as thick as maggots around an old dead horse. We will go out there on picket Tuesday. I expect we will have some fun. Old Captain Davis will be certain to go out on a scouting expedition, then we will have it.

All about the camp, several have died with pneumonia. We have lost but two members of our company. . . . It is a wonder to me that we have been so fortunate. We have to go at all times, rain or shine, but we have become accustomed to it. . . .

Ma, you must excuse all mistakes, as the boys keep so much noise that I cannot write. Give my best love to all the family and reserve a large portion for yourself and write soon to your loving son,

Hugh C. Dickson

☆ *James Johnson Kirkpatrick Diary*, March 9, 1862, Sunday:

Company C was waked up soon after midnight last night to go to Manassas to load cars and do guard duty. Worked all day, loading trains and destroying property. It was painful to see the vast destruction of stores that occurred today. The various state depots, crowded with . . . everything for the outer and inner man were scattered to the winds or trodden underfoot by the mass of unfeeling plunderers who collected during the day and gave license to these predatory proclivities. Barrels of whisky, molasses, etc., had their heads knocked out flooding the whole space around the buildings.

At dark, our regiment marched up, and we took our places in the grand retreat along the railroad towards the Rappahannock. This was General Johnston's second grand strategic movements. The march tonight is very tiresome. Having lost most of our sleep the night before, and being loaded down . . . it was with difficulty that I could keep my place in line. But . . . I must needs keep in ranks. My military conscience whispered that it was my duty. Halted about midnight and camped till morning, or rather, slept till morning for we observed no order of camping.

☆ *James Johnson Kirkpatrick Diary*, March 11, 1862, Tuesday:

Crossed the river today on the railroad bridge and camped on the south side, a mile back from the river. All much fatigued and used up by the march. Nearly one-half the troops straggling over the country, myself among the number. . . . Our camp here is on low, wet ground. Springs, or rather, impromptu cisterns, made all over camp by simply digging a hole. The worst inconvenience about them was stepping or falling into them after dark.

☆ *James Johnson Kirkpatrick Diary*, March 15, 1862, Saturday:

Aroused suddenly before day and ordered to get ready to move, not knowing whether to meet the enemy or retreat from him, or whether he had anything to do with it. Marched down to the railroad bridge through a cold, soaking rain and halted in it a few hours. Then crossed and marched up to Warrenton Junction. Rained all day. Made good time and reached our destination an hour or so before dark, completely worn out.

We camped amid a large quantity of cord wood and soon had splendid fires, but it kept raining too incessantly for us to dry our clothing and blankets. By stretching our blankets, we made us partial shelters and by laying sticks of wood together, we made beds "soft as down" to our wearied limbs.

☆ *James Johnson Kirkpatrick Diary*, March 16, 1862, Sunday:

About nine o'clock, this morning the long roll sounded in our ears. We were not thinking of an enemy, but there is no mistaking Old Jefferies. . . . "To arms," the cry. We are immediately formed and drawn up in battle array. All the preliminaries are fixed. Litter bearers detailed from each company, a field hospital designated. Some meager instructions about stopping blood imparted by our assistant surgeon and other directions how to act when wounded. All ordered to fill their canteens with water, as a wounded man is always thirsty. But after all—there is no engagement. . . . After remaining in line of battle till past noon, we are marched back to our camp. The alarm was caused by one of Stuart's scouts bringing word that the Yankees were crossing Cedar River.[3]

☆ *James Johnson Kirkpatrick Diary*, March 28, 1862, Friday:

Lay in camp, expecting all the time to move, till evening, when we were marched out near the railroad. The enemy advanced a force down the railroad from towards Warrenton Junction. . . . They located a battery on the opposite side and shelled a train . . . some of the shells falling not far from us. This was the first time we had been exposed to them, and their noise was somewhat peculiar. At dark, we deployed in line of battle below the railroad. The burning of the bridge and the enemy's camp fires across the river are the only demonstrations tonight.

☆ *Jesse Ruebel Kirkland to Lucinda Kirkland*:
   March 28th, 1862

   My Dear Wife,
   . . . Our regiment is now at Rappahannock Station, the rear guard of the army. I have not received a line from home for weeks and weeks, owing I know to the uncertainty of mails. I have written regularly when it was possible, which was two or three times a week at least. I sent Brother Joseph, a month ago or more by express, a hundred dollars for you. I do hope it went through safe for you must need money and, Ma, you must know how it distresses me to think of it, as well as not receiving a line from home. But such is the fact of war, thousands are in a similar condition.
   Since I heard from home, my division has been moving backwards and forwards all the time. After falling back from Manassas to the Rappahannock, we were ordered, at least our regiment, to Warrenton Station where the Yankees were reported to be in considerable force. We double-quicked it there, had a slight skirmish, then they fell back. . . .
   Mrs. Jayne tells me the baby is a fine looking child. . . . A thousand loves to you and the babies. . . . I kiss you goodbye. Your affectionate and devoted husband,

                                                                                                   Jesse

☆ *William Harris Hardy to Sallie Johnson Hardy*:
April 1st, 1862

My Dear Sallie,
     . . . Last Friday [March 28th], the Yankees appeared in full force on the opposite bank of the river, and commenced shelling every house and skirt of woods on this side. Major General Ewell cautiously concealed his force (eight thousand strong) behind the hills. Then lay our regiment in line of battle for six mortal hours, and the Yankee bombshells whistling around. Our boys were delighted and thought certain the hour for an exhibition of their prowess had certainly arrived. A few Yankees crossed over but during the night re-crossed, and the next morning (Saturday), not a Yankee Hessian was to be seen anywhere. Intelligence from Rappahannock this morning states that they are again back in still stronger force. Their first adventure was supposed to be merely a strong reconnaissance, and they have now come in force for the purpose of giving us battle, but I am satisfied that we'll not fight them unless we are reinforced. . . .⁴

     Two months from today I hope, my dear, to be with you once more. Oh, what a happy day that shall bring me safely to the bosom of my dear little family again! It seems to me that life would have no cares for me when surrounded by my wife and child. That, then, would be happiness enough to fill this frail bosom of mine, save the painful perturbations of my heart caused by my country's bloody struggle for liberty, the current of my life would run smoothly on to its final goal. What greater happiness can this earth afford than that springing from the devotions of a kind and loving wife and an interesting and dutiful child, the happiness and good fortune of both of whom is my greatest hope, my highest ambition? Oh, war!! Cruel war that is stretching its unhallowed wings o'er this once happy country of ours and like a besom of destruction sweeping all that is happy and dear to us from our grasp. I trust that merciful Providence, who stood by our venerated sires in their first great struggle for liberty, is still with us, their would-be oppressed and fallen sons and that our great struggle against despotism and for constitutional liberty will soon be crowned with success and our unfortunate country restored to peace, quietude and happiness!!!

     The day has turned off beautifully. Day before yesterday it sleeted all day, then rained and froze, and yesterday the whole forest was covered with icicles which hung pendant from the boughs in their diamond-like purity, presenting indeed a beautiful scenery. The sun, now the soldier's friend, came out and melted them all away, and today April ushered in, in all the loveliness of spring.

Give my love to all at home when you see them, also to Sister Mary and kiss my darling child for me and accept a thousand kisses and dear caresses for yourself from your affectionate husband,

W. H. Hardy

☆ *William Harris Hardy to Sallie Johnson Hardy*:
Lynchburg, Virginia at night, April 2, 1862

My Dear Sallie,

I have just arrived here on sick leave. I . . . have come here for variety sake first and to get some shoes for myself and some for my men. Besides, it didn't cost me anything to come, being on the sick list. I shall stay here tomorrow, then I return to my company.

I received a letter from you . . . giving me an account of your difficulties in getting things righted-up in Raleigh. It gives me much trouble to think that my dear was in Raleigh by her lone self, not even anyone to cook her a meal of victuals. Oh, my dear, I could see you in my mind, sitting there alone crying with no one to cheer you or dispel your gloom. . . . I long to get back home. I never have before given myself any uneasiness about you, but I must confess that I am now greatly uneasy for your welfare. I fear you will suffer, but, my dear, do try and content yourself, if possible, till I get home and then if it be in my power to do so, I will make you happy. . . . My dear, don't be uneasy about me, look on the bright side of things and remember that you suffer only in common with all who are subject to the calamities of this unholy war.

Give my love to all at home . . . and kiss my darling baby for me and accept a thousand kisses from your devoted husband,

W. H. Hardy

☆ *James Johnson Kirkpatrick Diary*, March 30, 1862, Sunday—April 18, 1862, Friday:

Moved out to some pine woods one-half mile off and went into camp. Snow on the ground and weather very severe. Remained at this place about three weeks, guarding Kelly's Ford. Two companies are kept on duty at a time, relieved every four hours. Here Company C immortalized itself by making a nocturnal raid. The intent was to capture some Yankees who were said to visit across the river. We reached the place and surrounded two houses before day-break and captured a contraband and a little boy, neither very hostile, but we must needs take back to camp some trophies of valor. Mrs. Smith, lady of one of the houses invested, entertained the whole company with a very substantial breakfast. One of the young ladies who presided made a permanent capture of one of the raiders. At this camp, those who had re-enlisted for the war and got furloughs, returned, much boasting of the good time they had enjoyed. The enemy never showed themselves during our stay. . . .

☆ *Jesse Ruebel Kirkland to Lucinda Kirkland*:

Camp Kellysville, Rappahannock River, April 4th, 1862

My Dear Wife,

. . . Our division is the rear guard of the army, and our regiment is the rear of the division, which is and has been on this post-picket duty for two weeks. The enemy are daily shooting and shelling our camp but without any material loss on our side. Our boys killed nine yesterday and captured twenty-nine, fourteen of which were officers.

I am now at the ford going over with a party scouting. Oh, that I could start home this morning instead of taking this trip. Tis useless, however, to talk about it. Lucy, I am writing on the horn of my saddle, and my horse will not stand still.

Good bye, dear Lucy. A thousand loves to you. God bless and protect you. I kiss you. Your affectionate husband,

Jesse

☆ *William Harris Hardy to Sallie Johnson Hardy*:

Culpeper Court House, Virginia, April 10th, 1862

My Dear Devoted Sallie,

While at Orange Court House day before yesterday, I was made happy by the reception of your affectionate letter. . . . You cannot imagine the pleasure, my dear, which your communications inspire me with. They are like the timely visitations of administering angels from heaven, who quell the sorrows and soothe the agonies of the heart and bring back the bright, sunny, halcyon days that once blessed me in the presence and association of my dearly loved and loving wife. Would that they came every day; for there is not a day, nay, an hour but what I think of my dear Sallie and sweet little Mattie. I say "sweet little Mattie" because you call her Mattie. If you have determined on that as her name, allow me to suggest that you do not give her any middle name, but plain, simple Mattie, and then if she ever gets married, she can put in Hardy as her middle name.[5]

I was indeed glad to learn that Sister Mary had arrived and that you were getting along very well, and I was glad to learn from Mr. Guthrie's letter (written in pencil—I hope you'll furnish him pen and ink next time he writes) that Sister Mary was well satisfied. This she may be, but I doubt if she is contented, having been driven from her home by the merciless vandals of the Yankee army, who, thank Heaven, have been most gloriously whipped near Corinth. This glorious news has electrified the whole country and everybody is in ecstasies. Sister Mary will be able to go home in a month or two now, as Generals Beauregard and Bragg will doubtless retake Nashville in their onward march to Cincinnati.[6]

I don't think our regiment will get into a fight at all, as the "Grand Army" have concluded they can't get to Richmond by this route and have consequently gone down to Fortress Monroe preparatory to advancing by Yorktown and Fredericksburg. They left one division here, and our division has been left here to keep them in check, the balance of our army having gone below to Yorktown and Fredericksburg, where there will be a great battle fought in a few days. Should we whip them there, I consider it will end the war, as it will be impossible for them to raise two more such armies as General Buell's in Tennessee and General McClellan's on the Potomac. We will then make it a war of aggression and push forward into their country and make them feel and know something of the ravages of warfare. . . .[7]

As you are so solicitous, my dear, on the subject of my reenlisting, I promise for your sake that I will not reenlist till after I return home. Then will be the proper time to decide that question. One month and a half more will bring the expiration of our term of service, and in that time much will transpire in the great bloody drama now being acted on this continent and will perhaps determine the fate of our youthful government.

My dear, write to me. . . . Give my love to Ma and Pa and Sister, also to Sister Mary and accept for yourself and darling baby the warmest love with a thousand kisses from your devoted and affectionate husband,

W. H. Hardy

☆ *Historical Sketch of the Quitman Guards*:

A Federal force of about twenty thousand men, under the command of General N. P. Banks, had penetrated the Shenandoah Valley as far as Strasburg and Front Royal, holding the city of Winchester. A small Confederate force under the command of General T. J. Jackson was all there were to oppose the progress of the Federal troops. A movement on Richmond from that quarter was looked upon as a very serious matter, and in order to check the enemy in this movement, General Jackson must be reinforced. For this purpose, General Ewell was ordered to join him in the Shenandoah Valley. The regiments being stationed at different points, General Ewell ordered them to concentrate at Gordonsville, from which place he took up his line of march for the valley.[8]

☆ *William Harris Hardy to Sallie Johnson Hardy*:
Gordonsville, Virginia, April 22nd, 1862

My Dear Devoted Sallie,
Our whole command arrived here . . . after having made a forced march . . . of thirty-one miles through the rain with nothing to eat but raw meat and parched corn. You may think it incredible when I tell you that I fared sumptuously on parched corn and raw bacon and was glad to get it. Talk of hardships. We have undergone the worse of them.

We have now given up at least a fourth of Virginia and have orders to march tonight in the direction of Richmond. We will likely be in a severe engagement in a few days. I am poorly fitted for either a march or fight, as I now have a fever on me and a cold. I have not been dry for days, and it is very cold. I marched with my overcoat on, which you know is very heavy, and carried my blankets on my back. I do not tell you of these hardships, my dear, to give you trouble but merely as an honest record of the campaign, for I bear up under these cheerfully. So many that suffer so much more than I do. . . .

I am now a candidate for lieutenant colonel of the Sixteenth Regiment, with fair prospects for election. How would you like to be called "Mrs. Colonel Hardy," eh?!! You see when I get to be lieutenant colonel, I can come home occasionally, perhaps.

My love to all and a thousand kisses for you and my darling Mattie. Your devoted husband,

W. H. Hardy

☆ *Jesse Ruebel Kirkland to Lucinda Kirkland:*
Gordonsville, Virginia, April 22nd, 1862

My Dear Wife,

    . . . You can better imagine my mortification at not having any of your favors to reply to than I can describe. . . . Tis more than a month since I had a letter from home, the last was the 18th of March.

Lucy, we have had an awful time of it for the past three days, marching and counter-marching day and night, all the while it rained incessantly and has but this moment stopped. Our boys stood it well. We were to have met Stonewall Jackson here. As yet, he has not reached here. Will be in tonight. Have just received orders to issue five days rations, saying there will be hard marching and hard fighting sometime this week. Our division, now under General Ewell, numbers twelve thousand, which we think will make its mark whenever we have an engagement. . . .

May Heaven bless and protect you and the babies. A thousand loves and kisses to you and them. I kiss you goodbye. Your devoted husband,

Jesse

☆ *Jesse Ruebel Kirkland to Lucinda Kirkland:*
Somerset, Orange County, Virginia, April 25th, 1862

My Dear Wife,

After an easy march yesterday, we reached here. Although the weather is very bad, snowing all day yesterday and now raining, our men have stood up remarkably well. We are now eighteen miles from General Jackson's army and expect to join him early in the morning, from which time we expect hard marching and fighting. Both Banks and Fremont's armies are immediately in front of General Jackson. Their combined forces are estimated at sixty thousand while ours will be twenty-five thousand. . . .[9]

Goodbye, a thousand loves and kisses to you and the babies. God bless and protect you is my prayer. I kiss you, Lucy. Your devoted husband,

Jesse

☆ *James Johnson Kirkpatrick Diary*, April 25, 1862, Wednesday:

Again started on march early this morning but marched leisurely and made little progress. Took the Madison Court House road and struck camp six miles from Gordonsvillle at Mr. Barnett's place near Liberty Mills. . . . Snow fell to depth of three or four inches. We had a reorganization and re-election of officers. None of Company C's officers retained their places. The re-enlisted men, acting in concert, carried the day. . . .

☆ *William Harris Hardy to Sallie Johnson Hardy*:
At Doctor Jones three miles from Gordonsville, Virginia, April 27th, 1862

My Dear Devoted Sallie,
I have not received a letter from you since yours of the 3rd of April. I can't imagine what's the matter. I am very anxious to hear from you. The last letter I wrote you I sent by Jasper Boykin, a discharged member of my company, in which I had given you a short account of our forced march of thirty-one miles in a day through the rain and sleet, on raw meat and parched corn. I told you, too, that I was sick. I was very sick. My fever lasted about five days, that with a drastic diarrhea, has made me so weak that I can't do duty now for sometime.[10]

Our company yesterday reorganized. . . . I was unanimously selected captain. Lieutenant Swittenberg was elected first lieutenant and Tom second lieutenant. . . .[11]

I am at a private house out here in the mountains, at a Doctor Jones' who is a man of wealth with a large and respectable family, three pretty, accomplished daughters. They all sing and play well. One of them, the youngest, Miss Mattie, is a lovely girl. I told her if I hadn't the best wife in the world, I would regret that I was married. They are all very kind to me. . . .

My love to all . . . and a thousand kisses for you and the baby from your devoted husband,

W. H. Hardy

☆ *Historical Sketch of the Quitman Guards*:

The expiration of the twelve months for which . . . the troops had volunteered being near at hand, orders were issued for their reorganization, and for that purpose the division was halted about five miles west of Gordonsville. . . . Colonel Posey was re-elected colonel of the regiment; Captain J. J. Shannon of Company F, Jasper Grays, lieutenant colonel; and Captain Samuel E. Baker of Company D, Adams Light Guards, was elected major. Many of the original officers returned to Mississippi and entered branches of service.[12]

☆ *William Harris Hardy to Sallie Johnson Hardy*:
Doctor Jones near Gordonsville, Virginia, May 3rd, 1862

My Dear Devoted Sallie,

This lovely Sabbath morning is the first time I have been able to sit up since I wrote to you last, which was last Tuesday. I have had the most severe attack of diarrhea I ever had in my life. . . . Doctor Jones says twenty years ago it would have been pronounced cholera. I feel very well now except I am very weak. I shall not be able to rejoin my regiment in a week yet. . . . If I continue in bad health, I shall quit the service and come home. I have not heard from the regiment since it left except that it had crossed the mountains. . . .

Well, this lovely Sabbath has passed away, the sun is now slowly falling behind the Blue Ridge Mountains. I have been in my room all day, read a little, slept a little, and eat a little. Mrs. Jones sent in with my dinner today a nice mint julep. Ah, twas excellent. You know how fond I am of them about eleven o'clock. This day had a very salutary effect on me, as I was very weak. It strengthened me very much.

I have learned from Doctor Jones . . . that we are evacuating Yorktown and . . . will be concentrated around Richmond, where the great Waterloo of this revolution is to be fought. Our division will hardly be in this fight. I think our campaign will be in the mountains of northwestern Virginia, a very hard and laborious one, though I can't tell. I think now the war will be a short one. It can't possibly last long with its present degree of magnitude. We have heard of the sad news of the surrender of New Orleans, which I presume could not have been prevented without a greater loss to the Confederacy than has occurred by its surrender. We must concentrate our forces so as to cut the invading armies to pieces. . . .

Give my love to all at home when you see them. Kiss my darling baby for me and accept a thousand kisses and kind caresses for yourself from your devoted husband,

W. H. Hardy

☆ *The Veteran's Story*:

From [Kelly's Ford], we were ordered to Gordonsville and camped there three days [May 2, 1862—May 4, 1862], having picket duties. Our march had been a weary one. The muddy roads over which we passed made us tired and stupid. On the march, we discarded all our belongings except a blanket, tent fly, haversack, and canteen.[13]

☆ *William Harris Hardy to Sallie Johnson Hardy*:
Gordonsville, Virginia, May 6th, 1862

My Dear Sallie,

Enclosed I send you a nice collar, a present from Miss Eddie Jones, one of the nice young ladies here where I board. It is to be prized the more highly because it is the work of her own delicate hands. The young ladies, three in number, call in to see me two or three times a day, doing everything in their power to make me comfortable and contented, and on their visit yesterday evening Miss Eddie brought in this collar to show me, remarking that "that was her day's work." I admired it very much. She asked me if you would wear it if she were to send it to you. I told her, "with the greatest pleasure," upon which she requested me to send it to you. . . . She says since the "Rebellion" broke out, they can't purchase such things, and she has from sheer necessity learned to make them herself, which is a noble example worthy of emulation.

I received a letter from Brother Tom yesterday. They are eleven miles beyond the Blue Ridge Mountains on the Standardsville and Harrisonburg Turnpike. . . .

Our regiment have selected field officers. Old Posey, by a "tight squeeze," was elected colonel. . . . I was sorry Colonel Clarke was beaten, for Colonel Posey beat him twenty-two votes. My being absent gave me no show as I anticipated, and on the first ballot my name was withdrawn.

Give my love to all. Your devoted husband,

W. H. Hardy

☆ *Jesse Ruebel Kirkland to Lucinda Kirkland*:
Camp on the Bank of the Shenandoah, foot of the Blue Ridge, Virginia, May 7th, 1862

My Dear Lucy,

I have just been awakened by the beat of the long roll and ascertained that we were ordered to fall back to intercept the enemy at Gordonsville, who had retreated from our front and taken the Fisher Gap Road down the valley with the intent to cross the Shenandoah, and, if possible, to cut us off, all of which they will be disappointed in. We are more than anxious and will doubtless, should they continue their march in that direction, meet them in the morning and are confident will, with the two divisions, Jackson's and ours (Ewell's), bag General Banks. General Jackson is in our rear.

Everything is kept dark. We know not who to trust, as so many of our move-ments have been telegraphed to the world. We are kept on the move all the time and, thank heaven, through all kinds of weather I have never been in better health. Although, Ma, you would hardly know me at first sight. I am not so fleshly as usual, awfully browned and hair all over my face.

Lucy, I am almost sure I will get a furlough in a short time, if only a few days, and will hasten home. . . . A thousand loves and kisses to you and the babies. May God bless and protect you all. Your affectionate and devoted hus-band,

Jesse

☆ *James Johnson Kirkpatrick Diary*, May 10, 1862, Saturday:

Companies C and D are sent out among the mountains to hunt up and arrest Union men and deserters. Had an interesting time. . . .

☆ *James Johnson Kirkpatrick Diary*, May 15, 1862, Thursday:

Started on the march today at ten o'clock. Commenced raining soon after and continued all day. Marched fifteen or eighteen miles which, considering the rain and want of rations, was as much as we were able to do. Halted shortly after dark.

— *Chapter 5* —

". . . DELUDED VICTIMS OF NORTHERN FANATICISM . . ."

By mid-May, 1862, the Sixteenth Mississippi reached the Shenandoah Valley of Virginia. Not only was the valley an important provisions source, its north-south corridor was a possible invasion route to the North. With Stonewall Jackson in the valley getting too close to Washington for comfort, Union generals Fremont, Shields, and Banks were sent to corral him, diverting strength from, and possibly delaying, McClellan's anticipated advance on Richmond. Ordered to reinforce Jackson, General Ewell's forces, including the Sixteenth Mississippi of Trimble's Brigade, moved its camp to New Market in the Hawk's Bill Valley between the north and south forks of the Shenandoah River. On May 21, 1862, they joined Jackson and immediately moved up the Shenandoah Valley, continuing one of military history's brilliant campaigns, one that made Jackson a legend. Here the Sixteenth, the only Mississippi unit to participate in the campaign, earned its reputation as part of Jackson's "foot cavalry," marching approximately four hundred fifty miles in less than thirty days.[1]

June 8, 1862, found the Sixteenth at the southern end of the Shenandoah Valley, two miles southeast of the village of Cross Keys, Virginia. As Fremont approached from the north, the Sixteenth and the rest of Trimble's Brigade were assigned to protect Courtney's Battery on the east end of the Confederate line, near the road to Port Republic. The aggressive Trimble, however, shortly moved the Sixteenth Mississippi, Twenty-first Georgia, and Fifteenth Alabama north and across Mill Creek. There the men of the Sixteenth would get their first taste of full-fledged infantry combat.[2]

☆ *James Johnson Kirkpatrick Diary*, May 21, 1862, Wednesday:

While in company drill this morning, received marching orders again. Struck tents immediately and marched at noon, re-crossed the mountains and encamped tonight one and one-half miles below Luray, having traveled six miles since noon. Saw "Old Jackson" today for the first time. He was stopped at a house and came out, by request, as we passed by. The Sixteenth gave him a good cheer. He was clad in an old sunburnt coat and cap.

☆ *Jesse Ruebel Kirkland to Lucinda Kirkland*:

Wednesday morning, May 21st, 1862, New Market, Page County, Virginia

My Dear Wife,

I had the pleasure on Sunday last on our march from the Blue Ridge to this place, which we reached yesterday at twelve o'clock. . . . The scenery and view from the mountains is truly magnificent, but, Ma, with all this before me, together with the noise of martial music and the regular heavy tramp of horse and foot-soldiering, you are still in my mind. No matter what the turmoil may be either in camp or on the march, you are never absent from my thoughts.

Captain Hardy has gone home on sick leave. It was my misfortune to be absent from camp when he started. I met him on the road and had no opportunity of writing. . . .

The health of the regiment is not so good as usual. Nearly all the new recruits are sick, which has again reduced our regiment from eleven hundred down to about eight hundred, all of which are in fine health and can stand hard and long marching. My health could not be better. I am not so fleshy as I have been. I only weigh 180 pounds, but I feel more energetic and more active than since a boy. . . .

Goodbye, Ma. May heaven bless and protect you and the children is my daily prayer. Kiss all the children for me a thousand times and tell them I am trying to get home to see them. . . . Goodbye my dear Lucy. I kiss you again and again. Your affectionate husband,

Jesse

☆ *James Johnson Kirkpatrick Diary*, May 23, 1862, Friday:

Started at sunrise towards Front Royal. Reached the place about three o'clock p.m. It is garrisoned by a regiment of [Union] infantry (First Maryland)

and some cavalry and artillery. We are immediately thrown into line of battle on left of the pike. The enemy's artillery commenced playing in our direction, but our line is formed behind the brow of a hill, and we are not exposed. Some musketry heard in advance. We are moved further to the left and advance. The First Maryland Regiment (Confederate) swept through the town in a charge, and the "Blue Coats" get further in haste. About this time, some of our artillery opens. Musketry roars louder, the air smells sulphurous, and things look real battle-like. The four right companies of our regiment are detached under Colonel Shannon to support a battery. Away it goes down the road at a gallop and we close behind, inhaling only clouds of dust and perspiring prodigiously. After keeping up this chase a mile or so, our battery takes a position, unlimbers and fires a few shots at the enemy. . . . The Yankees are in full retreat across the Shenandoah. They try to burn the bridges behind them but are prevented by too close pursuit.

After dark, we encamped two miles beyond Front Royal. No casualties in our regiment. The result of the engagement was the capture of five or six hundred prisoners; quite a number killed and wounded; the capture of two trains of cars loaded for Strasburg, a vast amount of commissary stores; some arms; quartermaster stores. . . . Everyone in high spirits.[3]

☆ *James Johnson Kirkpatrick Diary*, May 24, 1862, Saturday:

Started this morning for Winchester. Followed in the trail of the fleeing enemy last evening. It seems they threw away everything in this flight, even guns. Quite a number of them come in and surrendered to us today from their lurking places in the woods. We kept halting by the way till towards evening when we moved rapidly till within three miles of Winchester. Constant cannonading on our left and finally almost in our rear. Jackson is driving Banks from Strasburg down the pike towards Winchester. Slept on our arms tonight and came very near freezing. We had neither coats nor blankets, having left them at Front Royal, and the night is exceedingly cold. Continued firing among our pickets in advance of us.

☆ *James Johnson Kirkpatrick Diary*, May 25, 1862, Sunday:

In motion by daylight. Artillery opens at sunrise. We advance in line on the right of the pike. Meet no opposition except natural obstacles. One field of wheat that we passed through gave us the coolest of shower baths and performed a part of the morning toilet excellently. We are filed into a ravine on the right of town and remain inactive. The battle rages for nearly two hours with some sublimity, and then the Yankees are routed. We join in the pursuit and follow about eight miles; finding nothing to oppose, we are faced about and march back within five miles of Winchester and go into camp. . . .[4]

☆ The Veteran's Story:

. . . [May 25th] about daybreak, the line advanced towards Winchester. . . . When about a mile and a half of the march was made, the Twenty-first North Carolina Regiment commenced finding the Federals and drove their pickets back to their line of battle, which was posted behind a stone fence. The Twenty-first North Carolina dashed up to the line and was checked by a volley from the Yanks but was re-enforced by the Twenty-first Georgia. The Sixteenth Mississippi went to the right and just as we got in position, the Fifteenth Alabama . . . the Twenty-first Georgia and Twenty-first North Carolina routed the enemy, and the whole army set up the Rebel Yell and took after them.[5]

☆ Report Number 94. Report of Brigadier General Isaac R. Trimble . . . (commanding Seventh Brigade) of operations May 25:

The Sixteenth Mississippi (Colonel Posey), Twenty-first Georgia . . . and Fifteenth Alabama . . . followed [the Twenty-first North Carolina skirmishers] rapidly on the Winchester Road and all reached the hill a mile from town about seven a.m. . . At about eight o'clock, the fog dispersed . . . and the Sixteenth Mississippi was moved down the hill within view of the enemy and took a position on the east of the town in readiness to make a movement on the enemy's left flank. This movement, with that of the Twenty-first Georgia, no doubt had an immediate influence in deciding the result of the day as half an hour after a heavy force of the enemy . . . was seen to march in good order out of the town and take a northern direction behind woods and was soon lost to our view. . . .

About nine o'clock, a hearty cheer from that scene of conflict told the success made on the right flank of the enemy. . . . At this time, I received [General Ewell's] order to advance on the enemy's flank and cut them off. Had this movement been permitted half an hour earlier . . . the retreat of the enemy's reserves would have been completely cut off.[6]

☆ *Historical Sketch of the Quitman Guards*:

General Jackson pursued General Banks to Harpers Ferry, where he found the Federal forces stationed on the Bolivar Heights, an almost impregnable position. . . . General Jackson therefore abandoned further operations against Banks. . . .[7]

☆ *J. J. Wilson to James E. Wilson*:
Winchester, Western Virginia, May 27th, 1862

Father, Dear Sir,

I take the present opportunity of dropping you a few lines in answer to your letter. I received it about two weeks ago but did not have time to write since we have been on the march for the last ten days. The company is in very good health at this time. Marching agrees with them better than being still and doing nothing.

Our division is now under the command of General Jackson. He has whipped them three days in succession. He attacked them on Friday at Front Royal and gave them a very decent whipping, killed a good many and took some one thousand prisoners, and then on Saturday pursued them and whipped them again at Strasburg and Newtown, and Sunday morning at daybreak we advanced on them in Winchester and drove them out and followed them some eight or ten miles further, but we could not overtake them in their retreat. . . . I do not know how many were killed on either side. There was not a great many though. The Yankees took their killed and wounded off of the field, all that they could get. I reckon that I saw some fifty dead Yankees lying on the field.

Our regiment was placed back to support a battery if the Yankees should make a charge, but instead of them coming towards us, they went the other way as fast as their heels could carry them. They shelled us for an hour, but no damage was done to our regiment. Several shells fell within twenty feet of us and bursted there. It is not much fun in hearing the balls and shells a-coming. We can hear them from the time they leave the cannon until they burst.

I expect that they will reinforce from Harpers Ferry and advance on us, but

I think that Jackson is too smart for them. They lost a good deal of government property such as provisions and clothing. It was a complete victory over them. We took everything that they had except one house full of provisions which they set on fire as they ran off.

It is still very cold up here in the mountains, yet corn is just coming up. Good prospects for wheat and other grain crops. Give my love to all. Write soon.

J. J. Wilson

☆ *James Johnson Kirkpatrick Diary*, May 29, 1862, Thursday:

Started at daylight this morning. Passed through Charlestown, a beautiful place rendered lovely by the many pretty faces that welcomed us. Twas here that Old John Brown and his associates were tried and executed. Stopped to rest two miles from town and remained till two o'clock p.m., then advanced a few miles, halted, loaded and watched some Yankees till dark. Marched back and camped. . . .

☆ *James Johnson Kirkpatrick Diary*, May 31, 1862, Saturday:

Resumed the march this morning by day, passed through Winchester, Kernstown, Newtown, and Middletown. Saw some of the finest country I ever saw in my life. This valley of Virginia must once have been a paradise to live in. The buildings are ornaments, yards and gardens of excellent taste, orchards in abundance and the broad rich fields, waving with luxuriant grain. Plentiful springs of pure sparkling water. Everything indicative of wealth and happiness. In some places, the desolating touch of war has marred the prospect. No doubt this valley has added much to Virginia's far-famed hospitality for its people seem to possess this virtue in the highest order. Camped within two and one-half miles of Strasburg, after marching twenty miles.

☆ *James Johnson Kirkpatrick Diary*, June 1, 1862, Sunday:

Started again at day, marched to Strasburg, then making a detour of three miles northward, met and skirmished with the advance of Fremont's column which was trying to intercept us at Strasburg. They were a little too slow and . . . did not seem anxious for a fight. After confronting them for a few hours and exchanging a few compliments, we returned to Strasburg. . . . Remained here till after dark. Heavy rain this evening. Took up our line of march shortly after dark and marched nearly all night. . . . Halted a little before day within two or three miles of Woodstock. Slept the remainder of the night on the side of a hill in the rain. Quite uncomfortable. Traveled in all today, perhaps ten miles.

☆ *Historical Sketch of the Quitman Guards*:

[Jackson] arrived at Strasburg on the first of June. . . . General Fremont arrived a short time after . . . General Shields halted at Front Royal and cut off the retreat of Jackson in that direction. . . . Instead of giving Fremont battle at Strasburg, Jackson only made a feint and continued his retreat up the valley, burning the bridges as he passed over them, thus delaying the pursuit of the Federals.[8]

☆ *James Johnson Kirkpatrick Diary*, June 2, 1862, Monday:

Resumed march by daylight this morning. Some skirmishing in the rear today. General Turner Ashby, a most gallant officer, is covering our retreat. The force in our rear is estimated greater than Jackson's entire command. His force is about fifteen thousand, consisting of his own old division and General Ewell's, with a few companies of artillery and a small force of cavalry. Passed through Edinburg, Hawkinsville, and Mount Jackson. Heavy rain this evening continuing nearly all night. Roads very muddy. Day's march, seventeen miles.[9]

☆ *James Johnson Kirkpatrick Diary*, June 5, 1862, Thursday:

Aroused and . . . marched down to the turnpike and stopped in mud and water till day, waiting till the army passes by, then fell in and marched as infantry rear guard. Passed through Harrisburg this evening, leaving the pike and taking the road towards Port Republic. Camped soon after dark in an orchard. After getting comfortably settled, orders to fall in. Then might be heard curses loud and deep. We move a few miles and stop again for the night. Day's march over twenty miles.

☆ *James Johnson Kirkpatrick Diary*, June 6, 1862, Friday:

Started to Port Republic this morning, but on account of bad roads made little progress. Some heavy skirmishes in the rear this morning. The enemy, too, seems be pressing on with unusual courage. Their hope is doubtless to cut us off from crossing the river at Port Republic. General Shields has been marching up the other valley with a detachment from Fredericksburg, and we are almost between two armies larger than our own. All have the most unwavering faith in our leaders.

The noble Ashby was killed this evening in a skirmish. His daring charges on his milk white steed, his chivalrous and romantic disposition, his sublime courage had won to his admiration all who knew him. We hear of his death with melancholy regret. Brave hero! Who can take up thy mantle?

☆ *Historical Sketch of the Quitman Guards*:

Arriving at Cross Keys and having drawn the Federals from their base of supplies, he [Jackson] halted and determined on making a stand. The Federal army came up on the 7th of June.[10]

☆ *James Johnson Kirkpatrick Diary*, June 8, 1862, Sunday:

Today was fought the Battle of Cross Keys, and the Sixteenth Regiment, for the first time, made good use of their arms. . . . The Sixteenth, by a well delivered volley, decimated the Eighth New York. Fremont's forces were driven back with heavy losses wherever attacked. Only a small portion of our army was engaged, principally Trimble's (our) Brigade. . . . Lay on battlefield tonight. Part of our forces crossed the river at Port Republic this morning to hold Shields in check.

☆ *Historical Sketch of the Quitman Guards*:

The Federal army . . . formed in line of battle, General Shields being on the south side of the Shenandoah River. General Jackson, having different forces to contend against at the same time, determined to divide his command so as to operate as successfully as possible. Ewell's Division was left at Cross Keys. General Jackson moved about four miles distant and a little south of

Cross Keys to Port Republic in order to stop the progress of Shields, who was encroaching upon his right flank. Ewell formed his division, consisting of about eight thousand men, in line of battle to receive the attack of Fremont. Elzey's Brigade was posted on the left, Taylor's in the center, and Trimble's on the right.[11]

The Federals commenced the attack . . . [on June 8th] by skirmishing and cannonading and at the same time moving their line forward. Courtney's battery . . . was stationed on an adjacent hill and supported by the Fifteenth Alabama Regiment; and as that position seemed to be the main point of attack . . . Captain Courtney requested that General Trimble . . . send the Sixteenth Mississippi Regiment to his aid, which being immediately granted, the regiment took a position in front of the battery on the brow of a hill behind a string of fence.

The Eighth New York Regiment moved up in a beautiful line through a wheat field. They approached within thirty steps of the fence by which the Sixteenth Mississippi was concealed when they received a deliberate volley into the ranks. So sudden and so unexpected was this that . . . they immediately gave way. Colonel Posey . . . ordered his regiment forward. It crossed the fence, rushed forward, and kept up a rapid fire as it advanced. The whole line now became engaged. One of the enemy's batteries, which seemed to devote its attention to the Sixteenth Regiment . . . limbered up for the purpose of leaving that portion of the field. Colonel Posey . . . moved his regiment to the right to prevent the battery from making its escape, by which movement he placed his regiment in the rear of the Twenty-seventh Pennsylvania Regiment, which commenced a rapid and destructive fire upon him. Colonel Posey returned the fire and ordered his men to move forward, which they did, firing all the time. Here Colonel Posey was wounded in the breast. . . .

The attack was attempted to be renewed by the Eighth New York Regiment but, being met by the Fifteenth Alabama Regiment and having lost about two hundred and fifty men in the engagement with the Sixteenth Mississippi, was not able to stand against the earnest attack of the Alabamians and were driven pell mell from the field. . . .

Night coming on, the fighting ceased, and both armies went into camp. . . . General Trimble . . . requested General Ewell to allow him to make a night attack and urged that "as we had defeated them during the day, might easily put them to rout." Ewell referred the matter to General Jackson, who thought it unadvisable, as the Federals outnumbered him two to one.[12]

☆ *Report Number 94: Report of Brigadier General Isaac R. Trimble [continued]*:

I rode forward with [General Ewell] on the morning of the 8th [of June] at about ten o'clock to examine the ground most desirable for defense. I decided to post my artillery (Courtney's Battery) on the hill to the south of the small stream and immediately on the left of the road from Union Church to Port Republic. [General Ewell] directed my brigade to take the right of our line of defense and occupy the pine hill to the east of the road . . . en echelon position. Previous to assigning my brigade its position . . . I rode forward in front and to the right about half a mile and examined a wooded hill running nearly parallel to our line of battle. Finding this position advantageous, with its left in view and protected by my artillery and its right by a ravine and densely wooded hill, I at once occupied this position with two regiments (the Sixteenth Mississippi and the Twenty-first Georgia) about ten-thirty o'clock, leaving the Twenty-first North Carolina to protect [the battery]. . . .

Half an hour later, the enemy were seen to advance . . . (among the regiments, as prisoners informed us, the Eighth New York and Bucktail Rifles from Pennsylvania), driving in our pickets before a heavy fire. I ordered the three regiments [Fifteenth Alabama, Sixteenth Mississippi and Twenty-first Georgia] to rest quietly in the edge of an open wood until the enemy, who were advancing in regular order across the field and hollow, should come within fifty steps of our line. . . . As the enemy appeared above the crest of a hill, a deadly fire was delivered along our whole line, beginning on the right, dropping the deluded victims of Northern fanaticism and misrule by scores. The repulse of the enemy was complete, followed by an advance . . . in pursuit. As the enemy's rear regiments had halted in the woods on the other side of the valley, I deemed it prudent . . . to resume our position on the hill and await their further advance.[13]

Remaining in our position some fifteen minutes and finding the enemy not disposed to renew the contest and observing from its fire a battery on the enemy's left half a mile in advance of us, I promptly decided to make a move from our right flank and try to capture the battery. . . . I . . . moved the Fifteenth Alabama to the right along a ravine and, unperceived, got upon the enemy's left flank and in his rear, marching up in fine order as on drill. The Fifteenth Alabama completely surprised the force in their front (the enemy's left flank) and drove them by a heavy fire, hotly returned from behind logs and trees along the woods to the westward.

Meantime, the Twenty-first Georgia and Sixteenth Mississippi moved across the field and fell in with the remainder of the enemy's brigade, which had reformed in the woods to our left and delivered a galling fire upon the Sixteenth Mississippi. . . . The Twenty-first Georgia, came to their rescue . . . and drove the enemy out of the woods, killing and wounding large numbers. . . .

Perceiving the Sixteenth Mississippi and Twenty-first Georgia had advanced, I gave orders to charge the battery. Upon reaching the top of the hill, I found it had . . . retired. . . . Five minutes' gain in time would have captured the guns. This was lost by the Mississippi regiment misconstruing my orders. My regiments remained under arms all night, and I moved to camp at daybreak. . . .

I would call the attention . . . to the services performed on this occasion and previously by Captain Brown of Company A, Sixteenth Mississippi, who, with portions of his company, had within the last few weeks killed twelve of the enemy, captured sixty-four with their arms and some twenty-five horses with their equipments. . . .[14]

☆ *James Johnson Kirkpatrick Diary*, June 9, 1862, Monday:

Marched down and crossed the river this morning. A severe action is inaugurated with General Shields [at Port Republic]. . . . The enemy are completely routed and driven eight or nine miles down the river beyond Conrad's Store. Fremont's force came on after us to the river today, but seeming glad of the obstacle, made no attempt to cross. After deciding Shields's fate, we march up and camp in Brown's Gap.

☆ *Historical Sketch of the Quitman Guards*:

On the morning of the 9th of June, General Ewell was ordered to Port Republic where Jackson's Division was engaged against Shields. Ewell's Division was put in motion, and the Sixteenth Mississippi Regiment was deployed as skirmishers to cover the retreat to Port Republic. The Federals . . . advanced cautiously but frequently met the skirmishers, who contested every foot of ground. . . . They [the skirmishers] crossed the bridge at Port Republic and set it on fire, thus preventing the further pursuit of the enemy. In the meantime, Jackson had defeated Shields and compelled him to retreat down the valley.

Hearing that Jackson was receiving re-enforcements from Richmond, Fremont began a retrograde movement, and Jackson and Ewell went into camp near Weyer's Cave adjacent to the field of the recent conflict. Thus ended the Battles of Cross Keys and Port Republic.[15]

☆ *Dr. J. S. Davis to Mrs. Jessie R. (Lucinda) Kirkland*:
University of Virginia, June 12th, 1862

My Dear Madam,
It is my painful duty to inform you of your husband's death. He breathed his last at my home this morning about nine o'clock.

A train of wounded soldiers arrived here on the evening of the 9th, and among them was Captain Kirkland, who had been suffering from pneumonia and was said to be convalescing. I took him home but soon found that his case was extremely serious with symptoms of inflammatory rheumatism. Signs of typhoid fever with great prostration developed themselves during the night, and the next morning his mind began to wander, nor did he ever become rational again. He grew weaker and more restless through that and the following day and was unable to sleep at night, though anodynes were repeatedly administered.

We did what we could to render him comfortable. My mother stayed with him yesterday. The other members of my family persuaded him to take his medicine and food (his repugnance to both was almost insurmountable), and the whole of Tuesday night, I spent at his side. I have mentioned these details, dear Madam, because I am sure it will assuage the bitterness of your grief to know that your husband received that sympathy by those mentioned which you would have lavished on me in like circumstances.

His clothing and other effects will be entrusted to Colonel Posey who is here.

Believe me most sincerely and kindly yours,

J. S. Davis, [Surgeon]

☆ *James Johnson Kirkpatrick Diary*, June 14, 1862, Saturday

On guard duty at General Trimble's headquarters. . . . General Jackson's quarters are close by in some grove. He is a very devout Christian and makes prayer and reading his Bible a prominent part of his duty. Rises early and walks out alone every morning. Speaks on passing, without saluting. This little army thinks there is nobody like him. Everyone seems to regard him as a personal friend. Much reason, too, have we to admire him, for he never makes a blunder and is always acting.

☆ *J. J. Wilson to James E. Wilson*:
Craff Ford, Camp Jackson near Port Republic, Virginia

Father, Dear Sir,

I take opportunity of dropping you a few lines to let you know that I am well at present, and I hope that this may reach you all in good health. We have seen very hard times since I left home. We have been on the march nearly all the time. We have not stayed three days in the same place. We are now under the command of Major General Jackson in the [Shenandoah] Valley of Virginia. He has had five fights in the last three weeks and was successful in whipping them every time.

On Sunday last, we had a general engagement with the enemy; killed a great many and took about one thousand prisoners. The Sixteenth Regiment was in the engagement. It cut the Eighth New York Regiment all to pieces. There was seven hundred that come into the fight and only about two hundred of them that escaped. There was not very much damage done in our regiment. There was nine killed and about twenty-five or thirty wounded. . . .

Things is very backward up here. Corn is just large enough to work the first time [and] fine prospects for good wheat crops.

Nothing more at present. Write soon. Give my love to all.

J. J. Wilson

— Chapter 6 —

"... A REGULAR WAR OF EXTERMINATION"

While Jackson operated in the Shenandoah, McClellan maneuvered his Union troops on the other side of Virginia as a part of his Peninsula Campaign, the goal of which was to capture Richmond. Robert E. Lee, who took command of Confederate forces in the east following Johnston's wounding on June 1, 1862, summonsed Jackson to Richmond to help thwart the Union plan. The result was "... the Seven Days' fight below Richmond."

On June 18th, Jackson's troops and the Sixteenth received orders to march without revealing their destination. The latter, Ransom Jones Lightsey said, they didn't know themselves. The Sixteenth left its camp near Weyer's Cave and took the road for Gordonsville. Arriving at Gordonsville on the 20th, the Sixteenth boarded trains for Beaver Dam Station, then, after a three-day march, reached Ashland on the Richmond and Fredericksburg Railroad. By June 26th (the same day Lincoln appointed John Pope to replace McClellan) the Sixteenth reached Mechanicsville, five or six miles northeast of Richmond, where with the rest of Jackson's men they attacked McClellan's northern (right) flank. During the night, the Federals fell back to Cold Harbor and entrenched on an elevated position fronted by a boggy ravine and fallen timber.[1]

☆ **Report Number 255: Report of Brigadier General Isaac R. Trimble:**

On the 26th [of June], we moved with the army from Ashland in a southerly direction, passing to the east of Mechanicsville in the afternoon, and at four

p.m. heard distinctively the volleys of artillery and musketry in the engagement of General Hill with the enemy. Before sundown, the firing was not
more than two miles distant. . . .[2]

☆ *The Veteran's Story:*

We were then at Pole Green Church [near Hundley's Corner, about four
miles northeast of Mechanicsville]. . . . The Yankees made a bold stand at
Cold Harbor, fully determined to hold the place. . . . As we were going to the
front, we saw General Lee, Jefferson Davis, and Stonewall Jackson. We gave
them a hearty cheer. Davis tipped his hat and said, "Hurrah for old Missip!"

Jackson drove the Yanks from Cold Harbor and got their provisions and
whisky, too.[3]

☆ *James Johnson Kirkpatrick Diary*, June 27, 1862, Friday:

Warm today. Cannonading east of us soon this morning. Today is the Battle
of Gaines Mills. Company C lost two killed. . . .[4]

☆ *Historical Sketch of the Quitman Guards*:

On the morning of the 27th, the battle re-opened. . . . In order to gain the
brow of an opposite hill for the purpose of shelter until everything was in
readiness for a general charge, the Sixteenth Mississippi Regiment were
obliged to charge through this marshy ravine in the face of heavy fire from the
Federals. Several feints were made in order to attract the attention of the Federals from their right, where Jackson was executing a flank movement. About
sundown, a charge was ordered all along the line, and the Sixteenth Mississippi . . . rushed forward to the attack, and, notwithstanding the deadly fire to
which they were exposed, they continued to advance. . . . And in spite of the
breastworks, the strong abatis, and the galling fire, they succeeded in taking
the works and driving the enemy from the field. Though this was accomplished
in about fifteen minutes, the Sixteenth Mississippi Regiment lost about eighty
men in killed and wounded. . . .[5]

☆ *Report Number 255: Report of Brigadier General Isaac R. Trimble*
  [continued]:

On the 27th, line of battle was formed . . . by eight o'clock [a.m.], after
which we marched toward Cold Harbor, passing near [Pole Green] Church. At

this point, distant one and one-half miles from Cold Harbor, line of battle was again formed at about three-thirty p.m. and the advance ordered.

After marching half a mile, the front was changed considerably to the left, and orders were received to hasten to the front . . . in reaching the vicinity of Cold Harbor, our front was again changed toward the left under a heavy fire of the adverse artillery, and the point indicated where we were to engage the enemy. . . . I took the Fifteenth Alabama . . . down the road leading from Cold Harbor to McGehee's Farm, crossed the swamp and placed this and the Twenty-first Georgia Regiment . . . in position to advance. The Sixteenth Mississippi and Twenty-first North Carolina Regiments, in the confusion, were cut off and separated from us by several regiments which were marching out of action. . . . I returned to bring up the Sixteenth Mississippi and Twenty-first North Carolina Regiments. . . .

I decided to enlarge the front of attack . . . and led . . . [the Sixteenth Mississippi and Twenty-first North Carolina] across the road into the pines, one-third of a mile to the right (north) of the first point of attack. Here we met two regiments retiring from the field in confusion who cried out, "You need not go in. We are whipped. You can't do anything!" Some of our men said, "Get out of our way. We will show you how to do it!"

I formed my force . . . nearly parallel with the line opposed to us . . . and then rode along the line, distinctly telling the men in the hearing of all that they were now to make a charge with the bayonet and not stop one moment to fire or reload . . . and that the quicker the charge was made, the less would be our loss. . . . The regiments advanced . . . receiving heavy volleys of the enemy's fire from the opposite height without returning it; pushed on down the hill and over trees felled in the swampy ground to impede our progress, all the time under torrents of musketry fire; and . . . rapidly ascended the hill, cheered on by continuous shouting of the command, "Charge, men; charge!". . . .

The enemy were swept from the hill and retreated from his strong position. It was not until his fleeing forces presented a strong temptation that a destructive fire was opened upon them. Pursued to his camp . . . one regiment surrendered in a body; the others fled down a ravine toward the Chickahominy River. Reaching the plateau . . . I found a battery of seven guns (the First Pennsylvania Artillery) which had been captured a few minutes before. . . .

My brigade slept on the field from which the enemy had fled. . . . It is with just pride I record . . . that the charge of the Sixteenth Mississippi and the

Twenty-first North Carolina, sustained from the first movement without a falter, could not be surpassed for intrepid bravery. . . . The Sixteenth Mississippi
and Twenty-first North Carolina, numbering 1,244 men, passed under as hot
a fire and [one-half mile] distance in fifteen minutes, losing in killed and
wounded only eighty-five men.[6]

☆ *Letter from Major Samuel E. Baker*:

We were in the battles on Friday evening [June 27] . . . along the line from
Gaines's Mill on the right to Cold Harbor on the left. . . . We had hard fighting
to do, the enemy being in fine position and strongly posted, protected by
woods and breastworks.

On Friday evening [June 27], we were under fire till about half an hour
before sunset when the order was given to make a charge along the line from
right to left. The place where we had to charge was one difficult of access and
pregnant with danger. We had first to descend a ravine which ran into another
ravine which swept around the base of another high hill. In front of the hill,
there was a ditch about two feet wide, filled with water and mud waist-deep.
In the ravines, the enemy had cut down all the trees with the branches facing
us, so that our progress was slow and difficult. On the hill, the enemy had
posted three regiments—the first lying down on the brow of the hill, the second a little farther back, kneeling, and the third still to the rear, standing up.

Our line was formed with the North Carolina regiment on our left. The
Alabama and Georgia regiments of our brigade were separated from us early in
the evening. General Trimble led the charge. At the word "Forward," all
stepped off promptly. After going a short distance, we passed a regiment lying
on the ground just on the skirt of the woods from which we were emerging.
We now came to an open field. Over this we had to cross before we could reach
the ravine or hill on which the enemy were posted, and here the balls flew
thick and fast. But steadily we advanced to the ravine and were now at it. On
its brow lay a regiment. We were halted by its colonel and asked: "Where are
you going?" General Trimble answered: "We are going to charge the enemy
and drive them off." The colonel replied: "You cannot do it. Four attempts
have been made by different regiments, and each has failed." The general
answered, "We can and will drive them off. Forward, boys, and give them the
bayonet!"

With one loud cheer, we descended the ravine, falling and scrambling over the cut timber, each one anxious to be first. We now come to the ravine in which was a ditch. Into it we plunge under a most murderous fire of musketry. We cross it and commence the ascent of the hill and are met by a volley from the enemy; but now we charge up the hill furiously. Arrived at the top, the regiments lying on the brow fire upon us, and so close are they that the fire from their guns almost scorches and blinds us. Now for the first time, we fire. One general volley rolls along our whole line, and with a cheer, the men rush forward and charge. It is more than the enemy can stand. They waver, and they flee, hotly pursued, through the woods to their artillery. Here they are met by the Texas Brigade, which has broken their right, and they are driven back upon us. The slaughter here was great. Many escaped by running down a ravine . . . leading into the swamp. Many were taken prisoner.

It is now dark, and still the pursuit continues. The recall is sounded, our lines formed, and we lay down victors, sleeping on the field. But our victory is mixed with sorrow. Many noble have fallen. . . . The color sergeant was shot down as we neared the top of the hill. [Private] Irvine snatched the colors from the ground and, waving them proudly aloft, rushed to the front. The flag was pierced with eleven bullets. In this charge, we captured three batteries, over two thousand arms, large supplies of company stores, and about five hundred prisoners.[7]

☆ Report Number 255: Report of Brigadier General Isaac R. Trimble [continued]:

On Sunday [June] 29th, orders were received to march down the Chickahominy. . . . I halted about nine o'clock at a dwelling on the battlefield and sent an officer up a tree which had been prepared by the enemy as an observatory. . . . We continued our march about ten o'clock and after several halts, reached the York River Railroad near Bottom Ridge about two o'clock. . . . After marching and counter-marching several times, a halt of several hours was made two miles north of the railroad. Several times in the afternoon, I had called attention to the dense clouds of dust observed on the north side of the Chickahominy; and that it plainly was a rapid retreat of the enemy. . . . General Ewell had decided . . . to cross and attack them about four o'clock, but orders from General Jackson . . . prevented so important a movement.

About six p.m., the division was marched back up the Chickahominy,

crossed the stream in the night . . . and bivouacked at Reynoldsville, twelve
hours after the enemy and General McClellan had abandoned that place. . . .

On Monday [June] 30th . . . we marched at an early hour over the same
road taken by the enemy twenty-four hours before. . . . At about four p.m., we
reached the White Oak Swamp, where we bivouacked for the night. . . .[8]

☆ *Historical Sketch of the Quitman Guards*:

Jackson pursued the retreating Federals to Malvern Hill [on July1] where
the Sixteenth Mississippi was exposed to severe shelling for about eight hours.[9]

☆ *Report Number 255: Report of Brigadier General Isaac R. Trimble
[continued]*:

On Tuesday July 1, we marched . . . at sunrise; crossed White Oak Swamp,
the bridge having been destroyed by the enemy, causing some hours delay;
continued . . . and formed line of battle on Poindexter's Farm opposite the
Malvern Hills about two p.m., with [Trimble's] Seventh Brigade [which
included the Sixteenth Mississippi] on the extreme left.

We remained in position about three hours, during the greater part of
which time artillery and musketry firing was heard on our right a mile or two
distant. At five p.m., Courtney's Battery was put in position, opened a brisk
fire answered by heavy discharges from four or five batteries of the enemy
posted on Malvern Hill. . . .

After sundown, orders were received to march the Seventh Brigade to the
extreme right, where the battle had raged fiercely for some two hours and our
troops repulsed. I moved quickly . . . through a dense woods in the dark,
exposed for one and one-half miles to a continuous and rapid fire of the enemy's artillery and took up a position on that part of the field where . . . this
field was about half a mile broad, skirted by woods on the left and a high and
abrupt declivity to Turkey Creek on the right. . . . I occupied this position
until about twelve o'clock. . . . I retired the brigade into the woods to bivouac
for the night, as the men were completely worn out and no further action
expected.[10]

☆ *Letter from Major Samuel E. Baker [continued]*:

The fight on Tuesday evening [July 1st at Frayser's Farm, also known as
White Oak Swamp] was terrific, and we gained nothing. The enemy held their

position when the fight ended. It was continued until ten o'clock at night. We suffered terribly. We captured three batteries but were unable to hold them. My regiment was under a fire of shells but did not fire a gun. During the hottest of the fight, we were double-quicked from the extreme left to right under a terrible fire of round shot and shell. Here we acted as a support and kept the enemy in check. It was a trying position, for three batteries were playing upon us, and our artillery had been completely disabled.[11]

☆ *The Veteran's Story*:

We slept on the battlefield, expecting to renew the engagement on the morrow, but to our great joy and satisfaction the Yanks had left during the night. They certainly got off in a hurry for their food and all their dead and wounded were left behind.

This ended the Seven Days' Fight below Richmond. We moved . . . and went into camp.[12]

☆ *Report Number 255: Report of Brigadier General Isaac R. Trimble [continued]*:

The next morning [July 2] . . . in a drenching rain . . . the Seventh Brigade . . . prepared to move in a body by six o'clock. Orders were received from General Jackson . . . to march to the church, near which we remained all day, July 2.

Thursday July 3, we had orders to march to the front, did so, and encamped about eight miles from the James River opposite Westover.[13]

☆ *James Johnson Kirkpatrick Diary*, July 4, 1862, Friday:

Everything quiet. . . . No one seems to think that today was once an observed anniversary.

☆ *Report Number 255: Report of Brigadier General Isaac R. Trimble [continued]*:

July 4th, we again marched to the front; reached a point about four miles from James River where line of battle was formed and skirmishers thrown out half a mile in advance, who occasionally exchanged shots with the enemy's scouts. . . .

We lay in camp until July 8th, when we were ordered to move at dark to the rear, and on July 10th encamped four miles from Richmond, scarcely able to march from excessive fatigue and prostration, the result of constant fighting and marching in a country where air and water were both impure and rapidly breaking down the health of the army. . . .[14]

☆ *James Johnson Kirkpatrick Diary*, July 11, 1862, Friday:

Private Willie N. Robinson of Company C died in camp today very suddenly. Overcome by yesterday's heat and bathing in a pond in the evening was supposed to have caused his death. He was a good boy and is much lamented. . . . Our regiment, we understand, is about to be transferred from Trimble's to Featherston's Brigade.

☆ *The Veteran's Story*:

One night we [marched into Richmond and] serenaded President Davis. He came out on the portico of the Mansion and saluted us. We called for a speech. He responded very promptly. He said, "Fellow comrades, you are Mississippians. I am proud of the record you made, and I am satisfied that you will maintain your good record wherever you are called upon to meet the enemy." In his usual dignified manner, he bowed to us and retired. We gave him a hearty cheer and marched back to camp.[15]

☆ *J. J. Wilson to James E. Wilson*:
Camp near Richmond, July 11th, 1862

Dear Father,

I take this opportunity of writing you a few lines to inform you that I am well at present. . . . We are stopped for a few days for the first time since I came from home. I have marched at least five hundred miles since I got back to the regiment. The fight is over here at Richmond.

On Friday [June] 27th, our regiment got into the fight and drove the enemy from the field. We took a large amount of commissary stores, guns and ammunition, eighty pieces canon, some twenty thousand prisoners. . . . The Yankees loss in killed, wounded and prisoners is fifty thousand.

Nothing more at present. I remain, your son,

J. J. Wilson

☆ *James Johnson Kirkpatrick Diary*, July 13, 1862, Sunday:

Under marching orders. General Trimble bid farewell to the Sixteenth Regiment and turned us over to the tender mercy of General Featherston. The object in changing is to put us in a brigade wholly made up of Mississippi troops. All entertain a very good opinion of General Isaac R. Trimble . . .

☆ *James Johnson Kirkpatrick Diary*, July 15, 1862, Tuesday:

Marched to Richmond and thence to the camp of our new brigade two miles east of the city on the Charles City road. Extremely warm and dusty for marching. Camped in a field. Our brigade now consists of the Twelfth, Sixteenth, Nineteenth, and Forty-eighth Mississippi Regiments.

☆ *William Harris Hardy to Sallie Johnson Hardy*:
Camp near Richmond, July 22nd, 1862

My Dear, Dear Sallie,

I have concluded to write you a few hasty lines this evening. I am feeling better today that I have in a month, though I have a very bad cold. My general health is improving. . . .

I think it probable we will remain here for some time, though I can't tell. There is no accounting for the designs of our commanding officers. If I knew we would remain here long, I would write for you to come and spend a short time in Richmond, though it is one of the most unpleasant places I ever saw. Besides, the trip would be a difficult and arduous one.

I have no news to write you. Don't you be uneasy about me for if anything happens, I will telegraph to you, and if my health gets bad, I shall resign and come home.

If you have received any letters for me in relation to my candidacy for district attorney, show them to Mr. Spencer and then file them away.

My love to Sister Mary. . . . Kiss my darling Mattie for me and accept a thousand for yourself from your affectionate husband,

W. H. Hardy

☆ *William Harris Hardy to Joseph Kirkland*:

Camp of the Sixteenth Mississippi Regiment near Richmond, July 24th, 1862

Mr. Joseph Kirkland, Brandon, Mississippi

My Dear Sir:

As a friend to your brother Jesse and family, I have volunteered a statement of his affairs to you as near as I can get at them in the regiment.

1. He leaves here one horse worth about one hundred and twenty dollars.

2. He leaves here one horse worth about two hundred dollars.

3. He leaves here one horse in the Eighteenth Mississippi Regiment worth about one-hundred-seventy-five dollars.

Captain Jayne can inform you about this last horse, saddle, bridle and blanket, sword and belt, a Sharpe's carbine, one derringer pistol, and a few clothes. Most of his fine clothing he had with him. Also, he had with him one derringer pistol, all at Charlottesville, Virginia.

He has a good large sum of money due him officially by the officers of the regiment. He is owing Captain Hearsey, assistant quartermaster of our regiment, about five hundred for money advanced, two hundred dollars of which were advanced for the payment of his horse (Number 2). I would state that Captain Hearsey is willing to take the horse for the debt of two hundred dollars. He is owing other small sums in the regiment but none of any consequence.[16]

I have volunteered to give you this information and will do you any service in the premises that may lie in my power. Your brother was a warm friend of mine and indeed was universally beloved by the officers and men of the regiment. He was an excellent commissary and gave entire satisfaction and above all, an honorable gentlemen, a brave and chivalrous soldier which he clearly displayed at the Battles of Front Royal and Winchester. His death is universally deplored by the regiment.

Tender Mrs. Kirkland and family my kindest heartfelt sympathies in their bereavement to which Providence has subjected them. . . .

> Your friend and
> obedient servant,
> W. H. Hardy

☆ *Harry Lewis to Mrs. Nancy Lewis*:
Camp two miles below Richmond, July 30th, 1862

Dear Mother,

I commence this letter to you not that I have anything particularly interesting to speak of nor that I am bound by the established rules of correspondence to write as I have written twice since I've received any communication from you in the letter line, but simply because it is a quiet Sunday evening with me—a rare occurrence indeed! And further, because I well know it will cheer and please you to hear from us.

In the first place, we are all well, that is, none of us are really sick, though Fletch is complaining a little. Brother John . . . has been . . . in command of the company. Brother John is more popular than of old—that is, the company having experienced in the later battles the result of want of discipline and, seeing the evil consequent thereof, appreciate his strictness.

Mack, of course, returned to camp with Bud. He is not as homesick as he was two months since but still says he would like to go home sometime this fall. Mack [our slave] is very useful to us, and if anything is to be gotten, he obtains it for us. He is considerate and studies our wishes. . . .

We had preaching here this morning in the regiment. Reeves, our chaplain, gave a sermon which I did not hear because I had gone to take a bath and did not get back in time and besides, I don't think he is a man of the right stripe aside from ministering the Holy Gospel. One thing is certain, hypocrite or not, he exercised no moral influence in the regiment and commands not the respect of its members. This is a great pity for we sadly need the restraining influence of religion in camp, and a good holy man at the post would do untold good. In fact, two departments of our army sadly need to be cared for—the religious and the medical. One needs the presence of good men who command the respect of their fellows to attend the spiritual welfare of men fighting in a glorious cause.

And we suffer still more for the want of experienced and attentive surgeons. A great proportion of our assistant surgeons are men, or rather boys, of scarcely no knowledge or experience. Our assistant surgeon Groves showed cowardice three times in the field of battle. He could not be found till the battle was over and then away in the rear. He is irretrievably disgraced, not one of the regiment deign to notice him at all. He could have saved two poor fellows lives had he been at his post at Cross Keys. . . . One of these cases, a member of the Adams Light Guard from Natchez, had his leg torn off at the knee by a cannon ball, and if he had been properly tended doubtless would have recovered. As it was, however, he lay in the church for long hours until a Virginia surgeon dressed his wound in time to die.[17]

Another case of neglect was George Estes who died a few days since from the wound received at Cross Keys. A cannon ball took his leg off just above the ankle. A green physician amputated his leg, which George stood like a noble boy, as he was, but as the wound [was] healing . . . it was found that the bone protruded, so our young surgeon cut it off a second time just below the knee and neglected to secure the arteries properly, and when the wound commenced healing the artery bursted and threatened to bleed George to death, so the wise doctor concluded to saw the poor boys leg off a third time above the knee which caused his death. Poor George was a good boy and an excellent soldier. He told the boys when shot that he was sorry to lose his leg but was grateful his life was spared and told the surgeon after the second amputation he knew he was bound to die, and if his leg had been properly taken off at first, he would have lived. . . .[18]

The Sixteenth has been transferred to a Mississippi Brigade, the Sixth Brigade, under command of General Featherston, formerly colonel of the Seventeenth Mississippi Regiment. . . . We regretted to part with old "Stonewall" very much, for we had the utmost confidence in his skills and generalship, but we hated still more to part with our old Brigadier General Trimble. I believe there is not a man in this company or regiment who is not attached to him on account of his abilities and good qualities. . . .

Write to me soon. . . . Remember me to Aunt Alse and Judy and the colored population. Your affectionate son,

Harry

☆ *J. J. Wilson to James E. Wilson*:
Camp six miles east six of Richmond, July 31st, 1862

Dear Father,
I take the present opportunity of dropping you a few lines in answer to your kind letter. . . . There is no news of interest stirring about up here. The war

excitement is about over here at Richmond. It is reported that the Yankees are a-leaving James River. Jackson is in the valley and expect that he will stir the Yankees up over there. . . . I do not expect that there will be any fighting here again soon. We have got a good deal of work to do here. We have got to throw up breastworks. I do not see any of us in it for the Yankees will not come to fight us behind them.

You mentioned something about money. I do not want you to send me any as I have a plenty at present and will continue to have some as long as they pay off regular. Things is very high up here. They guess a man's pile and take it all at once.

We get a plenty to eat, such as it is, flour, bacon, beef, rice, and peas, but we get tired of that and want some vegetables. Peaches are one dollar a dozen, and they sell as fast as if they were twenty-five cents. . . .

Give my love to all relatives and friends. I remain, your son,

J. J. Wilson

☆ *James Johnson Kirkpatrick Diary*, August 5, 1862, Tuesday:

Called into line by the Long Roll at noon. Was just ready to sit down to a magnificent dinner of apple dumplings on which we had expended nearly all our resources, but orders will not admit of delay. Our repast is smoking hot and must needs cool before eating. With many regrets and unavailing tears, we leave our expected feast, a prey to the harpies that loiter behind. Marched four miles towards Malvern Hill and stop to await the issue. No hostile demonstrations. Learned that three thousand prisoners were exchanged today. Marched back to camp in evening, but as soon as we get there, are ordered to face about and march back again to our starting point. Evidently a misapprehension of orders. Very warm, dusty, and disagreeable. Slept quietly.

☆ *Hugh Carroll Dickson to Joseph J. Dickson*:
Camp near Richmond Virginia, August 7, 1862

Dearest Pa,

I now take my seat to write you a few lines to inform you that I am quite well at present. There is no news of importance worthy of communicating from this load of poles. All is quiet below Richmond. Our regiment is down here on picket while other regiments are throwing up breastworks. There was very heavy firing in the neighborhood of Drewry's Bluff last night. I think the enemy was trying to run the blockade through the darkness, as it was very dark, having rained pretty much all day, but it is mere surmise with me.[19]

General Jackson is up in the neighborhood of Gordonsville. I am listening to hear of a battle every day between him and Pope. It seems that the enemy have a great deal of confidence in him as a commander, but it will be with him like it has been with all of their other generals. When old Jackson defeats him, he will be lowered in the estimation of the people. . . .[20]

I am entirely out of clothes, have one pair of old breeches legs, no coat, one shirt, pair of drawers, one-half pair of socks. Someone stole my knapsack and everything I had, but what grieves me more is they stole my Mamma's and sister's ambrotypes. I hate that worse than anything that could have happened to me. I have kept them so sacred.

I must close, excuse all mistakes. . . . Give my best love to all of the family and reserve a large portion for yourself. I remain your loving son,

Hugh

☆ *Harry Lewis to Mrs. Nancy Lewis*:
Camp of Sixteenth Regiment, Mississippi Volunteers, August 9th, 1862

Dear Mother,

It has been over two weeks since I received a letter from you. . . . I have no valid excuse for not writing sooner but plead in the time worn and effete palliation of want of news and idle and lazy procrastination. . . .

The life of a soldier is in my estimation one of the meanest and laziest imaginable, and were not it for the cause we are battling for, I would not follow it a single hour longer. As a profession and a voluntary mode of livelihood, I would deride the idea and not allow it to engage my thoughts a moment, but as it is, I joyfully embrace it as a means of repelling a dastardly, plundering, oppressive and cowardly foe from our homes and borders. I grasp it as the only means of preserving all that is near and dear to me—home, family, friends, and country, and cheerfully I determine never to lay down my rifle as long as a Yankee remains on Southern soil—as long as the cry of subjugation and extermination is raised by the *"best government the world ever saw"* against a people of the same language and manners whose only offense is a desire of separation. Every day that passes strengthens the resolution of every Southern patriot. He sees the invaders overrunning a portion of his country and burning the houses of the most conspicuous Southern men and confiscating their property, compelling the old men and families to flee for their lives to the Southern lines. He realizes that wherever the track of the invader is, there everything Southern in sentiment is a perfect desolate waste. He sees the storm coming and sallies forth to dispense it or turn its course and resolved is he either to accomplish this or perish in the noble attempt, and this spirit will ultimately prevail—yes! The North may raise her volunteers and draft her conscripts by the hundred thousand and lavish her wealth by the hundred million, but to no avail. She may by her inexhaustible resources carry on the war for years and overrun the greater portion of Southern territory, still right will prevail, and in the end the Southern people—those that survive—will raise the triumphant shout of Freedom! Freedom! as the monstrous and decaying edifice of Union, undermined by debts and her own blind folly, collapses and forever settles into oblivion. But enough of this, I tire you with my ranting. . . .

Last night the moon was full and as bright, soft and mellow as I ever beheld even in our own Woodville. It was a beautiful night. . . . Chaplain Reeves held a well-attended prayer meeting in the next company to ours which was attended by a respectful as well as respectable audience. Although I have no confidence in the sincerity of Mr. Reeves as a true Christian, and the regiment as a general thing has less, still I attended and was gratified to see so many present. He will hold his meeting tonight in our company's camp. We had a splendid sermon from C. K. Marshall last Sunday, and he had a tremendous congregation. . . .

We have sent reinforcements to Stonewall Jackson from this point and large numbers of troops coming from the more Southern states have recently joined him, swelling his force to fifty thousand men, with which army we confidently expect him to defeat Pope, who is oppressing and trammeling the loyal people of Virginia in as base and unsoldierly a manner as the brute Butler tyrannizes the good people of New Orleans.[21]

The war is fast verging into a regular war of extermination. The repeated hanging and shooting of our citizens for trivial offenses and for protecting their homes has at length called forth a proclamation of President Davis, who in a manly tone says that if the murder of our citizens isn't stopped, he will retaliate upon their commissioned officers. Now it only remains for the Yankees to cease their outrages or enter in a war of no quarter, of a war to the knife. It is awful to contemplate such a state of things. Still, we are ready for the alternative.

Dear Mother, I am getting to hate the Yankees in earnest. Their treatment of prisoners is scandalous and insufferable. Although we have taken prisoners time and again, I have never seen one mistreated. On the contrary, I have seen our footsore, starving boys having only four crackers and a slice of bacon a day through, then give their only cracker to a crowd of begging Yankee prisoners who greedily played the game of grab. And I have noticed at other times our men ministering to wounded Yankees and voluntarily carrying cool water and seldom ever saying anything annoying to them as they passed by in squads to the rear. Yet these Yankees insult our boys when prisoners and, if they attempt to answer, resent it and strike them—the cowards!—and run a bayonet through them. I know of a case where a Yankee officer beat one of our brave men with the flat of his sword and then ordered him to a dungeon because he did not move quick enough. These are facts, for some of our own company who were taken at Winchester corroborate it.

McClellan is in his same old position at Turkey Bend which he took and fortified after the battles were over. No telling what he is about, but no doubt reorganizing and strengthening his army and probably awaiting the three hundred thousand recruits from Yankee Land. If he ever attempts to take Richmond again, it is thought he will advance on the south side of the James River where we are throwing up fortifications for defense, if necessary. I hardly think he will make the attempt before next spring, though he may make advances before that time. . . .

Write soon. Your son,

Harry Lewis

☆ *James Johnson Kirkpatrick Diary*, August 12, 1862, Tuesday:

Waked up a little after midnight last night to get ready to march. Formed and started at two o'clock [a.m.] Marched to Richmond and took the cars at sunrise for Gordonsville. Arrived here at three p.m. . . . marched out one-half mile into the woods and camped. A heavy rain in the evening.

— Chapter 7 —

". . . WE SWEPT EVERYTHING BEFORE US"

After failing to destroy Jackson's outnumbered army in the Shenandoah Valley, Union forces combined under General John Pope on June 26, 1862, the same day the Seven Days' Battles began. On July 14th, Pope moved fifty thousand troops toward Gordonsville, Virginia. With McClellan having ninety thousand men near Richmond, Lee saw the possibility of Federal forces converging and destroying his army. Seeing also, however, a Confederate advantage to be gained from McClellan's lethargy, Lee seized the initiative. He ordered Jackson and his twelve thousand Confederates, to be followed shortly by A. P. Hill's twelve thousand, to Gordonsville. Longstreet's Corps (which included the Sixteenth Mississippi, a part of Wilcox's Division, Featherston's Brigade) and Lee moved north, bringing a combined Confederate force of 48,500 to meet Pope's 75,000 on the Manassas Plains for the second battle at Bull Run.[1]

The Sixteenth spent their first night at Manassas, August 29th, in a cornfield. By four p.m. August 30th, they had relocated to a wooded area near the intersection of Sudley Road and an unfinished railroad. Featherston's Brigade was the farthest north of the four Confederate brigades facing the Ninety-seventh and One-hundred-fifth New York regiments. Just after six p.m., the Sixteenth and the rest of Featherston's Brigade emerged from the woods, intent on driving the Federals back.[2]

☆ *William Harris Hardy to Sallie Johnson Hardy*:
Camp near Gordonsville, Virginia, August 15th, 1862

My Dear Sallie,

I sent you a short letter. . . . It was written about midnight by a candle in the open air. That night . . . I did not sleep a wink. . . . At one o'clock, we took up line of march and by daylight we were in Richmond, having marched eight miles. Then we took the train, and at two o'clock p.m., we were in Gordonsville, having moved our whole brigade a distance of eighty miles in about twelve hours. . . . We bivouacked under the trees and, as usual, had quite a heavy rain on us, but we have plenty of splendid oilcloths captured from the Yankees and hence did not get wet. We remained in Gordonsville till yesterday when we moved out here, four miles west of Gordonsville between the two railroads, where we bivouacked last night.

My health is tolerably good. . . . The health of the company was never better. My men are devoted to me, and I have great confidence in them. I know they will do to depend on. I hated losing six of my best men. They were discharged . . . and although they were going home to their dear ones at home, the tear drops glistened in their eyes, and I could not restrain a tear myself.

Colonel Posey is still commanding the brigade, General Featherston's wound not having yet sufficiently cured up to enable him to take command. It is rumored in camps that Posey is to be promoted to brigadier general. If so, Colonel Shannon and Major Baker will be promoted, and I will then be promoted to major of the regiment.

A large and powerful army is concentrated in and around Gordonsville now, and you must not be surprised to hear of a desperate battle being fought here in a few days. Indeed, we do not know at what moment it is to begin. . . . Stonewall Jackson is here, General Lee, Longstreet and a host of other generals. The Yankees are reported to be advancing. It is thought that McClellan, Burnside and Pope are all concentrating their forces on this point, which I presume is so, as nearly our whole army has left Richmond and concentrated here to oppose them. . . .

God bless you, my dear. Be of good cheer. God will work out this great problem of our independence for us, and we yet will be permitted to live in peace and quietude. Good bye. Your devoted husband,

W. H. Hardy

☆ *J. J. Wilson to James E. Wilson*:

Camp Wood, Gordonsville, Virginia, August 18th, 1862

Father, Dear Sir,

There is a right smart of excitement up here now. They're expecting a large battle to come off now in a few days up on the Rappahanock River near Culpeper Court House. The Yankees has a very large force, and I expect that it will be a larger battle than the fight at Richmond. General Lee has a force of about one hundred thousand, and I think that he will make the attack. The Yankees have already fallen back a few miles, but I reckon it was to get behind their breastworks. I wish that they would end the war for I am getting tired of it.

If you can see any chance to send me one pair of shoes, I wish you would do it for I am nearly barefooted, and shoes cannot be had at any price. Shoes is from ten to twelve dollars a pair in Richmond. I do not want the other clothes yet, I have got as many as I can pack when . . . on a march.

Our company is in very good health at this time. We have about seventy-five men in [our company], and if we do get into a fight, we will give them the best that we have got, but I am tired of fighting. I had rather quit and let them alone if they would go home and tend to their own business.

I have not got time to write any more. Give my love to all relatives and friends. Write soon. I remain your son,

J. J. Wilson

☆ *James Johnson Kirkpatrick Diary*, August 19, 1862, Tuesday:

After a very cold night's rest in an old field, no fire and much dew, having had nothing to eat since early yesterday, I started out to forage for breakfast. Got a piece of one and filled up the balance on green apples and peaches. After getting back to the regiment, we drew and cooked three days' rations, flour and bacon. Formed to march a little before dark, but did not move. Received twenty additional rounds of cartridges, making in all sixty. Orders to be ready to march at three a.m.

☆ *Historical Sketch of the Quitman Guards*:

Arriving at Kelly's Ford [on August 21], the Twelfth and Sixteenth Mississippi Regiments, under the command of Colonel Posey, were sent forward to reconnoiter. Companies K and H of the Sixteenth were deployed as skirmishers. Those remaining were formed in a line of battle to repel the attack of the cavalry in case the skirmishers failed to drive them back. Two hours of fighting ensued when the two companies of skirmishers were compelled to fall back on the regiments for protection. The cavalry, being deceived as to the actual force against them and perceiving a portion of the Twelfth Regiment extending from a skirt of woods into an open field, immediately prepared to charge them. The Twelfth Regiment held its fire until the cavalry advanced within gun shot range then discharged a volley into their ranks which turned them in the opposite direction, killing a large number of them. The Federals, discovering the odds against them, retired to the north bank of the Rappahannock where they had the advantage of a hill upon which they placed their artillery. . . . Both sides commenced a fierce cannonading which did not cease until dark.

The Federals having crossed the Rappahannock at Kelly's Ford, General Wilcox moved on to Brandy Station on the Orange and Alexandria Railroad to rejoin the main body of the army. . . .[3]

☆ *James Johnson Kirkpatrick Diary*, August 21, 1862, Thursday:

A spy was caught and hung here this evening. . . .

☆ *James Johnson Kirkpatrick Diary*, August 23, 1862, Saturday:

Cannonading commenced early this morning up at the Rappahannock. Our guns on this and the Yankees on the other side of the river. Our troops move up and halt in supporting distance. A little before dark, we move back and camp at Brandy Station.

☆ *James Johnson Kirkpatrick Diary*, August 25, 1862, Monday:

On the march again by day. Greatly impeded as usual by trains and General Longstreet gets our blame for not keeping the trains out of the way of the troops. . . . They ought to be either before or behind the infantry and not mixed up with them on the march. There is no Yankee cavalrymen to attack them. Heavy cannonading in direction of Warrenton Springs. Came in sight of the enemy's wagons in the evening across the Rappahannock. Stopped to camp within range of a battery across the river. It fired a few shots at some of our ambulances, but did not annoy us. Drew some rations tonight—crackers and beans.

☆ The Veteran's Story:

We crossed the river at Ely's Ford and went to Rappahannock Station on the Rappahannock River. There we found Pope with his army stationed on the opposite side of the river to dispute our passage. Jackson paid very little attention to him. He gave them a few cannon shots and marched on to another crossing. Finding the Yankees posted on the other side, he would fire two or three big guns and resume the march, with Longstreet and Hill bringing up the rear. The march was continued till we reached Warrenton Springs, where a crossing was effected. A heavy thunderstorm with a downpour of rain caused Jackson to withdraw his troops. . . . We went into camp and drew three days' rations with orders to move at daylight.[4]

☆ *James Johnson Kirkpatrick Diary*, August 27, 1862, Wednesday:

After getting scarce two hours sleep, started early, as we learn, to support Jackson, who has made detour and got in the enemy's rear at Manassas. Were detained a few hours at Salem by the enemy's cavalry. After clearing the way, we pushed on and camped at a late hour three or four miles beyond. We never make much progress after night. Bad crossings and bad roads makes our progress so little that the distance gained is a poor compensation for our fatigue and loss of sleep.

☆ *James Johnson Kirkpatrick Diary*, August 28, 1862, Thursday:

Drew some beef this morning but hurried off before cooking it. As a consequence, most of it was left. Crossed the Bull Run Mountains at Hopewell Gap in the night, roads very rough and stopped late in the night in close proximity to the enemy. Slept on our arms in an old field covered with stones, ready for any emergency. Kept out two companies deployed as pickets. . . .

☆ The Veteran's Story:

Longstreet and Hill remained in front of Pope while Jackson and his corps moved around Pope's right flank and came down upon Manassas Junction in his rear. There [Jackson] captured the garrison and all of Pope's army supplies. . . . After being well supplied, [he] burned what was left and moved on to the Manassas Plains near the stone bridge on Bull Run Creek. There Jackson intended to stand till Longstreet and Hill could come to his relief. . . .[5]

☆ *James Johnson Kirkpatrick Diary*, August 29, 1862, Friday:

Off by day on a forced march towards Manassas. Brisk cannonading in that direction, and we understand that Jackson is being hard pressed. Passed through Haymarket and Gainesville amidst clouds of dust and the perspiration pouring off us in torrents. The country is now more open, and the display of Longstreet's columns is very imposing. Jackson may breathe easy for powerful aid is close at hand. After reaching the edge of the battleground, we halt. Load and form line on the left of the pike. After advancing about one-half mile in line of battle, we again halt. . . . Excessively hot and marching in close order of battle is too much for human flesh and muscle to endure. The firing in front is now more slack and desultory. The clouds of dust concentrating to Jackson's rear may have admonished the assailants to be prudent. In the evening, our brigade is withdrawn to the right of the pike and march up the old railroad embankment. . . . At dusk, Hood's Texas Brigade are sent to the front on our left, deliver a most musical volley in the enemy's face, and follow it up rapidly. The increasing distance tells who are giving way. We now march back to the left of the pike and advance by right of companies to the front a mile or two but meet with no obstacle, except ravine and fences. Halted in a corn field till after midnight, then retire to the rear and sleep in some woods till day. A force of cavalry attempted to charge down the pike tonight, but a volley from our line stopped their clamor and when it died away, only groans could be heard.[6]

☆ *James Johnson Kirkpatrick Diary*, August 30, 1862, Saturday:

One day's rations of meat and bread was distributed around this morning, and after relieving hunger, the brigade formed, marched down the turnpike and filed left to take its position for the day. Formed line in some woods and rested, sending forward a line of skirmishers. Ere long, we marched a few hundred yards to the front and occupy a stone fence. . . . The sharpshooters are busily employed, and occasionally a battery opens. There is one of these about twelve hundred yards in our front which occasionally speaks to us and the artillery behind us but in the main behaves very civilly. Clouds of dust all fore-noon approaching from the enemy's rear show that they too are reinforcing and maneuvering. The day is sultry, and about noon, almost a calm settles down in the field. The rattling of musketry has nearly ceased, and our troops all reclining, many asleep, some conversing and watching. No signs in front. Suddenly about three p.m., the earth fairly quivers from the shock of our artil-lery, and in a moment, the soundest sleeper is all attention. The enemy's lines, three in number, have emerged from the timber on the left of our front and are coming on with fixed bayonets and flying colors. But our artillery is making sad havoc in their dense columns. Every shot falls in their midst and bursting, strew the ground with blue. "Attention!" is heard for miles up and down our lines. Volleys of musketry rattle along our battalions on the left, and the enemy break in confusion and seek shelter in the woods behind them. "For-ward!" is the next command and the long lines of grey, with its battle flags proudly floating, death starts on its mission. The battery in our front gave us its special attention, but the undulating character of the ground saved us from much damage. Our direction is left oblique. From this time till midnight, the scene is sublime indeed, and many a soul is sent to its last account. Musketry rolls its incessant volleys, mingled with the deeper toned thunder of artillery, the swift rushing of shells, the hissing of shrapnel and canister, all combine to make a symphony most sublime. The enemy are everywhere routed, and night stops the carnage and our advance. We rest on arms on the field. Company C lost one killed . . . and thirteen wounded. . . .

☆ *Number 147. Report of Brigadier General Winfield S. Featherston . . . of [Second] Manassas:*

At an early hour on the morning of the 30th, my brigade was posted near a fence about a half a mile west of the main road running to the village of Groveton, uniting with General Jackson's command on my left at the railroad embankment. . . . The other brigades of General Longstreet's Division contin-ued our line of battle to the right, and extending a considerable distance to our right was an open field from half to a mile wide. The troops remained in position here from an early hour in the morning until about three o'clock in the afternoon. While in this position, my brigade was subjected to a very heavy fire from the enemy's artillery, which was placed in the woods on the opposite side of the field lying in our front. Two of our batteries, placed on a hill about the center of my brigade and just in the rear, returned the enemy's fire during the most of the time. The enemy were observed during the forenoon passing down the turnpike from the direction of the stone house and filing to the right and left of our lines.

About three p.m., one brigade was seen emerging from the woods on the opposite side of the field advancing in the direction of General Jackson's right and my left. The advance was steady and unchecked under a very heavy fire of the batteries supported by my brigade as well as from others placed on the right and left of the turnpike road. This brigade of the enemy was followed by two others . . . which advanced to within forty or fifty yards of our lines. Here they came to a halt and returned the fire of our infantry for about thirty minutes. When they commenced their retreat, our troops were ordered to advance. One of General Jackson's brigades advanced on our left, and my brigade . . . moved forward in line of battle on its right. We reached the works in front and passed through the skirt of woods over six hundred yards wide when we came to another old field some half a mile or three-quarters in width. Here we found on the opposite side of the field, the enemy drawn up in a line of battle with several pieces of artillery turned upon our troops and directing a rapid, heavy and destructive fire both upon the right and left of our lines. . . .

Very soon after, General Longstreet's staff announced to me [that] . . . a brigade of General Jackson's Division had been sent to reinforce me, and that other troops were coming up for the same purpose. General Pender and General Archer very soon arrived with their brigades, and I immediately directed my brigade to be moved to the left, so as to extend beyond the enemy's right, and Generals Pender and Archer to form on the right of my brigade. . . . As soon as our line was formed, an advance was ordered. The whole line moved forward. . . . The enemy fled after the first well-directed fire through the woods in the direction of the stone house. All their pieces of artillery were left upon the field and captured.[7]

These brigades continued the march in pursuit of the enemy. Passing through a skirt of woods, they reached another field some three-quarters of a mile wide, on the farther side of which the enemy were discovered again in line of battle with one or two pieces of artillery placed upon a commanding eminence, which were turned upon our troops as soon as they made their appearance. These brigades were again put into the line of battle in the edge of the woods. . . . These dispositions having been made, our lines advanced. The enemy fled precipitately, doing us no injury except with their artillery and scarcely returning the fire of our infantry. . . . It was now fully dark, and our troops bivouacked upon the ground until morning.

The enemy's artillery . . . served with great skill and effect upon our troops during the entire engagement, to which our greatest loss on the left must be attributed. Our troops . . . behaved with great coolness and courage during the whole engagement, which lasted about four hours. . . .

All of which is respectfully submitted.

W. S. Featherston,
Brigadier General
Commanding[8]

☆ *Historical Sketch of the Quitman Guards*:

General Wilcox desired to take a battery that was doing much damage to the Confederate ranks and . . . ordered General Featherston to move forward in order to attract its attention while he charged it with his own brigade. General Featherston obeyed the order, standing in front of his brigade apparently heedless of the iron hail that was falling thick around him and which inflicted instant death upon a large number of his men. The position of the Sixteenth was very much exposed, and they suffered greatly.[9]

☆ *William Harris Hardy to Sallie Johnson Hardy*:

[Dear Sallie]

I participated in the Second Battle of Manassas from start to finish. I again commanded the skirmish line in the second day's fight. It was in this battle . . . that I first saw effective use of artillery. Up until that time, we looked upon field artillery as just another arm of service, useful in its place but not of great and decisive power. That was all changed by this battle.

I was in a position where I could see the battle lines. Federal troops advanced to the attack in plain view from where my company was stationed. Batteries of artillery were behind us. When the Federals got within range, these batteries opened up. Great gaps were torn in the advancing lines, and as they came nearer, they were decimated by the murderous fire poured into them. They never got within rifle range of us. Those who survived turned and fled. Reserves were brought in to reinforce them. Thus reinforced, they returned to the attack. Again, their columns were broken up by the terrific fire of our batteries. We were then ordered to charge. At the time, our regiment was lying behind a low stone fence. My company was the first to leap over the fence. We charged down the hill, over the railroad cut and pursued the enemy through a clump of woods. When we reached the other side, they were going over the hill beyond. There was some confusion at this point in our ranks due to a conflict of orders. After this error had been corrected and while we were readjusting our lines, General Roger A. Pryor came up to me. He inquired my name and the identity of our troops. I informed him that this was the Six-teenth Mississippi Regiment, and that I was Captain Hardy of Company H. He then said he wanted to report to me and go into that charge as he had been cut off from his brigade. About that time, command was given us to change front forward on first company. I lost sight of the general and did not see him again in that battle. As soon as we got our regiment in position, we made a charge. These charges continued one after another as fast as we could get within gunshot of the enemy. We drove everything in front of us until night intervened. We lay down and slept on the field of battle.[10]

Our regiment made four charges, and we swept everything before us. I led the right. My company acted well, except a few. I must tell you, Henry Evans went out alone after we had halted for the night and presently returned with nine Yankees which he had captured by himself!

I have only twenty-five men left fit for duty. . . .[11]

[W. H. Hardy]

☆ *William Harris Hardy to Sallie Johnson Hardy:*
[September 7, 1862]

Dear Sallie,
[In the second Manassas battle on August 30th,] we drove the enemy about four miles, step by step, contesting every inch of ground till near night fall when they threw down their arms and fled in the wildest confusion. . . . Oh, could we like good old Joshua have commanded the sun to stand still for six hours, we would have killed, captured, or routed the combined army of Pope, Burnside, and McClellan. But we could not. Night closed the scene, and we lay down on the bloody field to rest our weary frames, which after the excite-ment was over, were completely prostrate and powerless.[12]

We slept in line of battle on our arms on the bloody field, and oh, the heart sickens at the thought. All the firing had ceased, everything was calm and still after the awful storm save the awful shrieks of the dying and wounded, which were great from every quarter in every direction. Cries for help, for water, brother calling for brother, comrade for companions, some calling on God to take their dying souls to heaven, others praying Him to take care of their wives and little children. In ten feet of where I lay was a Pennsylvania Yankee with his bowels shot out. He was lying in the branch. He begged for water and for a blanket and said that he was freezing. It was the cold hand of death. Some of the boys lifted him out of the branch and wrapped a blanket around him. We left before daylight. I don't know what became of him.

Brother Tom was wounded early in the fight by the cannon ball that cut Samuel Floyd in two. I caught Tom as he fell and led him to a tree. He was senseless, and the ball had severed flesh and blood from Floyd all over Tom's head and face, and I left him for dead, but fortunately, it was not serious. I have blood now on my coat which the ball knocked on me from poor Samuel Floyd. Dick Derrick was shot down right before me. How any of us escaped is a miracle. We marched by the flank four hundred yards with two Yankee batteries playing on us with grape and canister. I saw we would all be killed, so I ordered my men to take the trees, which they did. The little tree I got behind was struck with a canister shot. A man was killed right in front of it. . . .[13]

My love to all, kiss my darling for me. Your devoted husband,

W. H. Hardy

The men are sick and barefooted. I would write more but have no more paper.

— *Chapter 8* —

"... A LITTLE TOWN IN MARYLAND"

Following Pope's defeat at Second Manassas, Lee decided to move the war north and invade Maryland. He hoped to convince the people of the border state to rally to the Southern cause and strengthen the growing Northern discontent with the war. Further, Lee believed an invasion would relieve war-torn Virginia. With the Federal army now back under McClellan, Lee, knowing McClellan's slowness to act, split his forces and sent Jackson and forty thousand troops (including the Sixteenth Mississippi of Featherston's Brigade, now assigned to Anderson's Division) to Harpers Ferry. By capturing the Union garrison, Lee aimed to shift and secure his supply lines in the Shenandoah Valley. Learning of Jackson's success at Harpers Ferry on September 15th, Lee, with his back to the Potomac River and facing a Federal force twice the size of his own, decided to make a stand near the Maryland town of Sharpsburg. Jackson arrived in time for the Sixteenth Mississippi to join Confederate troops on the northeastern part of the battlefield in the eastern end of a sunken farm road that would come to be called "The Bloody Lane." Approaching from Henry Piper's farm to the south between nine and ten thirty a.m., Colonel Carnot Posey then led his Sixteenth Mississippi and the rest of Featherston's Brigade in a counterattack across the lane against the famous Irish Brigade and Sixty-fourth New York on the opposite side. Confederates would know the battle by the name of the town; the Union would know it by the creek that ran nearby, Antietam. Both would know it as the bloodiest day of the war.[1]

☆ *James Johnson Kirkpatrick Diary*, September 1, 1862, Monday:

Marched out to Little River Turnpike and thence within three miles of Fairfax Court House. Musketry this evening on our right. The Battle of Chantilly was fought in which the Federals' General Kearney was killed. Heavy rain, completely soaking us. Camped in a pine grove with orders to have our guns and ourselves ready for any emergency, or in other words, to sleep under arms with one eye open. Rested quietly.[2]

☆ *James Johnson Kirkpatrick Diary*, September 6, 1862, Saturday:

The sun rises bright and warm. "Get ready to move" is the order again this morning, so oft repeated. The many who had become bare-footed from the long march and rocky roads were left behind last evening at Leesburg in charge of officers. Marched slowly down to a ford on the Potomac. . . . Water very clear and channel firm and rocky on Virginia side, but somewhat muddy near Maryland shore. After partially undressing, we plunge and cross. It was an interesting sight to witness the mass of life in its unsteady crossing of the river. Sometimes an old horse, pressed into service, would upset his rider, and sometimes a footman, making a misstep, would precipitate himself and baggage into the water. Occasionally some unfortunate, to save his perpendicularity, would throw down his load in the current and then double-quick to overtake it. . . . After crossing, we marched towards Frederick City. Marched through ten o'clock tonight, passing through fine country. Very tired when we halted.

☆ **William Harris Hardy to Sallie Johnson Hardy**:
Monday, September 8th, 1862

My Dear,
. . . On the 7th, yesterday, we marched to this place and are now bivouacked on the banks of the Manoxie River, two miles from Frederick City and the Baltimore and Ohio Railroad. Where we will go next I can't tell. . . . I don't think we will have another grand battle soon.

Incidents of this march. We have made two-thirds of this march on roasting ears and green apples. Yesterday we drew rations, the first in three days. This morning we have drawn beef, bacon, flour, molasses, and coffee. We will live well for the future, as there is plenty in this country. Nearly one-third of the regiment are barefooted and left at Leesburg to be shod. Many fell out from hunger and weakness. Some of the men have not had a change of clothes since we left Gordonsville on the 16th [of June] and many not since we left Richmond on the 12th. Hence they are *lousy*. On the 5th [of September], I became so dirty that I stripped and boiled my shirt and drawers to kill the vermin and washed them out myself, going without till they dried.

Upon the whole, I have improved in health. . . . My company all express their great satisfaction at my conduct on the battlefield of the 30th and say that they did better than they ever did in their lives before.

Give my love to all and accept for yourself and precious little Mattie my love and devotions with prayers to God for your safety and protection. Your devoted husband,

W. H. Hardy

☆ *J. J. Wilson to James E. Wilson*:
Fredericktown, Maryland, September 8th, 1862

Dear Father,
. . . We have been on the march for the last three weeks and had several battles and whipped the Yankees in every instance. We fought three days, commencing on the 28th August. Our regiment was in the fight on the 30th and suffered considerable. There was about seventy-five wounded and fifteen or twenty killed in our company. . . . I was hit on the hip with a piece of shell while I was going into the fight. It was very slight. It made me lame for four or five days, but I soon joined the regiment again.

The battle was fought on the same grounds that the first Manassas battle was fought. We whipped the Yankees worse this time than they ever was whipped. Before, they lost ten men to our one. I never saw the like of killed and wounded before. The Richmond battle was nothing in comparison to it. The Yankees loss must have been fifteen or twenty thousand killed, wounded, and prisoners. . . .

After the fight was over, we marched over into Maryland. . . . I heard yesterday that the citizens was a-fighting the Yankees in Baltimore. I do not know whether it is so or not. There is some good secessionists over here and as fine a people as I ever saw.

I would like for you to send me a pair of shoes if you see anybody coming. Write soon.

J. J. Wilson

☆ *The Veteran's Story*:

From Manassas, we marched to Leesburg on the Potomac River, crossed at a ford by wading and then to Frederick City, Maryland. As we entered the city, our band played "Maryland, My Maryland" and finished up with "Dixie," and a loud Rebel Yell was given.[3]

☆ *James Johnson Kirkpatrick Diary*, September 10, 1862, Wednesday:

Roused by drums at four o'clock. . . . Got in motion at noon. Passed through Frederick City, a very handsome town, taking the pike towards Hagerstown. On reaching Middleton at dark, we took a road leading toward Harpers Ferry. Camped one mile from Middleton.

Very few symptoms of sympathy observable today. The houses are generally closed up as if deserted. In Frederick . . . were some indications of favor, but the awe of being reported to the Yankees when we leave, no doubt, kept the manifestations of feeling in check. Whenever a flag or handkerchief was waved, the holder was standing far back in the house. Our soldiers greeted them very fondly. Middleton was entirely Union, and some of the ladies expressed their opinions quite freely.

☆ *Historical Sketch of the Quitman Guards*:

General A. P. Hill was ordered to re-cross the Potomac and take possession of Loudon Heights. General Jackson was directed to move to the west side of the Shenandoah and take possession of Bolivar Heights. General Anderson's Division was taken to Sandy Hook on the Maryland side. General A. P. Hill took possession of Loudon Heights on the 14th of September and immediately placed twenty guns in position on Harpers Ferry. General Jackson secured Bolivar Heights. Cobb's Georgia and Barksdale's Mississippi captured Maryland Heights. Harpers Ferry was now completely surrounded, and there was no possible way of escape. A Federal garrison of eleven thousand men were stationed at Harpers Ferry. . . .[4]

The morning of the 15th was commenced with the firing of the guns from Loudon and Bolivar Heights. . . . The garrison, seeing themselves completely surrounded and no possibility of reaching their assailants and fearful of the consequences that might ensue, ran up the white flag and made an unconditional surrender. About fifteen thousand stand of small arms and large amount of quartermaster and commissary stores, a large number of wagons, and eleven thousand men, were surrendered to Major General A. P. Hill.[5]

☆ *James Johnson Kirkpatrick Diary*, September 15, 1862, Monday:

Our guns open rapidly this morning, but soon all is still. The news is brought that Harpers Ferry with its garrison had surrendered at about eight a.m. Our brigade is immediately formed and marched several miles up Pleasant Valley. . . . The enemy seem to have arrived in heavy force up this valley.

☆ *James Johnson Kirkpatrick Diary*, September 16, 1862, Tuesday:

Started by daylight, marched down through Sandy Hook and crossed the Potomac on a pontoon bridge, a novel structure to us. Took the Charlestown pike. Passed by the Yankee prisoners and camp. Halted two or three miles from town by the wayside and remained till evening. . . . The official report says we captured 11,500 prisoners, 73 pieces artillery, etc. In the evening, we start through the country towards Sheperdstown. March till after midnight, whence being very much fatigued, we halt. In an about an hour, we are aroused and again urged onward. Much straggling.

☆ *The Veteran's Story*:

After marching all night [September 16th and the early morning hours of the 17th], the Sixteenth crossed the Potomac at Martinsburg just at daybreak. We moved about half a mile and had stopped to close up the column when a courier dashed up with orders for us to move fast that the Yankees were pressing our line back. We were foot-sore and weary, but the booming of cannon and rattle of musketry suppled our joints. The wounded began to pass us saying, "Hurry up, boys, you are badly needed at the front." Just before reaching the battlefield, we saw one poor fellow kneeling behind a tree, praying earnestly for the cruel war to close. He seemed to be badly demoralized. We formed line of battle in the rear of Whiting's Division and advanced to his support.[6]

☆ *James Johnson Kirkpatrick Diary*, September 17, 1862, Wednesday:

We march down to the ford and cross the river, making no unnecessary delays, and start by nearest route for Sharpsburg. Artillery opened at sunrise. Tired and sleepy, we still march on, and as we come in proximity of the battle ground, the scores of wounded passing to the rear remind us that bloody work is going on. A little further on the left of the pike . . . halt and "load at will." No sooner done than in again. The enemy's batteries give us shot and shell in abundances, causing muscular contractions in the spinal column of our line. But all the dodging did not save us. Occasionally, a shell, better aimed than the rest would crack through our line, making corpses and mutilated trunks. A piece gave me a severe bruise in the shoulder. The brigade is halted in front of an old barn. Until dark, the battle rages in the most sublime fury, neither side gaining decided advantage. Our command suffers severely but maintains its ground. Meagher's Brigade opposing. Our army was very weak in numbers from stragglers and barefooted men who were left in Virginia. McClellan's very numerous. No advantage in position. The ground much broken by ridges, affording many excellent positions for artillery. The enemy used it very power- fully. Night stopped the flow of blood, and the army reposes on the battlefield.[7]

☆ *Report Number 232. Report of Captain A. M. Feltus . . . of the Battle of Sharpsburg*:

The [Sixteenth Mississippi] Regiment was on the left of the brigade. About ten a.m., being ordered to advance in the direction of the enemy, did so in good order. We advanced in line of battle, having the brigade of General Pryor in our front. Passing by a large barn, we proceeded under a heavy fire of artil- lery and small arms several hundred yards farther and came on General Pryor's Brigade and a brigade of North Carolina troops lying down in a road beyond the first cornfield after passing the barn. The regiment . . . passed over these troops and confronted the enemy . . . who were drawn up some three hundred yards from the road, pouring a destructive fire in our ranks. During this time, the losses in the regiment were heavy. A murderous fire of grape, canister, shell, and small arms played on us. Notwithstanding, this regiment gallantly held its position until ordered to retire, which it did in as good order as could be expected from its thinned ranks.

When we retired as far as the road, a scene of great confusion ensued from the mingling together of different brigades. We continued to fall back until we reached the barn, where the remnant of the regiment was rallied in its position on the left of the brigade. In this position, we advanced against the enemy and met them in the cornfield beyond the barn. Here, after a desperate fight, we fell back . . . to our original position on account of the terrific cross-fire of the enemy's batteries. We remained in this position under a heavy fire of shell and solid shot for about an hour, when the enemy advanced upon us in line of battle. This was about four or five o'clock in the afternoon. The remnant of the regiment, in its proper position in the brigade, moved forward and met the enemy in the orchard by the barn and drove them back. After this, night ensued and the fight ended.[8]

The number of men carried into the action was 228; of them, 144 were killed or wounded, leaving only 84 men.

> A. M. Feltus, Captain,
> Commanding Sixteenth
> Mississippi Regiment[9]

☆ *Historical Sketch of the Quitman Guards:*

General Featherston not having recovered from the wound he received at Richmond and having received a hurt from falling off his horse, Colonel Posey commanded his brigade which also went into action on the front and left of the town of Sharpsburg. . . .

The Federals were stationed on the brow of a hill, and nothing could be seen of them by the advancing Mississippians but their heads and shoulders. At the time of the charge made by the Sixteenth, the Federals were engaging troops who were stationed in an old road. Posey's Brigade charged up through a cornfield under a sweeping fire from the Federals in their front and an enfilading fire from their batteries on the right and left until they reached the troops in this old road. The slaughter was so great that it was deemed necessary to move them back two or three hundred yards to a more advantageous position. Perceiving disorder among the troops, Colonel Posey stopped the colors at the proper place, and the men rallied to them in perfect order and immediately began a destructive fire upon the Federals who had advanced when the Confederates were falling back. The brigade held its position throughout the day. The Federals were repulsed on the right and left, but stood firmly in their center. . . .[10]

☆ *James Johnson Kirkpatrick Diary*, September 19, 1862, Friday:

Last night our army re-crossed to the Virginia side. After all were safely over, the enemy advanced to the river and threw a few shells across.

☆ *J. J. Wilson to James E. Wilson*:

Camp near Sheperdstown, Virginia, September 20th, 1862

Dear Father,

I take this opportunity of writing you a few lines again. This leaves me in very good health at this time, and I hope this may reach you all enjoying the same.

There was fighting at Harpers Ferry and on the 15th the Yankees surrendered. . . . Then we marched into Maryland and had one of the hardest battles that has ever been fought since the war commenced.

Our regiment suffered more than it ever did before. There was twenty-six killed, ninety-nine wounded, nineteen missing. We supposed that they are killed or wounded. We had to fall back, and some of our wounded fell into the hands of the enemy. The fight was near a little town in Maryland. We have fallen back this side of the river. We had seven killed in our company and two that we suppose is killed or badly wounded. . . .

We were under the hottest fires that we ever was before. We went in with thirty-seven men [in our company] and twenty of them were killed and wounded. The Yankees had five men to our one. There is still fighting going on in the rear. The Yankees are following up our forces. The Yankees got a little the best of the fight over the river. We left a good many arms on the battlefield. We could not get them off.

I have nothing more at present. Give my love to all. Write soon. I remain, your son,

J. J. Wilson

☆ *Historical Sketch of the Quitman Guards*:

General Lee retired to Bunker Hill near Winchester where he went into camp. . . .[11]

☆ **J. J. Wilson to John N. Wilson:**
Camp near Winchester, Virginia, October 2nd, 1862

Dear Brother,

I take this opportunity of dropping you a few lines to let you know that I am yet among one of the living that belongs to Company C. The boys are all well, what there is left of them. . . . Our regiment suffered very much in the last fight near Sharpsburg, Maryland. . . . It was the hottest place I ever was in or ever want to be again soon.

I have got my fill of fighting and am willing to let them alone if they will go home and let us alone. I thought the battle at Richmond was a bloody battle, but that was not a circumstance compared to the battle in Maryland. We had to fall back and leave our dead and wounded in the hands of the Yankees. . . .

Where we went through Maryland, they were nearly all Union people and treated us very cool, but when we could find any secesh, we faired fine. We could get anything we wanted to eat or drink and very cheap at that. I never got any peaches until we got there, and then I got some as fine as ever I have eat at home for fifty cents, and I can get as many apples as I want all the time for nothing and fine grapes. As for watermelons, I have not tasted one this year. I got some muskmelons while I was in Maryland.

It was fun for me to fight at first when we could run the Yankees off and get in their knapsack and get hold of their love letters. It would amuse you to have seen some that I have read.

We have armed our regiment off of the battlefield with their Enfield and Springfield rifles, the best gun that the Yankees have in service.[12]

I have nothing more at present. Write soon. . . . I remain, your brother,

J. J. Wilson

☆ **J. J. Wilson to James E. Wilson:**
Camp Posey near Winchester, Virginia, October 18th, 1862

Dear Father,

I take this opportunity to drop you a few lines to inform you that I am in tolerable good health at this time. Our company is in very good health at this time. There is not much news stirring about up here. I d not think that there will be any more fighting in Northern Virginia this winter. Our company has had a few skirmishes with the Yankees lately. They drove them [the Yankees] back across the Potomac. . . .

When Bill Hughes comes back, you can send my clothes by him. I want two shirts, two pairs pants, my flannel drawers and socks. I will not want any coat, but if the cloth is for it in a gray color, I want an overshirt made out of it. Send one or two pairs of shoes. Shoes is hard to get up here. You can send them in a small box so that he can bring them without much trouble. . . . I remain your son,[13]

J. J. Wilson

— Chapter 9 —

"THE VALLEY IS STREWED
WITH BLUE . . ."

The Army of the Potomac moved slowly south after the Battle of Sharpsburg and crossed into Virginia on October 26th. General Ambrose Burnside, who replaced McClellan on November 7th, decided to move his line east and attack across the Rappahannock River at Fredericksburg, Virginia, half-way between Washington and Richmond. He then intended to move south to Richmond itself. Lincoln approved the plan. Foreseeing the Federal strategy, Lee moved quickly, beating Burnside to Fredericksburg and taking advantage of the excellent terrain on the river's south side. He then summonsed Jackson's Corps from the Shenandoah Valley and Longstreet's from near Culpeper Court House. Even after gathering his forces, however, Lee's troops numbered only half that of Burnside's. But Lee held the high ground (Marye's Heights) a mile southwest of town. From their vantage point about 750 yards north-west of Marye's Heights near the Orange Plank Road, the Sixteenth Mississippi helped carry out the later part of Lee's simple two-part plan: bait Union troops into charging up Marye's Heights—then shoot them.[1]

☆ **James Johnson Kirkpatrick Diary**, October 25, 1862, Saturday:

Efforts are being made to get our brigade transferred to the south. . . .

☆ *Petition from Brigadier General Winfield Scott Featherston to President Jefferson Davis*:

His Excellency Jefferson Davis, President, Confederate States

The undersigned officers of the several regiments comprising Featherston's Brigade of R. H. Anderson's Division would respectfully ask, if not in your judgment inconsistent with the public defense and efficiency of the same, that the brigade be transferred for winter operations to the State of Mississippi.

The following considerations make it desirable that such a transfer should be made. In case of serious illness on the part of any of the officers or men of the command requiring absence from camp and rest to restore health, such person would be in ready reach of home or friends and in whose hands he would receive the needful attention; especially would this be a consideration in case of battles resulting in the wounding of many men and officers.

As far as your petitioners are at present able to judge, an effort will be made by the enemy to possess himself of a very great portion of our home state of Mississippi this coming winter to prevent the accomplishment of which it will perhaps be necessary to increase the effective strength of our forces in such state. The probability of a period of inactivity during the coming winter in Virginia would make it seem reasonable that such increase might be made there by sending a force from the Army of Northern Virginia. In harmony with the desire of your petitioners herein expressed serves the public interest also in this respect.

As is known to your Excellency, the regiments of this brigade have been greatly reduced by losses in the many battles in which they have participated. The probability of filling the ranks of these regiments so long as we remain here seems very remote, whilst once in Mississippi the prestige and character which this brigade may claim without vain glory would cause the ranks to be rapidly filled even by those persons not subject to conscription.

The privations and endurance of the men of this command growing out of every march and battle made and fought by the army are pleaded by your petitioners as a cause to the granting of this request. Those toils and privations they are ready with resolute purpose to renew, though their preference is to do so on the soil of Mississippi.

Hoping that the desire of your petitioners herein expressed may be found to consist rather than to obstruct the public service, we remain,

Most Respectfully,
W. S. Featherston,
Brigadier General
Commanding[2]

☆ *James Johnson Kirkpatrick Diary*, October 30, 1862, Thursday:

Bid adieu to our camp at sunrise; marched down to the pike. Passed through Winchester; and took the pike towards Front Royal. Kept on steadily and camped at dark until within three miles of Front Royal. Day's march twenty-four miles. Very fatiguing. Many stragglers today.

☆ *James Johnson Kirkpatrick Diary*, November 2, 1862, Sunday:

Marched leisurely and camped in evening near Culpeper Court House. On this march, not half the army has kept up. Straggling has become a practice that needs to be visited by some punishment. It has gone so long unpunished that it has become popular. The stragglers will range through the country in the wake of the army and sometimes ahead of it, living off the citizens, plundering and pillaging and when they come back . . . are the lions of the day while relating their conquests.

☆ *Historical Sketch of the Quitman Guards*:

General J. E. B. Stuart . . . was constantly engaged with the Federal cavalry during the army's sojourn at Culpeper and was very often necessitated to ask the aid of a few regiments of infantry in repelling the frequent incursions of the enemy. After fighting them for eight days or ten days without success, he finally called for two large regiments of infantry to assist in driving them for one portion of his lines upon which they were making daily encroachments. The Sixteenth Mississippi and the Tenth Alabama were accordingly sent to Hazel [Run], one of the branches of the Rappahannock, for the purpose of supporting him, at which place they arrived about dark on the 9th day of November. . . .

On the next morning [November 10th], General Stuart began to advance with his cavalry. . . . Being supported by the infantry skirmishers from the Sixteenth Regiment, the Confederate cavalry were inspired with greater courage and fought with determination, making several charges. The infantry skirmishers were also hotly engaged. The Federal cavalry were driven from their position for a distance of about four miles when [they received reinforcements and] . . . General Stuart was compelled to return to his original position. The Sixteenth Mississippi Regiment lost eight or ten men wounded. . . .[3]

☆ *James Johnson Kirkpatrick Diary*, November 16, 1862, Sunday:

Preaching in brigade today. The soldiers of late have shown quite an interest on the subject of religion. Prayer meetings are held nightly among the encampments and well attended.

☆ *James Johnson Kirkpatrick Diary*, November 19, 1862, Wednesday:

Struck tents and got ready to march early. Formed brigade and awaited in suspense until noon. Started then, through Culpeper Court House and towards Racoon Ford on the Rapidan [River]. . . . Crossed the river a little before dark and camped immediately on the other side. Unpleasant march. Raining all day. Roads muddy and slippery.

☆ *Jerome B. Yates to Mrs. Obedience Yates*:
Gordonsville, Virginia, November 19th

Dear Mother,
As I have a few minutes, I will drop you a few lines. My health is not so good as it has been, though I have not got any fever this morning. I have had it for thirty-six hours.
The army has fallen back. It is thought it will go to Fredericksburg. I was not able to march and was sent down on the cars with a crowd. Everybody has got the smallpox. We have all been vaccinated. Mine is about well. I send you a scab if you should ever need it, but I hope you may never need it. It came off my arm last night.[4]

Jerome

☆ *James Johnson Kirkpatrick Diary*, November 20, 1862, Thursday:

Started at ten a.m. Heavy rains today and the roads getting worse for the web-foot. Halted about dark and camped in woods. A continuous rain all night. On guard at Posey's Headquarters. Slept none. A tree fell in one encampment, killing one of the brigade.

☆ *Historical Sketch of the Quitman Guards*:

The Federal army . . . about the 20th of November, began to move in the direction of Fredericksburg. General Lee left Culpeper Court House about the same time; crossed the [Rapidan River] at Germanna and Ely's Fords and moved in an eastwardly direction to Fredericksburg.[5]

☆ *James Johnson Kirkpatrick Diary*, November 22, 1862, Saturday:

Marched briskly to Fredericksburg. . . . The enemy's camps and wagons in plain view across the river. Many families from town passed us going to the rear. Filed to left of Plank Road and camped in line of battle. Received orders to have our guns unloaded and dried out. On account of the many rains to which we had been exposed, few of them would fire. . . .

☆ *Historical Sketch of the Quitman Guards*:

The Federal army was stationed on Stafford's Heights on the north bank of the Rappahannock and fronting Fredericksburg. The Confederate army was stationed on the south bank on a commanding ridge running parallel with the river. . . .[6]

☆ *J. J. Wilson to James E. Wilson*:

Camp near Fredericksburg, Virginia, December 8th, 1862

Dear Father,

I take the present opportunity of dropping you a few lines in answer to your kind and welcome letters. . . . There is not very much news stirring about up here. We are here in camp on one side of the river and the Yankees are on the other side in sight of each other. I do not believe that there will be any fight at this place this winter.

It is very cold now. There has been snow on the ground for four or five days, and we have not got any tents to stay in, and we come very near freezing out sometimes. It is enough to kill anybody, most lying out in the cold, but we have got used to it and can stand it as well as if we had houses to stay in. . . . Give my love to all and write soon. I remain, your son,

J. J. Wilson

☆ *James Johnson Kirkpatrick Diary*, December 11, 1862, Thursday:

Waked up about an hour before day by our signal. Guns were heard down towards the river, and we were called into line immediately by the long roll. Marched down towards town and took a position in rear of the batteries on the right of the Plank Road. The enemy kept up a heavy cannonading nearly all day, setting the town on fire in several places. Barksdale's Mississippians are picketing in the town. In the evening, the enemy completed one of his pontoon bridges and commenced crossing his troops. After dark, we were ordered down on picket, but arriving at our destination, the position was already occupied, and we marched back from whence we started. Extremely cold and very hard to acquire the warmth necessary for sleep. A great many of the town people—women and children—are moving back to the rear, leaving their dwellings to pillage and perhaps destruction.

☆ *Report Number 294. Report of Brigadier General W. S. Featherston*:

About five a.m. on Thursday the 11th . . . my brigade formed on the right of Anderson's Division and was posted . . . between the Plank Road and Hazel Run in front of the town. . . . Here we remained during that day and night, protected from artillery fire of the enemy by a continuous range of hills in our front.[7]

☆ *James Johnson Kirkpatrick Diary*, December 12, 1862, Friday:

Cannonading resumed this morning about eight a.m. Marched down to the left of the Plank Road and lay in a cornfield all day. From our secreted position, we can observe but little of what is going on. . . . Very little fighting done. The enemy have thrown over two additional bridges and have a very large force on our side of the river. It seems that very little effort is made on our part to oppose these preliminary movements. General Lee is no doubt anxious that in the coming battle they should top the weight of numbers.

☆ Historical Sketch of the Quitman Guards:

On the 12th, the two armies kept up a continuous cannonading and skirmishing. At night, the Federals extended their lines for the purpose of making a general assault. The Confederate army was thus arranged: Jackson's Corps composed the right wing with Stuart on his right to protect his flank; General Longstreet's composed the left wing and fronted the town; General Featherston's Brigade [still in Anderson's Division, a part of Longstreet's Corps] was immediately in front of the town and extended across the main road which leads from it in a southerly direction. The Federals on the right and in front of Jackson's Corps moved up under cover of the night and fortified themselves, building several lines of breastworks.[8]

☆ The Veteran's Story:

The next morning [December 13th], they moved upon our right flank. There they found General Jackson prepared to receive them. We were stationed upon the left, just in the rear of Cobb's Georgia Brigade, which was posted behind a stone fence. The enemy advanced upon our right and left about the same time and was repulsed with great loss.[9]

☆ Report Number 294. Report of Brigadier General W. S. Featherston [continued]:

About ten a.m. on Saturday [December 13th], we were ordered to advance in line of battle farther to the front and halted about one hundred yards in rear of our batteries on the left of the Plank Road, extending our line of battle up the river in the direction of the Taylor House. Here we remained during the day, subjected to a very heavy converging fire from the enemy's artillery immediately in our front and extending up the river to our left. My men were kept lying down during the day in an old road, protecting them as much as possible. The enemy's batteries immediately in front were numerous and skillfully served. Their batteries on our left completely enfiladed our position. . . . The fire of the enemy's artillery could not have been more rapid or galling on any part of the line than that which was brought to bear on our position on Saturday.

The right of my brigade was also within range of the fire of the enemy's small arms. My orders were to hold this position in support of the batteries immediately in my front and to advance to the batteries when the enemy advanced with small arms immediately in my front. There was no considerable advance of the enemy's small arms in our immediate front during the entire engagement. We remained in this position Saturday night, Sunday and Sunday night, Monday and Monday night. . . .

During the engagement of Saturday, the casualties in my brigade were forty-two killed and wounded. . . .[10]

☆ Historical Sketch of the Quitman Guards:

The dawn of the 13th exhibited to General Lee the position of the Federal army. . . . Fighting began in the morning by skirmishing and cannonading, which was kept up a good portion of the day. Charges were frequently made for the purpose of trying the strength of the Confederate lines, which was often repulsed. . . . General Burnside concluded to make a general assault. He opened his artillery from Stafford Heights with fearful effect and ordered the infantry to charge. The Confederate batteries on Marye's Heights and Lee's Hill did not often reply but reserved their fire for the advancing column of infantry. As soon as the Federal line approached . . . the Confederates discharged a volley of musketry but did not check the advancing column at once, but the rapidity of their fire, with that of the artillery, soon brought them to a standstill. The guns on Stafford and Marye's Heights and Lee's Hill thundered away . . . up and down the lines for four miles, the incessant roar of musketry, the booming of cannon, the bursting and whizzing of shell and solid shot, and the buzzing sound of grape and canister that plowed into the ranks of the contending armies were heard mingled with the yells and shouts of the enthusiastic soldiery. The Federal army was often driven back but . . . would rally again to the charge and again recoil before the incessant fire of the Confederate guns. . . .[11]

☆ James Johnson Kirkpatrick Diary, December 13, 1862, Saturday:

Lay in our position till noon then formed the brigade and started up over the hill towards the front. A shell fell in the regiment just before starting, inflecting some damage. The enemy's artillery is firing heavily and musketry is getting lively. Came to a halt close in rear of our batteries and without protection. Endured for two or three hours a very heavy shelling. Corporal Breeden was killed here by a Minie ball, shot perhaps from front of Marye's Heights.[12]

Towards evening, the Sixteenth was sent to support a battery on our right and remained in our position all night. The battle raged this evening with considerable fury, especially in front of Marye's Hill. . . . The valley is strewed with blue corpses, while our loss is but trifling. . . .

☆ *The Veteran's Story*:

One morning [about December 14th] at the roll call beat, we fell into line, answered the call, cooked and ate breakfast and were hustling around the camp generally when some of the officers looked at their watches and found it was only two o'clock a.m. In the east, there was no sign of daylight coming, but everything was bright as day. Finally, someone said that it was an Aurora Borealis. It was a grand sight.[13]

☆ *Historical Sketch of the Quitman Guards*:

The Federals did not renew the attack on the 14th, though both sides kept up a constant sharpshooting and shelling. . . . On the night of the 14th, the Federals withdrew to the north side of the river, taking up their pontoons. . . .[14]

☆ *Report Number 294. Report of Brigadier General W. S. Featherston [continued]*:

At a late hour on Sunday night [December 14th], I . . . threw forward to the rock fence on the right of the Plank Road, the Sixteenth Mississippi Regiment and five companies of the Forty-eighth Mississippi . . . to fill the place vacated by some of the troops withdrawn and to form a continuous line of battle. These troops . . . Sunday night, Monday, and Monday night remained in that position, declining on Monday night to be relieved by other regiments of my brigade.[15]

☆ *James Johnson Kirkpatrick Diary*, December 15, 1862, Monday:

Lay in the picket line all day. Nearly all the company exchanged compliments with the other side. A heavy gun over at Falmouth was very attentive to us and was unanimously voted a nuisance. It almost enfiladed on picket line and must have had an abundance of ammunition. A little after noon, a force of the enemy who had lodged themselves in front of the foundry was discovered and sent back in haste by our artillery and sharpshooters. . . . Relieved from this post at dark. . . . Dug a rifle pit to protect us from missiles that fly about so much. . . .

☆ *James Johnson Kirkpatrick Diary*, December 16, 1862, Tuesday:

A dismal morning, prospects for the day gloomy enough. Commenced rain about day and the sky overcast with perhaps sleet and snow. Our company all crowded up in a narrow ditch, the water running in on us and no chance to move for the sharpshooters in the foundry within less than one hundred yards. To get out would almost insure a discharge or least a long furlough. But the gloom is soon dispelled. The clouds break, the sun shines out, and the Yankees are found to be on the other side of the river. Our annoyers in the foundry surrender. We can move about without the accompaniment of Minie music and enjoy the consolation that another victory has "crowned our arms" and sent a thrill of joy throughout the Confederacy.

After supplying ourselves with blankets, overcoats, canteens, haversacks, tent flies, etc., and exchanging our rusty guns for bright ones—a thing we do in almost every battlefield—we march back to our camp, glad to enjoy once more undisturbed slumbers and that immunity from death and danger which can only be appreciated after a long time's imminent experience.

☆ *The Veteran's Story*:

A few days after the battle, we were sent out on picket duty just above Fredericksburg on the river. While there, late one evening, our band was playing "Dixie," and the Federals were playing "Yankee Doodle." When the bands finished the airs, the Yankees struck up "Home Sweet Home." Our band took up the strain, and when the bands quit playing, voice after voice caught up the song, and as far as we could hear on both sides, they were singing "Home Sweet Home."[16]

☆ *James Johnson Kirkpatrick Diary*, December 24, 1862, Wednesday:

Pleasant. Nearly everyone searching for liquor. Prices range from fifty to one hundred dollars per gallon; quality from bad to worse. Went out into the country to add to my mess commissaries. Purchased meal at four dollars per bushel and flour at twenty-five cents per pound.

☆ *James Johnson Kirkpatrick Diary*, December 25, 1862, Thursday:

Changed camp about a mile on account of wood. Some of the boys drunk this morning. Pleasant and warm. Spent the day chopping poles and building a bunk. Quite a contrast from the merry Christmases once enjoyed. May gentle peace soon smile over our land again. Bought some apples, the only luxury I enjoyed.

☆ *J. J. Wilson to John N. Wilson*:

Camp near Fredericksburg, Virginia, December 27th, 1862

Dear Brother,

I take this opportunity of dropping you a few lines in answer to your kind and welcome letter. . . . We have had another hard fought battle in which our men were victorious in every instance. Here at Fredericksburg, the Yankees had ten men to our one. . . . The dead men lay thicker on the ground than I ever saw before. Old Burnside acknowledges that he was badly whipped, and he said that his loss was fifteen thousand men. . . .

We had a six day fight of it, and we had to lay out in line of battle all the time, and there was snow on the ground, and we come very near freezing to death. We are lying out here without any tents, and we have not had any for six months, but we have got used to it and we can stand anything.

Give my love to all. I remain, your brother,

J. J. Wilson

☆ *James Johnson Kirkpatrick Diary*, December 29, 1862, Monday:

A number of the regiment drunk last night and sent to guardhouse. A balloon ascended across the river. Professor Lowe taking observations of the rebels for the benefit of some sensation journal.[17]

— Chapter 10 —

"EVERYTHING WEARS SUCH A CHEERING ASPECT . . ."

Following Burnside's disastrous charges up Marye's Heights at Fredericksburg, Union and Confederate forces sat for weeks, facing each other across the Rappahannock. Despite meager supplies of everything—wood, clothes, blankets, shoes, and rations—the Sixteenth suffered freezing rain, sleet, and snow in abundance with high spirits. This confidence was due in part, perhaps, to a second failed Federal effort to take Fredericksburg. The effort began on January 19, 1863, but by then the winter-wet Virginia clay had turned to slimy sludge, and the failed attempt came to be known as the "Mud March," again humiliating Burnside and further lowering Union morale. Thereafter, both sides seemed content to sit out the winter.[1]

Also in mid-January, the Sixteenth's colonel, Carnot Posey, replaced W. S. Featherston as brigadier, and Featherston transferred to Mississippi. Colonel Samuel E. Baker assumed command of the Sixteenth with Abram M. Feltus serving as it's lieutenant colonel and Edward Councill as major. The brigade remained assigned to General Richard H. Anderson's Division.[2]

On January 25th, Lincoln replaced Burnside with General Joseph Hooker, an officer whom Burnside had only earlier that day pressed Lincoln to relieve of command of the II and III Corps. As Hooker reorganized the Army of the Potomac, Confederate chaplains organized the Young Men's Christian Philanthropic Association (on March 28, 1863), with an eye toward improving troop morals. Confederate *patriotism and confidence remained high, and time was now available for transfers, inducting new conscripts, and furloughs.*[3]

☆ *James Johnson Kirkpatrick Diary*, January 3, 1863, Saturday:

Pleasant day. Amused ourselves by rolling ten-pins with cannonballs. . . .

☆ *Jerome B. Yates to Mrs. Obedience Yates*:

Orange Court House, Virginia, January, 1863

Dear Ma,

Yours of the 12th November came duly to hand and was received by me with gladness. . . . So you have got plenty to eat and wear. . . . That is more than any of the people up here have. Speaking of something to eat, we are getting rather at a low ebb in that line. We have not drawn any meat in three days, this is the fourth one. We draw one-fourth pound for tomorrow. I do not know when we will get any more. Something wrong must be the matter in the commissary departments. I can not believe that the Confederacy is playing out at that rapid rate, but we were astonished yesterday by the company commissary calling us to draw rations of coffee, sugar and rice—pure coffee at that. I did not believe so much coffee [was] in the country. I wish you had my share of the coffee, and I had a big potato in the place of it. I want potatoes more than anything else. . . .

You say you all are in the notion to move to some new country. Yourself, Aunt Patty, Eliza Cook, Tom Davis and Pole. A pretty good party. We could soon start a new colony of . . . Yates and Davises. I am in for such a thing, especially if we are whipped, which if we are, this country will be perfectly unbearable. I do not think I can stay in any such country as this will be. Ireland and Poland would be a paradise to this if we are subjugated, which God forbid, but let us look on the bright side of all things, hoping for the best. You will probably think I am despondent, but I am far from any such thing. I am full of hope, if every man will do his duty. . . .

Marie writes me that Buddy will probably have to go in the army. Tell him if he does to join the cavalry in Mississippi, if he cannot get into the commissary or quartermasters department, to never join as a private if he can do any better but by all means to join the cavalry and bear in mind that a private in the infantry is the worse place he can possibly be put into in this war. So if he wants to have a good time, join the cavalry. . . .

Ma, I have thought of the thing I wish to write to you about, and that is the debts we owe. I want you to write me how we stand. You know what a hurry and flurry I went off in when I left home. Write to me all about who we owe and how much. How do we stand with the old firm of Crutcher and McRaven and Dudley Mimms? They were the principal creditors. I am aware the stay law passed soon after I left home . . . but I would like to know how I stand with everybody. I would like to get home and have a settlement with everybody, Joe included.[4]

So you sold a load of cotton for thirty cents per pound. Pretty good, provided the money was any worth. A nice price for cotton. I wish times were as they used to be, and I was at home making it at that price. I would soon get rich and quit this country. I do not like it much any more. . . .

You must write me every chance and long letters. . . . Your son,

Jerome

☆ *J. J. Wilson to James E. Wilson*:

Camp near Fredericksburg, Virginia, January 12th, 1863

Dear Father,

I take this opportunity of dropping you a few lines in answer to your kind and welcomed letter. . . . This leaves me in very good health at present. Our company is in better health now than it ever has been since we left home. There has not been a man on the sick list for the last month. . . .

I would like to have been at home to spend this Christmas, but we had a very dull time in camp. Nothing to eat but beef and flour and some other things as we could buy at a very high price. I did not have any Christmas toddy, whiskey selling at sixty dollars a gallon and cannot buy anything for less than a dollar. . . .

I got the coat that you sent me. . . . Clothing is very high and cannot be had. Pants is seven dollars a pair . . . overcoats is fifty dollars. . . . They will ask anything, and the soldiers will buy it. . . . I remain your son till death,

J. J. Wilson

☆ *John S. Lewis to Mrs. Nancy Lewis*:

Charlottesville, January 12th, 1863

My Dear Mother,

I suppose it is about time for me to write you again. . . . My health on the whole is better than it has been for a long time, much to my surprise it is, for

I believed I should have to quit the army when I came back. Exposure, etc., may throw me out again. I hope not. I know if I could live as usual, I would be well enough.

Captain Feltus . . . is promoted to the office of major. I understand by the resignation of Lieutenant Colonel Shannon, Colonel Posey expects a brigadiership but has not been promoted as yet.[5]

I see by the papers that Banks is in camp [in Mississippi] with ten thousand men. It makes me rather uneasy, for if it is true, he could make a raid through all of southern Mississippi. I hope if he does, the people will move with everything they can and burn the remainder, it is the only way to deal successfully with an invading army. I know it is hard to move not knowing where to go to or how to provide for the future, but people and their Negroes will not be allowed to store, and anything is preferable to Yankees, and if Negroes are not removed, they will be stolen. If property is not destroyed, it will be taken. I hope if they ever get to Wilkinson, they will find the county [stripped], no grain, no cattle, no anything!

The chances of war are always uncertain, and we have, I am afraid, the most of our work before us yet. I think if all the men in the Confederacy were in the army, there is no doubt as to the result. If it is not done promptly and openly, we must suffer unavoidably. How much or how long, God only knows.

I have my things to fix up and nothing of interest to write, so goodbye. Your son,

John S. Lewis

☆ *Jerome B. Yates to Mrs. Obedience Yates*:
Camp Posey, January 19th, 1863

Dear Ma,

Your complaints of my not writing letters compels me to write you, though there is not a particle of news up here. Everything is quiet in the fighting line. The enemy still faces us on the opposite of the river. They do not seem to want to cross any more. A little excitement was raised in camp a few days ago. Orders came to get ready to move to the front at a moment's notice. We all packed up and got ready to march but was not ordered off. I was very glad to, for we are fixed up pretty comfortable in little split log huts with chimneys to them, and the weather is as cold as I ever saw it. Ice is two inches thick, everything froze up. The bread was froze so hard this morning that I could scarcely cut it for breakfast.

I received a letter from Pole Yates. He was on a big string about going to Texas. I think it a pretty good idea but have no notion he will ever go. He wants you and I to go with him.

The company drew for furloughs a week ago, but it was not my good luck to get one. They were drawn by Kirkpatrick, the schoolmaster that boarded at Broome's, the other by a fellow named Cowan. There is a probability of more when these get back. But they are so short that they are not desirable, only thirty days. . . . The boys are pretty bad out with the boys that has got furloughs and are staying out . . . so long over their time. . . .[6]

I will close as my paper is pretty scarce. You must write soon and often to your son,

Jerome

☆ *James Johnson Kirkpatrick Diary*, January 20, 1863, Tuesday:

Went over this morning to hear General Featherston's parting address. It has been agreed that he should go to Mississippi and Posey remain with us. He spoke highly of the valor of his brigade and expressed his regret at leaving it. Thought he could be more beneficial in Mississippi. Hoped that we would keep our fair name unsullied and said he would always be glad to meet us.

☆ *J. J. Wilson to James E. Wilson*:

Camp near Fredericksburg, Virginia, January 27th, 1863

Dear Sir,

I . . . was glad to hear that all was well. . . . The Yankees are still on the other side of the Rappahannock River. I do not know what there force is, but it is just enough to keep up the picket lines. I do not think that their design is of crossing the river at this place any more this winter, they got too badly whipped when they tried it before. General Lee is not asleep, and if they undertake to cross here again he will not let them off as well as he did before.

It is getting very bad weather up here. It is not very cold, but it is raining about most of the time. . . . I have got a very good hut to stay in, but when we go on picket, we have to lay out and take the weather for five days at a time. If it happens to be raining, we suffer very much. . . . Write soon. . . .

J. J. Wilson

☆ *Harry Lewis to Mrs. Nancy Lewis*:

Camp near Fredericksburg, Virginia, January, 1863[7]

Dear Mother,

I received your letter over a week since, but absence from camp on picket [near Falmouth, Virginia] and several days of busy work on payrolls have combined to defer and delay my answer until now, and even now, though the bright sun has been merrily shining for hours, it is so cold that I can scarcely command my pen. . . .[8]

We received our clothing and shoes on the 28th of December, and they came just at the right time, for we needed both and thankfully received them. After the distribution of the clothing, the whole company, ragged and dirty as they were, manfully withstood the application of cold water and promptly displayed, to the envy of the other companies of the regiment, their new duds, and many were the shouts that loudly arose for the ladies of Wilkinson County. In fact, I think the last shipment was more gratefully appreciated than any clothing formerly sent to our boys in Virginia.

The weather is extremely cold, today being the most severe of the winter thus far, but thanks to our homemade overcoats and abundant supply of tarps recently received, we managed to keep quite comfortable. Fletch and I have five blankets and our overcoats. . . . The whole company have more blankets and clothing than they can carry to save their lives. I only wish our whole army were as well provided for, even our regiment. It would be a matter of no small import. I can tell you I am pleased with my new overcoat. It fits me well, and the pockets are the most convenient I ever saw. . . .

We have heard of Bragg's fight at Murfreesboro and though the magnitude and importance of the original victory has been considerably cut down by subsequent dispatches, still all the considerate and thoughtful agree that he has gained a victory, and no inconsiderable one at that. Notwithstanding, all are disappointed at Bragg's not routing the enemy and at his subsequent retreat. This is rather unreasonable, for Bragg had to contend not only with odds of three to one, but against the very best material of the whole Yankee army. Bragg states in his dispatch to the War Department that he safely brought off the field four thousand prisoners, twenty-seven pieces of artillery, ninety-five stands of small arms and trains of the enemy's captured. The Yankee general admits a fearful loss of officers and their papers and a loss of eighty thousand men and trains of wagons. The thirty thousand men is probably exaggerated by their papers, but goes to show that their loss was truly terrific. I have been in this army long enough and have seen enough fighting to know that twenty-five thousand men cannot thrash out sixty or eighty thousand and follow up the victory, as military croakers who have never heard the hiss of the Minie ball or the scream of a shell, but sitting in the comfortable armchairs pretend, judge. The only alternative to Bragg was to fight and fall back to a better position where he could again engage the enemy to advantage and thus, by a series of hard blows, diminish his strength and numbers preparatory to his final overthrow. This is the policy preferred by our generals.[9]

The enemy . . . have not yet attempted to make a forward movement, though they have decided (so their papers say) upon a winter campaign. It is rumored that Burnside has been superseded by Fighting Joe Hooker. The former wishes to re-cross the river and attack again against the will of his own generals, but "Abram the First" wouldn't consent. So we may expect the Yankees to cross at any time and give no fight. Well, we are awaiting them here ready and . . . willing to meet them. . . .[10]

I suppose you have heard that Captain Feltus is promoted to major of our regiment, creating a vacancy which will be filled by Brother John as captain. . . .

We were paid off yesterday for two months. Everything is higher priced now than at any time before or during the whole war. In Richmond, a Confederate uniform is worth from one hundred to two hundred dollars. . . . Everything sells in this proportion, and everything is as scarce and dear.

Rumors of peace are afloat, and many sensible fellows think that the war will end before summer sets in. I don't let any of these reports trouble me for I hate to be disappointed and really won't believe any of them until it is certain and won't be certain and can't realize that peace will have been declared until I get home and cast aside stripes and all military gear forever.

Among the silly ablutions of Madam Rumor, I will relate one to you, dear Ma. Colonel Posey went to a fandango in the county about here somewhere and coming back, tells the following: an old Virginian relates that on his farm is a spring, which two months before the revolution broke forth in a copious stream of water and a few months prior to the end of that war dried wholly up. Two months before the War of 1812, the same spring again broke forth, and a few months before the declaration of peace, the fount a second time ceased to flow. Several months in advance of the Mexican War, the same spring again burst forth and as in former cases, a few months before peace refused to come forth. For the fourth time, and last, this same spring jumped forth in advance of hostilities between the South and North, and now the spring has disappeared. Their man is confident the war will last but a few weeks or months longer, and so infatuated is he that he will stake ten thousand dollars on it. This idle tale is hailed by the believers in the end of the war shortly. So anxious are some for the cessation of hostilities that they are willing to believe anything favorable.

I have been writing, dear Ma, with the determination to fill up these . . . pages, so you must excuse tawdry content of this letter. Your son,

Harry

☆ *James Johnson Kirkpatrick Diary*, January 28, 1863, Wednesday:

Rained all night and snowing this morning. . . . Exchanged posts at dark with Company G. Got a post without any shelter. Snowed worse than ever and all night. No sleep.

☆ *Harry Lewis to Mrs. Nancy Lewis*:

Camp near Fredericksburg, Virginia, February 6th, 1863

Dear Mother,

Knowing the fact that to a certain extent letters are valued as to their scarcity, yet I write again simply because I have nothing else to do. It has been raining quite steadily for thirty-six hours, confining us to our bunks most of the time, consequently no drilling or exercise, and hence, the want of employment causing me to write. It is at such times as present, of indolence and inactivity, that the minds of the volunteers naturally turns homeward and aided by imagination pictures in most pleasant colors all the varied imports and joys of "Home Sweet Home." On the weary march, the physical as well as mental powers are so taxed that home is almost driven from our thoughts, so on the battlefield in the wild excitement and confusion of the instant, there is no will or time for cherishing remembrances of home, unless it be to gather fresh energy and renew our determination. Enough of this, however. . . .

Fletcher has just made our corn coffee, of which Bud is very fond and declares he never will go to the expense of buying coffee when such a good substitute can be made. We eat but two meals a day. Though nearly dark, we haven't had dinner yet. . . .

I received the pair of gloves by Kann. They are very neat, and I am much obliged as they came just at the right time. The gloves Miss G. made for me were of more service than any I ever had before, I believe. Thanks to her industry![11]

We are looking for another attempt from the enemy as soon as the weather permits to force our position here. Our army is in a fine condition, healthy and full of fun and will render a good account of themselves when once more tried and . . . could be killed but never conquered unless through strange remissness on the part of our generals. Everything wears such a cheering aspect, and our successes by land and sea have been so uninterrupted and numerous that I am daily looking for some serious reverse, which I hope will never come, but I hope the same hand that has hitherto defended us and given us victory will maintain us still and by repeated defeats and failures on their part convince the enemy that they are battling against right and justice and that they cannot conquer us. How happy we would be if peace would once more beam forth through the clouds of war. What universal joy and satisfaction it would scatter broadcast over the lands! (This theme, so uncertain and vague, won't do to bear upon.) God grant us a speedy peace is my prayer. Your own son,

Harry

☆ *Harry Lewis to Mrs. Nancy Lewis*:
Camp near Fredericksburg, Virginia, February 15th, 1863

Dear Mother,
Your letter to me enclosed in Brother John's was received yesterday. I was pleased to learn that my letter cheered you. . . . I was not pleased with the idea of establishing a hospital in our native state for it seems to me that wherever soldiering predominates, decay and scarcity follow and a certain appearance of cheerlessness (as far as the inhabitants are concerned) seems to exist in proportion as the number of soldiers (locusts) increase. This is the case in Virginia, but I hope it won't prove so in Woodville. Anyway, as they are stationed upon you, do the best for them you can, for (poor fellows!) they have a hard time even when not sick.

Everything is quiet here and, as the weather is alternately sunshine, rain and snow, rendering military movements impractical, at least for the present. We are not apprehending an attack until good weather sets in. . . . Meanwhile, we are throwing up formidable lines of rifle pits with occasional redoubts for miles up the river and, should the enemy be blindly foolish as to again attempt the passage of the river, they will find to their cost it is a work fraught with loss of precious lives on their part. I hardly think the enemy will try us at this point a second time. . . .

At present, we are pleasantly situated, having good comfortable tents with fireplaces and generally enough to eat, besides occasionally something to read and sufficient clothing. I call this a "pleasant situation" because by experience I have learned what is truly hard and unpleasant. Dear Ma, if ever I get back home for good, I think I can put up with anything. I say "good" because I don't expect to come home again before the war is over unless severely wounded or something of this kind occurs. . . .

We have been confined to our quarters all day on account of rain and as it is Sunday, don't regret it much. I wish we had a good chaplain. No doubt he could effect much good in this regiment and brigade, both of which sadly need the services of some good man, I am sorry to say. Dear Ma, I am trying to lead a more consistent life than formerly, and I read my Testament and perform my duties more regularly than ever before, I am happy to say, and happy to be able to so live as to claim a home in heaven in case I am called upon to sacrifice my life for my country on the fields of battle.

I suppose you have heard ere this of my promotion to third lieutenant. George Pilant was my only opposition, and the vote stood forty-four to sixteen, and I can say with truth that as . . . sergeant for the past twelve months I have, by the sweat of my brow, earned my present place, and I will be gratified if I meet with the same opposition, and my conscience prompts me of duty discharged as freely when I lay by my sword as when I took up my orderly book and rifle. . . .[12]

Give my love to all. Your son,

Harry

☆ *J. J. Wilson to James E. Wilson:*
Camp—Posey's Brigade, February 20th, 1863

Father, Dear Sir,
   . . . This leaves me in tolerable good health at present. I have a bad cold and cough, but it is enough to kill anybody to have to go through with what

we have to do. The snow is on the ground twelve to twenty inches deep, and when it is drifted, it is deeper.

There is not much news stirring up here. The Yankees are still on the other side of the river, in what force I am not able to tell or what their design is. I do not think they will try to fight us here again, but if I have to fight, I had rather fight them here than anywhere else in the world. We have this place well fortified and can hold it one against five. We thought that we would leave for some place south, but the order was countermanded.

Things is very high up here. We cannot get anything for less than a dollar. Shoes is from fifteen to twenty dollars a pair. . . . I got my clothing some time ago, and it came in a good time, for if I had not got them I would have come near to freezing to death.

I have nothing more at present. Write soon. . . . Give my love to all relations and friends . . . I remain your son,

J. J. Wilson

☆ *James Johnson Kirkpatrick Diary*, March 17, 1863, Tuesday:

The regiment moved to U.S. Mine Ford [on the Rappahannock River] distant perhaps twelve miles up the river. . . .[13]

☆ *James Johnson Kirkpatrick Dairy*, April 6, 1863, Monday:

The regiment expected to go to work on fortifications. Prevented by snow.

☆ *J. J. Wilson to James E. Wilson*:
Camp near U.S. Ford, April 12th, 1863

Dear Father,

I take the present opportunity of writing you a few lines in answer to your kind letter. . . . There is not any news of importance stirring about up here. The cold weather is about gone, and it will not be long before the summer campaign will commence.

The Yankees are on the other side of the river, yet I do not think that they will fight us here any more. I heard yesterday that they were fighting among themselves, but I do not know whether it is too correct. I would not care if the whole Yankee nation would get to fighting, and maybe it would bring the war to an end sooner, but I fear that the war will go two or three years yet. I have lost all hopes of the war ending sooner. If it goes on much longer, I do not know what will become of some of the poor classes of people.

Things are getting higher every day. Butter is selling a dollar fifty per pound, eggs two dollars fifty cents a dozen, fresh pork a dollar fifteen cents a pound, corn meal two dollars, sugar two dollars a pound, tobacco two dollars fifty cents a plug, beans fifteen dollars a bushel, and everything else in the eating line are as high. It don't take long for a private to spend his money at those rates. . . .

If you get a good offer for my saddle, I reckon you had better sell it, too, and if I can come through the war safe, I can have another made.

I expect that there will be a good deal of hard fighting this spring and all. The Yankees say that they will not have to fight much longer, for they will starve us out in a month, but I think that they are very badly mistaken. The most of us men would fight without anything hardly to eat.

I have nothing more at present. Give my love to all relations and friends. Write soon. I remain your affectionate son until death,

J. J. Wilson

☆ *J. B. Crawford to Martha A. Crawford*:
Camp near Old United States Ford, April 12, 1863

Dear Wife

I seat myself down to let you know that I am well at this time hoping those few lines will find you and famley enjoying the same blessing of health. This is the third letter I have wrote and have received no word from you yet. I am thinking you have forgotten to write. I waunt to hear from you very bad and waunt to see you a heap worse than ever. I have sent three letters and one paper. I am on guard today and have not time to write but I have nothing of any importance to write. I can see the Yankey at work and we expect to fight every day. Tel the children that I hant forgotten them and would give the wourld to see then once more. If we never meet on earth meet me in heaven where we will part no more forever. Amen.

　　Poetry
How long sometime a day appears
And weeks how long they are
Months move along as if the years
Would never pass away

So I will close at this time. I remain your husband til death,

> J. B. Crawford to Martha
> A. Crawford

☆ **J. B. Crawford to Martha A. Crawford:**
Camp near the Old United States Ford, April 23, 1863

Dear Wife

I received your letter of the 14 which found me well and I was glad to hear from you but sorry to hear how Ben has done. The best way is to have nothing to do with him. I am glad you let Pippen have the mare. You waunted to know what I had to eat and to do. I have flour and bacon to eat and have to watch the Yankey. I see [Yankees] every day and we have taken three of them yesterday and brought them in camp.

I have nothing much to write. I wrote Martha and Mary a letter yesterday. I sent a paper to you. Let me know wether you got it or not. Tel Pippen that I haint forgot him. . . . Let me know who have gon from there. I must write Ben a note to tend to his own business. I waunt to see the children so bad I cant be still. Tel Jane and the boys all is well.

I am glad you sold the mare. Get somebody to take care of the wagon. Do the best you can til I return if I get off some. Give my best respects to my friends. Tel Molly I wood like to see her. So nothing more at present. I remain your loving husband until death.

> J. B. Crawford to Martha
> A. Crawford

I want to see Tomy so bad.

☆ **J. B. Crawford to Martha A. Crawford:**
Camp near the Old United States Ford, April 27, 1863

Dear Wife

I received your of the 16 which found me well. I hope those few lines will find you and famley enjoying the same blessing of health. I was glad to hear from you and the children. . . . Tel the children I waunt to see them. I have nothing of any importance to write. I stand on one side of the river and the

Yankee on the other side and we fish together. . . . Tel Jane the boys is all well and looks very well.

You said something about Bens conduct since I been gon. Tel Ben the next time he coms there cuttin up its only fifteen hundred miles home and if I cant com home I can run away and com and things will change there or somebodys neck will break. Dont let him have the mares and no harness. He is a Tory at best and a base coward. He thinks that I will never com back and he will do as he pleases. . . .

We expect to fight every day.Kiss the children for me. Tel them to send me some word and God bless the baby too. I will close at present until I hear from you again. Write soon.

> J. B. Crawford to M.
> Crawford and the
> children

☆ *James Johnson Kirkpatrick Dairy*, April 29, 1863, Wednesday:

. . . Started to go on picket in evening through the rain, but after going about half way, were halted by a courier and facing about, marched rapidly back past our camp, the brigade falling in with us and halted near Chancellors-ville. Formed lines of battle and remained watchful all night. The enemy crossed a force at Kelly's Ford, pushed on and crossed the Rapidan at Ely's and Germanna Fords. They are reported to be coming in larger numbers. No alarms tonight.

— Chapter 11 —

". . . ENOUGH TO MAKE THE OLD MASTER WEEP"

With the Army of the Potomac reorganized, Hooker took one-third of his army across the Rappahannock northwest of Fredericksburg and camped at the edge of a thickly wooded area known as "The Wilderness." One-third of the army was held in reserve, while General John Sedgwick took the remaining one-third to attack Lee in his entrenchments and divert his attention. Hooker would then move in behind Lee and annihilate his army. The plan was perfect.

The fifty-six-year-old Lee discerned that the main attack would come from Hooker and, absent bold action on his part, the Army of Northern Virginia would be destroyed. With less than sixty thousand troops, half the number of Hooker's, Lee ignored conventional military wisdom and split his forces. Leaving General Jubal Early to contend with Sedgwick, Lee took the remainder of his poorly fed, ill-equipped soldiers to meet Hooker at a lonely Virginia farmhouse known as Chancellorsville.

Hooker arrived first and stationed his cannons on the slight rises in the open fields. The level, thickly-wooded land around the fields left Confederate artillery virtually useless. Hooker formed his troops in three separate lines, entrenching each one, while Lee built only a few temporary works. Jackson, commanding the left wing, built none, his men would not be still long enough to need them. He planned to advance and attack, and the Sixteenth Mississippi and Posey's Brigade would be among the first he ordered to do so.[1]

☆ *Report Number 329: Report of Brigadier General Carnot Posey:*

On the evening of the 29th [of April], being then in camp . . . near the U.S. Ford, we were advised by our scouts at . . . Ely's Ford and Germanna Bridge, that the enemy had crossed in heavy force at those points and were advancing on the Ely and Plank Roads towards Chancellorsville. Upon consultation, we concluded to leave five companies of my brigade, the Nineteenth Mississippi, and one regiment of General Mahone's Brigade to watch and defend the U.S. Ford while we moved our brigades to Chancellorsville. On reaching that point, we posted my brigade on the right and left of the Plank Road at Chancellorsville and General Mahone's Brigade in Bullard's and Mexley's field, half a mile from Chancellorsville on the Ely Road. We remained in this position until about seven o'clock the next morning. . . .[2]

About seven o'clock the next morning, the 30th . . . we were directed . . . to move our commands back to a position where the Mine Road crosses the old pike and Plank Road. We remained in this position until the next morning about nine o'clock, May 1st. . . .[3]

☆ *The Veteran's Story:*

On Friday evening [May 1st], our division was in line of battle across the Orange Court House and Fredericksburg Plank Road. About three o'clock [p.m.], we saw Jackson coming up the road. Our boys commenced saying, "Get ready. Jackson is coming, we will soon be on the move." He rode up, saluted Generals Lee and Anderson and held a short consultation. He rode to the front and ordered our brigade to advance as skirmishers. We moved out briskly and did not go far before finding the Federal skirmish line. . . . The Federal skirmishers were soon in full retreat with Stonewall at their heels. They were pressed back upon their main line. We then halted to await orders. By this time, night was closing in on us. Jackson's men . . . were coming up forming on our left. We knew that something was going to happen soon, for Jackson never tarried when he went to battle. All night long the tramp of soldiers was heard as they went passing by, going to the left. In our front, we could hear the sound of the pick and spade. The Federals were preparing to receive us the next day. . . .

We halted near a large furnace, formed a line and were ordered to rest on our arms. Soon after halting, three of us were detailed to report to headquarters. There we found R. E. Lee, T. J. Jackson and R. H. Anderson holding a council of war. After reporting to them we were instructed to guard their horses and camp.[4]

☆ **Report Number 329:** *Report of Brigadier General Carnot Posey* *[continued]*:

About nine o'clock [a.m.] May 1st . . . I was ordered to advance my brigade up the Plank Road. After moving about two miles, I formed a line of battle in Aldridge's field between the Plank Road and Old Pike and sent out the Twelfth Regiment as skirmishers, moving the other three regiments forward as fast as the skirmishers advanced. The advance line of skirmishers soon encountered the enemy, when I advanced another line and drove the enemy's skirmishers back . . . until we encountered the enemy in heavy force drawn up in line of battle on the Furnace Road. This line was soon broken by the vigorous onset of my skirmishers. . . . I continued my advance across the Furnace Road through a dense wood thickly set with undergrowth, driving back the enemy's skirmishers through the woods until I reached a marsh and became much exposed to a rapid shelling from the enemy's artillery. . . . I halted my command and remained here until about eleven o'clock p.m., when I received an order . . . to advance as far as I could. I then pushed my skirmishers forward and with much difficulty crossed the marsh in front and advanced within a short distance of the enemy's lines of works, the enemy on my right being on my flank and somewhat in the rear of my right. I remained in this position until about seven o'clock the next day morning . . . [when] I was relieved . . . and withdrew my brigade to the field in the rear of the Furnace Road, where my command was allowed to rest for a short time.

Saturday, May 2nd, about ten o'clock a.m, my command moved down the Furnace Road and formed a line of battle with three regiments (the Forty-eighth being left behind as skirmishers) . . . on each side of the road about five hundred yards from the furnace. Here my skirmishers were hotly engaged with the enemy during the whole day and part of the night. The enemy, being in heavy force in my front, made frequent efforts to advance without success—on every occasion my line of skirmishers drove them back in confusion.[5]

☆ *James Johnson Kirkpatrick Diary*, May 2, 1863, Saturday:

Our brigade [was] sent back a short distance to the rear, being highly complimented for our action yesterday. General Jackson came up the Plank Road this morning at the head of his corps, looking as if something had to be done. After a hasty survey of the position, he files off to the left on an obscure road towards Catharine Furnace. After a short rest, we are again put in motion and march in to the left in front of the Furnace. The enemy is extending his right wing in this direction. Very hot. Extended our line of battle across the road on which Jackson had passed. Somewhat exposed to shell and Minies, but only our skirmishers replied. Some casualties in regiment. In evening, Company C is sent to the left on picket line. Received the especial attention of a battery a while—though it did us no damage. Only injured the trees. On picket all night. Some heavy cannonading and musketry before midnight in the enemy rear. . . .

☆ *The Veteran's Story*:

About three o'clock [a.m., May 2nd], Jackson was up, moving around, preparing for the work of the day soon to come. At sunrise, instead of advancing upon the enemy's works, he commenced moving to the left and thus continued moving till late in the evening. He then turned into the right and struck the Federal army, doubled up their right wing, put them to flight and presses them back to Chancellor House. It was now getting dark. Our army was halted and reformed. Jackson was at the front, placing his men in line. While examining the position of the Yankees, he rode into [Eighteenth North Carolina's] picket line [about 9:30 p.m.]. They called to him to halt. He about faced and galloped back toward out line. Our men mistook him and his aides for the Federal cavalry and fired into them, wounding him and killing some of his aides. The officers tried to keep the bad news from their men but did not succeed very well, for nothing happened in the army but what some ragged Rebel found it out. The news spread like wildfire all through the army. . . .[6]

☆ *Historical Sketch of the Quitman Guards*:

On the night of the [2nd] of May . . . Jackson executed his movement to the left. . . . He placed a battery on Hooker's right so as to enfilade his lines and then began to charge in his rear. Lee charged their front at the same time with the troops under his immediate command. Thus the Federals were placed between two fires and were also exposed to a destructive enfilading fire from the Confederate batteries on the right. They, however, had breastworks facing both ways. . . .

The Sixteenth Mississippi charged with unfixed bayonets. (Colonel Baker afterwards remarking that it never occurred to him to fix bayonets until the charge was over.) The Confederate army . . . swept over the breastworks of the Federals, carrying everything before it. . . . The works being carried, a hand to hand strife ensued. The artillery ceased, but the clashing of small arms told that the deadly strife was still progressing. . . . Clubbed muskets fell with crushing weight upon the victim warriors, and the mangled forms of the dead and dying covered the ground. The Federals were at length forced to yield, and the Confederates were masters of the extensive works. . . .[7]

☆ *James Johnson Kirkpatrick Diary*, May 3, 1863, Sunday:

Our skirmish line started forward early this morning to feel for the enemy. Find that the forces in our front have withdrawn. Formed our companies and started after the regiment which had marched from its present position. Rejoined them under a hill about a mile to left of Chancellorsville. A battery of ours on the hill above us is firing very rapidly. In a short time, we move a little to the right and start forward. The ground in our front is thickly timbered with pine and other small growth. Without the least falter, the brigade sweeps around, up to and over the enemy's rifle pits. They break and run pell mell, and we pursue, loading and firing as fast as possible, to within a short distance of the Chancellor's house, when we are ordered back to the rifle pits to reform.

About five hundred prisoners surrendered at the rifle pits, mostly to Company C. The works were well made of logs and earth with an abatis of from fifty to one hundred fifty yards in front. It looks like troops of any courage might have held them. After reforming and resting, we advanced to the Chancellor house, finding that the line has all been carried, we marched down nearly to U.S. Ford and are halted at our old quarters. . . . The casualties of the regiment were pretty heavy.

☆ *Report Number 329: Report of Brigadier General Carnot Posey [continued]*:

On the morning of the third, the enemy having disappeared from my front, I advanced my command by the furnace, capturing many prisoners and arms, until I reached a point in a field in rear of our batteries on the extreme right of the enemy's lines. Here I formed my command in columns of regiments and after a short time was ordered to advance by flank to the right and attack the enemy, who were in strong force in a field in front.

I deployed first the Nineteenth, then the Twelfth, Forty-eighth and Six-teenth, directing the commands to move by the right flank (which would bring them in line of battle fronting the enemy). As soon as they obtained sufficient room in the woods . . . they pushed forward their skirmishers vigorously against the enemy. The movement was made in fine order under heavy fire of shell and grape. As each regiment attained its position, the commands pushed gal-lantly and irresistibly through a dense wood, over a wide abatis and into the trenches of the enemy, driving them off with much slaughter and capturing many prisoners. . . .

Colonel Baker of the Sixteenth attacked the enemy's works on their extreme right. . . .[8]

☆ *The Veteran's Story:*

That morning [May 3rd] at nine o'clock, the signal gun fired, and we rushed upon the Federal lines with artillery and infantry. They were soon put to flight. The Rebel Yell was heard all along our lines.

After the Yanks had been routed, General Lee rode up where we were reforming. He was the grandest looking man that I ever saw. While he was there, a soldier boy with a wounded hand was passing by and said, "By God, General, the Yankees have done me up, but we have given them hell." Lee said, "Well, you are a brave soldier, but you must not swear." He dismounted, took a linen handkerchief from his pocket and wrapped it round the boy's hand, made a sling with a red silk one and placed the little fellow's hand in it and told him to go to the hospital and have the wound dressed. . . .[9]

☆ *Report Number 330: Report of Colonel Samuel E. Baker . . . on the loss of the Sixteenth Mississippi's battle-flag on May 3rd:*

The color-bearer was severely wounded and the flag-staff shot in two near the colors a short time after we got into the enemy's trenches. The colors were then passed to Color Corporal W. M. Wadsworth, who was shortly afterward wounded in the leg and who in turn passed these colors to Corporal W. J.

Sweeney, who came to me as we were following the enemy and reported that he had the colors safe. Soon after this the enemy opened on us with a destructive fire of grape when Corporal Sweeney was wounded and borne to the rear, taking the colors with him. He has since been sent to Richmond, and I am unable at present to state what became of the colors.[10]

I have heard that a member of the brigade who died of his wounds at our field hospital was wrapped in a battle-flag and think it not unlikely it may have been the one belonging to my regiment; and, as my regimental colors had no letters or distinguished marks upon them, it would be impossible to identify them. By the time Corporal Sweeney was wounded . . . the whole of my color-guard had been disabled with wounds more or less severe. One of them has since died, and the color-bearer had his left arm amputated. My center companies also were severely cut to pieces, and to these facts and these alone, I attribute the loss of the battle-flag of my regiment. . . .[11]

☆ Report Number 329: Report of Brigadier General Carnot Posey [continued]:

After storming the works, being somewhat scattered on account of the dense woods and vigorous pursuit, I reformed in an open field on the right and in a very short time was ready to move forward. In the afternoon of this day, my command was moved in the old pike, the left resting near Chancellorsville House, my right extended to the pike. I here sent out ten companies who penetrated to Bullard's and Mexley's Fields, where the enemy were in force and throwing up works of defense.

In the afternoon, my brigade, with General Wright's and Perry's, were moved near the U.S. Ford, where I sent out the Nineteenth and Twelfth Regiments and drove in the enemy skirmishers.[12]

The next day (Monday, the 4th) my command was moved . . . towards Fredericksburg in the afternoon and formed a line of battle near Hazel Run, fronting Dolmey's house. At the signal to advance . . . my command moved across the Plank Road opposite Guest House under heavy fire and at dark formed a line of battle and remained until about twelve o'clock, when I was ordered to move to a point up the Plank Road near Banks Ford. During this time, my skirmishers were engaged and brought in many prisoners. I remained near Banks Ford during the balance of the night. . . .

☆ *Historical Sketch of the Quitman Guards*:

After the Battle of Chancellorsville, General Lee's attention was drawn towards Fredericksburg, at which place Sedgwick had crossed twenty-five or thirty thousand men and was approaching the rear of Lee. He immediately detached a sufficient force for the purpose of driving them back across the river. This force met the Federals . . . and immediately began the attack.[13]

The Federals, not expecting an attack, were somewhat confused and consequently did not make their usual resistance. . . . The fighting began about the middle of the afternoon and lasted until dark. The Federals were driven back to the river and recrossed it at Banks Ford, three miles above Fredericksburg. Posey's Brigade was engaged in this brilliant affair. . . .

Some time after dark, the Confederate line of battle moved nearer to the ford at which the Federals were crossing. General Posey, wishing to be certain of their movements, called for volunteers to go out and see what discoveries could be made. Among others, John Walker and J. E. Simmons of the Quitman Guards volunteered. Shortly after leaving the line, they were halted by a company of Federal pickets. "Who are you?" said one of the pickets. They replied, "We are Confederate soldiers. You are now surrounded by our forces, and we have come to conduct you safely to our lines." The Federals immediately stacked their arms, and the company, sixty in number, were conducted by these two gallant young men to General Posey's headquarters.[14]

☆ *James Johnson Kirkpatrick Diary*, May 4, 1863, Monday:

Marched back to the back to the pike this morning and struck out for Fredericksburg. Filed to right of Plank Road at Salem Chapel, passed by our old winter quarters and formed line in a ravine near the . . . railroad. General Sedgwick occupied the Fredericksburg heights on Sunday, and it seems our object to send him back across the river. Expected a hard fight. Made our advance about two hours before dark. Drove the enemy with great ease towards Banks Ford. Pressed them on till late at night. Our artillery shelled the ford till after midnight. Slept more tonight.

☆ *James Johnson Kirkpatrick Diary*, May 6, 1863, Wednesday:

Started early. Proceeded up the Plank Road beyond Chancellorsville; and turned to the right towards Elys Ford. Stopped two miles beyond the town, faced about and marched to our camp near Fredericksburg. Rained nearly all day and everybody used up when we halted. Hooker had entirely disappeared from our side of the river. Our highly esteemed General Jackson was severely wounded on Saturday night.

☆ Report Number 329: Report of Brigadier General Carnot Posey [continued]:

Early the next day (May 6th), I was moved to Bullard's field and that evening returned to my old camp near Fredericksburg. My command was on foot from the 29th of April to [May] the 6th, inclusive, and bore the privations, fatigue, labor and fighting without a murmur. . . .[15]

☆ Historical Sketch of the Quitman Guards:

General Hooker again returned to Stafford, and General Lee's troops occupied their old camps, continuing to picket on the banks of the river. . . .[16]

☆ J. B. Crawford to Martha A. Crawford:

May 7, 1863

Dear Wife

I seat myself down to let you know that I am not well but I hope those lines will reach you and find you all well.

I have been on the battlefield eight days. The sight I saw I cant pen it down. It is a slaughter pen. It is enough to make the Old Master weep. The dead the dying the wounded they was stroad for ten miles in ever direction. Oh what a sight to behold. Our companie lost now ninety-five killed and wounded and missing in our rigement. Loss on both sides I cant tell but it looks like enough to make a wourld. I never waunt to see the sight again. The shot and shell and Minie balls came around me like hailstones but no time for dodging. I expected ever minute our companie would be blown into atoms but I think kind Providence smiled on us. If I could see you I could tell you more than I could write about it. It is so bad to talk about.

I cant write much now. We have to travel now after the Yankee so I will close at this time. I want to see you all so bad.

> J. B. Crawford to his
> dear wife and children,
> good by. God bless you.

☆ *Harry Lewis to Mrs. Nancy Lewis*:
Near our old camp opposite Fredericksburg, May 7th, 1863

Dearest Mother,

I know you have heard . . . of the battle that has been progressing here for over a week past, and I can imagine your anxiety, but you must not expect a good letter, as the battle was one, or rather a series of conflicts, so strange as to beggar all description.

Our lines of battle were formed to suit the occasion, one hour fronting one direction and the next an entirely different one, sometimes in front and rear simultaneously could be heard the popping of musketry and roar of artillery, and all in front could be heard the wild, desperate yell of our boys . . . crushing all obstacles, and perhaps on the right an hour before, we heard the hoarse but wavering "huzza" of the Yankee. We have fought over so much ground and our combinations have been so varied that it is utterly impossible to convey even an approximate idea of the various battlefields of the past days.

Wednesday, April 29th, the Yankees surprised a party of picket men from our brigade building a bridge at Germanna . . . [and] U.S. Fords and captured a majority of them. . . . About the same time, the enemy crossed near Fredericksburg and found Barksdale taking possession of the city and some of the surrounding heights. Wednesday evening, we hastily evacuated our quarters at U.S. Ford. . . .

The next morning [April 30th, we] retreated to a strong position about five miles from Chancellorsville toward Fredericksburg and commenced fortifying.

Friday morning [May 1st] dawned on us in our ample rifle pits, anxious for the enemy to advance. Though they maintained a constant picket firing a few hundred yards in front, they did not come up to our wishes, i.e., our rifle pits, but about ten o'clock that morning, Stonewall did come up and in a short time ordered a general advance much against our inclination. Our brigade took the Plank Road . . . and drove the enemy for three or four miles in such style and spirit as to elicit compliment from General Jackson himself, who attended on the whole route. Within a mile of Chancellorsville, we encountered heavy forces and batteries of the enemy in position in dense woods. Here we pushed the advance lines of the Yankees in and that night slept on our arms within forty yards of them.

The country in that section for miles in every direction around Chancellorsville is a wild, dense forest, generally undergrowth of oak, with an occasional house and clearing and roads running through it in every direction. This part of the world goes by the very appropriate name "The Wilderness."

Saturday morning [May 2nd] brought an ominous silence disturbed by an occasional volley from the pickets and the thunder of canons. Desultory fighting was continued all day Saturday at various points of the line. Line after line of our forces were coming up till noon and, taking the road to the left of Chancellorsville, were following the road "Old Jackson" took early that morning, leaving General Anderson's Division to guard the front which extended to the right and left of the Plank Road. About four o'clock[p.m.], our brigade was ordered around on our left line to protect our trains the Yankees were trying to cut off. We laid there till night, and in the evening heard a terrible commotion in the Yankee lines. Though their sharpshooters are knocking the bark off trees all around us . . . we listen in wonder and prepare ourselves for their reception. The sound passed to our left like a mighty rushing wind. It is the tread of closed columns of the enemy advancing to charge our left and break our line. Our front is weak, very weak. Jackson has gone off somewhere and unless something turns up, the enemy will ruin us irretrievably. But the huzza gradually ceased, and we can hear their officers plainly swearing at their men and shouting "forward." In vain! The Yankees won't charge, and we are considerably relieved I tell you. In half an hour, it is dark, and the startling flash of artillery away beyond the Yankee left and in their rear announces the fact that Jackson is in their rear. Then the solution of the mystery of their conduct a few hours ago. Remaining on picket till two o'clock [a.m.], we spent the last hours of darkness in building breastworks, which we left at sunup.

Sunday morning [May 3rd] the ball opened in real earnest, everything hitherto has been preliminary and now comes the work. . . . We must carry their formidable breastworks girded by an abatis of unusual strength. Fortunately, the whole of the left wing is detailed as skirmishers and to support our batteries. Our course throughout as skirmishers early in the day continued until just after the breastworks were taken. . . .

George Pilant was killed by a fragment of shell passing through his head. He was reading a Yankee newspaper and, unconscious of danger, passed into eternity. He was one of the best and bravest boys in the company. . . .

Our brigade charged the works . . . without a cheer or firing a gun until up to the works, but with heavy loss. They captured several hundred Yankees. Our regiment suffered most. After charging like "so many devils" over the abatis and works, they found double the number of Yanks still in them who surrendered unconditionally. But as soon as some of our men rushed on ahead to charge a battery in front, the scoundrels jerked up their guns and commenced shooting. The remainder went down without mercy. Company G was almost ruined here, the Yanks even shooting the men after they have surrendered. Companies D and I from Natchez lost men very heavily also. This was the key to the position at Chancellorsville, and we advanced to find the splendid brick building in flames and the orchard torn to pieces with cannon shot and the ground covered with the forms of men and horses mangled—all these were Yankees, however.

The next day [May 4th] we marched down opposite Fredericksburg by pass- ing to the right of the enemy, who had advanced several miles up the Plank Road, and gained their rear about dark. About dark, the battle commenced. The Yankees acted more cowardly here than ever before. . . . Everywhere . . . the victory was gained by raising a yell and charging, for the enemy wouldn't staunch. This fighting Monday night closed the scene, for then we marched up to Chancellorsville. . . . We found the Yanks had re-crossed the river . . . and yesterday we were ordered back here, near one of our old winter quarter camps opposite U.S. Ford. And here, I hope, we will stay till at least we are rested. The Yankees are now all across the river, and I don't see how they will have the assurance to attack us here again for some time.

We have captured between seven thousand and ten thousand prisoners and all of their baggage in shapes of knapsacks, blankets and tent flies. They depos- ited their baggage in lines and piles and were compelled to leave them. Each of their men had eight days rations which they carried in haversacks and knap- sacks. Our army are better supplied in the little necessaries than we were before. I don't know how much artillery we captured. I do not think we cap- tured many pieces.

We lost twelve hundred prisoners, I reckon, and several thousand killed and wounded. The Yankees lost near ten thousand prisoners and more heavily in killed and wounded than we. Our regiment lost, in killed, wounded and miss- ing, one hundred men, a little less than one-half of the number engaged. Twenty-two of this number were killed dead, besides those wounded who will die. I never saw dead men more terribly torn and mutilated on any other field. This was owing to the short distance we fought in, the woods being very thick. . . .

All the color guard were shot down. There were five of them, two of them were killed, one mortally wounded and one slightly. The sergeant charged over the works with his flag in his hand and commenced knocking the Yanks over the head with the staff, which was shot in two and himself was shot in the arm which afterward was amputated. . . .

Dear Ma, I have written you a longer letter than I thought I could. You must excuse the paper as I have been carrying it in my haversack, and it has become soiled—it is captured property.

Give my respects to all. Your affectionate son,

Harry

☆ *Jerome B. Yates to Mrs. Obedience Yates*:
Fredericksburg, May 8th, 1863

Dear Ma,

Being still alive, which I feel extremely thankful for to that all divine Providence, I will drop you a few lines. We have had another eight day fight and repulsed the enemy at all points and driven him across the river, perfectly disorganized, so says General Anderson our major general. I will not attempt to give you any description of the fight. . . . I came out all right without a scratch.

The victory was complete but not very disastrous. They would not stand before our troops when they charged. This brigade made a very gallant charge against . . . the enemy's twice our number. It was commended very highly by General Anderson for charging without any bayonets.

I send you a New York paper, thinking you would like to see it. Write soon to your son,

Jerome

☆ *Hugh Carroll Dickson to Joseph J. Dickson*:
Camp near Fredericksburg, Virginia, May 9, 1863

Dearest Pa,

I now take my pen in hand for the purpose of writing you a few lines to let you know that I am still in the land of the living. We have just had another severe battle, and our arms have been crowned with another victory, but as usual, a great many of our gallant boys have been consigned to their last resting places. . . . The loss of the enemy is heavy. We are now lying in camp resting.

We have had a severe time of it, marching and fighting in mud and rain for seven days. I assure you, I am completely played out for the present.

By the by, Pa, I came very near going up the spout on Sunday of the fight. Our company was ordered out to skirmishing through the pines. By some means or other, I got some fifty yards in advance of my company when suddenly I came upon a rifle pit full of Yankees. I was in twenty steps of them before I saw them. I then discovered some rails in front of me. I ran to this place and fell down with my head towards them. They then commenced firing on me, the balls flying like hailstones. One ball passed within two inches of my head while another struck my blanket, which I had rolled up and strapped to my back, passing entirely through, striking me on the backbone and tearing my coat, then glanced off without hurting me. While I was lying there, one man was killed. He fell on me. Another was shot in a few feet of me.

Our brigade was ordered to charge the enemy out of their works, which they did right gallantly, although a great many of our regiment were killed and wounded. The loss of our regiment is one hundred and five killed, wounded and missing. . . .

Give my best love to all of the family and reserve a large portion for yourself. I remain, as ever, your loving son,

Hugh C. Dickson

☆ *J. J. Wilson to James E. Wilson*:
Camp near Fredericksburg, May 10th, 1863

Dear Father,

I take the present opportunity of dropping you a few lines to let you know that I am yet among the living. . . . We have just got through with the Second Battle of Fredericksburg. It commenced on the 29th of April and lasted nine days. We were busy going all the time. We were one of the front lines, and all the time when there was any big fighting to do, our brigade was sent in. Last Sunday [May 3rd] was hard fought battle, but we were victorious in charging them from their rifle pits, killing a great many and took a good many prisoners. . . .

My love to all. I will write again in a few days as soon as I hear the report of the battle. I remain your son,

J. J. Wilson

☆ *Jerome B. Yates to Marie Yates*:
Fredericksburg, May 11th, 1863

Dear Marie,

As I have time and an opportunity, I will drop you a few lines. There is little or no news of importance with the exception of the rumor that General Jackson is dead, died from the amputation of his arm, which unfortunately was broken by one of our own men. The circumstances of the affair as I understand is that Jackson passed by one of his pickets on post without the knowledge of his pickets. On his return, he was fired into by them without ever being halted, his left arm broken and a bullet through his right hand. His loss to this country cannot be replaced by another in this country. Sometime I wish it had been Longstreet instead of the "Valley Soldier." Poor man. Would to God his life had been spared until this was over. It will be such a satisfaction to the enemy. I hate it more on that account. I think if we could spared him to of gone South, the armies down south would have been more successful. But now he is dead, and his services are lost to us all. I never seemed to appreciate his worth until he was killed. But enough of Jackson, I hope he has gone to heaven.[17]

What do you think of the Yankees getting into your part of the country? I hope they may never set foot on the home place nor anywhere in that country. I see that they have burnt the depot at Bahala and are en route for Hazlehurst, but that the Sixth Mississippi have been sent to intercept them, but I have a small opinion of that regiment. I am by the Mississippians in Mississippi like I am by the Virginians here. They are at home too often. They do not attend to their business.

I was glad to hear Van Dorn was killed. The Confederacy would have been a great deal better off if he had been killed twelve months ago.[18]

I heard all the commanding officers and gunners were at a party when the gunboats passed Vicksburg. I think such negligence should be severely punished by the government authorities, and I do most sincerely hope that the matter may be investigated and those in fault be shot. What is the use of us fighting so hard and whipping the enemy up here when through the neglect of those down at home we are to lose everything that we are fighting for? I for one am wishing to stop the thing unless the Southern army will give us a little help. If they would ever once whip them, they would never have any further trouble with them.

I will tell you what is the fact. After we let the enemy across the river and . . . the lines would give way before us without firing a gun. . . . They were in rifle ditches, but we made them skedaddle also. But enough of this bragging. I never did like anyone that bragged. . . .

> You must write soon to
> your brother,
> J. B. Y.

☆ *Harry Lewis to Mrs. Nancy Lewis*:
Camp near Fredericksburg, Virginia, May 15th, 1863

Dear Mother,

Since the eight days of constant fatigue and fighting, we have had ample time to become fully rested and are now as able as we ever were to undergo a campaign, being in fine health and good spirits. I think your discovery of "low spirits" in my letter must be the result of your own imagination worked upon by some depressing influences, for I must confess that of late I am troubled no more by "blues" than at any prior time since I belonged to the army, and as a general thing, I am visited less by fits of despondency in the army than before I belonged to it at all. Of course, anyone on the eve of a battlefield is serious and some even anxious and apprehensive, but every sensible and patriotic man knows that on the morrow, he must battle for his rights and on his deeds and bearing hangs the honor and existence of the Confederacy and the sanctity and preservation of home and family, and steeled with this idea and fired with determination to do his duty, every true soldier commits himself to the strife, confiding his fate to the Great Giver of Eternal Life. Dear Mother, I am trying to live in a manner more congenial to a Christian than heretofore, and though I am fully aware I fall far short of the proper mark, yet I will continue to try to perform my duties as best I can for I know man is full of imperfections and is not perfect.

I have been acting adjutant for several days and find it considerably easier than being attached to the company. Brother John is on court-martial duty again. The court adjourned during the fighting and Brother J. assumed command of his company and led it in every battle. Fletch is still on provost guard and is well pleased with it. You seem to cling to the impression that Fletch is very much dissatisfied in all your letters, but I can truthfully say that Fletch is very well contented, though during the winter he was somewhat discontented owing to so many persons visiting home, a privilege denied him. The guard of which he is a member consists of from ten to twenty men and every brigade has one. Their duty is to prevent straggling, especially in battle. So they do not go into a fight and, consequently, are but little exposed in times of danger.

We receive Richmond papers daily, some of which contain copious extracts from Northern files. The Yankee authorities have pursued their usual course of lying. They prohibit anything from the army to be published but their own absurd tales. But the truth will in time leak out, and then won't there be a dolorous howl in Yankeedom? As time unfolds the events of the late battles, it develops our victory in dimensions more grand and glorious than I at first expected or dreamed of. Besides incessant skirmishing and artillery drills, there were four distinct battles fought.

On the 2nd of May, "Stonewall," the beloved, flanked the enemy and with A. P. Hill's, Trimble's and Rodes's Divisions and defeated them with great slaughter at Wilderness Church, six miles above Chancellorsville. Here General Jackson was wounded by our own men.[19]

Sunday morning, May 3rd, the above-named divisions on the enemies' right and Anderson and part of McLaws in the front, made a grand combined attack upon the works around Chancellorsville, which were carried with considerate loss on both sides. On Sunday night, the Yankees had advanced six miles above Fredericksburg, endeavoring to break through our lines and form junction with their army above Chancellorsville. Here we attacked them and drove them a couple of miles, killing a number, to Salem Church.[20]

The next evening just before dark, Early's Division from Marye's Heights attacked the Yanks in the rear, while ours (Anderson's) attacked them in the flank and front. This was a pretty general fight, but the Yankees would not stand, yet some of our boys suffered considerably. This is called the Battle of Fredericksburg Number Two.[21]

To recapitulate, on Saturday, May 2nd, Battle of Wilderness Church; on Sunday May 3rd, Battle of Chancellorsville; Sunday evening, May 3rd, Battle of Salem Church; on Monday evening, May 4th, Battle of Fredericksburg Number Two. There was also a fight (but not deserving a place in the rank of general battles) at Fredericksburg on Sunday, May 3rd, where Barksdale fought the Yankees with fearful odds.

Yankee General Stoneman made a raid within four miles of Richmond but did no damage other than destroying thirty commissary wagons. Our communication with Richmond was unimpaired the next day. Of course, the Yankees boast greatly over this and with it attempt to veil their defeat.[22]

The result of the battles may be thus summed up. Hooker, with not less than one hundred fifty thousand men, surprised our pickets and crossed the river. This immense army was attacked (in some instances in fortifications) by Lee and Jackson with not over fifty thousand men and after five days fighting, [Hooker's men were] hurled demoralized and crippled across the river. History presents no parallel to this. In addition, we captured between eight and ten thousand prisoners, besides several thousand of their wounded. . . . I saw thousands of knapsacks and blankets, etc., scattered everywhere. Everything showed how panic stricken their men must have been, and Hooker will have to completely outfit the "finest army on the planet" again. . . .

The Yankees must have lost twelve or fifteen thousand killed and wounded. Our loss in prisoners, say twelve hundred; killed and wounded, about nine thousand. We lost five pieces of the Washington Artillery. Our regiment lost one hundred killed and wounded and prisoners. . . . Posey's Brigade acquired honor and great credit. Posey acted as well as a general could. . . .

Write whenever you get a chance, and I will do the same. Your affectionate son,

Harry

☆ *J. B. Crawford to Martha A. Crawford*:
Camp near Fredericksburg, May 16, 1863

Dear Wife

I received your letter of the 8 of May which found me well. I was so glad to hear from you but was sorry to hear how Ben have done you. You stated that he had whipped Tomy. . . . It almost broke my heart. . . . It hurt my feelings so bad. . . . I do not know for all the wourld what to say to you. . . .

I received a letter from Pippen the other day which gave me some comfort. He said he wood protect you all. He also said something about moving to our old place next fall. Maybe times will get better by then. I dont know what to say to you about it. If you can get [someone] to com in my place give everything we have got.

Martha take things as well as you can. I know it is enough to kill you and me the way things is going but take it easy as you can. I weigh one hundred and fifty pounds. Write how your corn and meat hold out and how the stock is doing. . . .

God bless the children and you. . . .

J. B. Crawford

☆ *Jerome B. Yates to Marie Yates*:
Fredericksburg, Virginia, May 19th, 1863

Dear Marie,

Thinking you would be more apt to get a letter than Ma, I will write you one. . . . The papers are giving gloomy accounts of the Yankees' conduct of the evenings in Hinds [County] and in Jackson. I suppose they burned and destroyed the railroad. But it is useless to write you anything about what you know so much about. . . .

There is positively nothing more to write, only what Henry Broome sends to his wife to be true and not follow the Negro liberators off, that we will be at home some of these days to claim her again. How is Mr. Swanson getting on? How does he feel about the Yankees making him a visit?. . . .[23]

I would like to hear from my little squad of darkies to see if any of them compose part of the three thousand that left Hinds County with the enemy. The Richmond papers report that many are from Hinds County. Write me if they took much from Ma or you. . . . If they did take anything, and I have a chance to, I will pay them with interest, that is if we ever go to Maryland or Pennsylvania, which I believe we will do this summer.

Tell my Darkies I want them to all behave themselves honorably in the hour of need. Tell Tom, if he has not already left, I want to find him at home when I get there. I believe he will stay if every one of the others go. Tell them all "Howdy" while giving them all my best. Tell them I would like to see how they act on such an occasion as when the Yankees made their appearance. I think we all have some that will not go with them. . . .

I want you to write to me everything in your camp. Your brother,

J. B. Y.

☆ *J. B. Crawford to Martha A. Crawford*:
Camp near Fredericksburg, May the 23, 1863

Dear Wife

I received yours of the tenth of may and I was glad to hear that you and childern was well.

I hope those few lines will find you all well. I have nothing of any importance to write you. I waulk over the battlefield yesterday and when I com back I received your letter. I go to church ever night. Wee have grate revival hear. preaching is going on now in our ridgement. today is Sunday and it look like some woman ort to be hear. It look odd without the lady.

They is some talk about our going to mississippi to Jackson and if wee do I will com by home if they dont chain me with a lock chain. The boys is well at this time and in hy spirit. Wee have to dril very hard hear every day.

Tel all the neighbours to write to me. I love to read letters from home and from the settlement. Wee are talking of sending for P. H. Napier to come and preach for us.

You said somthing about going to the old place. . . . I dont know what to say about it but I hope this ware will end by that time but some say it wount end in ten year. If Ben cuts up any more tel the neighbours to send him hear. I think I can cool him. Ever time I think of his whipping Tomy my blood boils to the top of my mettle. I think at that time I could murder him.

I send ten dollars in this and a pin and kneedle holder. I dont know what you would cal it. I picked it up on the battle field. Give the children a kneedle to remember me. There is four in it. Tel Tomy I have a little one for him if I ever com back to bring it to him.

Tel the children to send me some wourd. I want to see them so bad.

> J. B. Crawford to Martha
> A. Crawford
> For this time good by.

— *Chapter 12* —

"... A HARD FIGHT IN PENNSYLVANIA ..."

Having blocked Federal efforts to reach Richmond through Fredericksburg, and despite the loss of Stonewall Jackson, Southern morale was at its highest following Chancellorsville. In strategy and tactics, the South seemed invincible, and Lee turned his attention to an invasion of the North. Success on a Northern battlefield, Lee felt, would strengthen the growing Northern peace movement, induce Britain and France to formally recognize the Confederacy then offer military support, and move the Eastern Theater of war from Virginia to the Cumberland Valley. If Grant's forces had to be transferred from their six-week-long siege of Vicksburg to counter Lee, all the better. With these potential benefits in mind, in early June Lee began moving his re-organized but still underfed, ill-equipped Army of Northern Virginia north, temporarily leaving General A. P. Hill's III Corps (including the Sixteenth Mississippi) to deceive Hooker, who had re-occupied the heights opposite Fredericksburg on the Rappahannock.

As Lee moved into Pennsylvania, Lincoln lost confidence in Hooker and notified him to relinquish command to General George Gordon Meade on June 28, 1863. Unaware of Lee's exact location, Meade maneuvered his forces in south-central Pennsylvania and western Maryland to stand between Lee and Washington. With Meade looking for Lee and Lee looking for a fight, both would find their objectives in Gettysburg.[1]

The Sixteenth Mississippi and its brigade contended with the Twelfth New Jersey,

Eighth Ohio, and other Federal regiments for control of the William Bliss house, barn, and orchard on the northern end of the battlefield, midway between Seminary and Cemetery Ridges. The buildings, nearby orchard, and surrounding fields gained strategic importance once the battle lines were set on July 2nd. Situated on a slight hill, the buildings afforded the only real protection for troops maneuvering over the near-flat twelve hundred yards between Union and Confederate lines. Additionally, sharpshooters in the buildings and orchard would have unobstructed views of enemy gun placements, fortifications, and troop positions, and could safely pick-off enemy personnel. Control of the Bliss farm might determine the outcome of the battle—and the battle might determine the outcome of the war.[2]

☆ ***James Johnson Kirkpatrick Diary***, June 6, 1863, Saturday:

Company C went forward this morning as skirmishers. Halted our line on the railroad. Some of the company voluntarily went forward and engaged in sharpshooting. Towards evening, we are withdrawn, our brigade having orders to move up to the Howison House. Very warm. Rained this evening. Lay in trenches all night. The enemy that crossed are lying close to the mouth of Deep Run and don't seem to be at all hostile. . . .

☆ ***James Johnson Kirkpatrick Diary***, June 9, 1863, Tuesday:

Company C on the front again. Cannonading in direction of Culpeper Court House. Our army has all left Fredericksburg, except our (Hill's) Corps. Most of the enemy, too, have gone. . . .

☆ ***Jerome B. Yates to Mrs. Obedience Yates:***
Fredericksburg, Virginia, June 10th

Dear Ma,

As the papers say the way is open to Jackson, I will try to get this through to you. I am very uneasy for you as I have not heard a word from you. . . . Broome's letter states that you were the owner of only two Negroes. It is a truly sorrowful condition for one like you and Aunt Patty to be placed in after such hard work for a lifetime and then to have it all taken away in an hour. . . . I am in good health. Wilson [takes care of] me finely. I will have him to start with when this war is over. . . .[3]

We must look this matter boldly in the face and go to work again. You must do the best you can. Probably I will get home some of these days. I think I can repay all you have done for me since I was first in this world, which I think due every mother from her sons. If all our property is taken, we will yet get along in the woods. We will all go to Texas or some other new country where we all will be on our equal footing and make a new start. . . . You must trust to God, be of good cheer, as He does everything for the best. You must bear up under it. I will give you all the help in my power while I am in the army. I get eleven dollars for soldiering, so I can send you part of that. I will send you sixty dollars by the first opportunity. . . .

Write soon and tell me everything. . . . Put your trust in God. Your son,

J. B. Y.

☆ *Jerome B. Yates to Marie Yates Swanson:*
Fredericksburg, Virginia, June 11th

Sister Marie,

. . . I hear via Broome's letter . . . that [the Yankees] had taken all that Mrs. Watson had and completely broke Aunt Patty up, took all her Negroes and all of her meat, broke her carriage all to pieces and took her eleven horses and then burnt her house. Poor woman, I am truly sorry for her. We must look the matter bravely in the face and meet it with a good will and a firm resolve. All I pray for now is that I may get through the war without being disabled, which I hope to God I may. You must be of good cheer and do the best you can under the circumstances, but you are in good circumstances to what some are. . . . I am in favor of us all immigrating to Texas and all taking a fresh start. All I want is a sound body and good health, and I do not fear the worst.

Our company has been in the front lines for the last three days in skirmishes every day. I am in sight of not less than five thousand Yankees while I write. I would like to have them all in my power. I would send them to another world at a double-quick. I have been down this morning sharpshooting. I think of you every time I shoot at them. I wish I had a three hundred-pound cannon so I could speak louder tones to them and remind them they are invading a country where they are not very much liked. I hope this unholy war may soon terminate to the defeat of the enemy. . . .
Your brother,

Jerome

☆ *J. B. Crawford to Martha A. Crawford:*
Camp near Fredericksburg, June the 12, 1863

Dear Wife

I received yours today which found me well. I was glad to hear that you was all well. I waunt to see you and the children so bad that I am almost crasy. I thought I never would get another letter from you. I looked ever day til I got out of heart.

I am sorry to tell you that wee are in a line of battle today and has been eight days expecting a fight ever minute. I may never write to you again but as soon as the battle is over I will write if I am spared. I see hard times hear. . . . I am within two hundred yards of them ever night in picket post. I dont know what to write. I may be shot . . . . You must pray for me and tel all of my friends to pray for me. . . .

I dreamt last night of going home. I saw you and the children as plain as I ever saw you. . . . I pray ever day for you and the children that we may meet again on earth and enjoy the sweet [life] once more. Martha if we never meet on earth, meet me in heaven and raise the children to do the same. Martha if I could talk to you one day more I would be better satisfied than what I am. Write to me. . . . The boys is all well at present and doing well. So I will close by saying write soon. . . . May God bless us and save us now and forever is my prayer. Amen.

J. B. Crawford to his
dear wife and children

☆ *James Johnson Kirkpatrick Diary*, June 14, 1863, Sunday:

Went to the front. Found no enemy on our side of the river. They re-crossed last night. . . . Started at noon and marched to Chancellorsville. Went into camp before dark. Paid a visit to the battleground of May 3rd. Very offensive now. Rights of sepulture badly performed. . . .

☆ *J. J. Wilson to John N. Wilson:*
June 16th, 1863, Camp near Culpeper Court House

Dear Brother,

I take this present opportunity of dropping you a few lines in answer to your kind letter. . . . Since I wrote to you, I have had a hard time of it. . . . The

Yankees crossed over below Fredericksburg, and we had to stop and lay in rifle pits for ten days waiting for them to come from under the cover of their cannons on the other side, but they crossed back, and there were no general engagement. There was a good deal of sharpshooting every day but not much damage done on either side. . . .

Give my love to all. Write soon. . . . I remain your brother,

J. J. Wilson

☆ *James Johnson Kirkpatrick Diary*, June 17, 1863, Wednesday:

Reveille resounded through the woods at 3:30 a.m. Started a little after day. Very warm and tiresome marching. . . . Several cases of sunstroke proved fatal, reminding one of Longfellow's "They, the Young." Camped on the north side of Hazel River.

☆ *Jerome B. Yates to Mrs. Obedience Yates:*

Culpeper, June 17th, 1863

Dear Ma,

As we have halted to cook three days rations, I will drop you a few lines. We are on the move towards Winchester, and it is the opinion of the wise ones that we will go from there to Maryland and Pennsylvania, which I hope may be so. . . . I am in hopes we will gorge Lincoln with his own blood and put an end to the war, but I reckon you think it is most too late for us to gorge the lion since all of our property has been overtaken by the foe. I can fight them tomorrow harder since I have got a grudge against them. It is my honest wish that my rifle may draw tears from many a Northern mother or sighs from many a father before this thing is through. . . .

You must write me by the first opportunity. Give me all the particulars no matter how bad they may be. . . . Your son,

Jerome

☆ *James Johnson Kirkpatrick Diary*, June 19, 1863, Friday:

Resumed our march towards Front Royal. . . . Halted and rested three or four hours near Front Royal. Started again and encountered a soaking rain. . . . Night overtakes us soon after crossing the North Fork [of the Shenandoah].

Filed off into an old field close by. . . . Very muddy, so dark, so rainy. We rested ourselves by either standing, sitting, or lying in the mud and water. . . .

☆ *Harry Lewis to Mrs. Nancy Lewis:*
Camp near Berryville, Virginia, June 22nd, 1863

Dearest Mother,

We have been constantly on the march, this being the first day of rest since we commenced the march a week ago yesterday. During this time, we have come considerably over one hundred miles. The march from Fredericksburg to the mountains was attended with great fatigue and exhaustion, the sun being very hot and the roads dusty; and several men died of sunstroke in the division. When we reached the mountains, we were greeted by welcome showers which continued so long and so freely that they became as much a "bore" as the dust and heat of the previous days.

Having passed once more over the Blue Ridge, we emerged into the [Shenandoah] Valley, noted for its beauty of scenery, fertility and the loyalty of its inhabitants to the Confederacy. We again trod over the turnpikes over which we prodded over a year ago in our volunteer enthusiasm after the flying army of Banks. We viewed again the scene of our first encounter with our foes where we first heard the scream of the now familiar shell. Our whole division is encamped in a beautiful grove of oaks on the edge of the town of Berryville. Berryville is east of Winchester eight or ten miles and on a line with it, being nearer the mountains. Hooker is on the other side of the mountains, it is supposed, with his army. . . .

☆ June 23rd, 1863

Dear Ma, I resume my pen and letter which I was compelled to drop so abruptly yesterday morning. Having taken up our line of march yesterday noon, we proceeded eight or ten miles and encamped for the night. This morning early we fell in and marched rapidly to this camp, a distance of twelve miles, which we reached by twelve o'clock, passing through Charlestown. . . . We are now in sight of the white tents of the Yankees dotting the side of the mountain heights overlooking Harpers Ferry some eight or ten miles dim in the distance. . . .

I wish you could have seen how our army was welcomed in the little town of Charlestown. It would do any patriot heart good. And these people have suffered unspeakable misery from the tyrants who have oppressed them so often, and who have beggared them of all except honor and love of country. The more I see of this country, the more I admire it. Many places seem to me more like a dream of fairyland or a beautiful landscape than reality. The groves of tall fatherly oaks and chestnuts under the shade of which the grass seems to have grown purposely luxuriantly—the broad fields of waving wheat and rye undulating with the land—the pasture of sweet scented clover—the clear streams of water—the hills—the mountains—the beautiful residences here and there—all combine to form a scene at once indescribable and unsurpassed in loveliness. But this land, fascinating as it may be, could not persuade me to linger did not duty and honor bind me. Yes, though this land may be more attractive, still to every man home is dearer than foreign lands. . . .

General Ewell's Corps, after taking Winchester . . . crossed over into Maryland and at last accounts was at Hagerstown advancing on to Frederick City. Longstreet's Corps is about Winchester, and ours on the move—we suppose—to join Ewell in Maryland. We have three corps: Ewell, Longstreet, and A. P. Hill, and we belong to the latter. Our army is about seventy thousand, Lee, of course, being in command of all. We are all in the dark as to our movements and those of Hooker. We know but very little more of the army than that concerning our own division, with which we are always encamped. All the rest is guesswork and speculation. . . . I cannot say we are eager for a fight, but as veterans of many pitched battles, we are willing . . . trusting in God and the justice of our cause to again give battle to our foes when Lee gives the word. That the Lord has been manifestly in our favor heretofore, I doubt not, and I shall pray that He may continue to favor us and preserve us. . . .

Dear Ma, I must close as it is growing dark. . . Write soon. . . . Your affectionate son,

Harry Lewis

☆ *James Johnson Kirkpatrick Diary*, June 24, 1863, Wednesday:

Marched at sunrise. Crossed the Potomac at the ford below Shepherdstown. No pontoons as we had expected. The river is from two to four feet deep. The river is full of sharp rocks, which sometimes caused a fall, but such mishaps were rare. After crossing and redressing, we proceeded towards Sharpsburg. Halted and rested three or four hours near the old battlefield. In the evening, resumed our march through the much dilapidated looking town of Sharpsburg. Crossed the Antietam on a stone bridge near where the battle opened and camped within a mile of Boonsboro. . . .

☆ *James Johnson Kirkpatrick Diary*, June 26, 1863, Friday:

Waked up before day by drums but felt very reluctant to have my slumbers this rudely broken. Lay still till the drum again beat for us to fall in only a few moments later. No more delay now. Forthwith, I bundle up and call the company into line. Rained last night and this morning. Passed through Hagerstown and took the road to Middleburg, distant five miles. From thence to Greencastle [Pennsylvania]. Roads very muddy and the rain incessant. Saw some fine country, but very few sympathizers. Camped at noon two miles beyond Greencastle. A very large ration of whiskey was issued this evening. Nearly all the brigade more or less inebriated and boisterous. . . .

☆ *James Johnson Kirkpatrick Diary*, June 27, 1863, Friday:

Marched early this morning. Passed through the small town of Darion, thence to Chambersburg, the capital of Franklin County, a place of some note and elegance. Our bands gave the citizens an abundance of rebel music. Took the pike here towards Baltimore. Proceeded about six miles further and camped. The citizens look very coldly on us. Their rights are very strictly guarded. An old lady got loudly cheered for running a soldier out of her garden. He had intended to get some vegetables. A retaliation for the many thefts committed in the South carefully guarded against, and any injury that may be done is without sanction of the officers. Even the orchards on the way side are well guarded. But soldiers are hard to keep under restraint. . . .

☆ *The Veteran's Story:*

The inhabitants [of Germantown, Pennsylvania] were engaged in truck farming, their principal crop being onions, which were very tempting to a hungry Rebel, but we had positive orders from General Lee not to disturb anything. There was one old "Reb" who could not stand to see so many fine onions without trying some of them. So he lifted a picket from the fence, crawled in, and stooped down to pull up a very large onion. About this time, an old Dutch lady whacked him on the head with a long handled broom. He beat a hasty retreat with the old lady close upon his heels, whacking him every step. Finally, he reached the place where he went in. As he went to crawl out, she hit him with the broom handle, but he held on to the onion and brought it out with him.

Reaching Chambersburg, we marched through the principal street, our band playing "Dixie." There were a few small Confederate flags displayed. They were thrown out from windows and pulled back in a hurry. When our band played "Yankee Doodle," the Stars and Stripes could be seen floating from nearly every window in town. . . .[4]

☆ *J. B. Crawford to Martha A. Crawford:*
Pennsylvania, June the 28, 1863

Dear Wife

I received your kind letters of June the 7 and 14 which found me well but a long ways from home. I hope those few lines will reach you and famley well and doing well. Wee have been on the march three weeks and now are in the middle of Pennsylvania on our way to Boston in the middle of the enimy. The Yankey says they will whip us if it take them ten year but wee dont think so.

I have nothing of any interest to write now. I expect it will be two or three month before I can get to write any more. The mail cant go threw this country any more and wee dont know how long wee will stay hear. Some of us . . . never will get back to virginia and just [as well] me as any body. This is a hard road to travel. Wee have to go threw wet and dry cold and hot and sleep in mud. There is one thing I regret to write. D. O. Bankston have deserted us and gon in the mountain. The rest of the boys are well at this time.[5]

I waunt you to do the best you can. You said you had sold the wagon for one hundred and fifteen. You ort to had one hundred fifty the way things is seling now but I recon you done rite to sel it for I dont know when I will ever com back but I hope and trust it wount be long. God bless you and the children so I will close for this time by saying I remain your loving husband until death.

J. B. Crawford to Martha
A. Crawford

kiss the children for me. . . . Tel the children to do good.

J. B. Crawford

☆ *James Johnson Kirkpatrick Diary*, July 1, 1863, Wednesday:

Started at day on the pike towards Baltimore. Passed through Fayetteville.
. . . Halted several hours on the top of South Mountain. Encountered a heavy
rain. Artillery opened ahead of us. About ten a.m., General Lee passes, going
toward the front. The cannonading still keeps up briskly. Started on again
towards the noise, making frequent halts. Passed through New Salem and
reached the suburbs of Gettysburg a little before dark. Filed off into some
woods and rested for the night. Passed a considerable number of wounded
going to the rear. . . . General Reynolds (Yankee) was killed. The engagement
was a success to us, and the enemy were driven back out of Gettysburg. They
now occupy the hills on the west side of town. Most of our troops reached here
tonight.[6]

☆ The Veteran's Story

On entering the valley, some five miles from the town [of Gettysburg], the
booming of cannon was heard. Being ordered to hurry up, we knew what was
on hand. Lee had found the Yanks at last. Going up to Heth's Division, drawn
up in line . . . ready to advance, we formed upon his left, threw out skirmishers
and moved forward. Heth's men drove the Yankees through the town while we
supported his left. Night was coming on and we halted.[7]

☆ Historical Sketch of the Quitman Guards:

General Heth's and Pender's Divisions . . . attacked the Federals about
three miles west of Gettysburg and drove them back to town. . . . The Federal
army a took position at Cemetery Ridge east of the town. A beautiful valley,
about three-fourths of a mile in width dotted with beautiful farms and residences, lay stretched between the contending armies. There was nothing to
intercept the view except a number of beautiful orchards.

On the second of July, General Longstreet attacked the Federals on the
right, and Ewell moved forward on the left. A. P. Hill did not move from his
position in the center.[8]

☆ James Johnson Kirkpatrick Diary, July 2, 1863, Thursday:

Early this morning, our troops moved out for deployment, and the artillery
moved forward to take its respective positions. Longstreet's Corps passed by

going to the right, Ewell's took the left, and A.P. Hill's the center. The enemy occupy a very commanding position, having their artillery planted on a high ridge with their infantry in rear. The country is open and hilly. Anderson's (our) Division took its position about ten a.m. Posey's Brigade is posted in rear and in support of batteries. Company C is sent forward as skirmishers. Day very hot and we are much exposed. Towards evening, the sharpshooting is very animated. At times, our line advanced nearly to the batteries on the hill, and then the enemy, by being re-enforced, would force us back to the orchard, our starting point. Heavy cannonading and tremendous volleys of musketry on the right. Our main line in the center not engaged. Were relieved after dark and returned to our position behind the batteries. The company lost four men captured and four wounded this evening, among the latter Captain Slay.[9]

☆ Report Number 546. Report of Brigadier General Carnot Posey:

On the morning of July 2nd, my brigade was placed in position . . . in an open field with woods on my right and left flanks. My position was to the right of the cemetery about which the enemy's lines of battle were formed. In the afternoon, I received an order to advance. . . . Before the advance was made, I received an order . . . to advance but two of my regiments and deploy them closely as skirmishers. I had a thin line of skirmishers in front and at once sent out the Nineteenth and Forty-eighth Regiments. . . . These regiments advanced some two or three hundred yards beyond the barn and house which were burned. Later in the day, I sent out the Sixteenth and, receiving information that the enemy were threatening their right and left flanks, I took the Twelfth Regiment [to their support]. . . . When I reached the barn, I found my three regiments well up to advance. They had driven the enemy's pickets into their works and the artillerists from their guns in their front. It being nearly dark, I sent the major-general a message informing him of my position. He then ordered me to fall back to my original position. . . .[10]

☆ James Johnson Kirkpatrick Diary, July 3, 1863, Friday:

Company C is again sent to the front this morning. Our position is a little to the right of last evening—between the oppressing batteries—in an open field, exposed to shelling and to the hottest sun that ever shone on mortals. The quiet of the morning is broken at nine a.m. by artillery. The sharpshooters had previously commenced plying their small arms, but sun being so warm, they shoot lazily. Among the first shell that passed to and fro, one very unkindly carried away my gun and rendered it entirely unfit for duty. But there are plenty more lying around, ready for service.

About 2:30 p.m. nearly two hundred guns behind us belched forth their death and almost immediately as many, if not more, from the enemy's line replied. This continues until nearly all the enemy's guns cease to reply. Very soon our infantry make an appearance, coming forward to storm the crest. They make a very feeble effort and accomplish nothing. The troops in the movement were mostly North Carolinians. The distance they had to traverse was nearly a mile. There was no intermediate sheltered point to rally at and the sun's heat was intolerable, is the only excuse that can be plead in their behalf. Our skirmish line was immovable, according to orders, and the enemy made no attempt to follow. Company C lost one member this evening, killed by cannonball, several slightly wounded, and a good many contusions from fragments of shell. Were relieved at dark and slept behind the batteries.[11]

☆ The Veteran's Story:

Early on the morning of the third, we were advanced to the front and kept up a rapid skirmish fire till ten o'clock, when we were relieved. . . . We moved back behind our batteries to support them and as a reserve to be carried to any part of the line when needed. We crawled on top of the ridge and peeped over. The ridge in our front was lined with Federal batteries, also heavy bodies of infantry. In fact, the whole Federal army was there. We crawled back, threw up breastworks and got behind them, for we knew pretty soon we'd catch shot and shell and heavy. Our assaulting column had gotten in position when the signal gun fired. When the firing commenced what a tumult it was! The whole earth seemed to tremble. One of our boys was completely buried alive from a shell striking our works. We scratched him out in time to save his life. When the cannonading ceased, our assaulting column moved forward. They were not gone long and returned badly demoralized. We were ordered to the front to check the enemy if they should advance, but they did not come. . . .[12]

☆ Letter from unknown member of the Quitman Guards to his sister:

On the 3rd, skirmishing opened briskly during the forenoon with some hard fighting on the right and left. . . . Our brigade (Posey's) was ordered to support a battery of about thirty-five guns. . . . The signal gun was heard, and then commenced the fearful thunder. One hundred and fifty pieces of artillery opened on the Confederate side, which were answered by twice that number on the side of the Federals. The earth fairly quaked from the effects of the terrible storm. Thousands of shells burst around and about us, and the shrill whistle of long balls jarred upon our ears. The firmament seemed to be in a fearful blaze, and the smoke from the guns and shells hid the sun from the view. Not only did human beings feel and suffer this terrible shock, but the birds, attempting to fly, tumbled and fell to the ground. Everything save the undaunted soldier seemed to cling to the earth for protection from the terrible storm. Thus the dreadful conflict raged for two long and dreadful hours. The Federal batteries were silenced, then the order to charge was given. Our men were in line in a second and moved forward. . . . The charge was made through a field nearly a mile wide, under a raking fire of grape and canister from the Federal batteries. But the onward rush of the fearless soldiery could not be stayed. The breastworks were before them. A wild yell burst forth from the advancing column of Confederates, then began the work of small arms. Onward still advanced the column until they reached the breastworks. Thousands mounted them, and the Federals, leaving the first, took refuge in the second. Some of the cannoneers were drawn from their guns, but we were unable to hold them. The Federals were now reinforced. Then the work of death redoubled in its fury. Our men fell by hundreds, and we were compelled to retreat to our original position not in a solid line but in squads, bleeding with wounds, whole regiments cut to pieces. Thousands had fallen and were left on the field. The Federals suffered greatly and did not follow us. . . .[13]

☆ *James Johnson Kirkpatrick Diary*, July 4, 1863, Saturday:

All quiet on the lines this morning except a few sharpshooters. Raining nearly all day. A few guns fired on the right before noon. Evident preparations for a retrograde movement on our part. Artillery and wagons going back all day. We still occupy our old line and the enemy are very civil. Started to move back at dark. The branches are all full of water and the roads deep in mud and water. . . . Marched all night and stopped to rest at the foot of the mountains just before day.

☆ *James Johnson Kirkpatrick Diary*, July 5, 1863, Sunday:

Started about eight a.m. Roads very bad. Crossed the mountains and rested at their base on the other side. Went on picket (the regiment) in evening to Waynesboro. Cannonading down the mountains towards Hagerstown. Took a position on a high hill commanding the town. Had a battery located here. The citizens seem surprised at our presence. No alarms tonight, and I rested splendidly.

☆ *James Johnson Kirkpatrick Diary*, July 6, 1863, Monday:

Marched down the pike this morning and remained till evening. . . . Company C on provost duty tonight. Had some trouble. Many of the men found whiskey and got drunk. An officer of the Nineteenth Mississippi was shot by a private of the Twelfth Mississippi. Marched slowly, passed through Leitersburg at midnight. Halted at day in a little village and rested an hour or two. Feel very much fatigued and worried from loss of sleep, etc.

☆ *Historical Sketch of the Quitman Guards:*

[Lee] halted at Hagerstown for several days for the purpose of resting his troops and to make needful additions to his commissary and ordinance stores. . . . But having received a fresh supply of ammunition from Williamsport, General Lee arrayed his troops for battle. . . . The Federal army was drawn up in line of battle near the Antietam River with their lines running parallel with it. The Confederate army, being entrenched, quietly awaited the movements of the enemy. . . . Finding that the Federals did not intend to attack him at Hagerstown . . . General Lee quietly withdrew to the Virginia side of the Potomac.[14]

☆ *J. B. Crawford to Martha A. Crawford:*
Maryland, July the 8, 1863

Dear Wife

I seat myself down to let you know that I am well at present hoping those few lines will find you and famley well and doing well. I can say to you that wee have got back to maryland. Wee have had a hard fight in Pennsylvania and I think wee made a draw fight of it. boath armies move off at the same time in the night.

Wee had one hundred peses of cannon and the Yankey had two hundred . . . all firing at the same time. Wee taken prisoners and kild about fifteen thousand, and I thing the enemy don about the same as nigh as I can tel but some of our men says not. Says wee did not lose that many but they was a pile on boath sides enough to make one state and fill it ful

Wee are under canading all day. I [was] expecting to be shot in a thousand peses all day and wee expecting a fight tomorrow but I hope it wount come on. I never was scared as bad in my life. Some of our boys was wounded but non kild so fare. I am tiard of this ware [war].

If I live to get in virginia I will write to you soon. I have not time to write now. Wee expect to leave hear ever hour and we have to be reddy in a minet warning. Excuse this bad writing spelling I had to in a hurry.

So I will close by saing I remain you . . . husband until death. I would give the wourld if it was mine to see you and the children. Good by for this time.

J. B. Crawford to Martha
Crawford

☆ *Jerome B. Yates to Mrs. Obedience Yates and Marie Yates Swanson:*
Hagerstown, Maryland, July 8th

Dear Ma and Marie,
The army has halted, and I will drop you a few lines. I am still amongst the living of the Confederates that invaded the Union, thanks to the mercy of divine Providence. I cannot give you any of the particulars of the bloody fight that was fought on the 1st, 2nd and 3rd of July. Our loss was heavy. . . . We retreated on the night of the 4th of July, and the enemy did not follow. . . .

The whole loss of this company is fourteen, only one killed. . . . All of our wounded fell into the hands of the enemy with the exception of a few who were slightly wounded and were able to march. . . . It is the opinion of the knowing ones that we only came back here for ammunition. . . .

I received Marie's letter of the 7th of June. . . . I was glad to hear from you all, and that you were well and had enough to live on. Marie wrote me how Sam and Mahala acted when the Yankees visited you. Tell them if I live to get home, they will never be forgotten. Tell them all that stayed, when I am home that I will pay them for their services given in the hour of need. . . . I would write you all a separate letter if I had the paper, but as we did not whip the Yankees, therefore I have not the plunder. Better success . . . the next time.

[The Yankees] has pressed into service all the horses and provisions that was in the country we have passed through, besides what the men got for themselves. I am clear of taking anything, only what I paid for. You must write, all of you, to your brother and son,

J. B. Y.

☆ *James Johnson Kirkpatrick Diary*, July 13, 1863, Monday:

Got Richmond papers of the 9th stating that Vicksburg has capitulated. Still very few are inclined to believe. Heavy skirmishing on our lines yesterday evening and early this morning. A few heavy guns on the left in evening. Skirmishing animated at times today. Fell in at dark and marched to the Potomac. . . . It commenced raining soon after we started. With what had lately fallen, it put the roads in miserable plight. Mud and water from one to two feet deep, with a foundation at places slippery and again lined with sharp pointed rocks, made it very hard on the barefooted and half-shod infantry. Came to a halt at midnight and didn't get in motion again till daybreak. The entire distance to the river where we crossed could not have been over six or seven miles.

☆ *James Johnson Kirkpatrick Diary*, July 14, 1863, Tuesday:

Moved on slowly at dawn towards the pontoon bridge at Falling Waters. . . . Crossed the bridge, a fine structure, and halted about three-quarters of a mile from it on the Virginia side. The Yankee skirmishers soon came in sight on the opposite side, but a few shells from our batteries sent them out of sight double-quick. The report is today that Vicksburg is not yet taken. . . .

☆ *James Johnson Kirkpatrick Diary,* July 15, 1863, Wednesday:

Orders to march at five a.m. Moved out along the pike towards Martinsburg, distant six miles. . . . Many of the men are entirely without shoes and the stone pike is severe on their feet. Passed a small village and camped at four p.m. near Bunker Hill. Got Richmond papers of 13th stating again and more positively that Vicksburg capitulated on the 4th. The news is very discouraging. . . .

☆ *Historical Sketch of the Quitman Guards:*

General Lee . . . moved back to Bunker Hill, about fifteen miles from the Potomac and went into camp. The army was now without rations. The men had subsisted on short rations since they left their position at Hagerstown and were now suffering from hunger. The country around Bunker Hill and Winchester had been desolated by its constant occupation by one or the other of the hostile forces, and it was almost impossible to procure even one-third as much as was necessary to subsist the army now encamped in it. The army subsisted partially, during their week's stay at Bunker Hill, upon dewberries which . . . covered the ground.[15]

☆ *J. B. Crawford to Martha A. Crawford:*

Winchester Hospitle, July the 16, 1863

Dear Wife

I seat myself down to let you know that I am not well at present but I hope those few lines will find you and famley well. I taken the fever in a few days after the gettysburg fight. Wee left about darke and march all night. The mud and water was almost nee deep and then wee stop the next day and lad down in the water and I taken the fever and was send to Winchester but I hope it wount last long. The hardships wee have to go threw is enough to kill a mud turtle. I dont know any thing about the ridgement at this time. They have had a nother battle sence I left them but I dont know how they made it. I cant hear from them.

News reached hear that vicksburg has gon up the spout. If it has wee had just as well quit and give up the Confederacy. I dont know that I have any thing more of any importance to write.

I have an idea the ware will end in the next five years to come. . . .

I dont know wher you can read this or not. I am so weak my hand trembles so bad. So I will close by saying I remain your loving husband until death.

> J. B. Crawford to Martha
> A. Crawford fare well for
> this time.

☆ *John S. Lewis to Mrs. Nancy Lewis:*

Camp near Bunker Hill, Virginia, July 21st, 1863

My Very Dear Mother,

Van Easton starts home shortly, so I write these to send by him whenever he may start. I fear it will be the last you may hear from us in a long time. . . .[16]

If it were possible, I should wish . . . to have you into Alabama with such property, Negroes, etc., so you could get along, for I know if their army takes possession of any country, they pillage and plunder and will take all the Negroes, besides laying all its inhabitants open to insult and oppression. I had hoped that this might have been spared us, and if the whole country had done its duty, it would have been. Base and mean and pusillanimous must be the man who remains and allows the enemies' lines to encircle his home and find him within those lines while there is a musket in his reach.

The women of the South, I have often thought, have proved themselves its bravest defenders and the firmest enemies of our enemy. Let such of those whose hard duty it is to be left in the Yankee lines finish their good and glorious mission by spurning from among them such men as are able to bear arms. If this is done, the enemy can never hold our territory. . . .

We thank God we are safe after another hard campaign and hard fight. I was struck on the foot the second day of the fight at Gettysburg. It swelled up considerably but is all right now. If you will examine the map, you will see that General Lee made a rapid movement around Hooker's army from Fredericksburg to the Potomac. Our cavalry force protected and concealed our front by one or two hard fights and, by this means, General Ewell's corps was at Winchester before the enemy could determine our intention. . . . Our corps (Hill's) was then not much past Culpeper Court House coming up. The army finally was moved on and concentrated at or near Chambersburg, Pennsylvania, where we rested three days and moved forward about twenty-five miles to Gettysburg, and here let me remark that all were perfectly certain of a great victory whenever we should meet the enemy, and no army that he ever had, nor would any which he may be able to get, have been able to stand up before us as we were then for half a day in a fair field, but we did not have that.

Early on the morning of 1st of July, our division was put in motion. We had a narrow pass in the mountains to go through, and the roads were bad, but we pushed ahead, and as we proceeded through the pass, we could hear the cannon ahead. I did not think at the time that we were so close on their army. We marched nearly twenty miles by one o'clock and arrived on the battlefield. The fight was still going on. To our left, General Ewell's Corps and two divisions of our corps . . . had been engaged with haste, I suppose, with nearly half of the Yankee army and had whipped them badly, driving them two or more miles and capturing three thousand prisoners. Soon after we came up, General Longstreet's Corps came up also, and we rested that night about one mile to the right and east of Gettysburg. So ended the first day's fight. We all knew that the grand battle was yet to come off as half of our army had not been engaged.

On the morning of the 2nd, we moved further to the right and went into line of battle, our division joining the right of the troops who had been fighting on the 1st. We were just below the rise of a hill extending around in a semicircular form, our cannons in large numbers posted a few yards in front of us. About fifteen or eighteen hundred yards across were the enemy's batteries. Their lines conformed to ours but were more constricted and consequently shorter, and their guns in front of us were about as thick as they could work them. As soon as we got into line, orders were given for the men to make such protection as would shelter them. This, of course, could not be well done, but fences were pulled down and the rails piled up and a little dirt thrown up. About that time, the artillery began to play upon each other, and our frail breastworks stopped many a fragment of shell.

Soon Longstreet, on our right (now evening), pressed forward his corps. It was the most terrific musket fire for some two hours I ever heard on so short a line as his. He drove the Yankees steadily for two miles, I suppose. When the sun was getting low, the center was advanced, but unfortunately it lacked concert of movement, and though it was a large sacrifice, we charged and took some of the enemies' guns, but we were unable to hold them, and night found the center in the position it occupied in the morning. Ewell, on the left, attacked the enemy fiercely about dark and drove them a short distance. At night, we all knew that the battle was not yet decided and that the coming day was to be a bloody one. Our brigade did not get into the musketry fire. It was advanced in the evening over the hill and to within four or five hundred yards of the enemy guns, in fact, under them, where we remained until dark. Just after we got to the top of the hill, a piece of shell struck me in the boot but did not prevent me going ahead at that time. The next day, it was considerably swollen, and I couldn't march for some time.

By the morning of the third day, the enemies' lines were much contracted from a straight line. They now formed an acute angle, we a little to the right of the apex of it. They were well fortified all round and occupied a formidable range of hills or heights. Our men felt that to advance on them (double our numbers, strongly fortified, and their cannons in position to get a fair unrestricted range of us, while advancing a mile) was a desperate undertaking, almost a forlorn hope. So it proved. I have not the patience to write the particulars of this fight. It was most disastrous to us. We charged, the whole army charged and was driven back, though the cowards would not charge our shortened lines in turn. The lion, they knew, was hurt but not killed. Our brigade was out of the breastworks moving on the enemy when a courier dashed up and halted us. It saved many lives, and while we were willing to go to the last man, we were thankful for it.

Night again found us and the whole army in our old position, but how different from the preceding night. You see, we could inflict no serious damage upon the enemy's infantry as they were under cover all the time, though our artillery silenced many of their batteries. This attack commenced about three o'clock p.m. and was prefaced by the heaviest artillery duel ever heard on this continent. I believe no army ever heard one to surpass it, if it was ever equaled. Not less, I suppose, than three hundred fifty guns, and maybe more, kept up a continuous and rapid fire for two hours, then it ceased, and our infantry charged.

On the day of the fourth, we were quiet except the skirmishes, not wishing or able to make another attack and the enemy in the same condition. I believe on the fourth day even, if we could have swapped positions, we could have whipped them badly. . . .

[John Lewis]

☆ *James Johnson Kirkpatrick Diary*, July 22, 1863, Wednesday:

Troops in motion by daylight. . . . Marched towards Front Royal. Crossed the Shenandoah on pontoons, below the junction of the two branches. Camped on the hill above Front Royal about an hour before sunset. Warm and at times dusty. Saw a paper of 20th. Lengthy account of the riot in New York. Jackson, Mississippi is said to be evacuated. A renewal of the talk of European intervention. By some mischance, we drew a day's rations tonight. Very unusual occurrences of late.[17]

☆ *James Johnson Kirkpatrick Diary*, July 25, 1863, Saturday:

Marched at designated hour and made good time to Culpeper Court House. Went into camp at ten a.m. Day most oppressively hot. This march has been well conducted. . . . The men have necessarily suffered much from the heat and dust. . . . For the last week, our rations have been very irregular. Half our subsistence has been dewberries. Fortunately, there was a good crop of them this year. Heavy rain tonight.[18]

☆ *James Johnson Kirkpatrick Diary*, July 27, 1863, Sunday:

Warm and sultry with a heavy rain in evening. Received mail, the first in a long time. A letter from Mississippi gave me some very sad news. The disasters of late to our arms have been very depressing and, when added to private grief, makes the burden almost intolerable. Twere better perhaps not to live at all than to live without an aim. "Had I the wings of a dove," I would fly away and rest.

☆ *J. J. Wilson to James E. Wilson:*

July 27th, 1863

Dear Father,

I take this present opportunity of dropping you a few lines to let you know how I am getting along after the Battle of Gettysburg, Pennsylvania. I was wounded slightly in the leg by a piece of shell. The wound is getting nearly well. It was on the 3rd of July when I was wounded in the fight. . . . I think that I will be able to go back to the regiment in about two weeks.

Sorry to hear of the fall of Vicksburg. The Yankees been a-trying a good while to get it. . . . I wish that they would make haste and make peace, for I am getting tired of this fighting. I hope that it won't be long before peace will be restored to our beloved country. . . .

Give my love to all. I remain your son,

J. J. Wilson

☆ *John S. Lewis to Mrs. Nancy Lewis [continued]:*

Camp Near Culpeper, July 31, 1863

You see I have not yet finished my letter. . . . The whole army is here now after a long march from Gettysburg, in good health and spirits but barefooted. . . .

Our retreat was leisurely. We stopped at Hagerstown, Maryland, rested for three or four days and offered the enemy battle, which he respectfully declined. We will have another battle soon, and you will soon hear of another victory. We are all more or less discouraged about affairs elsewhere. Our men fight, and all will be well.

Frank and Ebb are both gone. They were captured I think, and I may yet get them back. I am almost sure to see Frank soon. Tell Aunt Alsie about it as if it was a certainty. It is hard on me, as I was going to sell him to pay my debts. I was offered thirty-five hundred dollars for him a few days before but did not take it, as I could have got four thousand dollars. I expect everything at home is gone too. All right, lets get through like we ought to, and I am satisfied.[19]

I hope all the cotton has been burned. If people fail to do so, they just offer an inducement for the balance of the country to be plundered, besides giving aid and comfort to the enemy. If they find you at home, I hope you will be able to live in comfort. It makes me out here feel more miserable than all and everything else put together.

Harry and Fletch are very well. I suppose one of them will write. Mack is here, and I don't know what we should be without him. I have to depend upon him now, too. The time is coming, I think, when I will have to wait on myself, pretty rough on a lazy man. . . . Answer soon if you can. . . . My respects to all friends. Your son,

John S. Lewis

☆ *James Johnson Kirkpatrick Diary*, August 1, 1863, Saturday:

Our regiment was mustered at eight a.m. This is another of those scorching days. About four p.m., the Long Roll calls us to arms. For a few moments, there is hurrying to and fro to get ready. We fall in and march. . . . We had heard cannonading in the morning towards Brandy Station. It gradually became more distinct until the time our drum beat, when it was in reach of Culpeper Court House. It proved to be only a cavalry force under Buford. They had crossed the Rappahannock . . . and speedily drove back the small cavalry force that was confronting them. When we came on the field, they took the back track. We followed almost to Brandy Station when, darkness coming, it was left to the cavalry to finish putting them across the river. We moved back after dark near Culpeper Court House and camped, in line, for the night. . . .[20]

— Chapter 13 —

". . . NOT VERY PLEASANT WORK,
BUT IT HAS TO BE DONE"

The North grew confident and the South depressed with Vicksburg falling the same day Lee withdrew from Pennsylvania. It appeared the tide had turned, and it was time for re-assessment. The Army of the Potomac camped on the north side of the Rappahannock, while the Southerners, spread between Culpeper and Orange Court House, bivouacked on the south. Lee and Meade sent troops west, while each wondered if the other would institute a major offensive. Though occasional skirmishing continued (the largest of which occurred on August 1st when a Federal cavalry force with infantry support crossed the river and came within a mile of the Confederate camp), the men of the Sixteenth turned their attention to problems back home and the future. While Lee re-assessed the military situation, the men re-assessed themselves spiritually, as religious revival moved through the camps.[1]

☆ *James Johnson Kirkpatrick Diary*, August 5, 1863, Wednesday:

Heard this evening that our Color Corporal W. J. Sweeney died of his wound at Richmond on July 30th. No braver or more gallant soldier ever trod a battlefield. He was ever gay and cheerful, whether in camp, or in battle. One by one our brave are cut down. . . .

☆ *James Johnson Kirkpatrick Diary*, August 6, 1863, Thursday:

Received pay for May and June. Had peas and potatoes today, scarce articles in the fare of "Lee's poor Miserables." A great many convalescents are returning to camp. The President's amnesty proclamation is bringing in some [deserters]. I feel very badly from a cold caught a few nights since.

☆ *J. B. Crawford to Martha A. Crawford*:

August the 9, 1863

Dear Wife

I seat myself to let you know that I am not well but hope those few lines will find you and the famley enjoying the best of health. I taken sick in maryland and was sent to whinchester and then to richmond. I am very low at this time and [have] nobody to fan the flies off of me. I miss you now I waunt to see you worse than ever but I hope god is with me. I tryed to get a furlow, but they wood see me dead first but if I die I think I am prepard to meet my god. Martha pray for me and tel all of my friends to pray for me. . . . Martha if wee never meet on earth my god I waunt you to meet me in heaven where wee never will part no more and raise the children to meet me there. I dont know that I ever will see you anymore on earth. Oh my god my god I wood give the world to see you once more on earth. . . . Martha dont let this greave you. It is a thing that cant be helped.

All I crave is buttermilk and cornbread. I have been sick since the first of July. Nobody can wait on me like you cood.

Our Confederecy has gon up the spout and I dont care how soon. The sooner the better for us. Wee are treated worse than dogs here.

I haint red a letter from you in two months. Your letters goes to the ridgement and I dont get them wright soon. . . . I dont feel like I will stay in the world very long.

Excuse my bad writing. I am so weak my hand trembles so bad I cant write. May God bless you and the famley. Direct your letters to general hospittle, howard grove, richmond, virginia.

> J. B. Crawford to Martha
> A. Crawford
> Farewell my dear. tel the
> children I waunt to see
> them.

☆ *J. J. Wilson to James E. Wilson:*

Richmond, Virginia, August 10th, 1863

Dear Father,

I take the present opportunity of writing you a few lines to let you know how I am getting along. . . . My wound has entirely healed up, but it is a little tender yet. I expect to start back to my regiment day after tomorrow. The army is somewhere near Orange Court House. They are expecting a fight again soon in that vicinity.

We had a good many men killed and wounded in Pennsylvania, but we are ready to meet them again. My company had one man killed. . . . Three were taken prisoners and are still in the hands of the Yankees. Another soldier and myself were surrounded, but we got off the field. . . .

When Vicksburg fell, it looked like the Yankees were going to try to take Charleston, Mobile and Savannah, but I hope that every man that is capable of bearing arms rush forward and fight for their country and home, but there is a good many young men about those cities and towns that had rather die than to face the Yankee bullets, which is not very pleasant work, but it has to be done.

Over in Pennsylvania, I heard at the time at least four hundred cannons shooting at one time. It beat all fights that ever I was in. I never want to be in any more like it. . . .

Well, I will close. Give my love to all relatives and friends. Write soon. I remain your son,

> ● J. J. Wilson

☆ *Jerome B. Yates to Marie Yates Swanson:*

Orange Court House, Virginia, August 10th

Sister Marie,

Yours of the 26th June came duly to hand and was happily received by me. . . . It brings the news I expected but not as bad as [it] could of been. Thanks to God. It must be galling to people of Mississippi to be treated in such a manner, so curt, and coming from a civilized nation who say their armies are fighting for an oppressed people. I would give all I am worth to hear from you all once more. I carefully preserved the last letters I got from you all, as I knew they would be the last that I would get for some time.

I got one from T. O. Davis at the same time. The old gentleman talks rather hard about the way the Feds treated him. I am sorry for brother or any other man that has worked as hard as he has for a little of this world's goods and then have them taken away from him as he did his. I reckon it is truly trying. I am more than troubled about his children. Would to God they were all boys. I would feel no apprehensions about them getting along in this world then, but as they are girls, I know what a time they will have to go through. Would to God this thing had been put off ten years longer when by that time they would of all been educated and could of made a living for themselves. But we should not grumble at the decrees of Providence. The Bible says all things happen for the best. . . . They are not to be pitied so much as the others . . . or . . . Mrs. Fulgham. But poor woman, I do not know what will become of her. I reckon it grieves her nearly to death to think of her sons, John, Jim, and Fay. Fay is reported missing. He was last seen in the charge his brigade made at Gettysburg. All the boys think he is taken prisoner and will be exchanged soon. I hope he may come out all right. I saw him just before going into the fight. He expressed an earnest wish that I might come out all right. I like that boy better than any boy living. I look on him as one of my best friends. I hope he is safe. . . .[2]

You must write me as often as you can. Kiss that pretty little baby for me that you brag on so much. I expect to take the little urchin on my knee yet and tell her what her venerable uncle did in the great rebellion. . . . Write soon if you can. Your affectionate brother,

J. B. Y.

☆ *Harry Lewis to Mrs. Nancy Lewis*:
Camp near Orange Court House, Virginia, August 10th, 1863

My Dear Mother,
Jeff Hamilton has received orders to report to Brigadier General Gholson commanding our state militia, as one of his staff and, of course, he will either visit home himself or find simple means to get our mail to Woodville, so we profit by present fortunes and send you a letter. . . .[3]

We are camped within sight of Orange, some ten miles from Gordonsville and but little from Culpeper. . . . Our encampment is in an exceedingly fine situation, being on a big, high, broad ridge well shaded with large oak and chestnuts and cooled by pleasant breezes, most acceptable these hot August days. We have a tent fly to protect us from the every day showers which so gratefully cool the atmosphere, while the thick leaves of lofty oaks is situated between us and the sun. . . .

The Yankee army, already far outnumbering ours, will be [waiting] for us until they have trebled our force in numbers and . . . the Yankee people clamor for "an advance" of their army. . . . I know that this army will do its whole duty as it has ever done; and confidently I expect the overthrow of the Yankees when they again try us in battle. Though there is no doubt that . . . the Yankees will be able to throw a . . . magnificent army against us, but God is for first the cause which is just and right!. . . .

We are in good spirits though it must be confessed for a while our southwestern disasters shed a cloud of gloom over us. . . . The prospect was enough to sadden our spirits, especially to men who have been fighting . . . the waves of war for over two long years. . . . Depression has had its day. The reaction has taken place, and we are determined to do our duty while we live and strike as we have strength. . . . The brutal and uncivilized policy of the Yankees to our citizens and soldiers will not tend to allay the flames already fierce burning in us. Dear Mother, be of good cheer. The Yankees can take our Negroes, but they cannot steal our honor and love of our own nation. . . . God will protect His and may He speedily bring this war to a happy end. . . .

By the bye, dear Mother, if it is possible, I wish you would send Claiborne (my boy) on to me. Since Frank and Ebb are gone, we can employ one other boy, and it is much safer here than it was. Please do this by all means if possible, and you will gratefully oblige your ever affectionate son,

Harry

☆ *Jerome B. Yates to Mrs. Obedience Yates*:
Orange Court House, Virginia, August 11th

Dear Ma,

I will start this with little hopes of it ever reaching you . . . but nevertheless I will try. Rumor says there is nothing between Jackson and Crystal Springs but Federal cavalry. . . . We have heard nothing definite from Mississippi in some time, and one or two men have come in since the fall of Vicksburg. They give glorious accounts of the condition of the citizens in the surrounding country. Some report you and all to have ten days rations and will be sent from their line if you refuse to take the oath of allegiance. Your condition must be truly a trying one. You do just as you think for the best without regard to the public as anything else. I do not know what will become of you all, but as the enemy have gained possession of that part of the state, I would rather they would hold it, as I notice here in Virginia when they hold the country, the people fare much better than when both armies are constantly traveling through it.

You all must trade with the Yankees and get something to live on. What little was left in the county before will be taken out of it now as they have complete possession of all the places. Put your dependence in divine Providence and do the best you can. I have heard it said that trouble never made a Christian unhappy. I hope to God it may be so. Our cause begins to look rather waning, but we will put our trust in the One that controls all things and fight the harder.

There is no immediate prospect of a battle up here. The enemy are on the opposite side of the Rappahannock. They are reported to be building up the railroad bridge burned by us some twelve months ago. When they finish it, so as to be easily supplied from the fountainhead, they will probably try and move on to Richmond, but with the assistance of God, I hope General Lee may whip them worse than ever before. The Richmond papers say we will have a few Negro regiments to fight in the next battle. It seems to please all the boys, as they only think they will be in the way more than anything. . . .

Your son,
Jerome B. Yates

☆ *James Johnson Kirkpatrick Diary*, August 13, 1863, Thursday:

Wet morning. . . . Corporal J. J. Wilson, wounded at Gettysburg, returned.

☆ *Jerome B. Yates to Mrs. Obedience Yates and Marie Yates Swanson*:
Orange Court House, Virginia, August 14th, 1863

Dear Ma and Marie,

Yours of the 20th July came duly to hand and was received by me with great joy and pleasure, as I thought I got my last letter from home. I am glad to hear you are all well. If you all can only remain well, I am satisfied. You say times are gloomy. I reckon they are gloomy. In fact, the gloomiest times Mississippi ever saw, and I hope the worst she may never see, but you all seem to be too despondent. Never give up in a just cause. . . . We will still battle for the right to have what we think we have a right to. I hope the enemy may leave what is left. With that I think you all can live very comfortably. You can not live in the lap of luxury as you have been living, comparatively speaking. Learn to do it on a little, it will be a good lesson. You may profit by it in years to come. . . .

But enough of public affairs. I reckon you all are in a peck of trouble about things inside the enemy's lines. Be of good cheer. . . . You will get all things to working well and get along finely. The people up here say they had much rather be inside the Yankee's lines . . . than have armies coming and going . . . twice a year. I am in hopes the enemy will hold that country as they have done all the others. . . .

Tell Lucy I am proud of her to prove herself so loyal to Ma in the hour of trial. Tell Sam Wilse is all right, and I do not believe he would go with the Yankees if he has a chance, which he has had several times. He had only to stop and wait for them to come up and go with them. . . . I expect you all have to treat the Negroes [differently] on account of the enemy's being so near. I would not do it. I would whip them when they needed it, though I do not know if talking would not do as much good. I took Wilse out the other day to chastise him and got to talking to him and made him cry. I think it done him more good than all the whipping I ever gave him. . . .

I am truly glad to hear that you have seventy bales of cotton to sell. If they will just give you anything for it. . . . I will not fear for anything if you can sell your cotton. I hope to God they treat you all as I did the people in their country. I did not take the first thing but what I offered pay for it, and I hope they may treat you the same way nor refuse to pay for anything. Take the money. If it is not worth a single cent to you now, it may be some day.

You and Marie did not write a word about Aunt Patty or the girls. Are they still staying with you? I hope so. You all will be company for each other, and I think you all will get along better together than you would separate. . . . Write soon to your son and brother,

Jerome

☆ *Jerome B. Yates to Mrs. Obedience Yates*:
Orange Court House, Virginia, August 16th, 1863

Dear Ma,
Being Sunday and a lonesome day and preaching being over . . . I will pen you a few lines. Nothing to do up in this part of the country. No prospects of

a fight soon, which is very pleasing to we soldiers. Fighting has become quite a task with most of us and a perfect hard job for some of us. . . . I reckon that the Northern army thinks as they whip Rebels so easy down in Mississippi, they will whip us very easy, but all they have to do is to try it. General Lee's army extends from this place to Fredericksburg, the distance of forty miles. That is the reason I do not think there is any likelihood of a battle in Virginia, which I hope is so, for I dread for the next fight to come off, though I feel confident of success. I have been through so many and never got a scratch. It seems like a miracle that I should have went through so many fights and come out safe. . . .

But I must begin to enquire how you all are getting along at home, that dearly loved place which it seems I am never to get to. But this war cannot last always. So I will be patient until winter. I am going to try Mars' Bob for a thirty days leave, then on the strength of having a widowed mother at home and of never received a leave of absence and a few more extra touches. If he does not give me one, I will always think he should.

How are T.O.D. and all the children getting along and all of Buddy's folks? I would like so much to hear from them all, especially from Sallie. Tell her I am not dead. She must not forget me because I do not write as punctual as if I was a clerk in a store or somewhere else where I could have all the conveniences for such things. Tell her I know how much she enjoys her good peaches and watermelons. I know what a dear lover she is of them. You all had better subsist of such things this summer and save your provisions for next winter. Tell me in your next letter how much meat and other provisions you have got to last you, and I can rest better satisfied. . . .

I will write regularly now that I know you receive my letters. Your son,

Jerome

☆ **J. B. Crawford to Martha A. Crawford:**
General Hospital, Howard's Grove, second division, richmond, Virginia, August 20, 1863

Dear Wife

I am happy to inform you that I am on the mend at this time. I hope those few lines will find you and the famley enjoy the best of health. I have nothing of any importance to write you at this time. I send you a soldier paper. If you get it write to me. I haint seen the boys in two months but I received a letter from them that they were all well. Write to me how you are gitten along in this world and how the stock is doing. Martha take care of the mare for horses is worth a fortune at this time. They are from three to four hundred dollars here. Write to me who have gon to the war and who haint. Tel the children I am gitten well and waunt to see them. So nothing more at this time only I remain your affectionated husband untel death so fare you well for this time. I hope to see you again.

J. B. Crawford to Martha
An Crawford

Tel the children I want to see them the worst in the wourld. I am mity weak, but I could wake [walk] ten miles in one hour to see them.

J. B. Crawford to the
children

Good by children god bless you my little ones forever amen.

J. B. Crawford

☆ *Harry Lewis to Mrs. Nancy Lewis*:
Camp near Orange Court House, Virginia, August 20th, 1863

Dear Mother,
Since I wrote you, I have received a letter of yours dated July 18th, which . . . I will now endeavor to properly acknowledge in the shape of an answer. . . .
I went to church in town last Sunday. . . . General Pendleton . . . preached. Generals Lee, Longstreet, and Ewell were present. It is the custom of our generals to act as preachers. Old Lee is the finest looking fellow I ever saw. Longstreet is a very fine looking man of six foot two. Hill is a medium sized man, rather thin, peaked face and resembles a planter rather a general. Anderson is a fine looking, dignified man; hair slightly touched with grey and with a very fine eye.[4]
We are living in better style than ever before as far as eating is concerned. Mack supplies us with vegetables and extras from town, which he visits every day as much for the benefit of his own pockets. . . .

Harry Lewis

☆ *Jerome B. Yates to Mrs. Obedience Yates*:
Orange Court House, Virginia, August 21st, 1863

Dear Ma,
Yours of the 4th came duly to hand and was gladly received by me . . . and I heard you all were all well and had plenty to eat, which is truly a great blessing these days. . . .

You wrote me you would like to know if I approved of your taking the Oath of Allegiance to the U. S.? You are the best person to decide that. I do not know whether it would be proper to take it or not. Under certain circumstances, I do not look upon it as binding in the least where people is in a destitute condition, and that is the only way to save what they have or get something to eat, then I do not think there is anything in it which is wrong. You do just as you think proper. Do not let any one influence you at all in the way you act. Tell Marie I am sorry to hear she has turned Union. I thought she was too good a Secesh for adversity to make her change so quick. I fear she is not very strong in her faith in Jeff [Davis] and the balance. Never fear, if it is a just cause, which I hope it is, we will come out all right yet.

Ma, how do you like the idea of sending all the Negroes to some of the interior states and selling them and buying gold with the money? All but two or three of the most trusty ones, so there will be no danger of our losing all by the war. Sell horses, stock, and everything, only a few cows are living on the place. That part of the country is subject to be overrun by the enemy at any time, and we may lose everything someday. Pole could take them to Alabama or Louisiana or some other state and sell them for a good price and not be gone from home very long. Negroes bring very good prices up here, and I reckon as good in those states. I think it must be the safer plan. But I will leave all to you, do as you are doing if you think it best. I do not think it a son's place to dictate to his mother. . . .

I am glad the Yankees are sending the Negro women home, they can make a living for you and themselves. Speaking of selling Negroes, if Tom should come back again, I want you to sell him as soon as you can get him off. Pole said he intended to sell Jake. He had better take both to Alabama or Louisiana and sell them, or they will be gone again and all the balance with them. . . . I want you to sell Tom at any price over seven hundred dollars and buy gold with the money. I expect you all will think of who will do all of this. Tell Pole to do it for me, or send him up here, and I will do it.

I have hired Wilse out, and now I do my own cooking with the other mess. I thought I had furnished a cook for them long enough. They never intended to offer pay for his services nor give him a thing except Jim Bolls and Bud. . . . Bud is one of the best and cleanest boys in the world. I would not give him for the balance of the company. This is the place to find out people. I can read every man that belongs to this company, and I find many wanting in what it takes to make a gentleman.[5]

You spoke of having some fine horses. You must look out for the Yankees that they do not get them. That is why I am in favor of selling them all and putting the money beyond their reach so as to make safe for something for you to live on in your old age. Suppose the Yankees were to come out and take everything on the place, what would you do with nothing to eat and no money to buy anything with? You see there is danger of your being in much worse condition than you are if you had $1000 in gold. If they broke you entirely up, you and Marie could leave and go somewhere else and do very well with the aid of Mr. Swanson, who I look on as yours and Marie's chief dependance, as he has no one but himself and Marie to attend to. Marie is much better off than many women who have not lost a single thing. I am truly glad she has such a husband to lean on in such times as this.

You spoke of having a fine dog for me. I am entirely out of the dog humor. I do not care anything for them. . . .

I reckon you all are fasting and praying today as it is the day appointed by the President. I hope that they may avail much towards the Confederacy gaining her independence.

Write soon. Your son,

Jerome

☆ *Harry Lewis to Mrs. Nancy Lewis [continued]*:
August 22nd

I don't know whether I will go to town to church or go to the same in the brigade, but rather think I'll go to Orange, as preaching in the brigade is generally very indifferent. We have service regularly in the different regiments of our brigade. I am told that in Mahone's Brigade there is quite a religious feeling. In fact, I think there is a growing interest in religion, not only in our brigade but also in the division and the whole army. Yesterday just as the regiment was forming for battalion drill, a gentleman on horseback with a pair of saddle bags and an umbrella behind his saddle came through camp distributing tracts and gave me a handful to give the boys when they came in from drill. The boys received them willingly. . . .

War is a strange scale for measuring men and brings forth strange developments in the character of men, who to all appearances in civic life are men of courage and sterling worth. You remember how disgracefully this unfortunate young fellow acted when returning to the army with me at New Orleans. Well, would you ever have thought he would make a reliable soldier? No, never!

Well, he made as good a soldier as there was in the regiment, cool and brave in battle and always on hand and never shirking duty in camp. Compare this soldier with others who occupied honorable positions in society . . . and as soldiers there is no comparison. Again, those mere boys as Frank Best, Johnny Stockett and whom everybody thought would not stand it, make excellent soldiers.[6]

Jeff Posey has just been telling how the Yankees visited Mrs. Posey. . . . Did the blue-bellied scoundrels molest you?

Harry Lewis

☆ *James Johnson Kirkpatrick Diary*, August 27, 1863, Thursday:

Read "The Autocrat of the Breakfast Table." The religious meetings are still kept up. Morning, noon and night can be heard songs of praise ascending from the varied encampments. These meetings will no doubt do much to improve the morals and discipline of our army.

☆ *James Johnson Kirkpatrick Diary*, August 30, 1863, Sunday:

Read *The Life of Stonewall Jackson*. Everything pertaining to this man is interesting to me. He was so mysterious and rapid in his movements as a leader and such a devout Christian. No one can help giving him this admiration. The Sixteenth Mississippi . . . held him in high esteem.

☆ *James Johnson Kirkpatrick Diary*, August 31, 1863, Monday:

Very cool last night as usual of late. . . . Heard of Captain Slay's escape from prison and arrival at Richmond.

☆ *James Johnson Kirkpatrick Diary*, September 5, 1863, Saturday:

Spent most of the day writing and reading. Heard a sermon to Christian Association by Dr. Broadus of Richmond. . . . Another week of fine weather for military operations has passed away and still lie guilty in camp. Whether constant fighting and blood-shed will hasten peace or not is a matter of some doubt to me. Perhaps quiet will allay the excited passions and restore the North to reason sooner than anything else. . . .

☆ *J. B. Crawford to Martha A. Crawford*:

General Hospital, Howard's Grove, Richmond, Virginia, September the 8, 1863

Dear Wife

I received your kind letter of August the 31 which found me on the mend. I think I will get well. I was rejoiced to hear from you and the children and to read your letter. I hope those few lines will come to hand and find you and famley well. I have nothing of any inturst to write you except our Confedracy is gon up the spout. I think the boys is all out of hart up hear.

I am glad you sending faney to scool. tel her to learn fast and I will send her a little book to read. T. H. Green got the letter you sent with some of your hair in it and it look like home to me but he did not send the letter to me.[7]

I make some mistakes. I leave out some wourd. I sent you the soldier paper. If you get them always write in your letter and then I will send some more. Direct your letter to the ridgement. I had like to forgot to tel you I received a letter from pippen the same day and he said brother ben was conscripted. poor old fellow he is in truble I know.

I waunt to see you and the children the worst in the wourld but there is no chance yet awhile. I hope I will see you and them before long. I got a letter from the ridgement day before yesterday and they was all well.

I wood give the Confedracy to the yankeys if it was mine to see you and the little ones. Write to me how you are making out in this dredful wourld and how the stock is doing.

I am sorry the old lady is crasy. tel her she must quit that way of doing. Martha take everything easy and do the best you can til I com home if it is god will for me to com back again and I hope it is. Martha take good care of the mare for horses is mity hy. So I will close for this time by saying I remain your very dear husband til death. goodby honey.

> J. B. Crawford to Martha
> An Crawford
> I send you some of my
> whiskers.

☆ *Jerome B. Yates to Mrs. Obedience Yates*:

Orange Court House, September 13th, 1863

Dear Ma,

. . . There is nothing new or interesting in this country. Nothing new in military circles, only General Longstreet has gone to Tennessee. . . . He got transportation for twenty thousand men in Richmond a few days ago for Bristol on the Virginia and Tennessee line. I think when he and General Bragg get together, they will whip old Rosy so bad he will not be able to get back into Yankee land. But you seem to think the Confederate States are going up anyway, so if we do whip them it will not amount to much. But I am not as desponding as you are yet. If the cause is just, we will succeed. Such reverses do not have such demoralizing affects on me as most people. If God is on our side, I am confident we will come out all right. He may suffer the wicked to prosper for a time, but vengeance will finally overtake them, and the right will triumph. So I am full of hope yet, which I pray to God may be fully realized and all of us can meet and be happy once more. . . .[8]

You say you will take the oath rather than sacrifice everything. You must be certain that everything will go before you take it. That is rather a knotty subject to decide on whether it would be proper to take it or not, but I think under the circumstances that you are placed under—a poor widow woman without any protection and no one to provide for things—I do not think it would be anything wrong. But it is very different with a man. I look on a man that takes it as good a Yankee as Abe has got. They can leave the country and make a living any where, but you do just as you think proper without regard to public opinion or anything else. . . .

You spoke of sending me money to get my winter clothes with. You need not do it as I can draw clothes from the government when I want them. I am allowed $130 for commutation, which is a plenty. The twenty dollars you sent me was duly received in my last letter from you and went like all the rest. Twenty dollars will only buy four watermelons. So you see, Confederate money will not go far. If you can make any use of it, you keep it as it is of no value to me. I can do as well without it as with it. If I get into a fight before winter, I will come out with plenty of clothes or a furlough. I never have failed to get anything in a fight that I wanted. If I can get hold of any U S. money, I will send it to you. If I was just only rascal enough to pick their pockets, I could get any amount I wanted. It is a temptation when I see them lying around, and I know their pockets are full of money and see other men taking it out. But when this war is over, I want to come back with a clear conscience, which I hope to.

You must write me . . . and give me all the news in the neighborhood and the country generally. Give my respects to all inquiring friends and my love to all the children. . . . Remember me to all the Negroes. Tell Sam, Wilse is doing finely. Write soon.

Jerome

☆ *J. B. Crawford to Martha A. Crawford*:

General Hospital, Howard's Grove, second division, Ward G, Sept the 17, 1863

Dear Wife

I . . . take this opportunity to tel you . . . that I am still on the mend. I hope those few lines will find you and famley in good health. I have nothing of any interest to write. I want to see you the worse in the wourld. I think if I could go to your house I could get a plenty of butter and milk to eat.

Take good care of the cows.

They is strong talk of our ridgement going to tennisee but I dont know where we will go or not. I wish they wood go then I wood be able to go home could run away and come home. It is easy to run away. I dont know any thing about the boys. I haint seen them sence . . . we left them in maryland after the battle in pennsylvania. That was the bloodiest fight I ever saw but god brought me out of it safe.

I wrote to moses the same day I wrote to you on the 8 I believe of Sept. let me know how much corn you made and who have gone from that settlement to the war and who haint.

Take good care of yourself and dont take things to hart too much. I want to meet you as fast as a beaver. I will send the children a few Confederate buttons to remember me by. Give my best to all my . . . friends and relations. So no more at this time. I will close by asking you to write all news you have.

J. B. Crawford to his
dear wife and children
Good by but not forever.

☆ *James Johnson Kirkpatrick Diary*, September 23, 1863, Wednesday:

All quiet in camp. No drilling. Heavy details for fatigue and guard duty. Weather cool, but pleasant. Blankets coming into active demand for comfortable sleeping. Colonel Baker read us a dispatch tonight from General Hill, announcing a complete victory to our arms at Chickamauga. . . .[9]

☆ *Harry Lewis to Mrs. Nancy Lewis*:

Camp near Rapidan Bridge, Virginia, September 23rd, 1863

Dear Mother,

. . . We have been prepared for a week, expecting a fight every day as there has been considerable skirmishing. . . . I have just learned that Stuart drew the Yankees into an ambush . . . and killed and captured many of them.

Our line of defense is along the banks of the Rapidan, which is very favorable to us on account of the ground on one side being higher and more commanding than that of the other bank. The river . . . runs through a high country and is much more difficult to cross than an ordinary stream. It furnishes a fine line of defense for us, and I think we can manage Meade, though his army more than doubles ours. . . .

We are fortifying the principal fords, especially at the station where the railroad crosses the river. We are (individually) well supplied with blankets, though many of the boys are nearly destitute. Still, we have a supply in depot at Richmond, which we will send for as soon as are we settled down permanently for this winter. I expect we will miss our supply of clothes which we have been accustomed to receive. Though the boys are pretty well clad, some of them are actually barefooted. . . .

Your affectionate,

Harry

☆ *James Johnson Kirkpatrick Diary*, September 24, 1863, Thursday:

Fine day. Read *Darvall Markham*, a novel of Miss Braddum. Started on picket at three p.m. The right wing on post first. About two p.m., the word passed along the lines that the Yankees were coming. They were approaching our lines a little on the left of my post, making a great deal of noise. A number of shots were exchanged, but no one on our side was hurt. They set fire to a house in our front and then retired. . . . Our division was put under arms, and the balance of our brigade turned out to support us. Night cold and no fires permitted. Some papers were exchanged with the Yankees. . . .

☆ *Jerome B. Yates to Mrs. Obedience Yates*:

Orange Court House, September 28th, 1863

Dear Ma,

I have found some time to drop you a few lines and so I will do so. There is nothing new or interesting. We are camped at Rapidan Station four or five miles from Orange. The enemy are on the opposite side of the river, and a battle may be looked for soon. We picket in four hundred yards of each other, but no firing is allowed. We have strong works on the opposite side of the river and have orders to be readied to march at a moment's notice. . . .

A letter from Pole came a day or two ago saying you would take the oath. I do not feel exactly right about you taking it. Though I say as I did before, do just as you think proper about it without being influenced by anybody. But I hope to God circumstances may be such that you may not have to take the detestable obligation upon yourself. Tell Pole I do not want him to take it by any means. Any man can make a living . . . without ever taking it. I see plenty of people up here doing it. But enough of such things, but they are the most important things. They occupy my mind from morning till night, and I do sincerely pray God you may never have to take it.

How are you all getting along at home? I am much interested about you all since I have heard that the Yankee general is going to extend his lines out to the Pearl River, and you all will be shut out from the Confederacy for good, but I am in hopes there is no truth in the report. If he does, goodbye to home until the end of the war, which does not seem to be coming in a very short time. . . .

Write soon,

Jerome

☆ **J. B. Crawford to Martha A. Crawford:**
October the 2, 1863

Dear Wife

I take the oppertunity to let you know that I am still on the mend and hoping those few lines will find you and famley well and doing well. Martha I want to see you and the children so bad I am almost crasy. my daly prey [prayer] is that I will live to see you all once more in this life. When I think if I should never see you and the children anymore it almost make my heart bleed to think about it amen.

I have nothing of any importance to write to you. times is hard hear and talk of the war lasting ten year longer and it looks like it wood from all appearance. They was ten men shot hear today for desertion. I did not go to see it. I could not bare the sight to see men shot more than I can help.

Martha get Pippen to spay . . . the hogs except the old sow and two gilts the ground squirrel one and the white one with the black spot on her back. Them is the two I picked when I was home.

I received your letter wrote the last of August and answered it and I am looking ever day hard for another one. Martha dont greave any more than you can help. I waunt you to be fat and harty so you can tend our little children. It almost kills me to thank if they should have to suffer.

I will send you a leaf of a songbook with two peaces of poetry. One is home home can I forget the. the other is be kind to thy father and I send Jane one the old folks at home. I found them on the battlefield a knapsack had them in it. So I will close by saying I will remain your dear husband til death parts us.

J. B. Crawford, good bye.

☆ **J. B. Crawford to Martha A. Crawford:**
General Hospital, Howard's Grove, Second Division, Ward C, Oct the 7, 1863

Dear Wife

I received yours of the 29 of Sept today which found me on the mend. I hope this will find you and the children well. You said ben waunted you to move. Dont do it except he pays you fifty dollars down. Martha dont let ben greave you. I wood not pay any attention to him. He is mean as hell wants him and everybody knows it. Dont let him bother your mind and dont move till he pays you fifty down and then I dont know where you wood go too. The old plase is so unhandy to ever thing and so fare to [the] mill and nobody to go for you. let Pippen keep the mare as long as he will.

I hope and trust I will live to com home. Martha dont let thangs greave you. I hope all thing will work out after a while and we will meet again. Oh what a happy meeting that wood be to us forever to think of.

Martha send ben word I love pippen like a brother and I love him like a Yankey. The boys is all well at this time. . . . Wee expect to fight here ever day. I wood like to write a long letter but I dont have nothing to write of any interest. when you write write a long letter. Maybe I will have somthing new next time. I waunt to see you all mity bad once more. Take good care of yourself and the children. Tel Jane and Molly hiddy for me. Good by for this time. So I close saying I remain your dear husband untel death.

> J. B. Crawford to Martha
> A. Crawford and the
> children

☆ *Jerome B. Yates to Mrs. Obedience Yates*:
Rapidan Station, Virginia, October 7th, 1863

Dear Ma,

. . . The army is still at the same place [as] when I wrote you before. . . . The enemy are reported moving towards us in three columns, trying to cross at the ford below and above this place, but as yet we have not been ordered out of camp or are under orders to be ready to march at a moment's notice. A fight is daily expected. We go on picket this evening. Probably the fight may come off before we get back. . . .

I wish the fight was over, and I had all the plunder. I expect to get it when it does come off. Rumors are afloat . . . that Meade has sent large reinforcements to Rosy in Tennessee. If such is the case, we may not have a fight at all. But appearances seem in favor of it so far. They are going to do something, I do not know what.

What are you all doing in Mississippi? I would like so much to see you all. Probably, I may get a furlough in the coming winter, who knows, when I will stay at home for a little while at any rate. But I hope to God I may go through this war without a single scratch which, thanks to Him, I have done so far. But, poor boys, many of them came from home . . . to be laid beneath the cold sod. Poor Fay F. He was missing at the battle of Gettysburg and never seen since. When last seen, he was twenty yards ahead in a charge. He was probably taken prisoner or wounded. . . .[10]

I have just heard of the death of Mrs. Davis, poor woman. I am truly sorry for her, but she is not that so much to be pitied as her husband and his children. She was a good woman. More than probable, she is in the place of rest where the mortal cease to be troubled. . . . God seems to punish him for his sins here on earth by taking away his wife. But I do not think the loss is so great to him as it is to his children, poor motherless things. They seem destined to be raised in this world without the fond, protecting, loving care of a mother. I should think Laura was nearly big and old enough to take care of her father's things.

All of you must write to me oftener than you do. . . . Marie was sick when I last heard from there, how is she by this time? She may be dead, and I never hear it. Tell her if she is able to write to do it, as I am anxious to hear from her. . . . You must answer this . . . letter by the first chance to your son,

J. B. Y.

☆ *James Johnson Kirkpatrick Diary*, October 8, 1863, Thursday:

Marched . . . towards Orange Court House. Thence took the road towards Madison Court House. . . . No one has any idea of our destination.

— *Chapter 14* —

"... WE MUST TAKE IT
THE BEST WE CAN"

In early October, 1863, Lee learned that Meade had sent two corps west with Hooker to participate in the Chattanooga Campaign. Still outnumbered eight to five, and amid rumors that the Army of Northern Virginia would follow Longstreet west, Lee decided to make a move. On the eighth of October, he put his army in motion, hoping to force Meade to withdraw from Culpeper. He planned to draw the Federals from their base of operations, then flank the Union forces from the west, employing the same maneuver that had worked at Second Manassas. Suffering from angina on October 9th, Lee adhered to his goal to surprise Meade on the 10th, capture his supplies, and drive him from the area. Meade's cryptographers, however, had decoded Confederate messages.[1]

On October 14, 1863, shortly after 3:10 p.m., Posey's Brigade and most of the Sixteenth Mississippi, coming to the support of General John R. Cooke's left, emerged from the woods a half mile west of Bristoe Station to find a railroad embankment with Colonel Alfred Thomas Smyth's Union troops on the other side. Union General Caldwell, seeing the threat to Smyth, ordered Battery G of the First New York Light Artillery to open fire on the advancing Confederates.[2]

☆ **James Johnson Kirkpatrick Diary**, October 10, 1863, Saturday:

Marched at seven a.m. Passed through Madison Court House, turning to the right along the base of the Blue Ridge. Marched across the country, following no particular road and camped a little after dark in an unknown locality. The campaign has now so far developed itself that it seems evident we are making a flank movement to get in rear of the Yankee army. The sorghum fields on our route are suffering extensively. There is nothing else in the country to eat. The nights continue cool.

☆ *James Johnson Kirkpatrick Diary*, October 12, 1863, Monday:

The enemy are reported all gone. Started early and took our backtrack a few miles, then left the road, turning to the right . . . towards Warrenton. Crossed Hazel River and camped at Amissville. Passed through a very desolate and forsaken country. . . .

☆ *James Johnson Kirkpatrick Diary*, October 13, 1863, Tuesday:

Resumed our march today. Crossed the Rappahannock at Waterloo. Our pioneers are doing some good on this march. Instead of fording all the streams, we now find them bridged. Went into camp a little after noon at Warrenton. . . . In passing the old Yankee camps today, many of our barefooted shod themselves by picking up old shoes. . . .[3]

☆ *James Johnson Kirkpatrick Diary*, October 14, 1863, Wednesday:

Had orders to march at midnight countermanded and did not start till nearly day. Passed through Warrenton and took the Gainesville Turnpike. Our brigade in front. After passing New Baltimore, we came up with the enemy's pickets and drove them back towards Buckland. Rapid cannonading commenced on our right at sunrise. Ewell's Corps had come up with their rear. Hill's Corps left the pike at Buckland, on the increase and stubbornness of the cannonading and musketry on our right, and marched towards the railroad at Bristoe Station. . . . The Sixteenth Mississippi remained observant and repellant on the pike below Buckland until a heavy cavalry force came up and relieved us. We then started to overtake our brigade. Heavy musketry and artillery firing ahead of us. We marched as rapidly as possible but [could] not reach the scene of action till after dark. . . . General Posey was severely wounded by a shell. Halted in the woods . . . in the edge of the battlefield till morning.[4]

☆ *Historical Sketch of the Quitman Guards*:

The Sixteenth Mississippi Regiment was in the advance, and the Wilkinson Rifles, under Captain John Lewis, supported by the Quitman Guards . . . were thrown forward as skirmishers. General Hill, having discovered that the Federal infantry had gone into camp at Bristoe Station about six miles to his right, left the Sixteenth Mississippi Regiment, under the command of Colonel Baker, at New Baltimore to guard the road and, if possible, drive the Federal cavalry from the place. . . . Colonel Baker moved his skirmishers forward, keeping the regiment in supporting distance. The Wilkinson Rifles had not proceeded far . . . before they came up with the Federal cavalry which they immediately engaged. The Federals fought with stubbornness. The Quitman Guards moved up rapidly and doubled the skirmish line when both companies rushed forward to the attack. The cavalry fell back until they crossed Broad Run when they formed in line on a commanding ridge. Companies K and E continued to advance, keeping up a rapid fire. The Federals discharged several deliberate volleys as they advanced but did not succeed in checking them. Arriving at Broad Run, the skirmishers, unwilling to be delayed by crossing the bridge, plunged into the stream, crossed over and drove the Federal cavalry from the ridge and compelled them to continue their retreat. . . .[5]

☆ *J. B. Crawford to Martha A. Crawford*:

Oct the 14, 1863, General Hospital, Howard's Grove, Ward D, second division

Dear Wife

I concluded to write you a few lines and I can send it by A. Langham. He has gon home on furlow.[6]

Dear wife I am not well. It looks like I cant get well any more. I am in a low state of health at present. I hope those few lines will find you and famley in good health. I have nothing of interest to write you except a fight going on up hear but I dont know how it will turn out but when I hear from it will write you the particulars of it.

You wrote about Net being with you. Tel her she must not run about. You said she was always gon. Tel her she must stay with you. They is talking a little of peace up hear. god send it wood be my prayer but I think it is all talk and no cider. Martha do the best you can. Dont let ben disturb you. I wood not bother my brain with him. he is nothing but a low life Tory no way at best. dont let him run you off. Stay til I come home if I ever come which I hope I will. So I will stop at present by saying I remain your husband untel death.

J. B. Crawford

God bless you.

☆ *James Johnson Kirkpatrick Diary*, October 15, 1863, Thursday:

A shower of rain this morning. All quiet in front. . . . The enemy retired last night towards Centreville. . . . Cooked some rations today and under orders to leave at dark. Changed our position about one-half mile and camped for the night. No movement at dark. Rain at intervals all day. Heavy cannonading tonight at Centreville. The flashes of the guns making a beautiful spectacle.

☆ *James Johnson Kirkpatrick Diary*, October 18, 1863, Sunday:

Waked up at one o'clock [a.m.] and sent on picket in rear of brigade. Started to march at the appointed hour. Roads very muddy and slippery. Very dark. Marched briskly. Passed through Greenwich after day, crossed the Warrenton Branch Railroad. Kept up a steady gait all day, making but few rests. Reached the Rappahannock at the railroad bridge soon after dark. Camped in an old field without crossing the river. Day's march, thirty miles. Some straggling.

☆ *The Veteran's Story*:

We moved out into an old field. While marching along we jumped a rabbit. The boys raised the Rebel Yell and lit out after it. It was soon caught. Then up jumped another one. Away went the boys after it, yelling as if they were making a grand charge. The march turned into a general rabbit hunt. . . .[7]

☆ *J. B. Crawford to Martha A. Crawford*:

General Hospital, Howard's Grove, Ward D, Oct the 18, 1863

Dear Wife

Today is Sunday and so I had nothing to do and very lonesome. I concluded I wood write you a few lines to let you know that I am tolerable well at this time and hoping that these words will find you and famley enjoying the best of health.

I never did waunt to see anybody as bad in my life as I waunt to see you and the children. If I had the whole world, I wood give it all to see you and the children. I keep the letters you send and read them once every day and look at your hair. It looks very natural, but I wood like the place it come off of much better. Martha I could talk with you a week and never get sleepy.

Martha I am afeared the cruel war will last ten year longer. It looks like it never will end. . . .

Write to tell me what ben is doing and . . . what the people is doing there.

The boys was all well the last time I heard from them. I heard today that our general got wounded and I fear some of the boys got hurt but I will hear in a few days and then I will write you.. There is a battle going on up hear at this time.

I wrote to Moses two month ago but dont get no answer from him. I am afeared he is dead and cant write.

You need not send me my clothing. I can draw them cheaper than you can make them. If you have got the wool you can keep it til I come if I ever get the chance to com which I hope I will and stay when I can. I dont think I could leave home two miles if I was at home without the whole famley with me. My prayer is to god daily that wee will meet again on earth and see each other once more. Home sweet home oh, how I long for thee. Martha I cant express my feelings to you. If I could come home I could tel you all about it. There is no place like home.

Give my best respects to brother, he and famley and Pippen and famley. Tel them to write to me. So I will close by saying write soon and let me hear from you. Tel the children I waunt to see them mity bad. May God bless you and family is my prayer. Amen.

> J. B. Crawford to his
> dear wife
> Fare well but not for
> ever

☆ *James Johnson Kirkpatrick Diary*, October 26, 1863, Monday:

A general quiet among our large armies. The elections in Pennsylvania and Ohio have been carried by the Republicans. Lincoln has called out thirty thousand men.

☆ *Jerome B. Yates to Mrs. Obedience Yates*:
Virginia, October 29th, 1863

Dear Ma,

The last letter I got from home stated that Margaret was with the Yankees. I have thought she was at home all the time. I am truly sorry to hear that she was gone. I thought she was one that would stay at home. [A letter from] Joe Murphy gives a gloomy account of things in general in Mississippi. I can not believe they are as bad as he represents them. If they are, you all must have an awful time to live. He says half the men are as good Yankees as Lincoln has got. If so, goodbye to Mississippi. . . .You say no Yankees had visited you since May. So far, so good. I hope none may pay you a visit at all.

So Sallie has been by the famed city of Vicksburg to buy from the Yankees. I am afraid she will get so fat on Yankee crackers and coffee she may injure her health. Tell her to be careful. She is not used to such things. This is not the first time I have heard of her drawing goodies from the [Yankees]. Tell Laura I am proud to hear of her good conduct. So much like a lady to keep her father's house and attend to his affairs and to supply the place of the poor dead mother. I was truly sorry to hear of Mrs. Davis's death, but he and the children seem to be fated in that way. . . .

I judge Mississippi to be the lonesomest place in the world, especially Hinds County. Henry has come round for me to write something home for him. Poor Negro. I am truly sorry for him. He seems so hurt since he found out his wife went to the Yankees. He says tell her to come home, that he will be at home shortly. He sends Howdy to all the Negroes and yourself. He has turned out to be a very good boy. I never saw a Negro hurt so in my life as when Cy told him Margaret was gone. I did not intend to tell him, but Cy came up and spoilt it all. He says tell Sam to take his children and raise them as if they were his own and to keep them under good control. I am sorry for him. . . .

You say the conscript officers caught Swanson, and you think he will not stay with us. Under the circumstances, I would not have him go to the Yankees for my right arm. You all know the circumstances our family is laboring under already, and God grant that never may . . . such a blow fall upon our heads. I blush whenever his name is mentioned. I do not think Mr. Swanson will go. He is a man of too much pride. I hope to God he may not for Marie's sake.

I wish to heaven I could get to see you all. I want to talk of family affairs and matters in generalities to the welfare of family in future letters. . . .

You must write often and long letters to your son who has not got back.

Jerome

☆ *James Johnson Kirkpatrick Diary*, October 30, 1863, Friday:

Drilling as usual. Went over to the band in the evening to hear some vocal and instrumental music. Our band is a great institution. It always keeps its numbers undiminished, and labors with the greatest assiduity at "tooting." Their music, however, is never the sweetest nor most harmonious.

☆ *James Johnson Kirkpatrick Diary*, November 1, 1863, Sunday:

Paid off for July and August. Pay day in the army is an important epoch. The soldiers generally spend this money in a week or two after being paid off. Then the sutlers vamoose, not being willing to credit, or they get out of stock and remain so till next pay day. Then once more trade is revived and begging tobacco ceases. Dress parade at sunset.

☆ *General Nathaniel H. Harris, Movements of the Confederate Army*:

After the wounding of General Posey, Colonel S. E. Baker, being the ranking officer present (Colonel N. H. Harris . . . being absent on sick leave), assumed command of the brigade. About the first of November, Colonel Harris returned and he being the senior officer, Colonel Baker relinquished the command of the brigade to him.[8]

☆ *James Johnson Kirkpatrick Diary*, November 7, 1863, Saturday:

Took a general wash at the spring. Just before dinner was ready, we received orders to get under arms immediately. Marched down towards railroad bridge, took a position near the river, and remained till morning. We observed artillery firing ahead of us at the river this evening, apparently only a few miles distant, yet the wind was so high we could not hear the reports. We learned that the enemy had thrown a heavy force against our pickets across the Rappahannock and succeeded in capturing portions of Hays' and Hoke's Brigades and a battery of artillery. There was no way for them to escape, as they left the bridge unguarded. . . .[9]

☆ *J. B. Crawford to Martha A. Crawford*:

Nov the 7, 1863

Dear Wife

I received your letter today which found me tolerable well at this time. I was glad to hear you was all well. . . . ben is hear but I have not seen him. He is [not] at the companey yet. . . . I have nothing of interest to write you. I dont think the war will close in five years longer.

I hope you will see some peace now ben is gone. I am glad the deserters is coming in. I received a letter from Caldwell today and all the boys is all well and going in winter quarters.[10]

Martha always date the letters you send and the date received one and then I can tel where you get all the letters I send or not. I have got the close I brout from home and wear them ever day. They are the best I ever saw. I have drawed a blue suit to wear of a Sunday to meeting.

Martha I want to see you and the children mity bad but there aint no chance yet but I hope the time will come soon when we can strike home once more. Martha keep in good heart and do the best you can. Tel Net to send me some of the pound cake in a letter to eat for supper.

I sent you two papers today. Write me if you get them. Excuse my bad writing. It is so cold here my hand trembles so bad I cant half write. . . .

I wrote on the 2 of Oct and I begin to think you were all dead. I am geting out of heart thinking you had forgot to write. I have to write to the camp today and to Moses.

Write often. I love to read your letters. So I must close by saying I remain your dear husband untel death.

> J. B. Crawford to Martha
> Crawford

P. S. My beard is six inches long. I will send you some of my hair . . . Kiss [the children] for me. Give my best respects to all my inquiring friends. . . . I wish I had a heap of good news to write to you. Write soon and often. So no more at this time.

> J. B. Crawford to Martha
> Crawford and all the
> children
> Good bye for this time.

☆ *James Johnson Kirkpatrick Diary*, November 8, 1863, Sunday:

Formed line and marched back to our old camps, reaching there at day. . . . We started on the march again by way of Brandy Station, down the railroad until within two miles of Culpeper Court House. Here we halted . . . and put up a line of temporary breastworks. Yankee cavalry came in sight a long distance off and seemed to like the distance well. . . . We remained here all day. At dark, the line of march was resumed toward the Rapidan. Night exceedingly cold and windy. Passed through Culpeper Court House at ten p.m. . . . Marched all night. Much of our way was across fields and through woods without any road. General Harris got lost and couldn't find the railroad. Had no guide to direct us. After a wearisome march, daylight found us on the road, three miles from the Rapidan. Many stragglers. Nearly every piece of timber was illuminated by their fires.

☆ *James Johnson Kirkpatrick Diary*, November 15, 1863, Sunday:

Some more rain this morning after which it cleared off. Cannonading at some of the fords down the river. Learned that General Posey was dead. Company inspection at the usual hour. . . .[11]

☆ *J. B. Crawford to Martha A. Crawford*:

Nov the 15, 1863

Dear Wife

I received your letter Oct 25 which found me tolerable well. I was glad to hear from you. I hope those lines will find you and the children well. . . . I have nothing new to write to you. ben is up hear but I have not saw him. he was consigned to the fourty eighth ridgement.

Martha I dont know what this world will com too. They have quit exchanging prisners. When they take them they keep them til the war is over. I think that will bring about peace before long. I am in hope so anyhow. Martha if they get me I am gon up til the war is over. They wount swap no more.

I am glad you made enough to fatten your hogs. I was uneasy about you making a crop to fatten your meat. I wood send you some money but I am afraid to risk it in a letter. Times is so hard people dont care what they do these days. If any of my company come on furlow I will send it. . . .

Martha you can take that little field now that ben is gon and cultivate it next year. Martha if the mare brings a colt take good care of them. Pippen wrote to me that he had put her to a fine horse.

I am in hopes Old Master spares me to get home. . . .

I wrote you a letter on the 7 of this month and sent two papers with it. I also wrote Moses a letter last week. You request of me to send you some of my hair. I forgot to put it in til I had sealed it up but I will send it in this.

I have red my testament threw three times and started threw again. Today is Sunday and I have nothing to do but to read when I get threw writing this letter.

I sent four buttons to the children. I cant send anything heavy or I wood send a heap of little things to them.

So I will close by saying I hope to hear from you soon. I remain your dear husband untel death parts us.

> J. B. Crawford to Martha
> Crawford
> Goodby once more my
> dear famley

☆ *Harry Lewis to Mrs. Nancy Lewis*:
Camp near Rapidan Station, Virginia, Sunday, November 15th, 1863

My Dear Mother,

This morning I read with pleasure the letter you sent me by Mrs. Posey. . . . I expect Mrs. P. arrived at Charlottesville in time to see the general before he died. I have not yet heard exactly when he died but have heard it through several sources, so that there is no doubt in my mind as to the fact. You doubtless have learned that General Posey was wounded in the fight at Bristoe Station, which was not a general engagement. The news is that he was one whose place could not be filled by anyone in the brigade at present. Though not personally a "brave man," still he would not hesitate to lead his men anywhere he was ordered, as I have frequently seen him in exposed positions on the battlefield. Though I esteem him a lot to the brigade, yet it is not in this light I deplore his death so much. It is on account of his family, for I know how devotedly Mrs. P. is attached to her husband and how many dependent and interesting children she would have to provide for. . . .

Claiborne renders himself quite useful, though very awkward and cornfieldish. Still, he is industrious and likes to work. . . . Remember me to the servants and accept my love to yourself. Your son,

Harry

P. S. General Posey was wounded in the thigh by a musket ball from a shelling and died of pneumonia, I expect, as I know he was suffering from that complaint prior to his death. . . .

☆ *Jerome B. Yates to Mrs. Obedience Yates:*
Orange Court House, Virginia, November 17, 1863

Dear Ma,

Cy Broome intends to start home in the morning, so I will send you a few lines by him, not that I have anything to write, but I know you will be expecting a letter by him. I am in good health, so is Wilse.

We are expecting a fight up here any day. The cannons are firing on the opposite side of the river telling us that the Feds are coming on in. Lucky for them, whomever may choose to come. We are almost compelled to have a fight yet before we go into winter quarters. . . .

I have got plenty of clothes to last me all the winter. Tell Aunt Polly I am surprised at what good pants she can make. Tell her I would not have any better than that. I expect to marry in a pair of pants of her make when I come home. The socks just suit. They are the kind I want for winter use. I got that twenty dollars you wrote about. . . .

Dave Hoover tells me [cavalry] scouts stole all of your mules. I am sorry to hear it. I only wish I had the rascals in my hands. I would not hesitate to cut their throats as quick as I would a dog. They are all deserters. The only two I know in desertion are Bob Carpenter and Adams. Dave tells me he has no doubts that they are part of the gang that is doing all the mischief through the country. News is this morning that one of their company stole a Negro and took him to Vicksburg. Reports says that young gentleman will suffer for it when he gets back.[12]

So you have only two mules left. How many horses have you to plow? Only two Negro men on the place. A sad difference between now and when I left you three years ago. But such are the fortunes of war. I wish the trouble had not of come upon us so soon, but as it is so, we will have to make the best of it. As I have embarked in the affair, I am going to see it through.

But enough of our misfortune. The letter you had written to General Posey has been received by me. The document is not put up in the right style. It is too long, for such an application should not cover over one page of common letter paper. Have it as short as possible. When you write it address it to R. H. Chilton, General R. E. Lee's Staff, Army of Northern Virginia, Richmond, Virginia. General Posey died the day your letter reached me from a wound received at the Battle of Bristoe. I will give you the way to direct your letter if you want to try and get a furlough for me. You should first state that you wanted me at home and for what purpose. Do it in as few words as possible. It would then go to him and if he approved it, it would come on down to General Hill to General Anderson and to the commander of the brigade and then to the regiment and company. If it was approved by General Lee, the others would be compelled to give their consent. . . . Such a document would reach him and probably some attention would be paid to it. Pole or Tom Davis could write it. It is nothing more than a common letter, only a very short one.[13]

You must excuse my taking up all my letter with furlough talk. Of the abundance of the heart the tongue will speak. You must write every opportunity. Your son,

> Jerome
> I'll get you some U.S.
> money if I can.

☆ *James Johnson Kirkpatrick Diary*, November 18, 1863, Wednesday:

A meeting today of the brigade was held today to pass resolutions on the death of our late commander, General Posey. I was appointed one of the committee from the Sixteenth Regiment. General Posey was well liked by his brigade and particularly by our regiment. He was remarkably kind and humane. The resolutions were drafted by his former legal partner, Major Hearsey.[14]

☆ *Harry Lewis to Mrs. Nancy Lewis*:
Camp near Rapidan Bridge, November 19th, 1863

Dear Mother,
I have just heard that Jeff Posey is in camp and will leave for Charlottesville in the morning and thence will conduct his mother home. I wrote you a letter Sunday . . . which stretched all the news to its amplest length. But knowing you

would be pleased to have a letter by Mrs. Posey and be disappointed by not getting one, I concluded to write anyhow. So you need not expect a good letter.

I sympathize most sincerely with Mrs. Posey in her bereavement and am exceedingly sorry that the general was wounded and died, more on account of his domestic relations that his services as a general, though he performed his duty as a soldier and made a very good brigadier, better, I fear, than we will get as his successor. . . .

The weather is cold and cloudy promising bountifully of rain and snow. We have built comfortable huts and desire nothing more than a long spell of bad weather that we may enjoy the fruit of our labor. . . .

It is growing dark and I close. Your affectionate son,

Harry

☆ *J. B. Crawford to Martha A. Crawford*:
Camp 16, Rapidan, Nov the 24, 1863

Dear Wife

I received your kind letter of Nov the 17 which found me well. I hope those few lines will find you and famley enjoying the best of health. I have nothing of any importance to write you. I have not saw ben yet and if I keep my eyesight I dont waunt to see him. he is consigned to the fourty eight ridgement.

There is something strange up hear. It has been raining blood. The people dont know what to make of it but I expect the next rain will be rain of Yankees or something else.

I sent you a letter and some tracks by Langham. Let me know if you got them. I enclose you a paper. I received your letter today. All is well in camp. Wee expect a fight soon up here. Our pickets is in sight of each other but wee expect to whip them very bad.

You need not look for me on furlough. They wount give furlough until wee are dead three days and then they have to examine the grave to see if he is there or not there.

I write once a week. I have contended to stay here five year if I should live that long. . . . If I could see you and the children once more I would be satisfied but they aint no chance and we must take it the best we can. So I will close by saying I remain your husband untel death. Fare well for this time.

J. B. Crawford to
M. A. C.
Write soon again

— Chapter 15 —

". . . THE MEN WOULDN'T COME TO TIME"

Though avoiding Lee's efforts to cut off his withdrawal, Meade failed to follow up on his success at Bristoe Station and took a defensive position near Culpeper Court House. Lincoln let his displeasure with this tactic be known to Meade, who was also advised that the President desired him to attack. Meade, reluctantly, took the offensive and decided to attempt to turn Lee's right flank, a maneuver similar to that intended by Hooker at Chancellorsville. After crossing the Rapidan at Ely's Ford on November 28th, Meade stationed his troops on the east side of Mine Run, a small stream emptying into the Rapidan.

Lee, kept informed on Federal movements by his scouts and anticipating Meade's strategy, had put his men in motion on November 27th with the intention of contesting the Federal advance. On the 29th, the Sixteenth Mississippi entrenched on a ridge on the west side of Mine Run and waited in a freezing rain.[1]

☆ *James Johnson Kirkpatrick Diary*, November 27, 1863, Friday:

Bid adieu to our comfortable homes at four a.m. and started towards Orange Court House. The roads are hard frozen and slippery. Many a laugh is occasioned at the expense of some unfortunate fellow slipping down. But sometimes it is not so amusing when a loaded gun goes off by contact with ice. . . . After traveling a mile or two towards the Court House, it is discovered that we have taken the wrong fork of the road. This is a very common thing for General Harris to do. We face about and make good time for the Plank Road from Orange Court House to Chancellorsville. Cannonading today towards [Germanna] and Raccoon Fords, also down the Plank Road in front of us. Left the road in evening, filing left to take our position in line. Groped about in the dark like blind men in a thicket for a few hours, not finding the right place. Late in the night, got orders to rest in a pine thicket but not to make any noise or fires. Aroused again after a short rest and countermarched some distance in direction of Orange Court House. Traveled two or three miles and went into camp. . . .

☆ Historical Sketch of the Quitman Guards:

On the 30th of November . . . the ground was covered with ice and the vegetation was drooping and dying from the effects of the winter's severity, the contemplation of which, mingled with thoughts of the coming struggle, caused a gloom to come over our spirits. . . . The indistinct sound of artillery was soon heard far away to the left. . . . As soon as the Federal line emerged from the wood . . . the Confederate skirmishers fell back to a point about one hundred yards distant from their entrenchments, closely followed by the Federals when, seeing the effect of their artillery, they faced about and with an enthusiastic yell charged the Federal skirmishers and drove them back to their battle line. . . .[2]

☆ James Johnson Kirkpatrick Diary, December 2, 1863, Wednesday:

Started at four a.m. to make a flank movement to the right and show the enemy that if they are afraid to charge breastworks, we are not. Daylight found us on their extreme left wing. We halted and after a short rest, started back to the Plank Road. Struck out and marched rapidly towards Chancellorsville. The enemy escaped us last night and retreated across the Rapidan. After pursuing six or eight miles and learning that they were across the river, we faced about and marched towards Orange Court House. Halted and camped on the Plank Road within fifteen miles of the Court House. . . . Our soldiers are severe in censuring General Meade for not giving us an opportunity of getting a supply of blankets, overcoats, etc. The weather is so severe and our supply so scant that we needed an engagement very much.

☆ *Historical Sketch of the Quitman Guards:*

The campaign lasted six days and though there was not much fighting, the troops suffered greatly from the severity of the weather, being compelled to pass the freezing nights without fire and . . . thinly clad. . . . The loss of the Confederate army in this affair did not amount to more than five hundred in killed and wounded.[3]

☆ *James Johnson Kirkpatrick Diary*, December 3, 1863, Thursday:

Started at four a.m. and marched back to our old camps near the Rapidan. . . . Very well pleased at getting back to our quarters. We have confronted Meade's army in line of battle nearly a week, but had no general engagement. One can scarcely imagine his object in coming over and giving back without a fight. Some prisoners stated the reason "the men wouldn't come to time."

☆ *J. B. Crawford to Martha A. Crawford:*

Camp near Gordonsville, Dec the 4 1863

Dear Wife

I received yours of the 5 of Nov which found me well at this time. I hope those few lines will find you and the children well. . . .

Ben is here. I saw him this morning. He come up and spoke to me and I spoke to him and then turned off and left him. I asked him no questions. I have no use for him. I wood whip him if I had been harty like I was when I left home but I haint got my strenh yet from my sickness. I am harty but haint got any strenth but I think I will gain it after a while if I can get enough to eat. Ever thing is scarce.

Dear you said you would not have no place to plant any thing if you stayed here. You can tend the little field at the house. Do not ask nobody for it just pitch in and tend it. Any thing people say if I was you it wood not bother me. I wood pay no attention to it. I wood not bother my brains with them. I wood think myself above any such. . . .

You said you wood have to sel some cloth to get some money. I will try and send you as much as a hundred dollars by January if I can get the chance and if not I will risk it in a letter. I have nothing more to write at present. I wood not bother myself too much or you will get down and then not do anything. I will close for this time. I hope we will meet again soon. Write often. I remain your husband untel death.

J. B. Crawford to Martha
A. C.

☆ *J. B. Crawford to Martha A. Crawford:*

Camp Baker, December the 7 1863

Dear Wife

I embrace the opportunity to write you a few lines to let you know that I am well at present hoping those few lines will find you and famley in the best of health. I have nothing to write you. Times is hard hear and the weather is cold. If you can see any chance I wish you could send me two pare of socks. We cant draw any thing but cotton socks and few of them.

D. O. Bankston and his wife is parted. She wrote to T. H. Green that she was don with him and shode the letter to D. O. and he don wrote to her to go wher she pleased that he was don with her forever. Not to write him anymore and he wood not write to her that they wood part while the time was good.

Martha I send you ten dollars in this letter. Let me know if you get it. Wee are now building winter quarters on the rapadan river. The boys is all well at this time. Martha I have got the same clothing I brought from home and one pare of socks but they are wore out.

No talk of peace up hear but talk hear of war. So I dont know when I can get the chance to come home but do the best you can and I will send you all the money I can spare. Wee have to by some things to eat or perish. Wee do not get enough rations and have to by some.

So I will close by saying kiss the children for me. I waunt to see you and them so bad I am almost crasy. I study a heap about you and them. good by once more.

J. B. Crawford to
M. A. C.

☆ *J. B. Crawford to Martha A. Crawford:*

Camp Baker, Dec the 12 1863

Dear Wife

I received yours of Nov the 24 which found me well. I was dobing my chimney and cood not write til now. I did not get the letter you first wrote about the land. it com to the companey while I was at the hospital. . . . I will send you a hundred dollars sometime this winter. I will send you all the money I can spar. I know it is hard with you to get along. I have to by something to eat. Wee dont get enough to eat and have to by a little to keep up but I am saving with it to send to you. I dont know what you will do for a living. I am almost crasy about you and the children. I am afeared you will suffer if times dont get no beter and I see no prospect of it going any beter at present. I hope those few lines will find you all well. If you cant do no beter . . . do the best you can. I draw a hundred dollars the first of January for clothing money and I will send that to you. . . .

I am glad you entered the land. Ben com to our companies and I wood not talk to him and he told some of the boys that he would not com any more. Me and him do not talk to one another.

So I have nothing of interest to write to you. I have made me a little home. All I lack is a little wife to go with it. So I will close by saying I remain your husband untel death. Fare well my dear for this time.

J. B. Crawford to
M. A. C.

☆ *Harry Lewis to Mrs. Nancy Lewis:*
Camp Sixteenth Mississippi Regiment near Rapidan Station, December 12th, 1863

My Dear Mother,

I write you a short letter by Stanhope Posey to let you know you need not expect me at home for some time to come. I made application for a furlough at the same time Stanhope did. Stanhope received his yesterday and starts home tomorrow. I have not yet received mine, but Stanhope just sent me word that he saw it, and it was returned disapproved for the present. So all my hopes of getting home by Christmas are knocked in the head. . . . Our company did not have a chance of drawing the furlough, though four were drawn in the regiment. This is owing to unfairness of Colonel Baker, who favors the small companies, his old company being among the number. . . .

Remember me to Eli and also Aunt Alsie and the rest of the colored. . . . Your affectionate son,

Harry

☆ *Jerome B. Yates to Tom O. Davis:*

Orange Court House, Virginia, December 12th, 1863

Friend T. O. D.[4]

As time and circumstances permit, I will send you a few lines by Parson Dobbs, Chaplain of the Twelfth Mississippi. He starts home in a few days on furlough, but this epistle will have to be very short and uninteresting. There is not a particle of news in this part of the Confederacy.[5]

All the Yankees have re-crossed the Rappahannock River falling back toward Manassas, tearing up the railroad as they go. They only got it built up a few days ago and are now tearing it up. This old railroad saw a hard time. It has been torn up no less than five times in the last twelve months. First by one party and then the other. But fortunately, we never have to build it up. The Feds always do the hard work.

We have had a slight skirmish with them since I wrote you last, but you no doubt have heard of it long before now. It is called the Battle of Mine Run. Nobody hurt much, Johnson's Division done all the fighting that was done. The Yankees crossed the Rapidan River at three different points and advanced out as far as the Plank Road leading from Orange Court House to Fredericks-burg. They remained on this side of the river just eight days, then they retreated back across without giving us a trial. I really wanted them to come on as we had such good ditches and redoubts for our cannons. I believe we could have whipped three to one.[6]

It was the awfullest coldest weather I ever saw. The Northern papers say that some of the pickets on each side froze to death, but that is all error. I stood picket but did not come anywhere near freezing to death, but I did get pretty cold.

How are you off for shoes to stand the winter in? Well supplied, I hope. You should see me, I am just deriving the benefits of my Pennsylvania trip. I've got the best pair of boots in the regiment. I got the leather over in Pennsylvania and had them made at Charlottesville. . . . Only $22 for making them and enough leather for another pair, cheap. C. S. money is not worth having. . . . Privates can't get many pairs in a year unless they capture them. Capturing things from the Yankees is about playing out with the Confeds, especially in the western army. They got considerably the best of the late fight with Bragg. Doggone, if I don't begin to think they are going to get the best of us in Ten-nessee and Mississippi. I wish to goodness the men would turn out and drive them from the country. If that army would only do as good as this one up here, we would get along very well. But when this army gets whipped as bad as Bragg ... the thing is about gone up. I hope to God we may never see such a thing happening as this army getting a whipping.

But enough of military affairs. What do you do at home all these long winter days and nights? I wish I could send you some powder and lead to hunt with. Is there any ducks? [I am told] there are lots of turkeys. If I were you, I would go to Vicksburg and trade with the Feds and get some ammunition or get somebody else and get it. . . . Trade with them and swindle them all you can . . . but I would not like for Ma to trade with them, no matter how lucrative it was, but if they pay you all another visit and treat you as roughly as they do, some you may have to trade with them in self-defense. But I hope you all may not see such times, but no telling the fortunes of war. You may be stripped any day. . . .

Marie tells me Laura keeps house for you. I am glad to hear such good accounts from her. . . . Tell your Darkies "Howdy" for me, and tell Uncle Tom that I hope to live to see him again in fine health and spirits. You must write often to me, a long letter. From your friend,

Jerome Yates

☆ *J. J. Wilson to John N. Wilson:*
December 15th, 1863, Camp near Rapidan Station, Virginia

Dear Brother,

I received your kind letter. . . . There is not any news of importance stirring about in this quarter. All is now quiet in front and likely to remain so for the winter. After Meade made his forward movement and then fell back across the river, he is going into winter quarters near Manassas, and I hope he may remain there for the winter. . . .

I have heard a good deal about Congress bringing out all able-bodied men from sixteen to sixty for state service. If you ever come out before you are eighteen, I would advise you to go into Norman's Cavalry. It is a good deal easier than infantry, but I would not come out until the conscript age was about to get you. There is not a bit of fun in fighting. I have tried it long enough to know all about it.

I would like for the war to end soon, but Lincoln's message don't look like there will be any peace while he is in office. He intends fighting on until the rebellion is crushed and the Union is restored, but I think that he will have to kill every man, woman and child that is in the Southern states before he succeeds in whipping the Rebels. I expect to remain in the army as long as I am able to shoulder a musket and march onto the battlefield.

I hear that Logan's Cavalry is playing a good hand down there with the girls. Several have already married and several more engaged I hear. Let them all marry if they want to, there is plenty up here and a heap better looking and plenty of the stuff. I have said enough for this time.

My love to all relations and the girls. You can tell them that I am not married yet but I expect to be soon. Nothing more at present. Write soon. I remain, your brother,

J. J. Wilson

☆ *Jerome B. Yates to Mrs. Obedience Yates:*
Rapidan River, Virginia, December 16th, 1863

Dear Ma,

One of the regiment is going to Westville in the morning, so I will send you a short letter though not very interesting. This company failed to get a furlough again, so we will have to remain content for the next thirty days. . . .

We are in regular winter quarters, four miles from Orange Court House on the [Rapidan] River. The enemy are nowhere to be seen. They have fallen back toward Manassas, tearing up the railroad as they go. So there is no more fighting for this year. There is a prospect of a fight in Western Virginia. A body of the Yankees are advancing on Stanton. . . . A portion of the troops from this army has been sent to drive them back. . . . It will be a very little affair if it comes off. Only three brigades have been sent from here. I wish it had been us. That part of the country is such a good country for something to eat. Rations are pretty scarce here at present. Only one [ration of] flour and one of meat per day, which is not more than half what a man can eat when he does not get anything else to go with it. Money is still scarce and what we have we can not buy anything with as everything is so high. . . .

The gloves and socks that was sent to Wilse came up to the company. He was glad to get them. He is getting on finely at his new place of labor. They all brag on him.

Have you acted on my suggestion about the furlough in my last epistle about writing to . . . R. H. Chilton? I want you to do it. Pole or Tom Davis either can do it. Write to him that you want me to have a furlough for thirty days and state your reason. Have it as short as possible with it in such a form that it will do for a furlough provided it is approved by him. Such a document would not reach him from me. They have issued orders against privates writing to him, the provost, or General Lee. So you see I am completely closed in. A letter from you would reach him. . . . Do so this minute. One fellow got a thirty day furlough last winter in the same way, by stating his father was in low health and wanted to settle his business, and it was necessary for him to be there.

I will close. . . . Your son,

Jerome

☆ *James Johnson Kirkpatrick Diary*, December 17, 1863, Thursday:

Commenced sleeting and raining before day. Times dull as they always are in bad weather. . . . There are, as yet, no indications of peace. Still more strenuous exertions for resistance and more levies raised by Lincoln for "crushing the rebellion."

☆ *J. J. Wilson to James E. Wilson:*
December 19th, 1863, Camp near Rapidan Station, Virginia

Dear Father,

This leaves me and all the rest of the company in very good health at this time. . . . There is not anything new up here. All is now quiet in front. . . . It is the belief here now that the fighting will be transferred to East Tennessee. I hear that Bragg has been relieved and Hardee has the command of the Army of Tennessee. If so, I am in hopes that things will go on better in that department. There is a rumor that one of the corps will go down to Tennessee and Lee will go with it. If so, I don't think that it will be long before Tennessee and part of Kentucky are redeemed and the foe driven from southern soil.[7]

Things look very gloomy at times. It looks as if we will have to serve the best part of our lives out in the army, but I am willing to fight as long as I am able to bear arms now rather than to give up and let the Yankees have the ruling of a free people.

I think that there will be a great deal of dissatisfaction next spring in the army. The President recommend that the regiment be consolidated and officers appointed over them. The men will not like that at all. Two-thirds of the army has not been home since the war commenced. I would like to get a furlough for a while, but there is not any chance for me without I get sick or wounded. I had rather stay until the war ends if I have to get a furlough in that way.

Everything is very high, almost takes a month wages to get a meal. Nothing more. My love to all. Write soon.

J. J. Wilson

☆ *James Johnson Kirkpatrick Diary*, December 24, 1863, Thursday:

Still cold. This evening at dark, some soldiers charged the sutlers at Orange Court House. They cleaned out everything as far as they went.

☆ *J. B. Crawford to Martha A. Crawford:*

Camp Baker, Dec the 24 1863

Dear Wife

I received yours of Dec the 13 last night. I was very sick but . . . I was glad to hear . . . that you were all well. I hope those few lines will find you and famley in good health. I have no news to write at present. Wee are at the rapadan doing picket duty. The weather is very cold. . . . It snowed all day yesterday but we have tolerable good houses to stay in.

I sent you ten dollars. . . . I sent Frances a testament. . . . I shipped it in her name. I aint got any thing to send the rest of the children. I will send you a hundred dollars as quick as I get it. I will get it sometime in January. Let me know if you get the money.

[This time of] year the men deserts hear. Three left our companey but they got them again. . . .

I cant think of any thing more to write at this time. I was joking about getting a wife. Tel Jim to com and take my place and I will give him my claim on the girls in this state. So I must close by saying I hope to hear from you soon. Fare well for this time. Give my best respects to all. . . .

J. B. Crawford to
M. A. C.

— *Chapter 16* —

". . . WE WILL HAVE OTHER FISH
TO FRY IN A DAY OR TWO"

Stalemated by the extreme cold, Lee and Meade waited out the winter. With no major military movement expected until spring, the Sixteenth occupied itself with picket duty, in full view of the Federals across the Rapidan River. What they did not see was Meade's visitor, General Ulysses S. Grant, conqueror of Vicksburg and recent guest of President Lincoln in Washington. During his visit with Meade, Grant learned Lincoln had appointed him commander of all United States forces. Though Lincoln retained Meade as commander of the Army of the Potomac, Grant made his headquarters with it in the field, giving him daily command as a practical matter.

The religious revival that commenced with the organization of the Christian Philanthropic Association in March, 1863, continued into the spring of 1864 and helped keep the patriotic spirit of the Sixteenth high. Conversions were frequent and hymns were heard at worship services in every camp. Meanwhile, a spirit of defeatism moved through the civilian South, and the Sixteenth's men used their renewed faith to encourage home folks.[1]

☆ *Jerome B. Yates to Mrs. Obedience Yates:*
Orange Court House, Virginia, January 14th, 1864

Dear Ma,

. . . I was glad to hear that you all were getting along well with plenty to eat and wear. I hope you may always have such. As for myself and Wilse, we are getting along finely, plenty of good clothes and lots of C. S. money. There is no news worth writing from this country. No movements being made in the army on either side except that General Meade is being reinforced from the armies down south, which will not trouble us until next spring, and then we will have the more of them to kill. As the old saying is, "the more the merrier.". . . .

I have not seen Joe in six months, but he is still well and holds his position at the Division Wagon Yard, which is a very good place, plenty to eat and nothing to do and a horse to ride on the marches and above all things, no fighting to do. But you may think from the tone of my short epistle that I do not like to fight Feds, which is not wholly true. I am perfectly willing to do my best but am very much opposed to doing any part of anyone else's. Gladly would I do my part if every man would come boldly forward and take part in the melee, but when so many are at home doing nothing, it goes very much against the grain for what's out here to do the fighting for the whole. . . .

There has been an order issued up here that every man who could furnish a recruit to this army would be granted a furlough for thirty days, but as I knew there were little hopes of any furnishing one, the order did not bother me much. . . . If one should chance to want to come to this company to join, try to prevail on them to go in my place.

Well, Ma, as I have told you everything I know, I will close. Remember me and Wilse to all the Negroes and the balance of the family and answer soon. Your son,

Jerome

☆ *J. B. Crawford to Martha A. Crawford:*
Camp Rapadan, January the 15 1864

Dear Wife

I seat myself down to let you know that I am well at present hoping those few lines find you and the children well. I cant tel you how bad I waunt to see you and the children but god knows when wee will meet but I hope soon. Wee are camped on the bank of the rapadan river doing picket duty. The weather is very cold hear. Ever thing is coverd with snow but wee do the best wee can. I am sorry to tel you that wee are in starvation. Wee have nothing to eat but a little bread and not enough at that. If times dont get any better wee will be liable to quit and do the best wee can. I dont see any prospect of peace for the next few years. My dear wife I am willing to give up my part of the Confedracy to get to com home. . . .

I havent any thing of importance to write you. All is quiet up to this time. I send you sixty dollars. . . . If you have any chance send me two pare of socks and one pare of suspenders.

I waunt to see you mity bad but I have no way of helping myself. I hope the time will soon com when wee will meet again. I sent you ten dollars last spring and ten dollars this winter but you never said wether you got it or not.

Give my best respects to . . . Pippen and famley and all inquiring friends. So nothing more at this time onley I remain your husband as ever. I hope to hear from you soon.

J. B. Crawford to
M. A. C.

☆ *Jerome B. Yates to Tom O. Davis:*
Orange Court House, Virginia, January 18th, 1864

Friend T. O. D.,

I was glad to hear from you and the children and to hear you were all well. . . . You may expect to hear stirring news from this quarter about next May or June, if they put off a forward movement so late as that, but rest in confidence of our success. You know this army hardly ever turns tail to the Feds.

Well, next to the Yankees comes rations which most interest a soldier. We are rather scarce. Meat is not very numerous, as the boys would say. They give it to us when they can get it. Do not have any regular times to draw. When they get anything for us, they blow the horn. It blew yesterday, and we drew one pound fresh beef. God only knows when we will draw any more. But as the old saying goes, "Providence provides for the lame and lazy." So it does for us.

Fortunately, the Yankees told an old man that he must move across the river with his plunder and Negroes but leave his corn and fodder. So one night, he slips over the river and goes to our company for volunteers to go over by daylight the next morning to bully the Feds and keep them off him until he could cross the river. . . . We crossed the river at daylight the next morning, and by the time the Negroes were up, we were around the house. They were all ready to go to the Feds, but we crushed their freedom in the bud by march-

ing them across the river. Then we moved the old man over. We had a fair
shot at all the hens, chickens, ducks, and geese. I soon captured chickens, two
ducks and one of the out-fighteness cocks you ever read of, whips all the chickens in camp. Well, we lived on our "clucks," as Virginians call them, a week.
And then, as good fortune did not desert us, the old man was compelled to
sell off all his stock. So we all went down to the sale armed with the where-
withal and bought two sheep for this mess and seven more for the company
and would of bought a cow, but just as we were bidding pretty lively, the commissary of the brigade rode up and pressed the lot. So we got the cows for fifty
cents per pound when we were just going to give two dollars per pound. We all
held a grand counsel and concluded to give two hundred dollars for a bull that
we had pitched upon, and, if we can make out until next spring, we are all
right until wild onions come up. You may think its all gas about the onions,
but it is so. Last spring they had them gathered for us by the bushel. They are
not as good as tame onions, but they go very well. Our bread rations are always
the same, and I hope our meat rations will come round all right after awhile.
I hate to think that we will have to [surrender or desert] for the want of something to eat.

I see in the morning's paper where the Lincoln Congress recommends calling out one million men for ninety days so they can liberate everyone of their
prisoners and plant their glorious Stars and Stripes on every prison wall in the
Confederacy. If ninety days is all they are going to call them for, let them
come. They can not get them organized and in fighting trim in so short a time.
But they will make a big show while they are coming, but so many more for
us to kill when they do come. Well time will tell everything, so we will drop
the subject.

You say you are have plenty to eat and wear. I am truly glad to hear such
good news from home as that. I can afford to live on half rations better than
you all. Good and cheering news from home does a soldier more good than
double rations. . . .

Sergeant Kirkpatrick has just come around to know how many canteens
and haversacks is wanting. . . . You know Kirkpatrick. He is our orderly. He
makes a splendid one, the best in the company, does all the commander's writing and all the captain's business. . . .

You must all write me soon. . . . So goodby. Answer soon, and a long letter
to your true friend,

                                                        J. B. Y.

☆ *J. B. Crawford to Martha A. Crawford:*
Camp Rappian, January the 20 1864

Dear Wife

I seat myself to answer yours of the 8 which found me well and I was glad to hear from you. . . . I have no news to write to you. I wrote you by John Loper and sent you seventy dollars by him. Wee are on starvation hear. Wee have nothing to eat but a little flour bread and not enough of that. I dont know what wee will do for something to go to sustain life. Times is hard hear.

You said something about your fat meat. I wood like to be there to see some of it. It wood be a show to me. If you have any meat at all you are better off than wee are. I am glad you have fat meat. That dont look like you will suffer.

Martha I waunt to see you and the children mity bad but I dont know when wee will meet. I hope soon. You asked me what I thought of your hog swap. I think you done very well.

You said Patsy wanted you to leave but I wood stay there if I wanted to . . . and tend that little field in the bargain and tel her I was mistress of that place and pay no attention to any thing she said.

Martha wee do bad hear. The weather is very cold and muddy. I lost my overcoat. I sent it to richmond last spring. Somebody stoal it and I have nothing . . . this winter. I [bought] a wool over shirt and make out tolerable well. Wee are camped on the rappian to do picket duty.

My fingers is cold and I must stop my short letter for this time by saying write soon. Fare well my dear for this time hoping to hear soon Martha good by.

                                                              J. B. Crawford

☆ *J. B. Crawford to Martha A. Crawford:*
Camp Rappian, January the 24 1864

Dear Wife

I seat myself to let you know I received your kind letter of the 10 which found me well at present. I hope those few lines will find you and famley well. I have nothing of any importance to write to you. I was glad to hear from you and that you was all well.

Today is Sunday and wee have just come off of inspection. Times is hard. The weather is very cold. Wee are in sight of the Yankee but nothing like a fight. I beleave the war will close next summer and wee can com home at least

I am in hopes so any how but wee expect a big fight next spring and if wee whip them I think they will quit warring. The Yankees are giting tiard of it as much as wee are.

My dear wife I hope wee will meet on earth again. May god speed the day to com. I waunt it to com and com right now. I waunt to see you and the children mity bad once more. All wee can do is to live in hope. I am messing with Hector Smith and Sergeant W. Caldwell. Wee have built a little house and have got a chimney to it and wee set by the fire and talk. talk of old times and sing old songs and some new ones.[2]

I wish I had something new to write you but I haint. The boys is all well and waunt to com home mity bad. I hope I will have something new to write the next time. I wrote Moses a letter yesterday. So I must close my letter and get dinner but I can soon get that. Nothing to do but bake a little bread and eat it as quick.

I remain your true husband as ever. Good bye honey.

J. B. Crawford

☆ *J. J. Wilson to James E. Wilson:*
Camp near Rapidan Station, Virginia, January 24th, 1864

Dear Father,

. . . All is now quiet in front. The Yankees have gone into winter quarters beyond the Rappahannock River, and I reckon that they will let us rest until spring. In fact, the weather is getting so bad that it would be impossible for troops to advance. The ground is covered with snow at this time. It was snowing all day yesterday and last night. We have a good deal of fun snowballing.

We are getting along very badly in the way of something to eat. We have been living on half rations for about three weeks. We only get one-half pound of bacon or one-half pound of pickled beef a day. We get full rations of flour, and when we can't buy anything, we have to starve.

Our money is not worth anything hardly. We cannot get more than a meal's victuals for a month's wages. I am in hopes that Congress will do something for our currency, but I do not see how they will make Confederate money a legal tender. Gold is selling for twenty dollars for one. I hope that everything may come down in the prices so that people can live.

Congress has done one good thing. They bring back into service all these men that have employed substitutes and all those that have claimed foreign protection will have to come into the service or leave the Confederate States within sixty days. I am glad that all able-bodied men will have to come into the service.

I do not care how soon this wicked war is over, but it do not look much like peace from the way old Lincoln talked in his proclamation. He was in for crushing out this rebellion.

Well I have nothing more at present. Give my love to all. Write soon. I remain, your son,

J. J. Wilson

☆ *J. B. Crawford to Martha A. Crawford:*
Camp Rapidan, Feb the 9 1864

Dear Wife

I seat myself to let you know I received your letter of the 20 and the 24 and the things you sent. I am well at the present hoping those few lines will find you and famley the best of health. Nancy Mcarty sent me a pair of yarn socks by O. C. Jones. I have a ful supply. I could get ten dollars for the gloves if I would take it but I would not take twenty for them. times is hard hear and I fear they will get harder. I am very soar to day. The Yankee com on our side of the river sunday and wee had to run them all day to put them back over the river. Wee kild twenty and capture fifty and that broke up the ball. Wee got the fiddler and they coudent dance no longer til they get a fiddler.[3]

Martha I cant tell you how bad I waunt to see you and the children but you may know it is bad enough.

You said you waunted me to reenlist so I could get a furlough. They dont give no furlough naren no bounty if I reenlisted. I know they would hold me any how. I think things this coming summer will change one way or the other. I think when Lincolns time is out something will be done towards peace but not untel then.

I will send you all the money I can and live hard myself. I cant stand to hear of you and the children suffer. That wood make me desert and com home. Tel me who have got conscripted sence the last law com out up to fifty.

The boys is all well at present. . . . So more at present onley I remain your loving husband.

J. B. Crawford
Good by honey

☆ *J. B. Crawford to Martha A. Crawford:*
Camp Rapadan Feb the13 1864

Dear Wife

I received yours of the 20 which found me unwell at present though noth-ing but bad cold. I hope those few lines will find you and famley enjoying the best of health. I was glad to hear from you and that you are well. I have nothing strange or new to write you. The boys all well except bad colds.

You stated you got no letters. I dont see the cause of it. I write once a week and sent three or four by hand. I sent one by John Loper and seventy dollars by him. He said he wood give it to you. He left here the 16 of January and I have sent money twice in a letter and you never wrote wether you got it or not. When you receive any thing always let me know it.[4]

Martha you dont [know] how bad I waunt to see you and the children but I hope god will hear my prayer. I sent Laura a little book. Tel Tomy the next one I get I will send him.

You said somthing about a little colt. If the mare has a colt and its a male call it Robert Lee.

Ever thing is quiet hear so I have nothing to write of any importance. I think if wee live by this time next year wee will have peace. That is the talk up hear. Tell Jim Brasher to make haste and com if he is going to take my place. Our men that has been home on furlough say the cavalry at home is worse than the deserters. They ride about and steal and the deserters hide from them and this army beleaves it.

So I will close by saying I remain your true husband as ever.

J. B. Crawford

☆ *James Johnson Kirkpatrick Diary*, February 22, 1864, Monday:

. . . Very sorry that drill is so early resumed. It interfered with our amuse-ments. Town Ball is all the rage.[5]

☆ *J. J. Wilson to James E. Wilson:*
March 6th, 1864, Camp near Orange Court House, Virginia

Dear Father,

I will write you a few lines by James Alford to let you know how I am get-

ting along. This leaves me . . . in very good health at this time. There is nothing new up here. . . .[6]

There was a good deal of excitement up here a while back about affairs in
Mississippi. I wish that some of this army had been down there. I do not think
that they would have went as far into the country as they did. They have not
got as good generals down there as we have up here or the men is not as good.
They never have as good discipline as they have up here.[7]

I wish you would send me a pair of drawers. The drawers is so coarse we
draw that I can't wear them. James Alford will bring them.

Nothing more at present. Write soon. Give my love to all. I remain, your son,

J. J. Wilson

☆ *Harry Lewis to Mrs. Nancy Lewis:*
March 12th, 1864, Camp Sixteenth Mississippi Regiment, Near Orange,
Virginia

Dear Mother,

. . . The quiet in this portion of Virginia has remained unbroken since the
last Yankee raid about the first of the present month, which had for its object
the taking and burning of Richmond, the liberation of some ten thousand
Yankee prisoners confined there and the wholesale murder of President Davis
and cabinet. It is needless to add that this nefarious project proved futile and
wound up in the killing of Colonel Dahlgreen, their leader, and the capture
of some four thousand of their number. Dahlgreen is nephew to Admiral Dahlgreen of Charleston notoriety and a relative to the Natchez Dahlgreens.[8]

It is the opinion of some that we won't have much fighting on this line in
the coming campaign. I don't think the Yankees will venture on the offensive
unless heavily reinforced, but I should not wonder if General Lee did not
assume the offensive and again advance into Pennsylvania, if the Yanks fail to
reinforce within two or three months. The boys are all anxious to visit Pennsylvania a second time . . . if the stakes are as large as they were at Gettysburg.

Thousands of veteran soldiers . . . are bound and firm in their belief that
the Southern states eventually will emerge from the smoke of the conflict covered with honor and fortified by the terrible ordeal through which she will
have passed. I believe if we hold our own until next year, we will see the dawn
of peace bringing joy to many hearts, and friends believe that there is no reason why we should not only hold our own but even beat back the enemy off

portions of our territory already in their hands. . . . I am led to hope great things for the present year. They are in good health and seem determined to endure to the end and die before yielding to our would be masters. But I know you have enough of this. . . .

We have heard of the Yankees being in Woodville again but have not the particulars. If they come by the plantation, I fear for your cotton, and I fear for your horses.

[Harry]

☆ *J. B. Crawford to Martha A. Crawford:*
Camp Rapidan March the 18 1864

Dear Wife
I seat myself to let you know I received yours of March the 5 which found me well at present hoping those few lines will find you and the famley in the best of health. I have nothing of interest to write you all things quiet hear. The weather is cold and windy. I have just come back from hauling a load of wood for my bunk and seting by the fire in my bunk. I wish it was at home by the fire I wood feel much better. I waunt to see you and home mity bad once more in life my Dear. I hope wee will soon meet again on earth. I think peace will be made this year I am in hopes so.

You seam to think wee are whip but I tel you wee ant half whip hear. The armey in miss and tennisee is too weak minded but I think they will do better this year. I expect wee will have a hard fight before long. The Yankee says on to richmond or to hell. I think it will be the latter with a grate many of them.

Wee have some deserters hear. . . . Wee suppose they have gon to the mountain to rob blockade runners. Tel patsy if ben comes back to have him hung in two hours after he get there. . . . The boys says if they live to get home they will kill the last one of them.

All is well so I will close to get dinner.

J. B. Crawford
Good by my love for this time

☆ *J. J. Wilson to James E. Wilson:*
Camp near Rapidan Station, Virginia, March 31st, 1864

Dear Father,
. . . There is nothing new of importance up here. All is quiet in front. The

Yankees are still in their old position, but how long they will remain so, no one knows. The weather has been very bad for the last two weeks. We had a heavy snow. It was twelve inches deep on a level, and then it has been raining nearly every day.

Since the spring campaign will soon open, I expect there will be some hard fighting in the Army of Northern Virginia. General Grant is up here and says Richmond must fall, but I think he will not be as successful as he was at Vicksburg. . . .

We have to go somewhere to get something to eat. We only get half rations of meat, but we get sugar and coffee, rice and lard. We can do very well on that while we are in camp. If we can get enough to eat, I think that this year will wind up the war.

Old Abe can't get any troops hardly to enlist, and when they are drafted they run away and go to Canada. There was an officer that escaped from Johnson's Island and came through reports that there is about eighty thousand Yankee deserters in Canada. . . .[9]

I am getting as tired of the war as anybody, but I don't think we ought to give it up after fighting this long. This army is in very good spirits, but they are as ready for a fight now as they ever was.

Well I will close. My regards to all relations. I remain, as ever, your son. Write soon.

J. J. Wilson

☆ *Harry Lewis to Mrs. Nancy Lewis:*
Camp Sixteenth Mississippi Regiment near Orange, Virginia, April 6th, 1864

Dear Mother,
I gave you all the news by Winans Hoard which holds good to the present time as nothing new in a military or any other sense has come to light since. . . .[10]

Grant is actually among the Yankee Army . . . engaged in reorganizing and reviewing those troops who are to meet us. . . . God grant that if we meet them in battle array, He may be with us. . . .

I was sorry to hear that Litmyer and Chapman deserted. Chapman was a very good soldier, but Litmyer was the best in the regiment and was invaluable to the company on account of his cool intrepidity in bringing the wounded off the field while under fire. Everyone was surprised at Litmyer, but not at all astonished at Chapman.[11]

You spoke in your letter of the deplorable state of religion at home among the people, and I am happy that the opposite is the case in this army. On returning from home, I was struck in the change of attendance of church in our regiment. I found where formerly scarcely none attended preaching, now crowds flock in. Our chaplain . . . is not a very intellectual and cultivated minister but is a sincere hard working Christian. He is in very bad health, though.

Our principal amusement is fishing, which sometimes proves to be quite as profitable as divertive. There is a seine in the regiment, which is the greater part of the day searching the bottom of the Rapidan and prying into its funny nooks in inexorable search of its slippery denizens. And no matter how cold the day or how chilly the North wind, an abundance of fish catchers are ever ready to undertake this (to me) disagreeable business, disagreeable only though in cold weather. . . .

Fletch has been writing to some fair maiden today, for he is indefatigably engaged with a little no-backed dictionary in correcting the jaw-breakers with which he has doubtly been wooing his Dulcinia.

I am sorry to learn that the Yankees robbed you of your carriage horses. What will Old Uncle Mack do without Prince? I think, however, you were fortunate that it is no worse, though a fine pair of horses are not picked up every day these times. . . .

I have been studying French over a month and am making some progress, though the novelty has worn off, and I find it not so interesting as at first. . . .

Peter Leatherman, who revisits home a second time this spring, obtained a recruit on the road and brought him to the regiment, thereby becoming entitled to a furlough of thirty days. If an individual could be found wishing to come to our regiment and army, Fletch could obtain a furlough on the strength of his enlisting in our regiment. . . .[12]

Remember me kindly to Aunt Alse and Judy and Fed and all the colored. And hoping the Yankees won't visit you again this year, I am in truth, your son,

Harry

☆ *James Johnson Kirkpatrick Diary*, April 8, 1864, Friday:

Fast day. Sermon by Chaplain Lomax. Weather spring-like. Went up the river as far as the bridge in a fishing excursion. Bad luck.[13]

☆ *Jerome B. Yates to Mrs. Obedience Yates:*
Orange, Virginia, April 20th, 1864

Dear Ma,

Having an opportunity to write, I will do so. Not that I have any thing of importance but because you expect one from me by any chance, I will not disappoint you. Your letter by George Nixon was handed to me by him. I was truly sorry to hear of Marie's illness, but I hope by the time this reaches you she will be well. But the measles generally go pretty long with old folks. . . . Have all the children had them? If not, you all [will] have a sickly time with all them down with the measles at once. But they are all yours, and it will not go hard with most of them.[14]

You probably wish to know what the war news is up here. We are all getting ready to meet the Yankees. General Grant, it is said, will make a onward movement to Richmond now soon, as soon as the roads will permit. The boys seem to be anxious for the fight. We feel confident of success, as we have received reinforcements from General Longstreet. Rumor says his whole corps is at Charlottesville. If that be true, we will have a bloody fight ere many days.

I was of the opinion . . . that the seat of war would be transferred from this part of our Confederacy to Mississippi, but it has all moved back this way. I was glad of it. You all should not be troubled. I wish the war will end in Virginia. I hope this is the dying struggle of the Yankees for our subjugation. God grant it may be. I hope the struggle may end this year. How hard we all would fight if we only knew it was the last year of the war. . . .

The boys get up considerable debates sometimes on the question whether . . . it is right that we will fight with the same ardor with which the young folks are discouraged at home. I can fight with the same spirit as I could if they prayed every day for our success. But I have no objections to their prayers and hope to be benefitted by them and our cause greatly helped. . . .

Orders came round for a detail of thirty men for regular sharpshooters to practice every day. . . . We all do very badly shooting. . . . I thought I was the best shot in the company, but I found out from amongst too many misses there is always someone . . . that will get ahead of me. . . . The life of a sharpshooter is much safer than in a battle . . . in ranks. But whether we have to go in the thickest of the battle is not known. The rumor is we will act as rear guard when the regular line advances, which if do, we will have an easy time.

Tell Marie she must write me as soon as she gets able. Kiss Annie for me

and all the children. Take good care of my saddle or let Tom Davis to do it.
... Write soon. Write a long letter. Your son,

Jerome

☆ *James Johnson Kirkpatrick Diary*, April 26, 1864, Tuesday:

Warm and pleasant. Company on fatigue duty at the rifle pits on the river.
Got very lazy. The river here is well fortified on our side, but it is not likely
that the enemy will make an attack at this point. U.S. Grant says the has no
idea of batting his brains out against these hills.

☆ *Hugh Carroll Dickson to Joseph J. Dickson:*
Camp Sixteenth Mississippi Regiment, near "Rapid Ann," Virginia, May
4, 1864

Dear Pa,

I wrote to you some days since and did not get a chance to send it off as
Billy Gray could not go to Mississippi until the man that he exchanged with
came to hand. I am still well and hope that this will find you all in the enjoyment of the same blessing.[15]

Doubtless before you get this, there will have been fought one of the bloodiest battles of the war. Grant is now advancing in heavy force and Massa Bob
Lee is preparing for him. We are all confident of victory. The troops are in fine
spirits. We all think that this battle will lay him on the shelf. A great many of
us may be killed, but we all think that Grant will be whipped unless he brings
three to one against us. We all believe that God will give us the victory.

It looks like the whole of our regiment are going to join the church. I never
saw as many conversions in such a short while in all my life. In the last month,
I do not know how many have joined. There was five, I think, joined yesterday
from one company. I wish the whole army were Christians.

Well, Pa, as we are expecting to leave in a short while, I must close. Give my
best love to all of the family and reserve a large portion for yourself. I remain as
ever your loving son,

Hugh

☆ *Jerome B. Yates to Marie Yates Swanson:*
Orange, Virginia, May 4th, 1864

Sister Marie,

As an opportunity offers, I will write this, thinking you would like to hear from me. Ma writes me you have had the measles. I am in hopes by the time you receive this you may be well again.

No news from this army. The enemy are just on the opposite side of the river. They have moved out of their old winter quarters but are still in the vicinity of Culpeper Court House, but we are expecting an engagement any day. We are so close together it will not take us long to arrange things when either party comes nearing.

The weather is unusually fine for this season of the year. I suppose you have heard of our success . . . in the Trans-Mississippi department. A bright opening for '64. God grant it may continue so through the balance of this year and until the end of this war. General Grant will make a definite attempt for Richmond, but with the help of the God of Battle, I hope we may be able to defeat him.

I will mention the revival that is going on in the army. The men seem to be awakening from their lethargy in regard to the salvation of their souls and joining the church rapidly. Five of our company have joined. . . . We have an excellent preacher to preach to us every day. He talks good sense, and, if he is right, that is an easy way to get to heaven. I hope all the boys may join the church before this revival is over. A man certainly stands much more in need of religion in the army than at home. . . .

How are you and Ma getting on? Well, I hope. You must write me everything you can think of—how much corn you have, how much meat, how much salt, how the garden is getting on, what for a chicken, the crop you will have, how the cows look—anything, no matter of how little importance, will interest me. You have no idea what little things I think of sometimes that will benefit you and Ma in the way of living. . . .

Ma writes me the Feds have drawn in their lines to Vicksburg. I hope the cavalry will be able to keep the enemy out of that country. How much better satisfied I would feel if I knew no Yankees would visit you any more. But such is the fortunes of war, and all who are unfortunate enough to be left prey to their raids. And truly the most unfortunate in the world . . . is all the young

Misses in Hinds [County] and thereabouts. Whenever I get time, my mind turns to the female part of creation—not that I class them least of all, forbid that I should be so ungallant, but I must admit that matrimony finds no little time in my mind at present. . . .

Marie, you must write me by every opportunity. Your affectionate brother,

J. B. Y.

☆ *Jerome B. Yates to Tom O. Davis:*
Orange, Virginia, May 4th, 1864

Friend T. O. D.,

Having time and opportunity, I will drop you a line or so by Mr. W. T. Gray who . . . will start home in a few days. . . . Nothing has transpired as yet, but an engagement is daily expected. Grant is reported to be moving. General Lee is moving up his rear. . . . All our cavalry have gone to the right of our position towards Fredericksburg. Our artillery has moved up in position. I have never realized that we would fight at this point, but circumstances go to favor such a belief at present. If Grant fights us at this place, his crown of laurels will soon wither, which God grant he may.

Uncle Jeff [Davis] says the war will probably end this year. I hope he may be right. As for myself, I am getting pretty tired of it but am not ready yet a while to say "enough." I think I can stand them three more years yet, and I think before that time they will get middling tired of it. But if Grant is successful, God only knows when the end will come.

So you and the balance of the Hinds natives are going to have a fish fry. I wish I was there to help you all, but we will have other fish to fry in a day or two. I hope I will fry mine up brown and [come out safe], but the men who get furloughs [by getting wounded] in this fight will miss all the campaigns this summer.

While writing, an [orderly] call has beat something up. . . . Oh, the devil, cook two days rations and get ready to leave is the next order. . . . Well, for Grant and glory. So goodbye. Write soon. Tell Laura, I will answer her letter as soon as the fight is over if I do not get a furlough. Yours truly,

J. B. Yates

— *Chapter 17* —

". . . THE PLACE RECEIVED THE APPELLATION BLOODY BEND"

Spring, 1864 brought a new campaign season, and Grant brought his bulldog-like tenacity to the Eastern Theater, putting the Army of the Potomac in motion on May 4th. Longstreet, who returned from the west on April 20th, remarked that Grant would fight every day until the war was over. Disadvantaged by inadequate food and equipment, and told by the Confederate Congress that they had none to send, it seemed the Army of Northern Virginia would be forced into a defensive position. This accommodated Grant's plan perfectly, for he intended to concentrate his efforts on destroying Rebel forces in the field instead of capturing Virginia cities.

Rather than attack Lee in his camp on the south bank of the Rapidan, Grant planned to pressure Lee out of his strong entrenchments and force a fight on ground of Federal choosing or cause Lee to retreat south to Richmond, where he could be bottled-up by Butler's forces approaching from the south. To accomplish this, Grant needed to slip down river past Lee's flank then get through the Wilderness as quickly as possible. He moved Meade's Army of the Potomac, plus Burnside's Corps, to the Wilderness, where they camped on May 4th to let their wagons catch up.

From the Chancellorsville battle, both armies were familiar with the seventy square-mile area of briars, brambles and second-growth timber known as "The Wilderness." Lee saw the area as an ally. By attacking there, he could get the most from his army of 65,000 and mitigate the numerical advantage of Grant's 120,000. Facing another "do or die" situation, Lee held true to his tactical style and moved east-

ward to intercept Grant, Meade, and Burnside. None of the Union generals thought Lee could reach the Wilderness by May 5th. They were was mistaken.[1]

By the early morning hours of May 6th, Lee's troops had formed a six-mile-long line with Longstreet's Division on the right, Hill's Division (including the Sixteenth Mississippi of Harris's Brigade) in the center, and Ewell's on the left. Around two o'clock p.m., Harris's Brigade attacked and fought until dark, driving the Federals about two miles. Being far in front of the main line, they were ordered back to construct breastworks. Late in the afternoon, Union troops struck the right end of the Confederate line without success but not before wounding Longstreet.[2]

Stalemated at the Wilderness, Grant side-stepped south, only to have Lee head him off at Spotsylvania Court House. There the Sixteenth Mississippi encountered the Federal troops of Hancock and Burnside at a curve in the breastworks called the "Bloody Angle."[3]

☆ **James Johnson Kirkpatrick Diary**, May 5, 1864, Thursday:

Sermon by Reverend Walthall soon this morning. All packed up and ready to fall in. . . . Formed line and left camp at three p.m. The enemy have crossed down above Germanna Ford and fighting is in progress by Ewell's Corps. Longstreet is coming up from Gordonsville. . . .

☆ **James Johnson Kirkpatrick Diary**, May 6, 1864, Friday:

Fell in at two a.m. this morning, marched out to the Plank Road at Vidiersville, and proceeded thence down it towards the scene of yesterday's engagement. Marched slowly till daylight and then increased our speed to a rapid gate. . . . We commence passing scores of our wounded going to the rear. The battle was renewed by daylight. Longstreet's Corps was . . . forced back the enemy's dense hosts. I recognized a number of friends among the wounded belonging to Barksdale's Brigade.

The afternoon is occupied by us in maneuvering as support to different parts of the lines. The musketry along the line is exceedingly heavy and at times a well known cheer tells unmistakably who is getting the best of it. Very few pieces of artillery used, as the ground is not suited to bring it into action. Low and densely wooded. A little after noon, while we were lying on the Plank Road at leisure among the enemy's dead and wounded, the Minie balls began to play unmusically to our ears, and very soon objects in blue were discovered in the woods on our left. General Lee, happening to be present, at once ordered our brigade to front and forward. We did so, meeting but little opposition, and halted on our front line, filling a gap that had been made in it by the withdrawal of some Floridians and Alabamians. . . . The boys went to work immediately and put up hasty breastworks. In half an hour, we were attacked, and for an hour or two we were under very heavy musketry. The enemy were careful to keep at a distance and shoot. Our protection made it an easy matter to hold our line and the storm of balls sent in fury against us. . . . Company C had three wounded. At dark, the company remained on picket, and the brigade moved back a short distance. Relieved from picket at midnight. . . . Just before day, we moved back to the Plank Road.

☆ *Reminiscence of Buxton Reives Conerly*:

We entrenched ourselves in this position during the night. The ground in front of us was covered by the dead and wounded Yankees, and the pine straw and leaves caught from the exploding shells, and long lines of fire lighted the woods and burned over the dead and wounded. The flashes of the exploding cartridge boxes on the dead and wounded could be seen as the long sweep of flame went over them, and [we heard] the cries of the wounded for help, which could not come. . . . Our ambulance corps did what it could and rescued many from death, at the peril of their own lives. . . .

The following morning [May 7th] was a most sickening scene of dead human beings with their clothes burned off. . . .[4]

☆ *James Johnson Kirkpatrick Diary*, May 7, 1864, Saturday:

Moved to the left after day and took a new position on the line of battle. Made rifle pits. Day very warm. Musketry close on our right, but none in front. At dark, we moved a mile or so to the right and halted till day among putrefied corpses. Very disagreeable to our olfactories. . . .

☆ *The Veteran's Story*:

It was expected that the battle would be renewed the next day [the 7th], but Grant had enough of the Wilderness. He moved his column towards Richmond. . . .[5]

☆ *Historical Sketch of the Quitman Guards*:

Anderson's Corps proceeded to Spotsylvania during the night to confront the forces sent in that direction by Grant. The remaining portion of the Confederate army was stationed in the Wilderness. This movement left a space between the Wilderness and Spotsylvania Court House. The Federals . . . took immediate advantage of it by occupying the road. This was Sunday, the 8th of May. General Lee's whole army was moving to the right on a line parallel with Grant and came up with him at Shady Grove where [Grant] had taken possession of the road leading to Spotsylvania Court House. . . .

On the 9th, the army moved to Spotsylvania Court House. Lee's line was formed in front of the Court House facing north toward the River Po. The Confederates strongly fortified themselves and quietly awaited the attack.[6]

☆ *James Johnson Kirkpatrick Diary*, May 9, 1864, Monday:

Marched briskly this morning towards Spotsylvania Court House. . . . Suffered considerably for want of water. Arrived at the Court House at noon and formed line a short distance beyond it and made earthworks. Sun very hot and we are entirely exposed to it. Feel badly used up. About four p.m., we started back to the left on a forced march. The enemy are advancing a column . . . to cut off the road on which we came up this morning. Reached the [Po] River and took a position in front of the bridge a little before dark. Brisk skirmishing in front and artillery plays on us from almost every direction. The pickets keep up a lively interchange of shots across the stream all night. Several times a volley leaped from the darkness on the opposite side. A steep ridge, behind the summit of which our regiment lay, made us rest as sweetly as if miles away from the rude blasts of war. . . .

☆ *James Johnson Kirkpatrick Diary*, May 10, 1864, Tuesday:

The sun rises clear and hot. Sharpshooting renewed with more spirit in front and cannonading at intervals. Some of the enemy's guns nearly enfilade our position. . . . Heth's Division is moving up the river. At noon, we moved off to the right. . . . Made entrenchments in an open field in front of the enemy's batteries and sharpshooters. Received a few compliments but no damage. Very warm and fatiguing. Dire necessity alone would get us to labor. Between three and four p.m., Heth, having struck their flank, came sweeping down parallel to the river on the opposite side. Our batteries played across on the fugitive masses with beautiful effect, and many a one rested from his labors forevermore. As soon as the bridge was uncovered, our division crossed over to join in the rout but night came on ere we found an opposing force. . . .

☆ *Historical Sketch of the Quitman Guards*:

In the afternoon [of May 10th] Grant brought a force to bear on Lee's left. He succeeded in placing a few guns in position and began to enfilade the Confederate line. Hill's Corps was on the left and was commanded by Major General Early who moved Heth's Division to the left and across the River Po so as to confront the Federals and at the same time flanked them with a heavy line of skirmishers. The Federals had fortified themselves, but being attacked in the front and flanked simultaneously, they were compelled to yield to their determined assailants. . . .[7]

☆ *Reminiscence of Buxton Reives Conerly [continued]*:

We arrived . . . on the 10th and were moved to about one mile west of town [Spotsylvania Court House] . . . as a support of troops in front of us. Some desperate charges were made by the Federals, and for some time the outcome seemed to hang in the balance. Our brigade courier . . . said, "General Early will fix them." We were immediately ordered across the river, and as we climbed the hill on the opposite side, the Federals quickly abandoned the ground and left pieces of artillery with spokes of the wheels cut out. This artillery had been annoying us for some time, and our troops swept forward in a magnificent line, meeting with but little resistance.[8]

☆ *Historical Sketch of the Quitman Guards*:

On the night of the 11th, General Grant massed a heavy force on the center in front of the division commanded by Major General Edward Johnson. They moved very quietly under protection of a hill and succeeded in gaining a point about thirty yards distant from the Confederate breastworks. At this place, the lines swung around so as to assume the shape of a horse shoe and from the desperate fighting there, this place received the appellation of "Bloody Bend."[9]

☆ General Nathaniel H. Harris to Colonel Charles S. Venerable:

On the morning of the 12th of May 1864, my brigade . . . was halted on the Court House Road near Spotsylvania Court House; in a half hour, General Lee in person ordered the brigade . . . to an attention, put it on the march . . . and moved in the direction of the salient . . . then moving at the quick-step, we were soon under a heavy artillery fire from the batteries of the enemy in front and on our right; that whilst thus advancing . . . a twelve pound (ricochet) shot passed just in front of General Lee, so near as to excite his horse very much, causing him to rear and plunge in such a manner as would have unseated a less accomplished horseman. The men . . . earnestly urged him to go back, and one or two of them caught hold of the bridle of his horse and turned the animal around. General Lee then spoke to the men and told them that if they would drive the enemy from the captured works, he would go back. The men responded with a hearty "we will!" . . . Almost a similar scene occurred on the 6th of May, 1864 in the Wilderness between General Lee and Gregg's Texas Brigade. . . .[10]

☆ Historical Sketch of the Quitman Guards:

General Grant, taking advantage of a thick fog on the morning of the 12th, charged the Confederate lines. There was not sufficient time for the firing of but one volley before the Federals were in the trenches in overwhelming numbers, capturing General Edward Johnson with about twenty-five hundred of his men. . . .

Harris' Brigade, with McGowan's South Carolina Brigade . . . were chosen to retake the works so captured by the Federals from Johnson's Division. The Sixteenth Mississippi Regiment was in advance of the brigade and . . . marched by the flank within a very short distance of the Federals and received a murderous fire. Fortunately, there was a row of breastworks near by sufficiently large to protect the brigade until it could form properly to make the charge. General Harris stood on top of these works exposed to a shower of bullets in order to ascertain the point of attack with as much exactness as the dense fog would permit and then ordered his men forward. Apprehending the desperate and bloody character of the prospective charge, the men at first hesitated, but seeing their colors moving forward borne by . . . Alexander Mixon, whose clarion-like voice resounded along the line urging the men to follow, they hesitated no longer, but rushed forward through a storm of bullets and were in a short time in possession of the trenches.[11]

☆ Report Number 294. Report of Brigadier General Nathaniel H. Harris:

On the morning of May 12th, I received orders to move by the right flank and at a double-quick across the Po River in the direction of Spotsylvania Court House. Halting near the Court House for a few minutes, orders were received from General Lee . . . to move by the flank on a road leading in the direction of the works lost by the division of General Edward Johnson. The command was soon under a galling fire of grape and cannister from the enemy's batteries, through which the men moved at a double-quick. . . .

Arriving near the lost works, Major General Rodes informed me that my command was expected to form on the right of Ramseur's Brigade . . . and recapture the works. General Rodes gave me as a guide a staff officer . . . I moved by the right flank on a road, which I afterward discovered ran at right angles with the line of works, and was soon exposed to a heavy musketry and artillery fire. At this point, the staff officer . . . deserted me in the most shameful and disgraceful manner, and I was thus left in total ignorance of our own lines as well as those of the enemy and was unable to discover anything in the smoke and fog. . . .[12]

At this moment, a gallant private of the Tenth Alabama Regiment . . . informed me of the position of Ramseur's right and of the enemy. Having advanced thus far by the right flank, when I should have advanced by the line of battle with my left resting on the road mentioned, no alternative remained but to file my command rapidly to the right and try to gain sufficient distance for my left to rest on said road. Moving with this view, the two right regiments had filed out of the road and were moving by the flank parallel to the line of lost works, when the enemy . . . opened a most terrific fire of musketry and artillery; and finding that I could move no farther to the right . . . I at once ordered the two right regiments . . . to charge up the works, and drive the enemy from them, which they did. . . .

In the meantime . . . the two regiments formed in line and, wheeling to the right, pressed up to the works and joined the left of the two right regiments, a portion of the extreme left regiment overlapping Ramseur's right. The whole command afterward gained sufficient front by moving to the right and driving the enemy from the works as they moved, but my force was not sufficient to regain the entire line, and a small portion was left in the occupancy of the enemy, from which was poured a destructive enfilade fire and this, in connection with the repeated assaults in front, had it not been for some traverses would have rendered the position untenable, one-third of my command being already killed or wounded.

At 11 a.m., McGowan's Brigade . . . arrived on the field for the purpose of recovering the works on my right, but . . . gained no ground to the right but halted in rear of my left and Ramseur's right. General McGowan being wounded soon after arriving on the field and unable to find his successor in command, I could make no arrangement by which that brigade could be moved to my right and press the enemy from the works. In this state and position, this command remained until three-thirty a.m. May 13th, repulsing desperate and repeated efforts of the enemy to dislodge them. . . .

Thus, from seven a.m. of the 12th to three-thirty a.m. on May 13th (twenty hours), my men were exposed to a constant and destructive fire, both front and flank, and during the hours of day to a heavy artillery fire in which mortars were used by the enemy for the first time during the campaign. A cold drenching rain fell during the greater portion of the day and night, and the trenches were filled with water.

Great difficulty was experienced in procuring supplies of ammunition, man after man being shot down while bringing it in. And here I cannot refrain from mentioning the gallant conduct of Courier A. W. Hancock and Private F. Dolan of the Forty-eighth Mississippi, who repeatedly brought in ammunition under this dreadful fire. As an instance of the terrible nature of the fire, trees twenty-two inches in diameter were hewn to splinters and felled by the musketry.[13]

☆ *James Johnson Kirkpatrick Diary*, May 12, 1864, Thursday:

Marched at day to Spotsylvania Court House. Halted on the roadside and began making protection against the numerous shells that were traversing the air. Got orders again very soon to face about and march to the left where musketry and artillery were rolling in beautiful sublimity. The enemy, under cover of a dense fog this morning, had found their masses over an angle of our works and captured a portion of Johnson's Division. To check these masses and recover the lost line was the duty assigned to our brigade. The enemy seems to have concentrated their whole urging of war at this point. Shell of every kind and shape from mortars and field pieces raked the approaches of reinforcements, while a forest of muskets played with awful fury over the ground itself. We advanced by the flank till at a close distance, then fired at right angles to the right, the brigade's length fronted and charged. All the lost line which our brigade covered was captured, but still a portion of the angle on our right remained in the enemy's hands, from which all day they passed on our flank a most galling fire. The fighting was terribly severe and against tremendous odds, but we maintained the position all day. . . .

Company C lost nine killed and eight wounded. . . . The casualties among the enemy must have been heavy, but we did not ascertain them. The heavy fog in the morning and the dense sulphurous smoke that settled down over the field rendered it impossible to note the effect of our volleys. The timber in our rear was almost devoid of limbs and bark, and one oak at our works nearly two feet in diameter was cut down by Minie balls. The day was showery, and our persons and faces became badly begrimed. We retired in the morning at three a.m. under a severe fire of musketry, which was kept up unremittingly through the night. . . .

☆ Historical Sketch of the Quitman Guards:

McGowan's South Carolinians were to take the works on the right, but having mistaken their course and being prevented by the dense fog from perceiving that Harris's Brigade had possession of the trenches, they fired into that brigade and moved up to the same point occupied by it, thus leaving the works on the right still in possession of the Federals. The Federals now fell back to the brow of the hill. . . . Charge after charge was made by the Federals. . . . Notwithstanding these desperate charges and the enfilading fire to which the Confederates were exposed, the [Sixteenth] held their own . . . for twenty hours. A continuous shower of rain fell during the time and the ditches were filled with water reddened with the blood . . . of the slain and wounded. Dead men literally covered the ground. . . .[14]

☆ Reminiscence of Buxton Reives Conerly [continued]:

About dawn the next morning [May 12th], we were aroused by the sound of cannon and musketry away to our right. Soon afterwards, we received orders to move and left the ditches, taking the road . . . to Spotsylvania Court House. We halted a short distance from the town, where the road went through an abandoned field. Looking northward, the grassy field sloped up to the crest of the ridge bristling artillery. While we were standing in line, solid shots and shells from the enemy's batteries were striking the top of the hill and came bouncing down the slope over our heads, coming just often enough to make us feel uneasy. . . .

We were ordered to move by the left flank, which placed the Sixteenth Mississippi in the lead, followed by the Twelfth, Nineteenth, and Forty-eighth Mississippi in succession. We took a narrow road which led by the left of the artillery in our front.

The Federal troops . . . had broken the Confederate line early in the morning, and under cover of a heavy fog just at the dawn of day, rushed upon the division under General Edward Johnson and captured him with about three thousand men. . . . This was the firing which aroused us from our position on the left early in the morning and to which we were now marching at double-quick.

We soon left the narrow road and crossed a freshly plowed field, made soft by the recent rain, and soon came to harder ground and where we crossed at right angles the Old Stonewall Brigade lying on the ground. The writer heard one of them say, "Boys, you are going to catch hell today. . . ."

The ground over which we were marching was strewn with the dead of both armies, showing that the Federals must have advanced some distance beyond the trenches and then been forced back and also that they were forced to shelter themselves on the reverse side of the captured trenches. A heavy fog and the smoke from the guns, screened our advance. Company K, being the leading company of the Sixteenth Mississippi, almost reached the enemy's position before they discovered us. They soon poured a murderous fire into our column and our men fell dead fast and thick. Archie Robertson, with whom I had only a short while back traded shoes, fell dead in front of me. Some skirmish pits furnished only temporary shelter. In this storm of shot, with the men falling on every side, General Harris rushed up and ordered the Twelfth and Sixteenth to wheel to the right and drive the enemy from the trenches. The Nineteenth and Forty-eighth Mississippi were turned in the same way. Our men rushed forward with cheers, following their flags which were planted in quick succession on the trenched works. . . . Our colonel, Samuel Baker, fell a few feet from me. His body, being in an exposed position, was riddled with rifle balls.

Lieutenant Colonel Feltus fell soon afterwards. I saw a man fall dead in the arms of General Harris. This brave and good man, in this hail of death, laid him gently on the ground with the exclamation, "Oh, my poor fellow!"[15]

Hundreds of the Federals threw down their guns and surrendered, while a triumphant yell rang out over the Confederate lines. The prisoners were ordered to the rear, numbers of whom fell dead from the shots of their own men, who were rushing on us with loud "huzzahs." Many of the Federal prisoners begged us to let them stay with us, as it seemed certain death to go to the rear. The line of works . . . was in a semi-circle, and the men, to protect themselves from enfilading fire of the enemy, were in traverses (little short works built of poles and earth at right angles to the main line). These traverses were from thirty to forty feet apart.

In carrying this position, our brigade joined General Ramseur's right. His brigade held that part of the line where we came in, and our left overlapped his right. Our line was not long enough to capture the whole line, and the Federal troops still occupied the trenches on our right. The guns which General Johnson's men used were left in the trenches, and the Federals threw down theirs on the same ground. When we recaptured this position, we gathered together quickly the guns found with the dead both in our front and rear, and with these guns loaded, we had practically the advantage of repeating rifles.

On the right, where the enemy was still in our trenches, the fighting was close and deadly, while the charges made on us in front came to hand to hand conflicts in spite of our rapid firing of so many guns. The enfilading fire from our right, where the men were fighting across the traverses, would have made our position untenable had not the traverses protected us. There was an incessant stream of rifle balls passing over us, as well as hundreds of exploding shells. The rain poured down upon us in torrents, and the ditches were filled with water reddened by the blood which flowed from the dead and wounded. We were forced to sit or stand on the bodies of the dead, covered with water. At this stage of the fighting, General McGowan's Brigade of South Carolinians . . . with their men falling thick and fast at every step, their cheers mingled with the roar of musketry (the heaviest heard during the war), cannon and bursting shells, over the dead bodies of hundreds who had fallen, rushed to our aid with the left of their brigade overlapping the right of ours, doubling our lines at this place, and drove the enemy out of the trenches, capturing a number of prisoners. The Federal troops now seemed to have renewed their efforts and made desperate charges. Hand to hand encounters occurred all during the day. The cold drenching rain continued. The flashing lightning, the bursting of shells, the tremendous and incessant roar of small arms, and the yell of the soldiers presented a scene indescribable in its terrible horror.

During the day, our ammunition ran short, and General Harris called for volunteers to go to the rear and inform General Ewell. Several men started to go, but none went far before they fell dead. Holden Pearson of our Company E, seeing these men fall, told General Harris he would go. The general gave his reluctant consent but looked as if he should never see him alive again. Keeping himself covered behind the trenches and moving rapidly from traverse to the left, he got to a point where he could leave the line in a depression in the rear. He arrived safely at General Ewell's headquarters on the field and informed him of the situation. He told General Ewell how to get the ammunition to us through the depression and soon, passing down the line from man to man, came a stream of cartridges tied up in pieces of tent cloth. . . .[16]

☆ *The New Orleans Times-Democrat, "The Death Angle":*

It was the early morning of the 12th of May, 1864. A heavy rain had fallen all night and Harris' Mississippi Brigade, without tent or any other protection whatever, had slept on the side of the road in the mud. The boys were just beginning to stir and occasionally could be seen a little column of smoke where some soldiers . . . was cooking their morning meal of corn mush. Just as it became light enough to see fairly well, we heard the galloping of a horse down the big road and directly there came in sight a courier, pushing his horse to its utmost.

"I am certain," said one of the boys, "that some kind of accident has occurred because I waked up shortly before morning, and I distinctly heard firing off somewhere toward our right."

By that time, the courier had arrived where we were and exclaimed in an excited way, "Where is General Harris?"

Word was passed up the line and General Harris, who was not far off (having slept on the ground in the mud like the men) said, "Here I am." The courier rode up to him rapidly and handed him a dispatch. General Harris glanced at it quickly, turned around and said, "Attention. Fall in line."

Word was passed to the right and to the left, and within ten minutes the cans of mush on the fire were snatched up, guns and accouterments were buckled on, and Harris' Mississippi Brigade was ready for the march. Five minutes more and we were going down the slushy road at a double-quick. We moved along rapidly for about four miles and then came within sound of musketry. . . .

Pretty soon we came upon some wounded men being carried out. Then we learned that Johnson's Brigade, which had occupied the angle, had been attacked . . . and the Confederate line broken. We soon turned out into a small cut road . . . and by that time the artillery fire had commenced, and shells were whizzing over our heads from the Confederate batteries on the right and Federal batteries on the left, and we were right between the artillery duel. We were halted under fire, and . . . every man lay flat on the ground. It was then General Lee came riding up accompanied by his staff and as he struck the head of our brigade, a shell passed over his body of regular attendants. . . . We saw he was going to speak. Stretching out his hand, [he said], "Men of Harris' Brigade. On you today depends the fate of the Army of Northern Virginia . . . and we must retake the works. I myself will lead the charge."

The soldiers gave a yell. Right at the head of General Lee's horse stood [a soldier], his gun strapped across his back. With his left hand he grabbed the bridle of General Lee's horse, and with his right, he waved his cap and said, "General, your life is of more value than all of ours. . . . Can't you trust us?"

General Lee said, "Yes, I trust you. Go and God be with you."

General Harris gave the command, "Forward. Forward!" Word was passed rapidly, and in a few minutes Harris' Brigade swung over the hill through the mud and the falling rain in a determined charge. We pressed forward . . . and as we came up through a field to a strip of woods, a tremendous volley was fired at us. Nine men in Company C, which was the extreme left of the regiment, fell. There was almost equal fatality throughout the entire Sixteenth Mississippi. Seven men were killed in Company K, but with the words of General Lee ringing in our ears, we gave a yell and rushed right at the enemy. They attempted to stand at the breastworks, but our fire was so deadly and our charge so determined that they fell back, and we took the position.

We had hardly time to throw the dead from the ditch and lay the wounded in the back of the ditch when with a "huzzah," the enemy charged to retake the works. The breastworks were slippery and the ditch was over ankle deep in mud. With courage, the Federal soldiers clambered up the slippery embankment, only to meet death from the guns and bayonets of the Confederates. The Federal line seemed to evaporate.

It was only a short distance from the breastworks to the decline of the hill, and under that cover, the Federal line was reformed. By the time we had succeeded in loading our guns and the guns of our fallen comrades, they were back at us again.

The battle flag of the Sixteenth Mississippi was right in the angle of the salient. The enemy clambered up the embankment and planted the United States flag and the flag of New York right on top of the embankment, but the man that held the Confederate flag did not move an inch. The Federal and Confederate flags flapped together, but not a man was left living around the Federal battle flag, and the Confederates pushed over the dead. Eight times the Federals picked up their flags and endeavored to place them on the top of the breastworks, and eight times the determined men were killed, and the . . . Confederate flag was in the hands of the third man who had borne that day, and he was wounded in the arm.

The Federal line fell back over the hill, and we had a moment's time to load all of the guns of fallen comrades and of the Federals and to throw the dead and wounded out of the ditch. In another desperate charge, many of the Federals rushed over the breastworks and down in the ditch among us, and there was hand-to-hand fighting. Major Councill ordered the men to fall back on the right and left and let the enemy have the [traverse]. We fell back, and they poured into the vacant space only to receive certain death. Then Major Councill ordered the men to take their places. From the right and from the left, we came back to the [traverse]. By this time, the blood had become so profuse that tramping back and forth in it, we were smeared with human blood from our faces to our feet.

The flag of the regiment had been shot completely off its staff, and one of the men picked up a limb from a white oak tree, which had been cut off by bullets, fastened the flag to it and held it up again in its original position in the salient. Then someone asked, "Where is Colonel Baker?" He was near by, lying under an oak tree a little in the rear of the breastworks, shot through the heart. "Where is Lieutenant Colonel Feltus?" He was by the side of Baker, shot through the heart also. Major Councill, who had been third in command . . . was now colonel of the regiment. He was wounded.

The enemy now adopted different tactics. A line of battle moved up over the brow of the hill and lay down upon the ground in front, not more than fifty yards off and opened up a terrific fire. Just behind the ranks of the Sixteenth Mississippi Regiment was a white oak tree about two feet in diameter, solid within and vigorous. The bullets of the Federals . . . struck the tree, and we saw that it was only a question of time when the tree would be cut down by bullets. . . . We soon saw that the limbs were being cut off in the front and that the weight of the branches in the rear would draw the tree from the breastworks. It slowly swayed and finally came down.

We had by this time lost nearly half of our men. Each soldier was shooting from seven to ten guns. Ammunition was passed up from hand to hand from the left, and there was no lack of ammunition among the Confederates. Then there came a singular lull in the fighting. Both sides commenced to cheer. The loud defiant huzzahs of the Federals and the weird yell of the Confederates rang through the battle smoke. Many of us climbed to the top of the embankment to look out over the scene. . . . In some places, the dead were in heaps, but the sight was nothing in comparison to the sound. The groans and moans of wounded men under dead men, the piteous cries for water, the feeble prayers of the wounded and dying—or at times the curses—made a pandemonium of terror.

An officer, evidently a captain from the Federal side, ran forward near the breastworks, waved his cap in the air and said, "Confederates, you made a gallant defense, but it is useless. Surrender."

The boys commenced to holler, "Come in, come in."

The officer said, "Are you going to surrender?"

Many voices cried, "No! Never!"

"If you will not surrender," [the Union officer said], "neither will I." He waved his cap in the air and turned to go, then a shot from the Confederate side crashed through his brain, and he was so close we could see the hair fly.

The Confederates scrambled into the ditch just in time to save themselves from a volley, and the Federal line charged again. There was a terrific struggle. A second line came up to the assistance of the first, and it seemed for a time that we would be overpowered, but so deadly was the fire from the Confederate side, so close the range, that with the advantage of being behind the embankment, we saw the gallant Federal line melt away.

The soldier who had killed the officer was asked why he had shot so gallant a man, and he replied that the officer would surely have reported how weak our force was, which would inspire his men with fresh determination to take the works.

A couple of bull bats sailed around over us, and their cries had been distinctly heard above the volleys of musketry. Night came on without cessation in the firing, but the charges of the enemy grew less frequent and less desperate. The soldiers were so weary that a man would shoot his guns, load them all, throw himself in the bloody mud and sleep for a few minutes in all the din and horror of the battle. Our suffering was terrific, not a mouthful of food, nor a drop of water had we had since early in the morning. In fact, no one thought of food.

A soldier from the Twelfth Mississippi came up from the left to see how we were faring. He sat down on the edge of the ditch to talk to the boys when a bullet struck him in the head. He sank to the ground, and we could plainly see the brains and blood ooze out of the wound. We thought he was dead, but he put his hand in his pocket, took out his handkerchief and wiped his forehead. Then he put his hand in his pocket again and took out a piece of tobacco and died attempting to take a chew of it. . . .[17]

☆ *Historical Sketch of the Quitman Guards*:

The casualties of the Sixteenth Mississippi Regiment were heavier in this than any other previous battle. Company F lost twelve men killed [including J. B. Crawford]. . . .[18]

☆ *Report Number 294. Report of Brigadier General Nathaniel H. Harris [continued]*:

At two a.m. on May 13th, I received orders . . . to withdraw my command and the brigade of McGowan as soon as the troops on my right and left had evacuated their positions, and at three-thirty a.m. . . . I withdrew. . . .[19]

☆ *Reminiscence of Buxton Reives Conerly [continued]*:

About daylight [May 13th] we withdrew from our position . . . with blackened faces and crisped hands from being in the water so long. Our clothing stained with red mud and blood, we marched out of this place where more than one-third of our men lay dead. . . . We stopped in a grove of trees where General Harris told us to build a fire and dry our clothes. Our men stood around in groups, inquiring of each other about their missing comrades—some in tears at the loss of a brother or near relative. Our colonel and lieutenant colonel both being killed, Major Councill became colonel of the Sixteenth Mississippi. . . . The loss in our command had exceeded that of any previous battle.[20]

☆ *James Johnson Kirkpatrick Diary*, May 13, 1864, Friday:

Remained here all day. Got some rations, washed our powder stained faces, discharged and cleaned up our guns and slept. Showery through the day. Got marching orders at dark. . . . We marched back to our old position and enjoyed one night's rest again.

☆ *James Johnson Kirkpatrick Diary*, May 14, 1864, Saturday:

Received marching orders in afternoon . . . and our brigade moved out to the front through our line and struck the enemy's left wing. . . . Advanced to the creek and held it till nearly dark, then fell back under orders. The enemy came charging over after we left, very noisy and no doubt highly elated at successfully gaining some ground that had been abandoned. The brigade moved back and took a position in the extreme right of our line. Dug rifle pits tonight. Some more rain.

☆ *James Johnson Kirkpatrick Diary*, May 18, 1864, Wednesday:

Slept but little tonight. Up at three o'clock. Rapid cannonading soon after sunrise on our left. The enemy made an assault on a portion of our lines but were easily repulsed. From statements of prisoners, General Grant has made a call for eight thousand volunteers to make a charge on our line. They say that they feel badly whipped. Our artillery fired at intervals today.

☆ *James Johnson Kirkpatrick Diary*, May 20, 1864, Friday:

Warm and clear. Unusually quiet on the lines. . . . Fighting has become an every day business. . . .

— *Chapter 18* —

"... A MAN CANNOT BE TOO GOOD TO DIE FOR HIS HOME, HIS COUNTRY"

Grant continued his southeast movement following Spotsylvania. Lee, with about 55,000 remaining troops, moved parallel to Grant and headed for the North Anna River to check him. Lee reached the river first, where the Federals attacked near Hanover Junction on May 23rd. After sustaining heavy losses at Ox Ford on May 24th, Grant abandoned his position and continued southeast on the 27th.

Correctly guessing that Grant would next move against the railroads near Richmond, Lee took a defensive position along Totopotomoy Creek on May 29th. The armies skirmished there three days, until both sides learned of fighting at Cold Harbor and both hurried to the important railroad crossroads ten miles northeast of Richmond. Arriving by June 2nd, Lee spent the entire day building fortifications for the attack he knew would come the next day. On June 3rd, Grant ordered a series of frontal assaults against the Confederates. It was an order Grant would regret the rest of his life, for within the first hour of the battle (perhaps as little as thirty minutes), he lost approximately seven thousand men.

The Sixteenth Mississippi, a part of Mahone's Division of A. P. Hill's Corps posted on the southern end of the battlefield between Breckinridge's and Wilcox's Divisions, helped support the Confederate right flank. Though they missed most of

the hard fighting at Cold Harbor, following the battle they endured skirmishes and
sharpshooters almost all the way to Petersburg.[1]

☆ *James Johnson Kirkpatrick Diary*, May 22, 1864, Sunday:

Rested an hour or two this morning and again resumed the march. Kept on
briskly all day, crossing the North Anna [River], encamping a few miles on the
other side. Day very warm. I suffered severely today, and it was with great difficulty that I could travel. Had it not been through fear of being captured by the
enemy's cavalry, I would have stopped. Slept in the woods just after crossing
the river, being unable to reach my command. Had a high fever and was delir-
ious.

☆ *James Johnson Kirkpatrick Diary*, May 23, 1864, Monday:

Arose today at dawn and made out to reach the brigade in camp. They
started soon after and I was, for the first time, so highly privileged as to ride in
an ambulance. Accompanied the brigade to Hanover Junction and was placed
in a field hospital. Remained here till next day, but received no medical attention. The brigade filed off to the left here, and in line about three miles distant. Fighting in progress at places along the line.

☆ *Historical Sketch of the Quitman Guards*:

On the 24th, the Confederate army moved back about a mile to prepare for
the advance of the enemy, who had crossed the [North] Anna River. The Federals began to advance in the afternoon and were met by skirmishers from Harris' Brigade and two regiments from an Alabama brigade. The Federals were
driven back, losing a considerable number in killed, wounded and prisoners.
The army then moved and took position on the Chickahominy River, being
nearly the same occupied by it during the Seven Day' Battle before Richmond.[2]

☆ *Jerome B. Yates to Marie Yates Swanson*:
Hanover Junction, Virginia, May 26th, 1864

Dear Marie,
Yours of 2 May came duly to hand and was received by me with pleasure. I
am glad to hear you and Ma are well. . . .

We are in line of battle, two miles from Hanover Junction, which is twenty-two miles from Richmond. . . . Em Lee was killed on the 24th in a skirmish. Em was a good soldier and a noble boy. Em would have made a good and useful citizen. He was buried of the 25th and the place marked with a board. Poor boy. I hope his soul rests in a better world. Sam and John Baskins were both killed. What a blow to their mother. Sam was her chief dependence. I am truly sorry for her, poor woman, though she is not the only one who has suffered by this cruel war. Fayette Kelly was killed on the 12th of May. Willie Gibbs from Raymond is supposed to be dead. George Nixon is either killed or captured. I hope they both may only be captured.[3]

Well, Marie, I must write you something about Bud to prevent a mistake. I wrote Ma that we did not get to bury Bud. We had not the chance when I wrote, but the next day the enemy abandoned that part of the field and a detail was sent back to re-bury our men. The enemy had buried them. Bud was taken up . . . some distance from the place and discreetly buried and the spot marked. I got his Testament, a lock of his hair and the buckle that Miss Kate White put on [his belt] when he was on furlough. Poor Bud, if any man deserved to live through this war it was him. He was such a noble and generous boy. He was loved by anyone who knew him. How I do sympathize with his mother and sisters. I hope God will give them strength to stand the sad blow. When Bud was killed, I lost the best friend I ever had. Nothing was too good for me from him. He would make any sacrifice for me. I loved him like a brother. Bud was a pious and good boy. I do not doubt that he has gone to the better world that is promised us all who walk in the straight and narrow path. God grant he has gone to that haven of rest where no wars nor troubles come. Marie, my letter is getting too sad. I must stop.

I envy you and Ma your good watermelons. This summer you all must think of me when you are enjoying them. I will close. You must give my respects to all inquiring female friends. I do not care about sending my respect to men who will stay at home such times as these. I will close. Goodbye, write soon to your affectionate brother,

J. B. Y.

☆ *The Veteran's Story*:

Grant assaulted our lines with his heavy columns. From the first to the twelfth of June, they were handsomely repulsed with heavy loss. Our loss was small. It was here that Grant decided to fight it out if it took all summer. He drew his army back from our front and tried to beat us to Petersburg.[4]

☆ Historical Sketch of the Quitman Guards:

On the 3rd of June, a considerable battle was fought at Cold Harbor (the scene of a great battle in the same month nearly two years before) which resulted in the repulse of the Federals.[5]

☆ Letter of General N. H. Harris to General William H. Mahone:

On the 4th and 5th [of June], skirmishing and cannonading was continuous.[6]

☆ Historical Sketch of the Quitman Guards:

On the 6th of June, the Quitman Guards lost one man, J. D. Stanford, killed in a skirmish charge at Turkey Ridge near the Chickahominy River.[7]

☆ James Johnson Kirkpatrick Diary, June 7, 1864, Tuesday:

The enemy are reported moving, has uncovered our left and center.

☆ Memorandum Book of Elijah Slay, Captain, Company C, June 8, 1864, Wednesday:

Let me die upon the field of battle in the front rank for an example to those whose duty it is to free the South from the iron hand of tyranny. What care I though my name never be put in print or my country never know I shed my blood for her freedom. What a worthless man is he who only acts to be seen of men! God sees and understands the honest heart.[8]

☆ John S. Lewis and Fletcher Lewis to Mrs. Nancy Lewis:
June 10th, 1864

My Very Dear Mother,
I would to God that Harry's pencil and not mine could write to you today.

Almighty God has willed it otherwise, and I hope and believe that you have trusted in Him for so many years will not feel yourself abandoned and forsaken in this great hour of sorrow. Our Harry died at eight o'clock yesterday morning, and I write to you now sitting by his body. We are at Major Hearsey's quarters and will bury him today, intending, if any of us are spared, to remove his remains to our graveyard when the war is over.

He was killed instantly and suffered no pain and is now where he will never suffer pain. How much consolation this is to me, I cannot express. This, with the remembrance of the cause he sacrificed his young manhood for, fills up to me much of his loss. For remember, he died that we might live free men and that the lives of our dear ones at home might be passed free from insult and oppression. The offering, my Mother, is great. Why should the best in every respect be taken? He was a thousand times more worthy to live than I. God was even here merciful, he was the best prepared to meet Him.

I will try to get Fletch to write some. I have refrained from writing during these fights, fearing something might happen.

The grand battle for Richmond is yet to come off. I hope for your sake, we will come out of it. Whatever may happen, Mother, do not forget that if all your sons are taken—many mothers have suffered the same, and a man cannot be too good to die for his home, his country.

I hope to write again soon and hope to assure you when I do that Grant is beaten, and the worst of our trials are over. Ever your son,

John

☆ Dearest Mother,

Bud has taken upon himself the painful duty of breaking the news of Harry's death to you, and it only remains for me to add my few lines to his of consolation. Harry died as a soldier and (most of all) a Christian, as I should like to die if the Almighty should see fit to take me from you. I never knew or had any idea of what an amount of consolation it is to one who has had the misfortune of losing one very dear to him to know that although he has been cut off in a bright and promising life, yet he is gone where the sorrow of an earthly life will never reach him, and there we all must in a few days (it may be a few days, Mother) follow him.

It is my most earnest wish that we may all be as ready to attend that awful summons as he was, for he was one of the few whom the temptations and the privations of the camp life here rendered a pious Christian and more devoted to his Bible and religious duties than ever he was before being enlisted as a soldier. He had no enemies, and his loss will be deeply felt both as an officer and as a companion. If he had been spared, no doubt he would have been a "bright light" and would have accomplished much good. But as he has been snatched from us, let us not question the justice of God but bear our affliction patiently. . . .

I suppose Bud has told you what he intends to do with the body, send it home if he can procure a metal coffin. If not, he will be interred in some safe spot near Richmond to be removed as soon as a good opportunity presents itself.

I will write soon again but must close for the present. Your son,

Fletch

☆ *James Johnson Kirkpatrick Diary*, June 11,1864, Saturday:

The weather continues warm by day and cool by night. Heard the unwelcome news that Captain Slay was killed yesterday by a sharpshooter. No officer now left with Company C.

☆ *Reminiscence of Sergeant George Bryant Ford, Company* C:

Captain Slay was killed on picket skirmish line at Turkey Creek, and when he was brought out, General Mahone shed tears and said, "My best man is gone."[9]

☆ *Jerome B. Yates to Mrs. Obedience Yates and Marie Yates Swanson*:
Richmond, Virginia, June 11th, 1864

Dear Ma and Marie,

Having time when on picket, I will drop you a few lines. I am still safe through this bloody strife. The two armies are facing each other. In some places, the pickets are only twenty or thirty paces apart. When I am on picket today, we are one hundred fifty yards from each other. It is pretty warm, no shade. We have to take our water with us in the morning to last all day. We can not leave our ditches during the day. Everything begins to assume the appearance of a siege. . . . Grant is thunder to dig but not better than Bob Lee. We are still hopeful and confident. . . .

We had a flag of truce on the 8th of June for two hours for Grant to bury his dead. That was in front of our lines. It was a novel scene to see our boys and the Yankees mixing up and talking together on friendly terms. The boys traded tobacco for coffee. I threw an old dirty Yank a piece of tobacco, and he threw me a little sack of coffee. . . .

Speaking of coffee makes me mention our rations. We are drawing splendid rations at present. We draw the following articles, coffee, sugar, one-half pound bacon, one and one-eighth pound flour, and onions. Pretty good, what think you? Every time the boys get anything extra they say Mrs. Jeff Davis gives it to them. Mrs. Bob Lee gave all the men in this brigade one pair socks a piece last winter of her own manufacturing. Pretty good for Madam Lee and her nine daughters. Did you ever hear of such big bugs having so many children? We used to say, "a fool for luck and a poor man for children."

I wish the time would come when we could sit on the gallery and eat peaches and laugh. . . . But the happy times will come someday when we will end this war and all be at home once more. "God speed the day," as the old man would say. How is the crops? Fine I hope. You must write me every particular of the crops, how high the cotton and corn is, where it is the largest, how fat the plow horses and how the cows look, how much milk you get, how the herd looks, hens look, colts look, how many chickens you have. Such things interest me. . . .

So Joe Murphy has killed John Watson. No more than I expected. It did not surprise me in the least. One more mean man gone from this world. . . .

You must all write often and long letters. Remember home matters and general news afterwards. Your son,

Jerome Yates

☆ *Letter of General N. H. Harris to General William H. Mahone:*

From the 8th to the 12th [of June], there was a continuous fire of sharpshooters and artillery and mortar firing, entailing on us a loss of ten or fifteen men a day. . . .

On the morning of the 13th, the enemy were found to have disappeared from our front and, being followed by our skirmishers a short distance, a number were captured. . . . The same day [Harris' Brigade, including the Sixteenth

Mississippi] crossed the Chickahominy and commenced moving toward Malvern Hill. . . .

On the 14th and 15th, we were in line of battle and fortifying near Riddle's
Shop on the Charles City Road. The enemy not advancing in this direction,
we received orders on the 16th to move to Camp Holly on New Market
Heights and encamped. Here we remained until June 18th, the men enjoying
a good rest and having an opportunity to wash for the first time since the
beginning of the campaign.[10]

— *Chapter 19* —

"MINING AND BLOWING UP
IS ALL THE TALK . . ."

On June 13th, Lee's skirmish line learned that Grant had moved the majority of his army from Cold Harbor on the 12th. Having predicted that Grant would cross the James River, which he did on June 14th, and attack Petersburg, Lee left with most of the Army of Northern Virginia (consisting now of only of Anderson's First and Hill's Third Corps) and moved south toward Petersburg. The Sixteenth Mississippi and the rest of Harris's Brigade followed on June 18th.

Petersburg, twenty-three miles south of Richmond and on the south side of the Appomattox River, was an important transportation center for the South. Five major railroads converged there, connecting the city to river ports, the ports of Chesapeake Bay and the Atlantic Ocean, and the lower South. When Grant was unable to take it by direct assault, he ordered his men to entrench east of the city, repeating the tactic that conquered Vicksburg. Thus began a 292-day siege, the most lengthy military undertaking mounted against an American city. More battles would be waged and more lives lost in connection with this siege than at Richmond, Atlanta, or Vicksburg.[1]

Leaving their camp near New Market Heights, the Sixteenth crossed the James River near Chafin's Farm and after a hot dusty march, reached the Petersburg fortifications at 2:30 a.m. on June 18th. They remained in the trenches for the next five months (except for occasional expeditions to check Federal raiders and advances), *daily exposed to cannon fire and sharpshooters, "losing more or less men every day."*[2]

Shortly after the Sixteenth arrived, Union soldiers, mostly former coal miners from Pennsylvania, commenced tunneling to a position twenty feet under a battery in the Confederate fortifications. Five hundred eleven feet later, the miners exploded four tons of black powder and began the Battle of the Crater.[3]

☆ *Jerome B. Yates to Marie Yates Swanson*:
In camp twelve miles from Richmond, June 18th, 1864

Dear Marie,

Your welcome letter came duly to hand and was received by me with joy. First, Marie, let us render thanks to kind Providence for the preservation of your brother through the fiery ordeal where so many brave boys sacrificed their lives on their country's altar. Poor boys. God grant they may be in a better world.

Well, Marie, we are through one campaign with the Northern hero, General Grant, who is precisely where General McClellan was after the Seven Days Battle in front of Richmond two years ago—in camp at west over on James River. He is quiet at present, but no telling how long he will remain so, but the North must admit that their "On to Richmond"[Campaign] has proved a failure, at least so far. Whether another onward movement will be made, we do not know.

We are in regular camp twelve miles from Richmond and have just washed up and put on clean clothes. You may guess how I feel. You would fancy my Yankee overshirts I know, if you could see them. I captured myself rich in the battle that has been fought in the last forty-one days. Grant is a hard knot. Just took Lee forty-one days to wind him up. . . .

Tom is all right, Dan also. Dan is one of my best friends. Kith and kin stick to each other out in these big wars, but when I think of friends, my mind always turns to Bud. He was indeed a true friend, such as are seldom found. Poor boy, God grant he may meet with the reward he so justly deserves. I can hardly mention him without shedding tears. . . . If an opportunity ever offers, I am going to visit his grave and place a headboard and enclose the place with a fence of some kind. I hope some day to be able to take his remains home. I would give anything but life for him back, but it is not our place to grumble at the will of God. So we will not say any more about the subject. . . .

Give all the children a kiss for me. . . . If I could be with you for one day only, but goodby. Write soon to your brother,

Romy

☆ *Letter of General Nathaniel H. Harris to General William H. Mahone*:

About 4 p.m. of the 22nd, we received orders . . . [to go] to the support [of] . . . an attack upon the flank of the enemy. This command [Harris' Brigade] left the trenches under a heavy fire from the enemy's guns and . . . formed lines on the right of the brigades engaged. Our skirmishers were heavily engaged. At 11 p.m., we returned to our original position in the trenches.

On the 23rd about 4 a.m., [we were] directed to occupy and hold the works captured from the enemy the preceding evening. On arriving near the works, the enemy was found holding a portion of them, but I occupied the portion not held by him and was making preparations to dislodge him from the remainder, when he was discovered to be moving in force on my front and flanks, and I deemed it best to withdraw. . . . My command returned to its original position and in the afternoon, was relieved . . . and ordered to move down the Weldon Railroad near the Nine-Mile House and form a line of battle on the Gurley Road. This done, skirmishers were advanced and . . . drove his [the enemy's] skirmishers into the entrenched line and held them there until they were flanked and captured by Perry's Brigade. Our loss was heavy for the time and force engaged. Late at night, we returned to the trenches in front of Petersburg.[4]

On the 24th, I was ordered to move down the Weldon Railroad to the Davis House and to picket the woods to the left of the road and observe the movements of the enemy. Nothing of importance occurring, we returned to the trenches at night.[5]

☆ *James Johnson Kirkpatrick Diary*, June 26, 1864, Sunday:

No change in temperatures. Made an arbor to shade us. Preaching in morning by Reverend Garrison, in evening by Reverend Morrison. Thermometer yesterday in shade one hundred degrees—today one hundred five degrees.

☆ *James Johnson Kirkpatrick Diary*, June 27, 1864, Monday:

Received orders at three-thirty o'clock a.m. to be ready to move at four a.m. Marched down the Weldon Railroad a few miles, and the brigade halted.

Company C went about a mile further and remained on picket till evening. Some skirmishing on our right and left. Returned to the fortifications at dark.

☆ *James Johnson Kirkpatrick Diary*, June 29, 1864, Wednesday:

Extended our line to left to occupy the works vacated by the brigade sent down the railroad. Received marching orders at noon. Marched down to the Davis House. Our object was to assist in capturing "Wilson's Raiders." We did not come in collision with them, but our cavalry and Finegan's Brigade captured most of them, their wagons, artillery, contrabands, etc. marched back to our position about midnight.[6]

☆ *James Johnson Kirkpatrick Diary*, July 2, 1864, Saturday:

Another warm day. Received orders this evening to be ready to march at seven-thirty o'clock p.m. Moved a mile to the left and took a new position in the works. Our picket line is close up to the enemy. Lively and continuous sharpshooting on our left. None in front. The pickets here had come to a mutual agreement to stop the "barbarous practice" of sharpshooting. One-third of the men required to be on watch all night in addition to the pickets.

☆ *James Johnson Kirkpatrick Diary*, July 7, 1864, Thursday:

No change. Company C infested largely in fleas. Rumors afloat of Early on the Potomac.

☆ *James Johnson Kirkpatrick Diary*, July 12, 1864, Tuesday:

Cloudy. All would welcome a rain. Companies C and A engaged in digging a well. Some of the others who have preceded us, struck good water at about twenty feet.

☆ *Jerome B. Yates to Marie Yates Swanson*:
Petersburg, July 19th, 1864

Dear Marie,
Yours of July 1st came duly to hand. . . . It is getting lonesome in the front.

The sight of hundreds of Yankees is a common sight. There is hardly a minute in the day or night without a cannon is firing on the line somewhere. The lines are as near as two hundred yards in some places. In our front, they are one thousand yards apart. They are on one side of a field, and we are on the other. We go on picket duty every seventh day. When we stand picket, our skirmishers are one hundred fifty yards on their battle line and one hundred yards from their sharpshooters. Firing has been agreed to by all parties as a senseless waste of ammunition, and we boldly stand and look each other in the face from daylight until night, then listen for each other to advance. We read each others papers in fifteen minutes after the newsboys bring them up from the offices. The boys deal considerable with them for various little articles such as coffee, knives, pipes, writing paper and envelopes.

We come off picket last night. . . . [There is] no more communication with the enemy. I was glad it was stopped. . . . I went on picket one day not long since, and a Yankee shot at me and shot a hole through my canteen. The worst picket I have had in the war. . . .

I will close. You must write soon to me. . . . Your brother,

J. B. Y.

☆ *Jerome B. Yates to Laura Davis*:
Petersburg, Virginia, July 21st, 1864

Dear Laura,

Your letter came duly to hand and was gladly received by me. I was happy to know you had not forgotten your old, gray, harried, war-worn uncle. I am well at present. As I always am, I am truly thankful for such favors from kind Providence.

Well, Laura, there is no war news nor anything else worth writing. The Yankees are still in shelling distance of Petersburg, the second city in the state. They burn a house every day or two, but they can never get the city.

So you are at home not going to school. I wish you were at school. You are spending the most precious moments of your life, you should be at school every day, but I suppose you can't help it. One thing you can do, you can read all the books your Papa's got and then get plenty from your Uncle Pole. You must do it, and above all things, you must try and learn to spell. You must follow my advice. You will not regret it in after years. If I should have the opportunity, I will send you some books. Study anything you can get hold of and try and inform Tish and the other children. Do everything in your power for this improvement. When you go to school, study hard and try to excel. Oh, how I wish we were going to the old Auburn School again. How much more I could learn than I did. If you do not study hard, in after years you will be wishing the same thing.

I will close. Tell Tish she must write to me. I enclose this in your grandma's for want of an envelope. You must write soon to your

Uncle Jerome

☆ *Jerome B. Yates to Mrs. Obedience Yates*:
Petersburg, Virginia, July 21st, 1864

Dear Ma,

Knowing you will expect a letter . . . I will drop you a few lines. . . . Things are as usual, no change in the military doings on either side. Our lines are from two hundred to three hundred yards [apart]. Skirmishing has been stopped in our front, but it is still kept up on the left as pickets are within two hundred yards of the Yankee line of battle. Trade has been going on briskly until the authorities stopped it. We read Washington papers in ten minutes after they come from the office. Our forces have had a small fight with the enemy in the Northern portion of this state and whipped them badly. You can always rest easy about this army. . . .

I will bring my conversation down to more personal things. I am still in my tent within range of Yankee canons and Minie rifles. I have not finished patching my pants in the place where a lazy man first wears them out. I will get a pair from Richmond in a few days. I wrote to Marie for them. You need not think because my pants are patched that they are worse than anybody else. The colonel of this regiment would not be a fit subject to enter a ball room at present, so you can rest easy about my clothes. What you have for me, send them by the first opportunity.

You wrote me you would send me clothes by the wounded Irishman at Mr. Brown's. You must not trust him. He is the grandest rascal in this regiment. You need not say anything about him but just make an excuse of some sort and send them by someone else. He would sell them to some people before he got back. I never look for him back. He was under arrest for two months before he left here for robbing a man. So you know how far you can trust him. . . .

You all must write soon and a long letter. I will write you any chance I have.

. . . Give my respect to all my kith and kin, and tell Phebie I would like to hear from her. Write soon to your son,

J. B. Y.

Wilse says Howdy to all.

☆ *James Johnson Kirkpatrick Diary*, July 22, 1864, Friday:

Very cool last night. Sharpshooters and artillery very noisy. Our band came up this evening and commenced fortifying in our rear. Late Yankee papers from the picket line have Grant still alive. Lincoln has made a call for five hundred thousand more men.

☆ *J. J. Wilson to James E. Wilson*:

July 24th, 1864, In line of battle at Petersburg, Virginia

Dear Father,

I received your kind letters . . . a few days ago, and I now hasten to drop you a few lines in answer. This leaves me and all the rest of the company in very good health and fine spirits at this time.

There is not any changes up here. The Yankees are still in front of us here, lying still and seem to be fortifying. There has not been any regular engagement for the past two weeks but sharpshooting and cannonading going on both night and day. I don't think there will be a regular fight at this place. We are too well fortified for Grant to attack us here. He will be apt to try at some other point. It is rumored here that Grant was killed by a shell. I hope it is true, but he was the best general for us. He would fight us behind our breastworks, and that is more than the rest ever have done.

There is cheering news from all quarters. General Hood has whipped the Yankees in Georgia, Forrest [whipped them] in Mississippi, and General [Early] has just returned from Maryland having gone in a few miles of Washington City. He tored up the railroads and brought off a great many beef cattle and horses which was very much needed.[7]

At this time, we are getting tolerable good rations of flour, bacon, tea, rice, sugar and coffee. Things is very high up here. A month's wages will not get a man's dinner. Peas is selling at two dollars a quart, onions a dollar fifty and two dollars a piece, and every other thing at the same proportion. I don't see how some people do to live at such prices. It don't make any difference with the soldiers. We have not had any pay since the first of January. . . .

I believe that Grant is going to stay here, if he is allowed, until the president's election. The Yankee papers say seems to think there will be a split up in the North and run a peace Democrat. It don't make any difference with us who is elected. It is generally believed that the present campaign will bring the war to a close.

I want a pair of pants (woolen) and cotton overshirt, and I don't care how many socks for I am entirely out. . . . I wish you would have some nice gray cloth ready to have a coat made. I will send my measurements, and it can be made to fit. Also, a pair shoes. I will not want them until winter.

Nothing more. My love to all. Write soon.

J. J. Wilson

☆ *James Johnson Kirkpatrick Diary*, July 30, 1864, Saturday:

Orders this morning to have all the men in the trenches at three a.m., as an attack was expected. Just at sunrise, a heavy explosion on our left was followed by a fierce cannonade all along the line. Then there was "running to and fro" by those who had left the trenches and gone back to their tents to sleep. The shells, in quick succession, came crushing through our camps, and the sleepers waited not long at their toilets. Very soon the news comes up the line that a portion of our works, including a redoubt, had been blown up by a mine. The Yankees immediately rushed in and occupied them. A portion of the charging column were Negroes of Burnside's Corps. Mahone, with his old brigade, was sent down to see after them. He formed and charged at eleven o'clock, restoring the line but not dislodging quite all from the crater. Wright's Brigade went down to assist him and at one p.m., all the line was restored, and the shelling nearly ceased.

Our loss was trifling while that of the enemy was about eight hundred killed and one thousand prisoners. Harris'(our) Brigade did not leave the trenches but stretched out in one rank to fill up the space vacated by Mahone. A mortar battery in our front hurled many a huge sphere over our way, but we had no mortalities. Before dark, we took our old positions, quiet being restored and the result of the day's operations vastly in our favor.

☆ *The Veteran's Story:*

During the siege of Petersburg, General Anderson was sent south and General Mahone was made major general [on July 30, 1864] and placed in command of our division and continued till the close of the war. . . .

The Yanks tried very hard to drive us out of our works. They dug a mine under our lines, blew up one of our posts, killing a number of our boys. They got possession of a short space in our lines, but little Billy Mahone . . . soon drove them out and re-established the lines. . . .[8]

☆ *James Johnson Kirkpatrick Diary*, August 1, 1864, Monday:

Another hot day. A flag of truce was granted this morning. Went down while the "emblem of peace" was flying and took a view of the scene. The crater was perhaps one hundred feet long and thirty feet deep. The lines exactly where they were before. Saw a few wounded Negroes. One of our guns was lying bout midway between the lines. After gratifying my curiosity, I returned by a pond and took a bath. Company C for picket duty tonight.

☆ *Jerome B. Yates to Marie Yates Swanson:*
Petersburg, Virginia, August 2nd, 1864

Dear Marie
    . . . The news from Petersburg is scarce. Both . . . [armies] confront each other in the same old trenches, no changes in our lines. . . . The nearest Yankees to Richmond are within fourteen miles. Grant could have been there two months ago and seven miles more without firing a gun, but I was glad he tried the road he did. . . . All I have to say for Grant is bully for him. He is the man to fight this war out.
    Lincoln has called for five hundred thousand more men. If he got them all on the line, how a lively time [we would have] in the country in the fall. Some Yank is volunteering today who [will wound me] to give me a furlough to spend the winter at home. Talking of furloughs, lots of our men are getting furloughs for being blind at night. They can see as well in the day as anybody, but not a thing at night. I have seen four or five along at night holding on to each other's coattails, led by one who can see. They fall over everything in their way, which is much. . . . Three left our regiment yesterday. This is a good trick to play off,

as the boys call it. I have no doubt some does it. They see food coming. . . .
But I could not play it off. I would betray myself. I cannot keep my mind on
any one thing long enough at a time.

Well, let me tell you what I had for my dinner yesterday. First, sweet cakes
and apples. Next, blackberry dumplings. . . . We are living very well at present
on . . . cornbread, bacon, coffee, sugar, peas, and some . . . rice. Pretty good
for Jeff in these besieging times. We drew lots of good food four days ago when
seven trains of cars come into Petersburg loaded with blockade goods. The
government has taken the blockade running into their own hands, and they
make it profitable. . . . But when our cotton is all gone, I don't know how we
will stand. . . . I think our friendly [trade] will end when the . . . money runs
short.

You must write soon to your brother.

J. B. Y.

☆ Extra—August 3rd, 1864

Dear Marie,

. . . Grant has made his brilliant move that was to astonish the world. You
have doubtless heard of the grand blow up of the Army of [Northern] Virginia
on Saturday, July 30th. About daylight, Grant touched off . . . powder which
he had placed under Elliot's South Carolina Brigade and six guns. The explosion was awful. . . . They charged the blown up part of the works with two
lines. They gained the works formally occupied by Elliot's Brigade which they
held until two of our brigades of this division was sent for. Then they charged
and recaptured the works and with them one thousand prisoners and twenty
flags. Most of the Negroes were killed after they surrendered. The ground was
covered with dead Negroes. Some was killed after they were taken to the rear.
Only sixty or seventy was saved from the river. The Yankee loss is estimated at
three thousand, ours at six or seven hundred. Mining and blowing up is all the
talk. . . . The men in the fight say the Negroes fought better than the whites.
So it is all stuff about them not making soldiers. The very thing of Grant trying
to blow up [our fortifications] admits on his part that he will not take Petersburg by charging. Mortar shells are all the go. . . . The enemy asked for permission to bury their dead, which was granted, then they put one hundred in one
grave. They were all killed in one hole, the place where they blew our line

up. Such blow ups do not pay. A few more such and Grant will have a corps less. . . .[9]

I will close my extra. I will write you another if Grant blows us up again before this leaves. Write soon to your brother,

Jerome

— *Chapter 20* —

"... DAILY THERE WAS A LIST OF CASUALTIES"

In August, Lee's seemingly solid lines around Petersburg were dangerously thin. The Army of Northern Virginia was woefully outnumbered and Grant knew it. With Cold Harbor and the failure of his initial direct assaults on Petersburg fresh in his memory, Grant may have been reluctant to attack Lee's well-entrenched forces head-on and decided instead to extend his flanks. This would force Lee to extend his to match, further thinning Confederate lines, perhaps to the breaking-point.

Atlanta fell the first of September, and Petersburg, Richmond and the Confederate government itself was in a precarious position, even though military matters around Petersburg were deadlocked. This deadlock was due in large part, if not entirely, to Confederate regiments, including the Sixteenth Mississippi, moving in and out of their trenches from August through October to repulse continuous Federal efforts to destroy Petersburg's railroads. By November, winter weather ended all thoughts of serious military movements until spring.[1]

☆ *James Johnson Kirkpatrick Diary*, August 4, 1864, Thursday:

No change in atmosphere. The Yankees admit their defeat on Saturday [in the Crater]. The boys all indulging in apples, onions, peas, pies, and etc. Their money will soon all be spent. . . .

☆ *James Johnson Kirkpatrick Diary*, August 13, 1864, Saturday:

Occupied our new position in the trenches. Some of Company C had a very narrow escape this evening from an enfilading shell. It exploded in my tent and wounded Mike Noll. . . .[2]

☆ *The Veteran's Story:*

One day there was a detail of men working on the breastworks. Directly after the work was started, the bullets commenced to whistle around them, killing one man and wounding two. The men were ordered to scatter, which they did in double-quick time. We spied around to find out where the bullets were coming from. Just about a mile in our front was a tall pine tree. Some of the boys saw a puff of smoke in the top of the tree and yelled, "Lie down boys!"Just as we lay down, the ball passed over us. Now we had him treed. One of our officers stepped over to a battery to report him to the captain, who searched for him with his spy glass. He spied him and a rifled gun was turned on him, which brought the young man down from his lofty perch. After that he worked on without being disturbed.[3]

☆ *Jerome B. Yates to Marie Yates Swanson:*
Petersburg, Virginia, August 14th, 1864

Dear Marie,

Yours by Cain came to hand yesterday. I was agreeably surprised to see him back at all, much less for him to hand me all the clothes. . . . He brought me one pair pants, one pair drawers, two pair socks and one fine shirt. You all must not send me such fine clothes. They cost too much. A common dyed cotton shirt could answer as well. Such things cost too much money for these hard times.[4]

I am truly glad to hear you had gotten entirely well, but you speak of not standing the kind of life you have to lead. You must bear nobly up under the trials and afflictions that are in this short life of ours. It will only be for a few short years, and then all will be well for us if we live the life pointed out to us in the Good Book set before us by our Maker. Besides, we all hope for better things when this cruel war is over. Trust to God and be cheerful. No telling what is in store for us in the future. I am glad the Yankees did not bother you and Ma any more than they did. Your full account of the raid has not come to hand. . . .

I am truly sorry to hear of the suffering from the good old people of Utica. So Mr. Brown is broken up. I was in hopes that as he had escaped so far, he would be as lucky through the war. But everybody has to bear their portion of the evils of this war. God grant they may fall lightly upon my mother and sister. All the balance of the family seems more able to stand it than you and Ma. . . .

Remember me to all the children and teach them all you can, Tish especially. She is backward. Make Laura pay attention to her spelling. Teach Yates in figures, they are the things men most need. But I reckon you thank me but little for my advice as you are a teacher. You know what they need.

You must write me soon and a long letter. Your brother,

J. B. Y.

Tell Miss Maggie many thanks for the nice shirt she has made me. I will pick her out a sweetheart up here in [Virginia], provided she wants one.

J. B. Y.

☆ *James Johnson Kirkpatrick Diary*, August 16, 1864, Tuesday:

Orders to be ready for brigade inspection. All indulging in green corn. Received orders after noon to get ready to move. Marched from the trenches at four p.m. Passed through Petersburg and took the cars on the [South Side] Railroad a few miles north of the Appomattox [River] for Richmond. Arrived at the capital about midnight. Marched through the sleeping city to the music of our bands and halted . . . till day.

☆ *General Nathaniel H. Harris, Movements of the Confederate Army:*

August 16th, General Harris . . . withdrew the brigade from the trenches in front of Petersburg and proceeded by train to Richmond, thence by steamer on the James River to Chafin's Farm. Disembarking at daylight at that point, General Harris reported to General Lee and was ordered by him to report to Major General Fields near Fussell's Mill on the Darbytown Road. Reporting to General Fields as directed, General Harris, in addition to his own [brigade], was placed in command of [Sanders] and Girardey, these brigades having already arrived from the south side and formed line of battle. . . . Remained quiet until the afternoon of the 18th. . . .[5]

☆ *James Johnson Kirkpatrick Diary*, August 17, 1864, Wednesday:

Went on board a transport this morning and steamed down to Drewry's Bluff. Disembarked on the north side and marched across the country perhaps six miles and rested till dark. Heavy rain this evening. After dark, we moved three or four hundred more yards and occupied a line of rifle pits. Stretched our tents and lay down to sleep, leaving details to watch, but no rest for the weary. After getting comfortably settled for the night, we are aroused with the inexorable marching orders. Traveled all night and reached our destination a little after day.

☆ *James Johnson Kirkpatrick Diary*, August 18, 1864, Thursday:

On the lines near Fussell's Mill. Dense timber in front and our pickets advanced only a few yards. Some skirmishing. Heavy rain in evening. Cannonading last night towards Petersburg. Received orders this afternoon to get ready to move but to leave our tents standing. Heavy musketry commenced on our left, rapidly raining down on us. Soon we advanced. Passed over ground badly broken by rains and in places precipitous. The brigade acted badly under guidance of Colonel Jayne. Fell back before reaching the enemy's works. Essayed another change, but did very little better. . . .

☆ *General Nathaniel H. Harris, Movements of the Confederate Army:*

Remained quiet until the afternoon of the 18th when . . . General Harris advanced his own brigade, under command of Colonel Jayne . . . to feel the enemy. Advancing but a short distance through thick woods and driving in the enemy's skirmishers, we encountered the enemy's line of battle entrenched. Holding the position until dark, the brigade was withdrawn to its original position.

The brigade in this affair met with some loss in killed and wounded. Among the killed was Lieutenant John B. Coleman of the Sixteenth Regiment. Though young in years, he was a veteran soldier and efficient officer. . . .[6]

☆ *James Johnson Kirkpatrick Diary*, August 19, 1864, Friday:

Our pickets advanced this morning and found the enemy had left the works in our front. Some skirmishing today. Got marching orders in evening and started again towards Petersburg. About dark, we were deluged with a perfect torrent of rain, but onward we groped our way through mud and water. Crossed the James [River] on a pontoon bridge at Chafin's Farm and took the cars perhaps three miles beyond. Disembarked near Petersburg crossed the Appomattox [River] and pushed on towards our old situation on the line.

☆ *James Johnson Kirkpatrick Diary*, August 20, 1864, Saturday:

Reached our trenches just after day, wet and tired. Stretched a tent, ate breakfast and lay down to sleep. Soon orders came to move again. Fell in and marched back to some woods. All loaded guns discharged and cleaned. The enemy has again cut and now occupy the Weldon Railroad. Troops are being massed here to attack them. Rain again today. The men are much worn out and in need of rest. Lay down to sleep on some brush under cover of an oil cloth with orders to march at half past two o'clock.

☆ *Historical Sketch of the Quitman Guards:*

On the 21st, [the Sixteenth] engaged in a fight on the Weldon Railroad. During the absence of some of Lee's troops on that portion of the line, the Federals moved in, took possession of the road and fortified themselves. Mahone's Division [including the Sixteenth] attacked them for the purpose of driving them out, but being somewhat mistaken in their position, his division suffered greatly and did not succeed in getting possession of the road. . . .

After the fight on the Weldon Railroad, [Harris'] brigade returned to its position in the trenches before Petersburg. . . .[7]

☆ *James Johnson Kirkpatrick Diary*, August 21, 1864, Sunday:

Marched out this morning. Moved down and to the right of the Weldon Railroad. Finegan's Brigade led the attack but soon came back in confusion. Harris's Brigade (my) next made the attempt but failed to carry the works. Our total force carried into action did not amount to over four hundred men and

very much scattered. About seventy-five of us were captured and a large number killed and wounded. We were taken by Warren's Corps near the "Yellow
House" [Yellow Tavern]. They were strongly entrenched, four ranks deep in
the breastworks and well supported by artillery and reserves.

We were escorted to the rear under fire of our artillery, counted and started
for Bermuda Hundred under a squadron of cavalry. Roads very muddy.
Marched to . . . where our names were taken, and we were put up for the night.
Drew a day's rations of coffee, sugar and hardtack.[8]

☆ General Nathaniel H. Harris, Movements of the Confederate Army:

On August the 21st, the brigade under command of Colonel J. M. Jayne . . .
(General Harris being sick) . . . marched to a point near the Davis House on
the Weldon Railroad. Turning to the right, they moved on the Dinwiddie
Road to get position on the left flank and rear of the enemy, who had seized
and held a strong position on the railroad near the Yellow Tavern. Marching
some distance on the road mentioned, the brigades of Finegan and Sanders
were formed in line of battle on the left of the road and moved forward to
attack the enemy, Harris' Brigade moving by the flank in support of Finegan's
Brigade with orders to assist promptly. Pushing forward rapidly, through the
thick and tangled woods and swamps, Finegan and Sanders soon encountered
the enemy strongly entrenched. Finegan was repulsed by the heavy and galling
fire of musketry and artillery poured upon him by the enemy and fell back in
confusion and disorder. Harris' Brigade was rapidly formed in line and moved
forward at a double quick to the support of Finegan, passing through and over
that brigade as it retired. Harris' Brigade charged right up to the face of the
enemy's works, but the fire of the enemy was so severe, and being unsupported,
the brigade was compelled to retire. By the confrontation of the enemy's
works, the left of the brigade first encountered the enemy, and a number of
the officers and men of the Twelfth and Sixteenth Regiments—the left regiments—passed into the works of the enemy and were captured. After retiring,
the brigade formed a line of battle a short distance from the enemy's position
and at dark withdrew with the division to the lines in front of Petersburg.

In this engagement, the loss of the brigade was severe in officers and men.
Colonel E. C. Councill of the Sixteenth Regiment, a gallant and admirable
officer, was mortally wounded and died in the hands of the enemy. . . .[9]

☆ *James Johnson Kirkpatrick Diary*, August 22,1864, Monday:

Marched down this morning to the railroad and embarked for City Point. Our names were again taken here, and we were put in a place styled the Bull Pen. Feel very uncomfortable. Clothing all dirty and none to change. We left everything behind previous to making the ill-fated charge. Day warm. Received bad treatment. The soldiers at the front treated us well. Only a few were permitted to go after water at a time, consequently, the many had to endure thirst. No protection from the sun. Our crowd is a mixed one, consisting of Rebel prisoners, Yankee deserters, criminals, and Negroes. Rain this evening and after dark. Took it as it came. Slept on the wet ground.

☆ *James Johnson Kirkpatrick Diary*, August 23, 1864, Sunday:

After the fog cleared away, the sun shines out intensely hot. The officers who were in our crowd left this morning for Johnson's Island. About three p.m., we were marched down to the river and put on board the Utica. Very much crowed and uncomfortable. Steamed down stream until dark and anchored. Little sleep tonight.

☆ *James Johnson Kirkpatrick Diary*, August 24, 1864, Wednesday:

Started again at daylight. Cloudy. Passed Fortress Monroe at ten a.m., making no halt. Reached Point Lookout at dark. Disembarked and marched into an enclosure for the night. Very thirsty and hungry, but the water is not drinkable, and no rations are given.[10]

☆ *James Johnson Kirkpatrick Diary*, August 25, 1864, Thursday:

Waked up at day. . . . Drew some rations. Marched down to a grove . . . to be searched. All valuables and dangerous looking pocket knives were taken from us. Not permitted to keep any U.S. property. After being thoroughly searched and plundered, we were marched into the prisoners camp and went to work putting up tents for habitations. The tents given us are small "A" tents, five men to each. Prospect before us very gloomy. . . .

☆ *James Johnson Kirkpatrick Diary*, August 26, 1864, Friday:

Waked up at dawn—tried to sleep longer but in vain. Time hangs heavily on my hands, and I would gladly know some method to forget its passing. Changed quarters at ten o'clock. Were put into old Sibley tents full of holes, ready to admit all the rain. Sixteen men to a tent. Drew some bread at noon. Our mess is all Mississippians from the Sixteenth Regiment, good men and true. . . .

☆ *Jerome B. Yates to Mrs. Obedience Yates:*
Point Lookout, Maryland, August 29th, 1864
Direction: J. B. Yates, Company B, Sixth Division, Point Lookout, Maryland

Dear Ma,
I am a prisoner at last. I was captured with eight of the company on the 21st of August. . . . We fare very well. This winter will be hard I fear. . . .
You must all write often, letters, money or anything can come through safely. I have written to Owen to take charge of anything you may send to me. Send all to him, and he will send it safe to me. You had better not try to send me any clothes. Owen will send me clothes when I want them. If you can get any U.S. money without too much trouble, send me some, a small sum, and see if it comes safe at first. Direct all to Owen, he will send them. . . . Do not try to send anything, only by Owen. . . . Write soon to your dutiful son,

Jerome

☆ *Jerome B. Yates to Dan Yates:*
Point Lookout, Maryland, August 30th, 1864

Dear Dan,
. . . We are all well with the exception of myself. My arm is very sore, the ball is still in the left arm just above the elbow. A good sixty days furlough. Dan, I want you to attend to Wilse for me. Hire him out and spend the money or keep him with you, just as you please. Send my knapsack to the Mississippi Depot or some place of safety. Get my portfolio and send it to Laura Davis, or to Ma and tell her where I am. Do not mention my wound. . . .

Anything sent to any of us will come safe. . . . Tell all my friends greenbacks would go mighty well. Your friend,

J. B. Yates

☆ *General Nathaniel H. Harris, Movements of the Confederate Army:*

[Through September and] until the 27th of October, [the Sixteenth] occupied what was known as "Rives Salient" in the line in front of Petersburg. [They were] daily exposed to a heavy artillery fire and a continuous fire day and night from the enemy's sharpshooters, and in addition, at night a constant hammering from the enemy's mortar batteries, and daily there was a list of casualties. But notwithstanding all this and the heavy labor the men had to perform in repairing the old [works] and building new works and the meager fare and scant clothing, they faced the enemy with undaunted spirits.

On the 27th of October, General Harris received orders to withdraw his command from the trenches . . . to follow the division on the Boydton Plank Road in the direction of Burgess Mill. At twelve o'clock [noon], the brigade was relieved and moved on the road and in the direction indicated. Soon firing in front announced the cause of the movement and that the conflict had begun. Hastening forward as rapidly as possible, the brigade arrived at the scene of action about three o'clock p.m. General Harris was first ordered to support a battery that was in position near the bridge across Hatcher's Run, but before the order was obeyed, he was ordered by General Heth . . . to take position on the bank of the run . . . to make a demonstration against the enemy when General Mahone . . . (with the intention to flank and strike the enemy in the rear) made his attack. . . . In obedience to this order . . . General Harris formed the brigade on the left of Dearing, but owing to the distance to be covered, nearly the whole of the brigade was deployed as skirmishers. When Mahone made his attack, the line was advanced to make the required demonstration, but [due to] the weakness of the line, the enemy was not pressed to advantage. The brigade held the position during the night.[11]

At daylight on the 28th, it was discovered that the enemy had withdrawn and General Harris, pushing forward three companies, captured nearly one hundred prisoners. The loss of the brigade was not large. . . . We returned to the position held in front of Petersburg the afternoon of the 28th.[12]

☆ *Historical Sketch of the Quitman Guards:*

The two opposing lines were about two hundred yards apart and kept up a continual picket firing and cannonading. The suffering of the army while quartered here was intense, the men having nothing to shield them from the rain and snow. Great scarcity of wood prevailed. We had but few blankets and they inferior in quality. . . . We were, in this condition, compelled to pass this freezing winter in trenches knee-deep in mud or filled with ice and snow. Railroad communication with the South was at length cut off, thus causing a greater scarcity of provisions and supplies. This, together with the known constant and large accessions of the Federal army, caused despondency, if not despair, for the first time to settle upon the Army of Northern Virginia.

On the 12th of November, [Harris' Brigade] was then again taken out, moved about three miles to the right and built winter quarters but was almost constantly on active duty in repelling advances made by the Federals on the front and right.[13]

☆ *Official Records:*

[On November 12, 1864, the Sixteenth was] relieved from the trenches in front of Petersburg and went into winter quarters on the Boydton Plank Road, two miles from Petersburg. . . .

[On November 30, 1864, the] Sixteenth was commanded by Lieutenant Colonel James H. Duncan [of the Nineteenth Mississippi].

[On December 7, 1864,] Companies C and K marched for Belfield. The enemy retired without fighting, then we took up line of march for camp. Company H marched to Jarrett's Station on the Petersburg and Weldon Railroad to meet a party of raiders, but they retired immediately on our approach. Then we came back to quarters.

[On December 13, 1864,] Companies C and K arrived at camp after absence of six days. They encountered very severe weather. Severe rain and sleet; since remained in camp.

Companies B, D, F, and I marched to within four miles of battlefield in pursuit of a raiding party. They returned via Jarrat's Station on the railroad.[14]

— *Chapter 21* —

". . . FORT GREGG WILL
NEVER BE SURRENDERED"

By January 1865, the South had little left but grit and determination. Its commercial and industrial institutions were in ruins, and the Confederacy controlled only isolated sections of the country. Desertion in the Army of Northern Virginia rose as tired, cold, and hungry soldiers abandoned their trenches. Lee petitioned the Confederate Congress for help, but returned empty-handed, telling his son, Custis, ". . . they do not seem to be able to do anything except eat peanuts and chew tobacco while my army is starving." Between February 15th and March 18th, Confederate records reflect that nearly three thousand deserted. According to Federal records, over 1,750 came over to their side, thus leaving about 1,250 who probably just went home. Anxiety about families back home no doubt contributed to the desertion rate, as troops in Petersburg were all but surrounded, and little mail, if any, from Mississippi got through.

The peace negotiations that began at Hampton Roads, Virginia on February 3, 1865, broke down the same day when Confederate representatives insisted on independence and Lincoln refused to acquiesce to any plan that perpetuated slavery. Two days later, Grant launched an offensive on Hatcher's Run (also known as Dabney Mills), being driven back initially but finally extending his lines across Vaughn Road. Lee lost Weldon Railroad and the battles at Fort Stedman and Five Forks by April 1st, while Grant worried that the roads would dry enough to allow Lee to escape. On April 2nd, Grant ordered a massive attack on Petersburg, and Lee called on

Harris's Brigade to buy him time to evacuate the city. At Fort Gregg, a square earth-work with steeply sloped walls ditched around three sides, the Sixteenth would strug-gle for its own life, as well as that of the Army of Northern Virginia and the Confederacy itself.[1]

☆ *Report of Lieutenant Colonel James Henderson Duncan, Commanding Sixteenth Mississippi Regiment, January 22, 1865:*
Brigadier General Joseph Finegan, Commanding Mahone's Division:

General:

I have the honor to respectfully report the result of my tour on picket as division field officer of the picket-line of Mahone's Division. . . . Everything remained quiet on the line.

I regret to have to report a loss of nine men by desertion—seven from the Florida and two from the Virginia brigades. These desertions are becoming amazingly numerous, and I beg leave to submit for your consideration what I esteem to be the main cause of this dissatisfaction, and is, in my opinion, the controlling influence that prompts our men thus to desert. It is the insuffi-ciency of rations. Our men do not get enough to eat. I have been long con-vinced of this important fact from my own careful observation. I have conversed with the field and line officers of different regiments on this subject, and their statements all concur in establishing the above facts, and unless something is done soon to remove this evil, which of all others weighs most heavily on the minds of the troops, I fear that the number of desertions will be greatly increased during the winter.

I have the honor to be, sir, respectfully your obedient servant,

J. H. Duncan,
Lieutenant Colonel[2]

☆ *General Nathaniel H. Harris, Movements of the Confederate Army:*

Marched . . . once in January to the vicinity of Hicksford on the Meherrin River to intercept cavalry raids on the Weldon Railroad, the troops suffering from exposure and intensely cold weather.[3]

☆ On the 6th of February, the brigade, whilst returning to camp from a position . . . [near Armstrong's or Dabney's Mills on Hatcher's Run[4]] . . . was
ordered to about face and move at the double-quick on the Boydton Plank
Road in the direction of Hatcher's Run. Arriving at Burgess Mill, a distance
of four miles from the point where the order was given to about face . . . heavy
firing was heard to the left and down the run, crossing which [the brigade]
moved in the direction of the firing and pushed on over swamp and morass
through woods and thicket—the men marching . . . a distance of over two
miles from the bridge—the brigade arrived upon the scene of action.

It was discovered that the enemy was making a bold and determined effort
to reach the Boydton Plank Road and was gradually pushing Gordon's Corps
back towards that road. Being the rear brigade of the division, on arriving on
the field it was found that the other brigades had been put into action as fast
as they arrived. General Harris, reporting to General A. P. Hill, was ordered
by him to report to General Gordon, by whose order General Harris moved
without delay to the support of his [Gordon's] left. Aligning the brigade and
obliqueing to the left, General Harris reached the desired position and,
ordering the brigade to charge, pressed the enemy from the field he occupied.
After crossing the field, the brigade formed a junction with the left of the
division which had also attained a position well to the front; and the whole
division moved steadily and earnestly forward, driving the enemy a distance
of near one mile and a half to his works, when night put an end to the conflict of the day. During the night of the 6th, the line was perfected and
entrenched.[5]

Early in the morning of the 7th [of February], the enemy pressed upon the
skirmish line of Harris' and Sorrel's Brigades, which was near a mile in advance
of the main line, but it resulted in their being driven back. At twelve o'clock
p.m., the firing becoming rapid and severe. . . . The enemy pushed back the
line of the Georgia Brigade, leaving the skirmish line of Harris' Brigade
exposed on the left and pressed with great vigor endeavoring to intervene and
capture the line. This was stubbornly resisted. . . . The enemy was repulsed,
and the skirmish line re-established. The brigade returned with the division
to quarter near Petersburg after seven days of severe and trying service, the
weather intensely cold all the while. . . .[6]

About the middle of February, Mahone's Division [including the Sixteenth

Mississippi] relieved the division of General Pickett and occupied the lines between Swift Run Creek and the James River, Harris' Brigade being in the extreme left and next to the James River.[7]

☆ *Official Records*:

February 24—March 1, 1865:

Forty officers and five hundred one men [are] present for duty [in Harris' Brigade].

N. H. Harris, Brigadier[8]

☆ *General Nathaniel H. Harris, Movements of the Confederate Army*:

Early in March, General Harris received orders to move his command to Chesterfield Station and from there via train proceeded to Richmond. . . . Arriving at Richmond, General Harris reported to General Ewell on the Brook Turnpike and was assigned to the command (in addition to his own brigade) of the forces holding the inner line of defenses composed of the City Battalion, the Corps of Cadets . . . of the Virginia Military Institute, two regiments of militia, and a body of convalescents from the Richmond hospitals, and one or two batteries marshaled to meet the threatened raid of Sheridan.[9]

Sheridan abandoned his movement on Richmond, turned the right of the army and rejoined Grant before Petersburg. General Harris returned with his command to the lines between Swift Run Creek and the James River and was assigned a position next to the brigade (Finegan's) holding the right of the division.

On the night of March the 24th, General Harris, commanding the division in the absence of General Mahone, received orders from Army Headquarters to maintain a close observation, and if a favorable opportunity offered, to attack the enemy. . . .[10]

☆ *Historical Sketch of the Quitman Guards*:

The Federals finally succeeded in flanking General Lee at Hatcher's Run and at the same time, succeeded in breaking our lines on the right of Petersburg held by Heth's and Wilcox's Divisions. Early in the morning of [April 2nd], Harris' Brigade left its position between the Appomattox and James Rivers . . . to reinforce the troops which had lost their works on the right of Petersburg. Arriving at that place, they immediately went into action but were compelled to fall back slowly before the overwhelming numbers of the Federals until they arrived at Fort Gregg, where they made a stand. . . .[11]

☆ *General Nathaniel H. Harris, Movements of the Confederate Army:*

At one o'clock a.m. of the 2nd, orders were received "to march at once to Petersburg, cross at the upper pontoon bridge and report to General R. E. Lee." The brigade was at once put in motion in obedience to said order, the officers and men in fine spirits and marching with a quick, lively step. As the brigade reached the turnpike . . . to Petersburg, the enemy made a heavy demonstration on the front of the division. . . .

As the brigade approached Petersburg, the deep, heavy and incessant roar of artillery and the sharp rattle of musketry announced a more than ordinary conflict on the lines around . . . the city. Crossing the upper pontoon bridge, General Harris reported to General Lee and by him was informed that the enemy at daylight had pierced the lines of General Wilcox and ordered General Harris to report with his command to General Wilcox near the Newman House on the Boydton Plank Road.

Moving at the double-quick, General Harris reported to General Wilcox at the point designated. The enemy could be seen as far as the eye could reach, moving in great and imposing force to seize the advantage gained. The brigades of Wilcox's Division occupying the lines had been scattered, and there was no other organized body of troops to meet this immense host but Harris' Brigade, numbering about four hundred muskets. General Wilcox ordered General Harris "to take position in front of the enemy and detain him as long as possible." With this object in view, General Harris advanced about four hundred yards and formed line of battle at a right angle with the Boydton Plank Road. The ground being undulating, General Harris threw both flanks of the brigade back behind the crest, on which the command formed and exposed the center, in order that the enemy might believe there was a continuous line of battle behind the ridge, and advanced a line of skirmishers well to the front. The enemy was evidently misled by this device as he made the most careful dispositions, forming two lines of battle and advancing with the utmost caution. This position was held until the enemy was in easy range when the brigade opened a brisk fire. At this juncture, General Harris received an order from General Wilcox . . . "not to suffer himself to be cut off, but to hold the enemy in check as long as possible and when compelled to retire, to fall back slowly and to throw two regiments into Battery Gregg and two regiments into Battery Whitworth." These were two contiguous earthworks between the front line and the Appomattox River; the first situated on the Boydton Plank Road and nearest to the front lines; the latter about two hundred paces to the west and on an almost direct line to the Appomattox River.

The enemy pressing on the brigade slowly and far reaching on both flanks, the command with great steadiness gradually retired, General Harris placing the Twelfth and Sixteenth Regiments, numbering about one hundred fifty muskets in Battery Gregg. . . . Lieutenant Colonel James H. Duncan . . . was placed in command of Battery Gregg. . . . The Nineteenth and Forty-eighth Regiments [were placed] in Battery Whitworth.[12]

☆ "The Defense of Battery Gregg" by General N. H. Harris:

I rode to the front of Battery Gregg and instructed Colonel Duncan to have plenty of ammunition brought into that work, telling him where the ordnance wagons were located . . . and that he was to hold the work to the last extremity. After having the cabins (quarters of my brigade the preceding winter) located in front of Whitworth set on fire so that they would not be a cover for the enemy, I assumed immediate command of Whitworth. . . .[13]

☆ General Nathaniel H. Harris, Movements of the Confederate Army:

Ammunition was brought in and preparation made for the deadly struggle to ensue. The enemy made dispositions for the assault. At this moment . . . orders came to withdraw the artillery. The execution of this order General Harris protested against, but it was to no avail. The four guns were withdrawn from Whitworth, but the enemy had approached so close, the guns in Gregg could not be withdrawn. Perceiving the guns leaving Whitworth, the enemy at once moved to the assault on both works. He assaulted in columns by brigades, completely enveloping Gregg but approaching Whitworth only on the front.

Gregg repulsed assault after assault. . . . Gregg raged like the crater of a volcano, emitting its flashes of deadly battle fires, enveloped in flame and cloud, wreathing its flag in honor as well as in smoke of death. . . . The enemy continued to press forward fresh troops. Whitworth gave Gregg all the assistance possible by pouring a heavy flank fire on the assailants. . . .

For two hours this bloody work went on, the assailants falling like leaves of an autumn forest swept by fierce winds before the accurate and deadly fire of the defenders. In close array, the enemy push forward against Gregg, constantly filling the gaps in his ranks with fresh troops. Once gaining a foothold, he is driven out with the butt of the musket and bayonet, but . . . the enemy, gathering in numbers, again reach the ditch, climb the parapet—and overpowered by numbers, their ammunition expended, the noble little band of heroic defenders are compelled to surrender after inflicting a loss of seven times their number on the enemy.

The enemy now prepared for a final assault on Whitworth, massing his troops in front and moving to envelope it, but before his dispositions are completed, General Harris received orders from General Lee to evacuate Whitworth, as time had been gained for Longstreet to arrive from the north side of the James and the inner line formed.[14]

☆ *"How Fort Gregg Was Defended" by Buxton R. Conerly*:

Fort Gregg was situated about two miles southwest of Petersburg, Virginia, and was one of the many earthworks, or redoubts, that General Lee had constructed for artillery in the rear of his main line of defenses covering the cities of Richmond and Petersburg. Its form was semicircular, and a space was left open in the rear for the entrance of wagons and artillery. The earth was thrown up from the outside, forming a ditch twelve or fourteen feet wide and from four to six feet deep. The walks were from six to eight feet wide at the top, and the ground on the inside next to the wall was raised for the men to stand on. A considerable quantity of artillery ammunition was in the fort, consisting of grape, canister, bombshells, and solid shots stacked in pyramid form.

The disaster on the right wing of General Lee's army at Five Forks, causing the loss of the Southside Railroad, forced the evacuation of Petersburg and Richmond. The position at and near Fort Gregg evidently increased and became of importance from this time to that portion of our army in the trenches around Petersburg, as it covered the pontoon bridges that had been thrown across the Appomattox River west of town, over which our artillery wagon trains and troops were crossing in their retreat.

During the latter part of March, 1865, our brigade, the Twelfth, Sixteenth, Nineteenth, and Forty-eighth Mississippi Regiments, commanded by General N. H. Harris, occupied a position between the Appomattox and James Rivers, watching and guarding the line from Dutch Gap on the James. . . . About two o'clock on Sunday morning, April 2, 1865, we received orders to move, leaving about one-third of our men on a picket line in front of this position. We marched rapidly in the direction of Petersburg, following the Richmond and Petersburg turnpike road until within about two miles of Petersburg, when we left the main road, turned to the right, and crossed the Appomattox River on a pontoon bridge about two miles west of the town. We then crossed the Southside Railroad and marched by Forts Gregg and Alexander (or Whitworth as it was called by some). We moved to a position about four hundred yards in front of these forts and formed in line of battle with skirmishers well thrown out to the front. Every foot of ground was familiar to us, for we had spent the greater part of the preceding winter and had guarded this part of our line for several months. Our old uncovered winter quarters were just behind us. Long lines of Federal infantry were advancing on our front, batteries of artillery were coming into position, and as far as we could see to the right and left the enemy's guns and bayonets glistened in the rays of the morning sun, now well up over the hills in the east. Our skirmishers soon became hotly engaged in our front, and the leaden hail was striking our ranks.[15]

"Stand like iron, my brave boys!" said General Harris as he walked along the line. "Stand like iron!"

Our skirmishers were soon driven in, and our brigade opened fire on the advancing Federal line with deadly aim and effect. They gained the shelter of a sunken road about one hundred and fifty yards in front of us. Continuous firing was kept up from this position for about one hour. On the right and left of this position, the Federal troops continued to advance, threatening to enfilade us in both flanks. Quite a number of our men fell killed and wounded in this position.

General Harris, seeing that our position was untenable, ordered us to fall back to the shelter of Forts Gregg and [Whitworth], leaving a skirmish line to hold the enemy in check. Our brigade began the backward move in a storm of shot from the enemy's sheltered position in the sunken road and the crest of hills on the right and left flanks, behind which they were rapidly increasing in strength. General Harris led the greater part of the brigade into Fort [Whitworth], and Lieutenant Colonel Duncan of the Nineteenth Mississippi Regiment led the remainder . . . into Fort Gregg. The enemy, discovering this movement, rushed forward with loud huzzas, and our skirmishers were pressed back over the open field by overwhelming numbers, but taking the advantage of every protection the ground offered to rest a moment and load, they never failed to give them a parting salute as they retired from one position to another.

During this time, the men in the fort had gathered all the loose guns they could find scattered over the field around and near the fort. The Federal forces had advanced to this place early on the morning before we arrived, but had been driven away by General A. P. Hill, leaving quite a number of rifles scattered over the field. The men quickly gathered them together, not forgetting their experience in the "Bloody Angle" at Spotsylvania, May 12, 1864, where they used the captured guns against the enemy . . . as they had from two to four guns each all loaded. In addition to the artillery ammunition in Fort Gregg, there were also several boxes of rifle ammunition—about one thousand rounds to the box. . . .

The Federal troops at this time had reached a point about three hundred yards in front of Fort Gregg and were moving on Fort [Whitworth] at the same time behind or under cover of our winter quarter huts, which had been set on fire, and the smoke obscured their movements. Fort [Whitworth] was about three hundred yards to the right of Fort Gregg and was at this time under the command of General Harris. The fighting on the other parts of the line to our right and left stopped for a while, as if the men were watching the results of the movements about Fort Gregg.

Colonel Duncan watched the men and told them not to fire until the word was given. With his sword flashing in the sunlight . . . he insisted (with his appeals to the state pride of Mississippians) that we should obey his orders. All around the walls of Fort Gregg was the cry of the officers with drawn swords, "Keep down, men; keep down"—officers who had never quailed on any field. . . . Soldiers that knew them . . . yielded to the order and waited . . . until that magnificent line of Federal soldiers was within less than one hundred yards of us and not the flash of a single rifle had yet defied them. The last order of our officers, "Steady, boys!" was interrupted by the cracking of rifles sending their death-dealing missiles with telling effect. Gibbon's men fell fast and thick; his line staggered and finally broke in confusion, seeking shelter behind the crest of a ridge. A great cheer went up from our lines on the right and left, and our boys responded with their customary yell of triumph and defiance from Fort Gregg.[16]

Reinforcements were hurried forward by the enemy from their sheltered position behind the hill, and the second line came forward at a double-quick in broken and scattered ranks. We opened on them at a distance of three hundred yards, firing as fast as we could. They staggered up to within one hundred yards of us when the greater part of their line broke and [they] ran back under cover; the others (perhaps three of four hundred) reached the ditch in our front. They were not strong enough to take us and could not retreat without running the gauntlet of death. Before we could turn our attention to the enemy in the ditch, reinforcements were hurried to their assistance, and a third line came rushing on us with loud huzzas from their covered position behind the hill, but in broken and scattered ranks. The greater part of them succeeded in getting in the ditch and completely surrounded us. . . .

Our men deployed so as to cover every part of the walls of the fort and detailed twenty-five men to hold the gate in the rear. Now the solid-shot and bombshells found in the fort came into use. Our men hurled them on the heads of the enemy in the ditch. The fuses of bombshells were fired and rolled on them. This work did not stop until all, or nearly all, of the solid cannon balls and shells were gone. Brick chimneys built to tents for artillerymen were thrown down and the bricks thrown at the enemy. Numbers of efforts to scale the walls were made, but the Federal soldiers would not act together and, consequently, the most daring ones were shot down on the walls and fell on their comrades below. A color-bearer fell on the fort with his flag falling over on our side. . . .[17]

The Federal troops . . . then began pouring in from the rear and firing as they came. So many of our men had now fallen that the resistance was weak all around, and the Federal troops began pouring over the walls, where a hand-to-hand encounter ensued on the crest, and our brave men went down in death by overpowering numbers. Quiet soon followed, and about thirty survivors were marched to the rear as prisoners of war and sent to Point Lookout Prison. . . . Lieutenant Colonel Duncan was left on Fort Gregg wounded . . . and in an unconscious condition rolling in the blood of his fallen comrades when we were marched out.[18]

☆ "The Defense of Battery Gregg" by General N. H. Harris [continued]:

A few moments after the fall of Gregg, I received an order from General Lee, at least I understood it as coming from him (General Wilcox says he sent the order), to abandon Whitworth and retreat to the inner line. The enemy had nearly surrounded Whitworth and, under a heavy cross-fire, I withdrew the two regiments [the Nineteenth and Forty-eighth Mississippi] and retired to the inner lines running . . . to the Appomattox River.[19]

☆ *"The Last Engagement of Lee's Army" by J. B. Thompson, Sergeant, Company F, Sixteenth Mississippi Regiment*:

The Battle of Fort Gregg, near Petersburg, Virginia, on the morning of April 2, 1865, was fought by . . . the famous [Twenthy-fourth] Army Corps on the Federal side, nine thousand strong, or thirty Federals to one Confederate. Harris's Brigade of Mississippians was deployed as skirmishers a short distance in front of Fort Gregg. General Harris stationed his men ten feet apart with instructions to maintain that distance and each man in his work must represent ten men. . . .[20]

The first charge was checked with heavy casualties. The second charge came in greater numbers, and many reached and took refuge under the outer wall of the fort. Then there came a lull. . . . When the third assault came, the fort was quickly filled by the enemy. We had no time to load and fire. We broke our guns and used the barrels for clubs. But what could we do against so many?. . . .

There were left of that three hundred Confederates heroes only twenty-seven alive, nineteen of them badly wounded. Among the eight unwounded was M. G. Turner, a Freemason. He gave the Masonic sign of distress to a Federal colonel who grasped him by the hand and drew him from the crowd and protected him from massacre.[21]

I received a blow upon the side of my head and a bayonet thrust at the base of the brain which well-nigh ended my life. I was taken prisoner, though unconscious, to City Point Hospital. . . .[22]

☆ *The Veteran's Story*:

A few men from each regiment made their escape. I was one of that number. As I ran out of the fort, Colonel [Duncan] was shot down right in front of me. I rolled over him and went running on as fast as I could. We surely did some good old running. . . . We learned afterwards that Colonel [Duncan] was only shot through the hip and not killed. We fell back to our reserve line, remaining there till after dark, when we were ordered to march. . . .[23]

— Chapter 22 —

"... THE LOSS OF ALL—
SAVE HONOR"

As a practical matter, after Fort Gregg the Sixteenth Mississippi no longer existed as an organized unit. Through their efforts, and that of the Twelfth Mississippi, the Army of Northern Virginia escaped Petersburg and gained new life. It would be short-lived. Lee's army left Petersburg and Richmond in four separate columns, traveling west toward Amelia Court House. There, where the Richmond and Danville railroads intersected, Lee planned to consolidate his forces, get rations, and move south to unite with Johnston in North Carolina.

Instead of pursuing, Grant, perceiving Lee's dire straits, moved to intercept him and block any chance to move south. After cavalry actions at Namozine Church on April 3rd and Amelia Springs on April 5th, Lee's rear guard under Ewell was annihilated at Sayler's Creek on April 6th.

Lee finally found rations for his starving army at Farmville on April 7th (those due at Amelia Court House inexplicably never arrived), and though he placed his remaining troops in a defensive position, they were unable to prevent the Federals crossing the Appomattox River at High Bridge. Sheridan, in the meantime, positioned his cavalry to cut off Lee's line of retreat at Appomattox Station. When Lee was unable to break through Sheridan's line on April 9th, he found his Army of Northern Virginia, now reduced to less than thirty thousand, surrounded near Appomattox Court House.[1]

☆ *General Nathaniel H. Harris, Movements of the Confederate Army*:

The evacuation [of Fort Whitworth] was accomplished but not without loss, as the enemy made every effort to intercept the retreat. The brigade . . . took positions in the newly formed line, the enemy making no attempt to press his advantage at this point of the lines with infantry but brought artillery and kept up a constant fire throughout the remainder of the day [April 2nd].

The disaster to the Army of Northern Virginia was fully realized by officers and men, and it was apparent that Richmond and Petersburg . . . were to pass into the hands of the enemy; and the Army of Northern Virginia, its ranks thinned by bloody conflicts and disease . . . would have to retire to the mountain fastness of Virginia, then to struggle on for the cause in which their comrades had so bravely died.

Late at night [on April 2nd], the brigade, moving with the remnant of Wilcox's Division, withdrew from the lines and passing through the silent streets of Petersburg—a silence broken only by the low wail of anguish from the hearts of women wrung by the partings from husband, brother, son, or lover—crossed the Appomattox River and left the devoted city to darkness and the enemy. All night the march was continued.[2]

☆ *The Veteran's Story*:

We crossed the north side of the Appomattox River and headed upstream. For five days and nights, we tramped, scarcely knowing where.[3]

☆ *General Nathaniel H. Harris, Movements of the Confederate Army*:

Halting for a short time on the morning of the 3rd of April, a junction was formed with the division and with weary step, without food, the march was continued until late into the night of the 3rd.

On the morning of the 4th, [Harris's Brigade] arrived at Amelia Court House. Here a sore disappointment awaited the army. It was found that the trains that were to supply rations to the army had passed southward without unloading. The march was resumed, the troops suffering from the pangs of hunger, the country affording but little to forage parties sent in search of food. During the afternoon, the enemy intercepted the march and his cavalry occupied the road. General Harris . . . dislodged the enemy, capturing some prisoners. Without halt, save but for a few hours at a time, the march was continued wearily throughout the night of the 4th and the day and night of the 5th.

[Harris' Brigade] crossed Sayler's Creek noon of the 6th [of April] and, halting for a few hours in the afternoon, returned to the hills overlooking Sayler's Creek and with the division formed line of battle to resist the advancing enemy who, overcoming the corps of General Ewell, was pressing hard upon the retreating army. As night closed in, the darkness was illuminated by the lurid glare of burning trains, fired to prevent their falling into the hands of the enemy and the deafening reports from exploding ammunition and bursting shells added a fierce accompaniment to the scene of destruction. On the night of the 6th, [Harris' Brigade] crossed the Appomattox [River] on the High Bridge and went into bivouac on the opposite side.

At early dawn [April 7th], the enemy made an attack on the troops holding the bridge. Firing the bridge, [Harris Brigade] retired along the railroad in the direction of Farmville, taking a right hand road when within about a mile of that place . . . formed a line across the road. Here, on the morning of the 7th, rations were issued to the troops for the first time since leaving Petersburg. About noon, the enemy advanced against the division and was repulsed with great loss. The march was resumed and continued without serious molestation until late in the night.

On the 8th, the march began at an early hour and continued steadily through the day, at dark going into bivouac within four miles of Appomattox Court House. Not a hostile gun had been heard during the day, but soon after sunset the ominous sound of cannon is heard in front.[4]

☆ *Historical Sketch of the Quitman Guards*:

Sherman was approaching from Wilmington by way of Goldsboro, North Carolina, with a force of seventy-five thousand men; Thomas was moving with a force of fifty thousand by way of Knoxville, Tennessee into North Carolina. . . .[5]

☆ *General Nathaniel H. Harris, Movements of the Confederate Army*:

At three o'clock a.m. on the 9th, the roll of the drum aroused the weary troops to resume their toilsome and painful march. Marching some two miles, after many halts the division was filed to the left and right of the road and ordered to rest. Day had dawned . . . and firing, both of musketry and artillery, was heard in front, then everything became quiet. After the lapse of an hour, strange rumors were brought back from the front by stragglers. At first, the men were terribly excited and swore they would shoot the coward who fled from the front and talked of white flags and surrender, but later in the day the story came in such shape as to leave no doubts on the minds of the listeners, and then it was that strong, bearded men, veterans tried by every ordeal of four years of relentless war, threw themselves prone upon the earth and wept as women.

At sundown [on April 9th], the enemy made the welkin ring with salvos from all his batteries. The vanquished, drenched, cold, shivering and hungry huddled around their bivouac fires, realizing the loss of all—save honor.

On the 10th and 11th, it rained, and without rations, except a ration of beef issued on the tenth, the men were exposed to a pitiless storm, without shelter.[6]

☆ *The Veteran's Story*:

When General Lee was paroled, he mounted his old gray war-horse—Traveler—and started towards his war-blighted home. As he passed through our camps, we all cheered him for the last time. The grandest chieftain the world has ever known gave us a farewell salute. He was gracious and gallant in the sorest hour of defeat.[7]

☆ *General Nathaniel H. Harris, Movements of the Confederate Army*:

On the 12th, Mahone's Division, under command of General Harris, marched to a point near Appomattox Court House and stacked arms. Harris' Brigade stacking about one hundred and fifty muskets. On the night of the 12th, the division of Mahone, assembled, formed a hollow square and after being addressed by General Mahone, General Harris and other officers, and the men took final leave of each other.

On the morning of the 13th [of April], General Harris called the remnant of his brigade together and after considering the impoverished condition of the country, the destroyed lines of railroad and the difficulty of subsisting a body of men, it was determined by officers and men to divide into small squads and thus try to reach their homes.[8]

☆ *The Veteran's Story*:

The soldiers were paroled as fast as possible and turned loose to get home the best way they could. We had known nothing but war for four years, but the home-journey was the tug of war. No transportation, no rations, no money, ragged and heart-sick, with miles and miles between us and our homes "away down south in Dixie". . . .[9]

☆ *"The Last Engagement of Lee's Army" by J. B. Thompson, Sergeant, Company F, Sixteenth Mississippi Regiment*:

Fifty-two years later, at the peace jubilee of the Blue and the Gray at Vicksburg, Mississippi, I met G. L. Kern . . . [one of the Union soldiers who helped capture] Fort Gregg. . . . Then he and I stood face to face as bitter foes; today we stand side by side, as friends in a photograph.[10]

POSTSCRIPTS

Samuel E. Baker—Colonel Samuel E. Baker was killed at Spotsylvania on May 12, 1864.[1]

Buxton Reives Conerly—After the war, Conerly moved to Marshall, Texas, and wrote extensively about his wartime experiences and possibly authored *An Historical Sketch of the Quitman Guards, Company E, Sixteenth Mississippi Regiment, Harris' Brigade, by One of the Quitman Guards.*[2]

Luke Ward Conerly—Captured in the Shenandoah Valley on June 27, 1862, and confined in a Washington, D.C. prison for forty days, Conerly rejoined the Sixteenth after his parole (or exchange). He was wounded at Spotsylvania Court House on May 12, 1864, but survived the war and married Emma Euline Quinn in December 1867. They had fourteen children. Conerly wrote *The History of Pike County, Mississippi, 1798–1876* and possibly the Quitman Guards history. He was reported living in Gulfport, Mississippi, in 1906 and died there in 1922. He is buried in the Old Soldiers Cemetery at Beauvoir, the last home of Jefferson Davis and now a museum and library in Biloxi, Mississippi.[3]

John Berryman Crawford—Crawford was killed in the Bloody Angle at the Battle of Spotsylvania, May 12, 1864. His widow, Martha Ann, married Thomas Henry Green, a member of the Jasper Grays to whom Crawford referred in his letters as T. H. Green.[4]

Hugh Carroll Dickson—Dickson survived the war but died from unknown causes a year after returning home. He is buried near Utica, Mississippi, in the family cemetery.[5]

Winfield Scott Featherston—Upon his return to Mississippi in 1863, Featherston commanded a brigade in Loring's Division in the Yazoo River delta and served in the Vicksburg Campaign. At Atlanta and Nashville, he occasionally commanded Loring's Division. He surrendered with Johnston's army in North Carolina and was paroled April 26, 1865.

After the war, General Featherston practiced law in Holly Springs, Mississippi, and was elected to the state legislature in 1876, 1877, and 1890. While in the legislature, he served as chairman of the Judiciary Committee. Appointed judge of the Second

Circuit Court in 1887, he later served as grand commander of Confederate Veterans of Mississippi. He died May 28, 1891, in Holly Springs.[6]

Abram Morrell Feltus—Colonel Feltus was killed in the Bloody Angle at Spotsylvania Court House, May 12, 1864. His body was found next to Colonel Baker's.[7]

William Harris Hardy—In late 1862 or early 1863, Hardy resigned from the Sixteenth Mississippi due to chronic illness. When he recovered, he re-enlisted and served in the Western Theater as aide-de-camp to General James Argyle Smith. Hardy survived the war and practiced law in South Mississippi. Sallie died in 1872 at the age of twenty-nine.

Hardy went on to build South Mississippi's railroads and served the state as a legislator and circuit judge, becoming one of its leading citizens during the Reconstruction period. After he founded the city of Hattiesburg (named for his second wife, Hattie Lott), Forrest County, Mississippi, was nearly named Hardy County in his honor, but Anselm McLaurin, governor at the time and fellow former Smith Countian, vetoed the bill. Hardy died shortly after his eightieth birthday in Gulfport, Mississippi, which he also founded.[8]

Nathaniel Harrison Harris—General Harris resumed his law practice in Vicksburg after the war and later became the president of the Mississippi Valley and Ship Island Railroad. Later, he served as registrar of the U.S. Land Office in Aberdeen, South Dakota. After 1890, Harris made his home in California where he engaged in business with John Hays Hammond. Harris died on August 23, 1900, while on a business trip. At his request, his remains were cremated and the ashes buried in Green-Wood Cemetery, New York City. He never married.[9]

Jesse Ruebel Kirkland—Captain Kirkland died of pneumonia on June 12, 1862, at the home of Dr. J. Staige Davis in Charlottesville, Virginia.

James Johnson Kirkpatrick—On August 21, 1864, Kirkpatrick was captured and sent to the Federal prisoner of war camp at Point Lookout, Maryland. At the end of the war, he returned to Mississippi where he farmed cotton and dealt in the cotton market. After a poor market left him nearly bankrupt, he moved to Missouri and farmed. Kirkpatrick served as a Presbyterian Elder for many years and died in June 1924 at the age of eighty-five.[10]

John South Lewis—Captain Lewis returned to Woodville after the war and bought the local newspaper, *The Woodville Republican*, now the oldest continuous business and newspaper in Mississippi. He married Mary Lawton Gildart, and together they had three children. At the time of his death in Woodville on September 9, 1900, Captain Lewis still edited the paper. It is still owned and operated by his descendants.[11]

Fletcher Drake Lewis also survived the war and returned to Wilkinson County, Mississippi, and married Elizabeth Harris. They had four children and owned and successfully operated a 3,500 acre plantation. He died on March 3, 1923.[12]

William Henry Harrison Lewis—Harry Lewis was killed at Turkey Creek near Gaines Mill, Virginia, on June 9, 1864.[13]

Ransom Jones Lightsey—Lightsey escaped Fort Gregg and surrendered with Lee at Appomattox. He returned to Jasper County, Mississippi, and married Mary Elizabeth

Beard on December 7, 1865. With their eight children, they lived near Hickory in Newton County, Mississippi, where Lightsey ran a grist mill and cotton gin. The family moved in 1885 to Daleville in Lauderdale County, Mississippi, where Lightsey died on September 9, 1919 at the age of eighty-one.[14]

Carnot Posey—Posey was wounded at Bristoe Station, Virginia, and said to his son Stanhope, "Well, Son, it looks like they got me this time." He died from his wounds on November 13, 1863, in Charlottesville, Virginia, at the home of his friend, Dr. J. Staige Davis, surgeon at the University of Virginia.[15]

Isaac Ridgeway Trimble—Trimble lost a leg in the Pickett-Pettigrew charge at Gettysburg and was captured there July 3, 1863. After the war, he was a consulting engineer in Baltimore, where he died in 1888.[16]

Jefferson J. Wilson—J. J. was captured at Weldon Railroad on August 21, 1864, and imprisoned at Point Lookout, Maryland. He died there of acute diarrhea.[17]

Jerome Bonaparte Yates—Yates was captured August 21, 1864, at Weldon Railroad and sent to the Federal prison at Point Lookout, Maryland. Records show he returned to the Sixteenth (whether by escape or exchange is unknown) and was paroled at Appomattox. After the war, Jerome farmed near Edwards, Hinds County, Mississippi. While returning home from Vicksburg, where he had sold his cotton crop in October 1877, he was robbed and murdered.[18]

Notes

Introduction

1. H. Grady Howell, Jr., *For Dixie Land I'll Take My Stand! A Muster Listing of All Known Mississippi Confederate Soldiers, Sailors and Marines*, vol. I (Madison, Mississippi: Chickasaw Bayou Press, 1998), p. v. "See the elephant" was a popular phrase for participating in a battle. Henry Woodhead, et al., editors, *Soldier Life* (Richmond: Time-Life Books, 1996), p. 160.

2. James McPherson, *The Battle Cry of Freedom* (New York: Oxford University Press, 1988), pp. 91–9; Bruce Catton, *America Goes to War* (New York: MJF Books, 1958), p. 88; James Ford Rhodes, et al., *The Causes of the Civil War*, ed. Kenneth M. Stampp (New York: Simon & Schuster, 1991), pp. 49, 58, 86–8, 151, 178; Emory M. Thomas, *The Confederate Nation, 1861–1865* (New York: Harper & Row, Publishers, 1979), pp. 4.

3. Thomas, *Confederate Nation*, pp. 7, 11; James McPherson, *For Cause and Country: Why Men Fought in the Civil War* (New York: Oxford University Press, 1997), p. ix; McPherson, *Battle Cry*, p. 243.

4. McPherson, *Battle Cry*, p. 21.

5. Ibid.

6. Bell Irvin Wiley, *The Life of Johnny Reb* (Baton Rouge: Louisiana State University Press, 1943), p. 347; Catton, *America Goes to War*, pp. 48–57.

7. John Berryman Crawford Letters, Mississippi Department of Archives and History, Jackson, Mississippi. (The Mississippi Department of Archives and History will be hereinafter referred to as "MDAH.")

8. H. Grady Howell, Jr. and Terrence J. Winschel provided valuable editorial assistance in the preparation of the "Introduction," and their contributions are greatly appreciated.

Writers

1. Elwood Christ, *The Struggle for the Bliss Farm at Gettysburg, July 2nd and 3rd, 1863* (Baltimore: Butternut and Blue, 1994), p. 30; Terrence J. Winschel, "Posey's Brigade at Gettysburg: Part I," *Gettysburg Magazine*, Issue Number 4 (January, 1991), pp. 7–15;

Howell, *For Dixie Land*, Volume I, p. 103; Robert K. Krick, *Lee's Colonels: A Biographical Sketch of the Field Officers of the Army of Northern Virginia*, 4th ed. (Dayton, Ohio: Morningside House, Inc., 1996), p. 43.

2. Miss Mamie Yeary, *Reminiscences of the Boys in Gray* (McGregor, TX, 1912; reprint, Dayton, Ohio: Morningside Publishing, 1986), pp.146–50; Luke Ward Conerly, *Pike County Mississippi, 1798–1876* (Nashville Tennessee: Brandon Printing Company, 1909; reprint, Easley, South Carolina: Southern Historical Press, 1978), p. 111. Buxton R. Conerly, "Defense of Fort Gregg," *Confederate Veteran*, Volume XV, Number 11 (November, 1907), pp. 505–6.

3. Howell, *For Dixie Land*, Volume I, p. 552; Luke Ward Conerly, *Pike County*, p. 111.

4. Letters of John Berryman Crawford, MDAH.

5. Karen B. Taylor to editor, May 4, 1999; Letters of Hugh Carroll Dickson, private collection of Karen Taylor.

6. Howell, *For Dixie Land*, Volume I, p. 863; Mark M. Boatner, III, *The Civil War Dictionary* (New York: Vintage Books, 1991), p. 276; Bobby Roberts and Carl Moneyhon, *Portraits of a Conflict: A Photographic History of Mississippi in the Civil War* (Fayetteville, AR: The University of Arkansas Press, 1993), p. 137; Dunbar Rowland, ed., *Mississippi: Comprising Sketches of Counties, Towns, Events, Institutions, and Persons Arranged in Cyclopedic Form*, vol. 1 of *A History of Mississippi* (Atlanta: Southern Historical Publishing Association, 1907; reprint, Spartanburg, South Carolina: The Reprint Company, Publishers, 1976), pp. 700–1.

7. Civil War diary of James J. Kirkpatrick, Center for American History, University of Texas at Austin, initial entry (undated); Eugene M. Ott, "The Civil War Diary of James J. Kirkpatrick, Sixteenth Infantry, C.S.A." (Master's Thesis, Texas A&M University, 1984), p. 19; Krick, *Lee's Colonels*, p. 137; David E. Holt, *A Mississippi Rebel in the Army of Northern Virginia: The Civil War Memoirs of Private David Holt*, ed. Thomas D. Cockrell and Michael B. Ballard (Baton Rouge: Louisiana State University Press, 1995), p. 257.

8. William Harris Hardy and Toney A. Hardy, *No Compromise With Principle: The Epic Story of William Harris Hardy and the Mississippi He Loved* (New York: American Book—Stratford Press, 1946), pp. 6, 57, 342; Dunbar Rowland, editor, *Biographical Sketches of Mississippians*, vol. 3 of *A History of Mississippi* (Atlanta: Southern Historical Publishing Association, 1907; reprint, Spartanburg, South Carolina: The Reprint Company, Publishers, 1976), pp. 367–76; Mrs. Edwin K. (Margie) Myrick to editor, May 5, 1999; Civil War Letters of William Harris Hardy to Sallie Johnson Hardy, private collection of William Harris Hardy Family and McCain Library and Archives, University of Southern Mississippi, Hattiesburg, Mississippi.

9. Winschel, "Posey's Brigade," p. 10; Howell, *For Dixie Land*, Volume II, p. 1031; Boatner, *Dictionary*, p. 378; Roberts and Moneyhon, *Portraits*, p. 361; *A Historical Sketch of the Quitman Guards, Company E, Sixteenth Mississippi Regiment, Harris' Brigade, by One of the Quitman Guards* (New Orleans: Isaac Hinton, Printer, 1888, photocopy), p. 28.

10. Letters of Jessie Ruebel Kirkland, MDAH.

11. Terrence J. Winschel, "The Gettysburg Experience of James J. Kirkpatrick," *Gettysburg Magazine*, Issue Number 8 (January, 1993), pp. 111–19. Kirkpatrick Diary, initial entry (undated); Ott, p. 8.

12. Harry Lewis Papers, Southern Historical Collection, University of North Carolina at Chapel Hill; John South Lewis, telephone interview by editor, April 9, 1999; Howell, *For Dixie Land*, Volume II, p.1751.

13. Lewis Papers; Lewis, telephone interview; Howell, *For Dixie Land*, Volume II, p.1754.

14. Rowland, *Biographical Sketches*, p. 452; Hon. Norman Gillis, Jr. to editor, December 15, 1999; Lewis Letters; Lewis, telephone interview; Howell, *For Dixie Land*, Volume II, p. 1748.

15. Patricia Lightsey Davis, *The Lightsey Family History* (n.p., 1990), p. 61.

Ada Christine Lightsey, *The Veteran's Story: Ransom Jones Lightsey* (n.p., 1899, photocopy), p. 19; Howell, *For Dixie Land*, Volume II, p. 1756.

16. Winschel, "Posey's Brigade," p. 7; Boatner, *Dictionary*, p. 663.

17. Winschel, "Posey's Brigade," p. 7.

18. Winschel, "Posey's Brigade, p. 7; Kitty Day Papers; Day, "Brigadier General Carnot Posey," p. 26.

19. Boatner, *Dictionary*, p. 849.

20. Rev. J. William Jones, "Reminiscences of the Army of Northern Virginia, Paper Number 3: Down in the Valley After Stonewall's Quartermaster," *Southern Historical Society Papers*, Volume IX (1881), pp. 185–9.

21. Muster Rolls of "Crystal Springs Southern Rights," Records Group 9, Volume 132, Folder T, and the Wilson (J. J.) Papers, MDAH; Howell, *For Dixie Land*, Volume III, p. 3222.

22. Letters of Jerome B. Yates, Center for American History, University of Texas at Austin; Ott, p. 28.

Chapter 1

1. James C. Davis, age 52, Baptist minister and organizer of Company C. Howell, *For Dixie Land*, Volume I, p. 673; Dunbar Rowland, *The Official and Statistical Register of the State of Mississippi, 1908* (Nashville: Press of the Brandon Printing Company, 1908), p. 459; Ben H. Fatherree, "John Wall Fatherree and the Jasper Grays, 1861–1865" (unpublished manuscript, date unknown, photocopy), p. 15; Wenschel, "Gettysburg Kirkpatrick," pp. 111–19; Ott, "Diary Kirkpatrick," p. 14.

2. John J. Pettus, Governor of Mississippi, 1859–1863. Rowland, *Statistical Register*, p. 148.

3. Yates is obviously referring to James Johnson Kirkpatrick, the only Kirkpatrick in Company C. Howell, *For Dixie Land*, Volume II, p. 1667.

Myers could be either Francis Marion Myers, fifth sergeant, Company C or Private John Myers of Company C. Howell, *For Dixie Land*, Volume II, pp. 2151, 2152.

"Cy" is likely Cyrus LaFayette Broome, private. Howell, *For Dixie Land*, Volume I, p. 310.

"Tom" could be one of several "Thomases" in Company C or others who have "T" as an initial.

"Throgmorton" is likely John W. Throckmorton, corporal in Company C. Howell, *For Dixie Land*, Volume III, p. 2951.

Mimms could be either George A. or Martin M., both privates in Company C. Howell, *For Dixie Land*, Volume II, p. 2052.

Bolls is Private (later corporal) James Bolls of Company C. Howell, *For Dixie Land*, Volume II, p. 232.

4. "Mac" Mimms, is likely Martin M. Mimms, private, Company C. Howell, *For Dixie Land*, Volume II, p. 2052.

5. Thomas J. Hardy, sergeant; third lieutenant, first lieutenant, then captain of Company H when his brother, W. H. Hardy, resigned and joined the staff of General Argyle Smith. Hardy, *No Compromise*, p. 61; Howell, *For Dixie Land*, Volume II, p. 1277.

6. Mrs. Kirkland was pregnant when Jesse left for the war. Kirkland Letters, MDAH.

7. Kirkpatrick meant Robert Clarke of Company I, who had commanded the militia company since 1838. He was dropped at the May, 1862 reorganization because he was not re-elected. Hardy, *No Compromise*, p. 62; Howell, *For Dixie Land*, Volume I, p. 499; Ott, "Diary Kirkpatrick," p. 18; Krick, *Lee's Colonel's*, p. 92.

Thomas Jefferson Bankston, lieutenant, Company F, April 27, 1861, elected major June 8, 1861; later promoted to colonel. Hardy, *No Compromise*, p. 62; Howell, *For Dixie Land*, Volume I, p. 113; Krick, *Lee's Colonels*, p. 45.

Thomas Ringland Stockdale (1828–1899), was born in Pennsylvania and a graduate of Washington and Jefferson College, living in Holmesville, Mississippi. He was dropped from the roster at the May, 1862 reorganization but later served in various other Mississippi units, including the Fourth Mississippi Cavalry. He served on the Mississippi Supreme Court, 1896–1899. "Colonel Thomas Ringland Stockdale," *Confederate Veteran*, Volume 7, Number 4 (April, 1899), pp. 176–7; Ott, "Diary Kirkpatrick," p.18; *Quitman Guards*, p. XI.

8. James D. Blincoe; company mustered in at Summit, Pike County, Mississippi, April 20, 1861; Blincoe later resigned and did not re-enter service with the company. Howell, *For Dixie Land*, Volume I, p. 220; Luke Ward Conerly, *Pike County Mississippi*, p. 183.

George J.D. Funchess; company mustered in at Westville, Simpson County, Mississippi, April 20, 1861. Howell, *For Dixie Land*, Volume I, p. 939; Rowland, *Statistical Register 1908*, p. 459.

James C. Davis, see endnote above; company mustered at Crystal Springs, Copiah County, Mississippi, April 25, 1861; this was the largest company with 107. Howell, *For Dixie Land*, Volume I, p. 673; Rowland, *Statistical Register 1908*, p. 459; Fatherree, "Jasper Grays," p. 15.

Samuel A. Matthews; Ohio-born lawyer; residence in Holmesville, Mississippi; company mustered in at Holmesville, Pike County, Mississippi, April 23, 1861; retired, April 26, 1862. Howell, *For Dixie Land*, Volume II, p. 1995; Rowland, *Statistical Register 1908*, p. 460; James F. Brieger, *Hometown Mississippi* (n. p., 1980), p. 394; L. W. Conerly, *Pike County*, p. 179; *Quitman Guards*, p. XI.

James J. Shannon was thirty-six when the war began. His company mustered in at Paulding, Jasper County, Mississippi, April 27, 1861. Rowland, *Statistical Register 1908*, p. 460; Ott, "Diary Kirkpatrick," p. 38; Krick, *Lee's Colonel's*, p. 339.

John Taylor Moore; company mustered in at Port Gibson, Claiborne County, Mississippi, March 10, 1861; this was the smallest company, with 68 men; Moore later resigned and was replaced by Benjamin Humphreys. Howell, *For Dixie Land*, Volume II, p. 1489; Rowland, *Statistical Register 1908*, p. 460; Fatherree, "Jasper Grays," p. 15.

William Harris Hardy; company mustered at Raleigh, Smith County, Mississippi, April 29, 1861; forty-one additional men were mustered into C.S.A. service at Corinth on June 17, 1861. Rowland, *Statistical Register 1908*, p. 460.

This was company number 1 of Adams Light Guard; Douglas Walworth, elected after Captain Robert Clarke of Natchez was elected lieutenant colonel; company mustered in at Natchez, May 25, 1861. Rowland, *Statistical Register 1908*, p. 461.

Abram Morrell Feltus was elected captain after Carnot Posey was elected colonel; company mustered in at Woodville, Wilkinson County, Mississippi, April 21, 186. Ott, "Diary Kirkpatrick," p. 19; Rowland, *Statistical Register 1908*, p. 461.

9. Peter G. Feltus, also known as "Gad" Feltus, first sergeant, third lieutenant, first lieutenant, Company K. Howell, *For Dixie Land*, Volume I, p. 864.

10. Jefferson Hamilton, Company K, later field staff. Howell, *For Dixie Land*, Volume II, p. 1252.

11. Battle of First Manassas (Bull Run), July 21, 1861. Boatner, *Dictionary*, p. 99. Pierre Gustave Beauregard (1818–1893) of Louisiana graduated the U.S. Military Academy in 1838, second in a class of forty-five. In the Mexican War, he was an engineer on Scott's staff. In January 1861, he was superintendent at West Point but resigned in February to accept appointment as brigadier general in the C.S.A. Though J. E. Johnston was in over-all command at First Manassas, Beauregard commanded the line. Described as selfish and petty yet brilliant, he had a talent for making enemies and counted Jefferson Davis among his most bitter. After the war, he turned down command of the Rumanian and Egyptian armies to work in the United States as a railroad president and supervisor of the Louisiana lottery drawings. Boatner, *Dictionary*, pp. 54–5, 99. Noah Andre Trudeau, *Bloody Roads South: The Wilderness to Cold Harbor, May-June, 1864* (Boston: Little, Brown, & Co., 1989), p. 251.

12. *Quitman Guards*, pp. 8–9.

13. Henry W. Evans of Sylvarena, Smith County, Mississippi, corporal, Company H; brother-in-law of Hardy; promoted to sergeant, but preferred the rank of private; he died at his home near Macon, Mississippi on January 24, 1912. "Henry W. Evans," *Confederate Veteran*, Volume unknown, number 5 (May, 1912), p. 237; Hardy, *No Compromise*, p. 61. Howell, *For Dixie Land*, Volume I, p 837.

Chapter 2

1. *Quitman Guards*, p. 13.

2. Joseph Eggleston Johnston (1807–1891) of Virginia graduated West Point in 1829, thirteenth in a class of forty-six. He served in the Black Hawk Expedition, the Seminole War, Mexican War, and on the frontier, but resigned when the war began and commanded the Department of the Potomac. Senior among the officers who resigned to join the Confederacy, he felt he should retain it even though he was fourth in seniority in the C. S. Army. He and Davis feuded over the issue, and after being wounded at Seven Pines, was replaced by Lee on June 1, 1862 and later transferred to the western theater. After the war, he entered the insurance business and served a term in Congress. Boatner, *Dictionary*, p. 441.

3. The battlefield was that of First Manassas (First Bull Run), July 21, 1861. E. B. Long with Barbara Long, *The Civil War Day by Day: An Alamanac 1861–1865* (New York: Da Capo Press, Inc., 1971), p. 98; Boatner, *Dictionary*, p. 99.

4. William was, apparently, a slave.

5. George Britton McClellan (1826–1885) of Pennsylvania graduated second in a class of fifty-nine at West Point 1846. Winning three brevets for gallantry in the Mexican War, he resigned the army in 1857. When the war began, he was vice president of Illinois Central Railroad. After being appointed major general, he commanded the Department of the Ohio. He excelled at organizing, administrating, and training, and Lincoln gave him command the Division of the Potomac and later made him Commander-in-Chief. When he failed in the Peninsula Campaign, he was relieved but reinstated when Pope failed at Second Manassas. Lincoln removed him again in 1862, and he sat out the rest of the war. McClellan ran for president in 1864, relying on the vote of the army, which held him in high regard. After the war, he was governor of New Jersey. Boatner, *Dictionary*, p. 524.

6. George Bibb Crittenden, major general and son of Kentucky senator John J. Crittenden, who authored the Compromise of 1861and worked to keep Kentucky in the Union. After Crittenden's defeat at Logan Cross Roads in 1862, he was arrested, censured and forced to resign. He served the rest of the war without rank on the staff of General John S. Williams. Shelby Foote, *Fort Sumter to Perryville*, vol. 1 of *The Civil War: A Narrative* (New York: Random House, 1958), p. 87; Boatner, *Dictionary*, p. 208.

7. James E. Griffith, sergeant, brevet second lieutenant, first lieutenant, Company H. Howell, *For Dixie Land*, Volume II, p. 1207.

8. Robert Augustus Toombs (1810–1885) of Georgia. A lawyer, Congressman, and Senator, Toombs was one of the wealthiest men in Georgia when the war began. He wanted to be C. S. A. president but accepted the post of Secretary of State, resigning in July, 1861 to become brigadier general. Failing to get the promotion he felt he deserved, he resigned in May, 1863. In 1865, he fled to Cuba and England but later returned to build a large law practice. He never asked for a pardon. Boatner, *Dictionary*, pp. 841–2.

9. James Longstreet of Virginia, known as "Pete" and "Lee's Old Warhorse," was born in South Carolina in 1821 and appointed to West Point from Alabama, graduating in 1842, fifty-fourth in a class of sixty-two. After serving in Florida, Mexico, and on the frontier, Longstreet resigned to accept a Confederate commission. In October, 1861, he was made major general and commanded a division. He disagreed with Lee's strategy at Gettysburg and was later considered responsible for the loss. Sentiment developed against him after the war which forced him to rely on political appointments for his livelihood. Following the war, he was an insurance company president, cotton factor in New Orleans, and member of the Republican Party. He was said to be slightly below average height, broad shouldered and heavy. Longstreet died in 1904. Boatner, *Dictionary*, pp. 490–1.

10. Doctor Joseph J. Holt, Surgeon, Second Mississippi Infantry. Howell, *For Dixie Land*, Volume II, p. 1434; Holt, *Mississippi Rebel*, ed. Cockrell and Ballard, p. 9.

Chapter 3

1. Kirkpatrick (and Kirkland's October 22nd letter) is referring to the battle of Ball's Bluff at Leesburg, October 21, 1861. A Union brigade crossed the Potomac, hoping to dislodge Rebels from the area. Confederates, waiting on top of the bluff, routed the Federal forces, driving them back across the river. James M. McPherson, editor, *The Atlas of the Civil War* (New York: MacMillan, 1994), p. 33; Long, *Day by Day*, p. 129; Boatner, *Dictionary*, p.41.

2. Clement Anselm Evans (1833–1911) of Georgia, a lawyer, judge, and legislator before the war, enlisted in November, 1861. As a result of the carnage he saw at Fredericksburg, he became a Methodist minister after the war and edited the multi-volume *Confederate Military History* in 1899. Boatner, *Dictionary*, pp. 267–8. William Barksdale (1821–1863) of Mississippi. A Congressman, he resigned when Mississippi seceded. Wounded and captured in the Peach Orchard at Gettysburg July 2, 1863, he died the next day. Howell, *For Dixie Land*, Volume I, p. 121; Boatner, *Dictionary*, p. 44.

Erasmus R. Burt, colonel, Eighteenth Mississippi Infantry; born in South Carolina. He served as Mississippi's state auditor and is credited with founding the Deaf and Dumb Institute of Mississippi. On October 26, 1861, he died of abdominal wounds received at Leesburg. Howell, *For Dixie Land*, Volume I, p. 374; Rowland, *Statistical Register 1908*, p. 475.

Otho R. Singleton, captain, Company C, Eighteenth Mississippi Infantry; after the war, he served in Congress. Howell, *For Dixie Land*, Volume III, p. 2704.

3. Cornelius B. Lancaster, private, Company H. Howell, *For Dixie Land*, Volume II, p. 1695.

4. Edmund Kirby Smith (1824–1893), a Floridian, graduated West Point in 1845, twenty-fifth in a class of forty-one. After the Mexican War, he taught mathematics at West Point, resigning in March, 1861 to become a Confederate cavalry colonel. Promoted to brigadier general in June, 1861, he was wounded at First Manassas. While commanding the Department of East Tennessee, he was promoted to full general in February, 1864, he appointed several generals, only to have the appointments revoked because such authority lay only with the President. Smith surrendered the last Confederate forces on June 2, 1865, then fled to Cuba but returned in November, 1865. He served as president of the University of Nashville from 1870–1875 then taught math at the at the University of the South (Sewanee) until his death. Boatner, *Dictionary*, pp. 769–70.

5. John W. Hughes or Walter Hughes, both privates in Company K. Howell, *For Dixie Land*, Volume II, pp. 1482, 1483.

6. Chatam Roberdeau Wheat (1826–1861) graduated the University of Nashville in 1845. He practiced law in New Orleans and was a legislator. When the war began, he became major of the First Louisiana Battalion, later known as "Wheat's Battalion." Colleagues described him as six foot four, uncouth, wild, and passionate for adventure. His men, apparently, followed his example and continued to bear his name after he was killed at Gaines' Mill, May 25, 1861. Krick, *Lee's Colonels*, p. 391.

7. John J. Norwood, private, Company B. Howell, *For Dixie Land*, Volume III, p.2243.

8. The Battle of Dranesville, December 20, 1861, in which the Confederate forces were led by James Ewell Brown Stuart (1833–1864) of Virginia. Kirkland was obviously unaware that Stuart had been made brigadier on September 24, 1861. Stuart graduated West Point in 1854, thirteenth in a class of forty-six. He was wounded fighting Indians on the frontier and was Lee's aide-de-camp during John Brown's raid at Harpers Ferry. In May, 1861, he resigned the Army to become lieutenant colonel of the Virginia Infantry but two weeks later was appointed a cavalry captain. At Yellow Tavern (May 11, 1864), Stuart was wounded and died the next day. Boatner, *Dictionary*, pp. 812–13; Long, *Day by Day*, p. 150.

9. Daniel W. C. Murray, private, Company B. Howell, *For Dixie Land*, Volume II, p. 2145; Judge Bee King, "Unpublished Notes," MDAH, p. 2.

Chapter 4

1. *Quitman Guards*, pp. 15–17.

2. Zack Royals, private, Company H. Howell, *For Dixie Land*, Volume III, p. 2579. Hardy, *No Compromise*, p. 72.

3. David G. Jefferies, drummer, Company K. Howell, *For Dixie Land*, Volume II, p. 1538.

4. Richard Stoddert Ewell (1817–1872) of Virginia; graduated West Point in 1840, thirteenth in a class of forty-two; served in the Mexican and Indian Wars. Resigning in May, 1861, he was a division commander in the Shenandoah Campaign. He lost a leg at Groveton and indecision at Gettysburg tarnished his reputation. After a fall from his horse at Spotsylvania, he was unable to return to field service. He was described as "bald, pop-eyed and long beaked, with a piping voice. . . ." Boatner, *Dictionary*, pp.268–9.

5. Mattie was born December 17, 1861. Hardy, *No Compromise*, p. 72.

6. Hardy was referring to the Battle of Shiloh (Tennessee) fought April 6–7, 1862. The Yankees were not, however, "gloriously whipped," as he suggests. Both sides claimed victory. Beauregard withdrew to Corinth, Mississippi, approximately twenty miles south, and Halleck pursued leisurely. Boatner, *Dictionary*, pp. 752–7.

7. Don Carlos Buell (1818–1898) of Ohio; graduated West Point in 1841, thirty-second in class of fifty-two; served in the Mexican War. He arrived at Shiloh late but in time to help claim a Union victory. In June, 1864, he resigned amidst investigations of his Tennessee and Kentucky campaigns. After the war, he was president of Green River Iron Company. Boatner, *Dictionary*, p. 96.

8. Nathaniel Prentiss Banks (1816–1894) of Massachusetts; congressman, 1853–1857; Massachusetts governor, 1858–1861. Banks took command of the V Corps in March, 1862 and defeated Jackson at Kernstown but was outgeneraled in the remaining Shenandoah Valley Campaign battles and Cedar Mountain. In 1863, he commanded the Department of the Gulf. He left the army in 1864. Returning to Massachusetts after the war, he served several terms in Congress, retiring in 1890 "owing to an increasing mental disorder." Boatner, *Dictionary*, p. 42.

Thomas Jonathan Jackson (1824–1863) of Virginia graduated West Point in 1846, seventeenth in a class of fifty-nine. Distinguished in the Mexican War, he left the army to teach at the Virginia Military Institute in 1851. He was appointed to brigadier general in June, 1861, and at First Manassas, he won the nickname "Stonewall" for his bravery. In 1862, he was promoted to major general. Boatner, *Dictionary*, pp. 432–3. *Quitman Guards*, p. 17.

9. John Charles Fremont (1813–1880) of Georgia explored the Rocky Mountains and arrived in California in 1846, saving it for the U.S. After serving as California's governor, he was its Senator and ran for President as a Republican in 1856. Following Cross Keys on June 8, 1862, his command became the I Corps under Pope. Fremont refused to serve under Pope and was relieved on June 26, spending the rest of the war "awaiting orders." After the war, he built railroads and was governor of Arizona. Boatner, *Dictionary*, pp. 314–15.

10. Jasper Boykin, born November 9, 1834 in Pineville, Smith County, Mississippi,

private, Company H; dismissed due to illness; one of ten Boykins (all brothers or first cousins) in the eighty-man company; later enlisted in the 37th Mississippi. Howell, *For Dixie Land*, Volume I, p. 264; Olivia Skaggs Killian, *Boykins: Branches and Roots* (Tupelo, Mississippi: Richardson Publishing Company, 1979), pp. 109–10.

11. On April 16, 1862, the Confederate Congress passed a conscription act, drafting into service for three years all white males between the ages of 18 and 35 not otherwise exempt. Long, *Day by Day*, p. 200.

John C. Swittenberg (or Swettenberg), second lieutenant, captain, Company H; lost leg at Spotsylvania. Howell, *For Dixie Land*, Volume III, p. 2878; "History of Mississippi Troops," J. L. Power Scrapbook, MDAH, p. 40.

12. *Quitman Guards*, p. 17.

13. Lightsey, *Veteran's Story*, pp. 10–11

Chapter 5

1. Boatner, *Dictionary*, pp. 432–3, 739–40; *Quitman Guards*, p. 18; McPherson, *Atlas*, pp. 66–9; Kitty Day Papers, p. 5; Winschel, "Posey's Brigade," p. 10; Rowland, *Statistical Register 1908*, pp. 461–2; William Allan, *History of the Campaign of General T. J. (Stonewall) Jackson in the Shenandoah Valley of Virginia from November 4, 1861 to June 17, 1862* (Philadelphia: J. B. Lippincott & Company, 1912; Reprint, Dayton, Ohio: Morningside House, Inc., 1991), pp. 91–2, 152.

2. Robert K. Krick, *Conquering the Valley: Stonewall Jackson at Port Republic* (New York: William Morrow and Company, Inc., 1996), pp.145–6, 158–82; Robert G. Tanner, *Stonewall in the Valley: Thomas J. "Stonewall" Jackson's Shenandoah Valley Campaign, Spring, 1862* (Mechanicsburg, PA: Stackpole Books, 1996), p. 385.

3. On May 23, 1862 at Front Royal, Jackson brought his force of 16,000 against Colonel John R. Kenley's one thousand. After Belle Boyd met General Dick Taylor outside town and advised him of Federal positions, Taylor attacked. Kenley was wounded and captured, the First Maryland Confederate Regiment captured the First Maryland Union Regiment, and 900 of Kenley's men were killed or captured. Boatner, *Dictionary*, pp. 317–18.

4. First Battle of Winchester, May 25, 1862. The Federal lines held the first few hours of the Sunday morning attack, then retreated. Jackson was unable to mount an effective pursuit. Boatner, *Dictionary*, pp. 936–7.

5. Lightsey, *Veteran's Story*, pp. 13–14.

6. United States War Department, *The War of the Rebellion: A Compilation of the Official Records of the Union and Confederate Armies*, 70 volumes in 128 parts (Washington, D.C.: U.S. Government Printing Office, 1880– 1901), Series 1, Volume XII, Chapter XXIV, pp. 794–5. [Excerpts from the *Official Records* are hereinafter cited as "O. R."]

7. *Quitman Guards*, pp. 20–1.

8. Irish-born and educated Union General James Shields (1806–1879) once challenged Lincoln to a duel, but they later became close friends. He served as a state legislator and state supreme court justice before being appointed governor of the Oregon Territory. After serving as U.S. Senator from Oregon, he served as Minnesota's senator. He was mining in Mexico when the war began and was made brigadier general on August 19, 1861. During the Shenandoah Campaign, he commanded a division. After the war, he returned to the U.S. Senate. Having served as senator for Minnesota, Illi-

nois, Oregon, and Missouri, he is possibly the only individual to represent four states. Boatner, *Dictionary*, p. 752. *Quitman Guards*, p. 21.

9. General Turner Ashby (1828–1862), a wealthy planter, grain dealer, and politician in the Shenandoah Valley prior to the war, raised a cavalry company then was appointed brigadier general on May 23, 1862. By the time of his death near Harrisonburg, Virginia on June 6, 1862, his leadership skills had made him near legendary. Boatner, *Dictionary*, p. 28.

10. *Quitman Guards*, p. 21.

11. Richard "Dick" Taylor (1826–1879) of Kentucky, the son of Zachary Taylor, educated in Europe, Harvard and Yale, then became a planter in Louisiana. Appointed brigadier general in October, 1861, he commanded the Louisiana Brigade in the Valley Campaign. Promoted to major general in July, 1862 and lieutenant general in May, 1864, he commanded the Department of East Louisiana, Mississippi and Alabama in August that year. He surrendered May 8, 1865 in Cintronelle, Alabama. Boatner, *Dictionary*, pp. 827–8.

12. *Quitman Guards*, pp. 22–3.

13. The "Bucktails," the Thirteenth Pennsylvania Reserves, consisted of lumbermen who wore the tail of a buck deer in their hats, representing their skill with a rifle. Boatner, *Dictionary*, p. 636.

14. James A. Brown, private and later captain. Howell, *For Dixie Land*, Volume I, p. 320. O.R., Series 1, Vol. XII, Chapter XXIV, pp. 796–7.

15. *Quitman Guards*, p. 23.

Chapter 6

1. Lightsey, *Veteran's Story*, pp. 17–19; *Quitman Guards*, p. 26; McPherson, *Atlas*, pp. 70–1; Stephen W. Sears, *To the Gates of Richmond: The Peninsula Campaign* (New York: Ticknor & Fields, 1992), pp. 197–204; Boatner, *Dictionary*, p. 659.

2. O. R., Series 1, Vol. XI, Part 2, Chapter XXIII, p. 614.

3. See Clifford Dowdey, *The Seven Days: The Emergence of Lee* (Lincoln, NE: University of Nebraska Press, 1964), p. 195; Lightsey, *Veteran's Story*, p. 18.

4. Lee attacked McClellan in mid-afternoon and succeeded despite large losses. Long, *Day by Day*, pp. 231–2.

5. *Quitman Guards*, pp. 26–7.

6. O. R., Series 1, Vol. XI, Part 2, Chapter XXIII, pp. 614–18.

7. E. Steele Irvine, private, Company D. Howell, *For Dixie Land*, Volume II, p. 1513.

Baker's letter was written from Charles City Road, eighteen miles from Richmond on July 6, 1862. "Flag of the Sixteenth Mississippi Regiment," *Confederate Veteran*, Volume XXVI, Number 2 (February 1918), pp. 75–76.

8. O. R., Series 1, Vol. XI, Part 2, Chapter XXIII, pp. 614–18.

9. *Quitman Guards*, p. 27.

10. O. R., Series 1, Vol. XI, Part 2, Chapter XXIII, pp. 614–18.

11. "Flag of the Sixteenth Mississippi," pp. 75–6. See also Boatner, *Dictionary*, pp. 914–16.

12. Lightsey, *Veteran's Story*, p. 19.

13. O. R., Series 1, Vol. XI, Part 2, Chapter XXIII, pp. 614–18.

14. Ibid.

15. Lightsey, *Veteran's Story*, p. 20.

16. Henry J. Hearsey, private, Company K; assistant quartermaster; major; Posey's law partner prior to the war. Howell, *For Dixie Land*, Volume II, p. 1340; Kirkpatrick Diary, November 18, 1863 entry. See also Nathaniel H. Harris, *Movements of the Confederate Army in Virginia and the Part Taken by the Nineteenth Mississippi Regiment: From the Diary of General Nathaniel H. Harris* (Duncansby, MS: W. M. Harris, 1901, photocopy), pp. 20–1.

17. James Alston Groves, surgeon, Companies F and K. Howell, *For Dixie Land*, Volume I, p. 1213.

18. George K. Estes, private, Company K. Howell, *For Dixie Land*, Volume I, p. 830.

19. Drewry's Bluff is a ninety-foot high cliff on the south bank of the James River, seven miles south of Richmond, atop which sat a Confederate fort. Sears, *Gates of Richmond*, p. 93.

20. John Pope (1822–1892), of Kentucky, appointed to West Point from Illinois, graduated in 1842, seventeenth in a class of fifty-six. He fought in the Mexican War and on June 26, 1862 replaced McClellan as head of the reorganized army. Lee disliked Pope intensely due to his harsh treatment of Southern sympathizers. After his defeat at Second Manassas, Pope was relieved of command and McClellan reinstated. Pope retired from the army in 1886. Boatner, *Dictionary*, p. 659.

21. Benjamin Franklin Butler (1818–1893) of New Hampshire practiced criminal law and was in politics prior to the war. In May, 1862, he was appointed military governor of New Orleans. While there, he was extensively criticized and nicknamed "Spoons" (for allegedly stealing silverware) and "the Beast." December 16, 1862, he was replaced by General N. P. Banks. Considered incompetent, Butler's political influence prevented Lincoln from relieving him until after the 1864 election when Grant convinced him that Butler's inaction and blunders at Petersburg contributed to the disaster at Fort Fisher. Elected to Congress in 1866, he was active in President Johnson's impeachment. Governor of Massachusetts in 1883, he unsuccessfully ran for President in 1884. Boatner, *Dictionary*, pp. 109–10.

Chapter 7

1. Boatner, *Dictionary*, pp. 103–5; John J. Hennessey, *Return to Bull Run: The Campaign and Battle of Second Manassas* (New York: Simon & Shuster, 1993); David G. Martin, *The Second Bull Run Campaign, July-August, 1862* (Conshohocken, PA: Combined Books, Inc., 1997).

2. Hennesey, *Return to Bull Run*, pp. 427–8; Martin, *Second Bull Run*, pp. 217, 224.

3. North Carolinian Cadmus Marcellus Wilcox (1824–1890), appointed to West Point from Tennessee, graduated in 1846, fifty-fourth in a class of fifty-nine. Wilcox, a groomsman at Grant's wedding, taught tactics at the Academy after serving in the Mexican War. In the Second Manassas Campaign, he commanded a division in Longstreet's Corps and his own brigade. After the war, he declined commissions in the Egyptian and Korean armies and held various government positions in Washington, D. C., authoring several books on military tactics. At his funeral, eight former generals, four Confederate and four Union, served as pallbearers. Boatner, *Dictionary*, pp. 918–19; Hennessey, *Return Bull Run*, pp. 561–2; Martin, *Second Bull Run*, pp. 280–1.
Quitman Guards, pg. 30.

4. Lightsey, *Veteran's Story*, p. 21.

5. Ibid., p. 22.

6. John Bell Hood (1831–1879), of Kentucky graduated the U.S. Military Academy in 1853, forty-forth in a class of fifty-two. After his failure at Franklin, Tennessee in November, 1864, he was relieved at his own request. He surrendered at Natchez, May 31,1865. After the war, he was a factor commission merchant in New Orleans. Hood, his wife and daughter died in the summer of 1879 of yellow fever. Boatner, *Dictionary*, pp. 407–8.

7. William Dorsy Pender (1834–1863) of North Carolina graduated West Point in 1854, nineteenth in a class of forty-six and resigned in 1861. A Confederate major general at age 29, he died July 18, 1863 following a wound received at Gettysburg. Boatner, *Dictionary*, p. 631.

James Jay Archer (1817–1864) of Maryland attended Princeton and the University of Maryland. He resigned the U.S. Army in May, 1861 to accept a Confederate commission. He was captured at Gettysburg, held for over a year, then served in the Army of the Tennessee until his death on October 24, 1864. Boatner, *Dictionary*, p. 23.

8. O.R., Series 1, Vol. XII, Part 2, Chapter XXIV, pp. 602–4.

9. *Quitman Guards*, pp. 30–2.

10. Roger Atkinson Pryor (1828–1919) of Virginia graduated the University of Virginia School of Law and published a newspaper before going to Greece to investigate American claims against the Greek government. A Congressman in 1861, he resigned for a Confederate commission. He declined the invitation to fire the first shot at Fort Sumter and resigned the Confederate Army in August, 1863, then enlisted as a private in Fitzhugh Lee's cavalry. Captured in November, 1864, Lincoln ordered him freed shortly before Appomattox. A lawyer and newspaper writer in New York in 1865, he was later appointed to the New York Supreme Court. Boatner, *Dictionary*, p. 674.

11. Hardy, *No Compromise*, pp. 67–8.

12. Ambrose Everett Burnside (1824–1881) of Indiana graduated West Point in 1847, eighteenth in a thirty-eight-man class. He served in the Mexican and Indian Wars, then resigned in 1853 to manufacture the breechloading rifle he invented. Treasurer of the Illinois Central Railroad when the war began, he resigned to lead the First Rhode Island Volunteers. After being promoted to major general and twice refusing command of the Army of the Potomac, he accepted at the urging of other generals. Relieved in December, 1862 after the Union disaster at Fredericksburg, he commanded the Army of the Ohio, but returned in time to fight at Spotsylvania. He was again relieved following the Petersburg mine fiasco in July, 1864. In 1866, he was elected governor of Rhode Island, serving two terms before being elected to the U.S. Senate where he served until his death. His mutton-chop whiskers gave rise to the style and phrase "sideburns." Boatner, *Dictionary*, pp. 107–8.

13. Samuel H. Floyd, private, Company H. Howell, *For Dixie Land*, Volume I, p. 893. Dick Derrick is probably William E. Derrick, private, Company H. Howell, *For Dixie Land*, Volume I, p. 709.

Chapter 8

1. Stephen W. Sears, *Landscape Turned Red: The Battle of Antietam* (New York: Ticknor & Fields, 1983), pp. xi-xii; Boatner, *Dictionary*, pp. 17–21, 241–5; John Michael Priest, *Antietam: A Soldier's Battle* (New York: Oxford University Press, 1989), pp. 163, 319.

2. Phillip Kearney (1814–1862) of New York joined the Army in 1837 and served as a cavalry observer in the French Algerian War in 1840. In the Mexican War, he lost an arm in the Mexico City battle. Resigning in 1851, he fought in the French army in Italy, winning the Legion of Honor. He re-enlisted in the U.S. Army and was appointed brigadier general in 1861. At Chantilly, he accidentally rode into Confederate lines and was killed attempting to fight his way out. Boatner, *Dictionary*, p. 449.

3. Lightsey, *Veteran's Story*, p. 23.

4. Richard Heron (Dick) Anderson (1821–1879) of South Carolina, graduated West Point in 1842, fortieth in class of fifty-six. He served in Mexico and the Utah Expedition, then resigned to accept a Confederate commission. In July, 1861, he was appointed brigadier general. His command was destroyed at Sayler's Creek on April 6, 1865. He failed as a planter after the war and was at one point reduced to day labor. Boatner, *Dictionary*, p. 14. Howell Cobb (1815–1868) of Georgia was a Whig Congressman who opposed secession and urged compromise on the slavery issue. He served as governor of Georgia (1851–1854) and as Buchanan's first Secretary of the Treasury. Upon Lincoln's election, he changed his position and supported secession, serving as chairman of the Secessionist Convention in Montgomery. He was appointed brigadier general in February, 1862, and returned to Georgia in 1863 to command the state's reserve forces. Boatner, *Dictionary*, p. 160.

5. *Quitman Guards*, pp. 33-4.

6. William Henry Chase Whiting (1824–1865) of Mississippi graduated Georgetown College and later West Point, first in a class of forty-one in 1845. An army engineer, he accepted a Confederate commission in February, 1861. Wounded at Fort Fisher in January, 1865 and captured, he died on March 10, 1865. Boatner, *Dictionary*, p. 916.

Lightsey, *Veteran's Story*, p. 24.

7. Thomas Francis Meagher (pronounced "marr"; 1823–1867) was banished from Ireland to Tasmania for sedition. Escaping to the United States in 1852, he became a leader in New York City. In 1862, he was commissioned brigadier general and commanded the famous "Irish Brigade" he raised. The brigade was decimated to the point of ineffectiveness in May, 1863 at Chancellorsville, and he resigned. In December, the resignation was canceled, and he commanded of the District of Etowah, serving with Sherman at Atlanta. After the war, he served as governor of Montana. In 1867, he drowned in the Missouri River. Boatner, *Dictionary*, pp. 427, 540.

This was the Battle of Sharpsburg, known also as "Antietam," the bloodiest of the war. Federal casualties were estimated at 2,010 killed; 9,416 wounded; and 1,043 missing. Confederate casualties were about 2,700 killed; 9,024 wounded; and 2,000 missing. Long, *Day by Day*, pp. 267-8.

8. The road mentioned was the infamous "Bloody Lane," a landmark in the battle. Boatner, *Dictionary*, p. 79.

9. O. R., Series 1, Vol. XIX, Chapter XXXI, p. 885.

10. *Quitman Guards*, pp. 34-5.

11. Ibid., p. 36.

12. Springfield rifles were American made .58 caliber; Enfields were British .577 caliber 1853 Enfield Rifle Muskets. The Enfield, considered the better weapon, was fifty-five inches long and weighed nine pounds. It was accurate up to one thousand yards and fired either Enfield .577 or the Springfield .58 caliber cartridges. Ott, "Diary

Kirkpatrick," p.185; Henry Woodhead, editor, *Echoes of Glory: Arms and Equipment of the Confederacy* (Alexandria, Virginia: Time-Life Books, 1996), pp. 36–7.

13. William Patterson Hughes, private, Company C. Howell, *For Dixie Land*, Volume II, p. 1485.

Chapter 9

1. Edward J. Stackpole, *The Fredericksburg Campaign: Drama on the Rappahannock*, Second Edition (Harrisburg, PA: Stackpole Books, 1991), p. xxii; Carl Smith, *Clear the Way: Fredericksburg, 1862* (Sterling Heights, MI: Osprey Publishing Co., 1999), pp. 18, 22, 32, 47; Boatner, *Dictionary*, pp. 312–13.

2. Seventy-six officers of the brigade signed the petition, and Davis forwarded it to Lee, asking his views. Lee denied the request November 3rd. Record Group 109, Letters received by the Confederate Secretary of War, National Archives, Washington, D. C.

3. *Quitman Guards*, p. 37.

4. Yates was apparently familiar with variolation.

5. *Quitman Guards*, p. 37.

6. Ibid., p. 38.

7. O. R., Series 1, Vol. XXI, Chapter XXXIII, pp. 615–16.

8. *Quitman Guards*, p. 39.

9. Lightsey, *Veteran's Story*, p. 26.

10. O. R., Series 1, Vol. XXI, Chapter XXXIII, pp. 615–16.

11. *Quitman Guards*, p. 40.

12. Richard L. Breeden, private, corporal, Company C. Howell, *For Dixie Land*, Volume I, p. 286.

13. Lightsey, *Veteran's Story*, p. 25.

14. *Quitman Guards*, p. 40.

15. O. R., Series 1, Vol. XXI, Chapter XXXIII, pp. 615–16.

16. Lightsey, *Veteran's Story*, p. 27.

17. Thaddeus S. C. Lowe, a twenty-nine year-old New Hampshire professor whom Lincoln had made chief of army aeronautics in August 1861, piloted a hydrogen-inflated balloon at Fredericksburg to ascertain Rebel troop movements, artillery and infantry placements, and roads. While Lowe provided information, Burnside's correct evaluation of it is questionable. Stackpole, *Fredericksburg*, pp. 43–4; William J. Miller, *The Battles for Richmond, 1862* (Washington: Eastern National Park and Monument Association, 1996), p. 9.

Chapter 10

1. *Quitman Guards*, pp. 42–4; See *Constitution, By-Laws and Catalogue of Members of the Christian Philanthropic Society*, MDAH.

2. Edward G. Councell (also appears as E. C. Councill and Counsel), first lieutenant, major, Company D, field- staff, lieutenant colonel; wounded and captured at Weldon Railroad on August 21, 1864 and died in Alexandria, Virginia at the military hospital the following September. Howell, *For Dixie Land*, Volume I, p. 587; Holt, *Mississippi Rebel*, ed. Cockrell and Ballard, pp. 207, 308.

Harris, *Movements*, pp. 20–1.

3. Long, *Day by Day*, p. 315; Carl Smith, *Chancellorsville: Jackson's Lightning Strike* (Oxford: Osprey Publishing, Ltd., 1998), pp. 7, 9, 14–15.

4. The "stay law" was probably similar to the Soldiers-Sailors Act which prevents suits for collection of debts owed by those on active military duty during wartime.

5. Shannon, age 36, resigned December 20, 1862 due to diarrhea, neuralgia, and hemorrhoids. Ott, "Diary Kirkpatrick," p. 38.

6. Calvin A. Cowan, private, musician, Companies C and F, field- staff. Howell, *For Dixie Land*, Volume I, p. 590.

7. Harry originally dated this letter "January 7, 1862," but the reference to Hooker indicates it was written in late January, 1863.

8. See Harris, *Movements*, p. 21.

9. Harry is referring to the battle also known as "Stones River" fought December 31, 1862-January 3, 1863 in which Braxton Bragg led the Army of Tennessee. Bragg was born in North Carolina in 1817 and graduated the U.S. Military Academy in 1837, fifth in a class of fifty. He fought in the Seminole War and in Mexico, then resigned the army in 1856 to return to his Louisiana plantation. On March 7, 1861, he was commissioned brigadier general in the Confederate army. His leadership at Chicka-mauga and Chattanooga was viewed as inept, and he was relieved of command, being called to Richmond to act as military advisor to Davis. After the war, Bragg moved to Texas and worked as a civil engineer. He died in 1876. Boatner, *Dictionary*, pp. 78, 803–8; Long, *Day by Day*, pp. 302–3.

10. Joseph Hooker (1814–1879) of Massachusetts graduated the U.S. Military Academy in 1837, twenty-ninth in a class of fifty-nine. After serving on the frontier and in the Seminole War, he was adjutant at West Point and then won three brevets in the Mexican War. He resigned in 1853 after becoming involved in a feud between General Winfield Scott and General Gideon Pillow and farmed in the far west. He also quarreled with Halleck. When the Civil War began, the War Department initially ignored his offers of service but finally commissioned him brigadier general in May, 1861. At Fredericksburg, he led the Centre Grand Division and replaced Burnside as head of the Army of the Potomac on January 25, 1863. Boatner, *Dictionary*, pp. 409–10; Long, *Day by Day*, p. 315.

11. Gustavus (Gus) Kann, corporal, Company K, Sixteenth Mississippi. Howell, *For Dixie Land*, Volume II, p. 1615.

12. George S. Pilant, sergeant, Company K; see letter of Harry Lewis dated May 7, 1863. Howell, *For Dixie Land*, Volume III, p. 2368; Holt, *Mississippi Rebel*, ed. Cockrell and Ballard, p. 167.

13. Kirkpatrick was promoted to first sergeant on March 11, 1863. Winschel, "Gettysburg Kirkpatrick," p. 113. See Harris, *Movements*, p. 21.

Chapter 11

1. Stephen Sears, *Chancellorsville* (Boston: Houghton Mifflin Company: 1996), pp. 27, 187, 193; Smith, *Chancellorsville*, pp. 16–17; Boatner, *Dictionary*, p. 27; Ernest B. Furgurson, *Chancellorsville, 1863: The Souls of the Brave* (New York: Vintage Books, 1992), pp. xv, 124–8; Lightsey, *Veteran's Story*, pp. 28–9; *Quitman Guards*, pp. 44–5.

2. William (Little Billy) Mahone (1826–1895) of Virginia, graduated Virginia Military Institute then taught at a military academy. In 1861 he was president of a railroad. After the war, he returned to the railroad business, and in 1880–1882, he served in the U.S. Senate while controlling Virginia's Republican Party. Boatner, *Dictionary*, p. 502.

3. O.R., Vol. XXV, Series 1, Part 1, Chapter XXXVII, pp. 870–3.

4. This was Catharine Furnace, an ironworks two miles south-southwest of Chancellorsville. Holt, *Mississippi Rebel*, ed, Cockrell and Ballard, p. 162; Furguson, *Chancellorsville*, p. 127. Lightsey, *Veteran's Story*, p. 30.

5. O.R., Vol. XXV, Series 1, Part 1, Chapter XXXVII, pp. 870–3.

6. See Furguson, *Chancellorsville*, p. 202 and Long, *Day by Day*, p. 346. Lightsey, *Veteran's Story*, p. 30.

7. *Quitman Guards*, pp. 45–6.

8. O.R., Vol. XXV, Series 1, Part 1, Chapter XXXVII, pp. 870–3.

9. Lightsey, *Veteran's Story*, pp. 31–3.

10. William M. Wadsworth, color corporal, Company A. Howell, *For Dixie Land*, Volume III, p. 3032.

William J. Sweeny, corporal, Company C. Howell, *For Dixie Land*, Volume III, p. 2875.

11. O. R., Vol. XXV, Series 1, Part 1, Chapter XXXVII, p. 874.

12. Edward Aylesworth Perry (1831–1889) of Massachusetts practiced law in Florida. He was commissioned a Confederate brigadier general in August, 1862 after recovering from a severe wound received at Frayser's Farm. At Fredericksburg and Chancellorsville, he led his brigade but missed Gettysburg due to typhoid. Wounded at the Wilderness, his three-regiment brigade was reduced to one regiment then placed in another brigade. Transferred to the reserve forces, Perry served the rest of the war in Alabama. After the war, he returned to law practice and was elected governor of Florida in 1884. Boatner, *Dictionary*, p. 642.

Ambrose Ransom Wright (1826–1872) of Georgia was a lawyer and Democratic politician who remained neutral on secession until Lincoln was elected. Made brigadier general in June, 1862, and major general in November, he was then ordered to Georgia. After the war, he remained in Georgia and worked as a newspaper editor. He died shortly after being elected to Congress. Boatner, *Dictionary*, p. 949.

O.R., Vol. XXV, Series 1, Part 1, Chapter XXXVII, pp. 870–3.

13. John Sedgwick (1813–1864) of Connecticut graduated West Point in 1837, twenty-fourth in a class of fifty. He served in the Mexican War, the Seminole War and on the frontier prior to the Civil War. Appointed brigadier general, he was often called "Uncle John" by his men as a term of affection. He was a bachelor described as genial and generous but a strict disciplinarian. At Spotsylvania in May, 1864, he was killed by a sharpshooter. Boatner, *Dictionary*, pp. 730–731.

14. John A. Walker, corporal, Company E; wounded at Turkey Ridge, Virginia in June, 1864. Howell, *For Dixie Land*, Volume III, p. 3044; *Quitman Guards*, p. XI.

Jefferson E. Simmons, private, Company E. Howell, *For Dixie Land*, Volume III, p. 2692. *Quitman Guards*, pp.47–8.

15. O.R., Vol. XXV, Series 1, Part 1, Chapter XXXVII, pp. 870–3.

16. *Quitman Guards*, p. 48.

17. Jackson died when pneumonia set in following amputation of his arm. Boatner, *Dictionary*, p. 432.

18. Earl Van Dorn (1820–1863) of Mississippi graduated the U.S. Military Academy in 1842, fifty-second in a class of fifty-six and was described as small and elegant. After being wounded four times by Comanches on the frontier, Van Dorn served in the Mexican War, where he received another wound and two brevets, and in the Seminole War. He resigned in January, 1861 to serve as brigadier general of Mississippi

troops and succeeded Jefferson Davis as major general of those troops. He took command of the Trans-Mississippi Department in January, 1862 then commanded the Army of the West until May, 1862. Though an inquiry acquitted him of blame for the loss of Corinth in October, 1862, he was transferred to command the cavalry. Van Dorn was shot and killed in Spring Hill, Tennessee on May 8, 1863 by a Doctor Peters, who claimed that Van Dorn had "violated his home." Boatner, *Dictionary*, p. 867, quoting Stanley F. Horn, *The Army of Tennessee* (Indianapolis: The Bobs-Merrill Company, 1941), p. 453.

19. Robert Emmet Rodes (1829–1864) of Virginia graduated from Virginia Military Institute and taught there until T. J. Jackson was given the position Rodes wanted. After resigning, he worked for railroads as a civil engineer. In October 1861, he was appointed brigadier general. He was wounded at Gaines's Mill and Antietam in 1862. He recovered sufficiently to command his brigade at Fredericksburg in December, 1862 and at Chancellorsville the following May then was promoted to major general that same month. After the battle at Spotsylvania, he moved to the Shenadoah Valley, where was killed at Winchester on September 19, 1864. Boatner, *Dictionary*, pp. 706–7.

20. Lafayette McLaws (1821–1897) of Georgia graduated West Point in 1842, forty-eighth in a class of fifty-six. He was appointed brigadier general in September, 1861 after serving in the Mexican War and fighting Indians. After the war, he was in the insurance business in Augusta and worked for the Internal Revenue Service and Post Office. Boatner, *Dictionary*, p. 536.

21. Jubal Anderson Early (1816–1894) of Virginia graduated West Point in 1837, eighteenth in a class of fifty. Following the Seminole War, he resigned the army in 1838 to practice law but re-enlisted to fight in the Mexican War. As a Virginia legislator, he voted against secession but enlisted in Confederate military, being appointed brigadier general in July 1861. Promoted to major general in April of 1863, he led a division at Chancellorsville, Gettysburg, the Wilderness and Spotsylvania, then took over for Ewell as commander of the II Corps in May 1864. Reaching the outskirts of Washington in July, 1864, he withdrew when he learned that the U.S. VI Corps had arrived to re-enforce the city. Being out-generaled in the Shenandoah Valley, Lee relieved Early in March 1864, concurring with public outcry. After the surrender, he went to Canada, where in 1866 he wrote *A Memoir of the Last Year of the War for Independence in the C. S. A.*, then went to Mexico. He returned to his Lynchburg law practice before being employed by the Louisiana Lottery. He was described as six feet tall (but stooped by arthritis in his later years), 170 pounds with black eyes and beard. Boatner, *Dictionary*, pp. 254–5.

22. Harry is referring to the cavalry raid into Virginia (April 29—May 8, 1863) led by General George Stoneman as part of Hooker's strategy. It had little effect. Boatner, *Dictionary*, p. 803.

23. No Henry Broome connected with the Sixteenth Mississippi could be located.

A. B. Swanson, soon to be Marie Yates's husband and Jerome's brother-in-law. See later Yates letters.

Chapter 12

1. Mark Grimsley and Brooks D. Simpson, *Gettysburg: A Battlefield Guide* (Lincoln, Nebraska: University of Nebraska Press, 1999), pp. 3–6; Carl Smith, *Gettysburg, 1863: High Tide of the Confederacy* (London: Osprey Publishing, Ltd., 1998), p. 16; Furguson,

Chancellorsville, p. xv; Long, *Day by Day*, p. 374; Harris, *Movements*, p. 22; Boatner, *Dictionary*, pp. 331–2.

2. Christ, *Bliss Farm*, pp. x, 2, 4, 6, 31–5, 60, 71, 85, 87.

3. Wilson, also referred to later as Wilse, was Yates' slave.

4. Lightsey, *Veteran's Story*, p. 34.

5. Daniel O. Bankston, private, Company F. Howell, *For Dixie Land*, Volume I, p. 113.

6. John Fulton Reynolds (1820–1863) of Pennsylvania graduated West Point in 1841, twenty-sixth in a fifty-two- man class. After receiving two brevets in the Mexican War, he fought Indians in the West and was commandant of West Point when the war began. Described as six feet tall, courageous and self-reliant with dark hair and eyes, he was killed by a sharpshooter at Gettysburg. Boatner, *Dictionary*, pp. 694–5.

7. Henry Heth (1825–1899) of Virginia graduated the U.S. Military Academy in 1847, last in his class. He served in the Mexican War and on the frontier, resigning in April, 1861 for a Confederate commission. From captain, he rose to brigadier general by January, 1862. Lee requested that he be transferred from the Department of East Tennessee to the Army of Northern Virginia in January, 1863. After Chancellorsville, he was promoted to major general. On July 1, 1863, his troops unexpectedly clashed with Union troops at Gettysburg, and he lost half his men within the first twenty-three minutes of the encounter, being wounded himself. After the war, he was in the insurance business and a surveyor with the Office of Indian Affairs. Boatner, *Dictionary*, p. 398.

Lightsey, *Veteran's Story*, p. 35.

8. *Quitman Guards*, p. 50.

9. Elijah Slay, captain, Company C. Howell, *For Dixie Land*, Volume III, p. 2712.

10. O.R., Series 1, Vol. XXVII, Chapter XXXIX, pp. 633–4.

11. Kirkpatrick is describing the Pickett-Pettigrew Charge.

12. Lightsey, *Veteran's Story*, p. 36.

13. *Quitman Guards*, pp. 51–2.

14. Ibid., p. 52.

15. Ibid., p. 54.

16. Hy Van Easton, private, Company K. Howell, *For Dixie Land*, Volume III, p. 3010.

17. Names were drawn July 13,1863 in New York City pursuant to the controversial new Federal draft. Draft headquarters and residences were attacked and businesses looted as fires broke out in the city. Blacks became targets and an African-American church and orphanage were burned. Not until Federal troops arrived, some from Gettysburg, on July 16th was the riot brought under control. Estimates are that one thousand people were killed or wounded. Long, *Day by Day*, p. 384.

18. The Sixteenth traveled nearly one hundred miles in five days. See *Quitman Guards*, p. 54.

19. The Lewis brothers apparently had three slaves with them, Frank, Ebb, and Mack.

20. John Buford (1826–1863) of Kentucky graduated the U.S. West Point in 1848, sixteenth in a class of thirty- eight. After fighting Indians on the frontier, Buford served on Pope's staff and was appointed brigadier general in July, 1862, taking command of a cavalry brigade. He was wounded at Second Manassas and was Chief of Cavalry in the

Maryland Campaign. He held McPherson's Ridge at Gettysburg until Federal infantry arrived and prevented a Confederate victory. Buford died of typhoid December 16, 1863. Boatner, *Dictionary*, p. 97.

Chapter 13

1. William D. Henderson, *The Road to Bristoe Station: Campaigning with Lee and Meade, August 1-October 20, 1863* (Lynchburg, VA: H. E. Howard, Inc., 1987), pp. 1–77; Long, *Day by Day*, pp. 393, 422; *Quitman Guards*, p. 55.

2. Probably John A. Fulgham, sergeant, and James M. Fulgham, captain, both of Company K (the Dixie Guards from Copiah County, Mississippi), Thirty-sixth Mississippi; and Fenton Taliaferro Lafayette Fulgham, private, Company E (Mississippi College Rifles), Eighteenth Mississippi. The Eighteenth was at the Peach Orchard at Gettysburg. Howell, *For Dixie Land*, Volume I, pp. 934–5; Rowland, *Statistical Register 1908*, pp. 482, 706.

3. Jefferson Hamilton, private, Company K, field-staff. Howell, *For Dixie Land*, Volume II, p. 1252.

Samuel Jameson Gholson (1808–1883), born in Kentucky, was a Mississippi lawyer, legislator, Congressman, and federal judge who strongly supported secession. When the war began, he enlisted as a private and moved up the ranks to be appointed brigadier general of Mississippi's State troops.Wounded and captured at Fort Donelson, he was later promoted major general of the state's troops in 1863 and Confederate major general in May 6, 1864. Following a wound received at Egypt, Mississippi on December 27, 1864, he lost his arm. He returned to his law practice and the state legislature after the war. Howell, *For Dixie Land*, Volume II, p. 1114; Boatner, *Dictionary*, p. 340.

4. William Nelson Pendleton (1809–1883) of Virginia graduated West Point in 1830, fifth in a class of forty-two. Before he resigned the army in 1833, he was a mathematics teacher at West Point. In 1838, he was ordained an Episcopal minister and in 1844, moved to Baltimore and ran a school. He served as minister for a church in Fredericksburg from 1847 until 1853 when he moved to Lexington, Virginia. On July 13, 1861, he was appointed Artillery Chief for Johnston, and on March 26, 1862, brigadier general and Chief of Artillery for Lee. Boatner, *Dictionary*, pp. 631–2.

5. This "Bud" is not Captain John South Lewis.

6. Francis F. Best, private, fifth sergeant, Company K. Howell, *For Dixie Land*, Volume I, p. 189.

John D. Stockett, private, Company K. Howell, *For Dixie Land*, Volume III, p. 2829.

7. Thomas H. Green, private, Company F. Howell, *For Dixie Land*, Volume II, p. 1191.

8. "Old Rosy" is William Starke Rosecrans (1819–1898) of Ohio who graduated West Point in 1842, fifth in a class of fifty-six. After resigning a teaching position at West Point in 1854 to become a civil engineer, architect, and coal refiner, he reenlisted and was appointed brigadier general on June 16, 1861, serving in West Virginia. Promoted to major general in March, 1862, he commanded the Army of the Mississippi, but his defeat at Chickamauga cost him command, and he was left "awaiting orders" until January 30, 1864, when he was assigned command of the Department of the Missouri. He resigned the army in 1867 and served as Minister to Mexico from 1868 through 1889. Upon completion of that service, he was a congressman and rancher in

California. He was said to have a testy disposition and temper and was known for his ability to go without sleep during campaigns. Boatner, *Dictionary*, p. 708.

9. The Battle of Chickamauga was fought September 19–20, 1863 in North Georgia, southeast of Chattanooga, Tennessee and resulted in a tactical Confederate victory. Long, *Day by Day*, pp. 411–12; Boatner, *Dictionary*, pp. 151–2.

10. Fay F. could be Henry F. Foster, private, Company C. Howell, *For Dixie Land*, Volume I, p. 909.

Chapter 14

1. Boatner, *Dictionary*, p. 87; *Quitman Guards*, p. 55; Lightsey, *Veteran's Story*, p. 37; Henderson, *Bristoe Station*, pp. 74, 123;

2. John R. Cooke (1833–1891), a Harvard engineer, was wounded at Seven Pines, then appointed brigadier general in November 1862 and commanded a North Carolina brigade. He was wounded again at Fredericksburg, Bristoe Station and the Wilderness. After the war, he a merchant and political leader in Richmond. His father was Union General Phillip St. Cooke. Boatner, *Dictionary*, pp. 173–4.

Born in Ireland, Thomas Alfred Smyth (?–1865) was a Wilmington coachmaker when the war began. He was promoted to brigadier general in October 1864 for his bravery at Cold Harbor the previous July. On April 9, 1865, he died of wounds received two days earlier near Farmville, Virginia. Boatner, *Dictionary*, p. 777.

John Curtis Caldwell (1833–?) of Vermont was promoted to brigadier general in April 1862. After the war, he was a Maine senator, Minister to Uruguay and Paraguay, and Consul at Valparaiso. Boatner, *Dictionary*, p. 112.

Henderson, *Bristoe Station*, pp. 181–91.

3. Pioneers were soldiers who built roads, bridges, defenses, etc. Michael Varhola, *Everyday Life in the Civil War* (Cincinnati: Writer's Digest Books, 1999), p. 138.

4. A. P. Hill met the U.S. III Corps near Bristoe Station, Virginia. In a hurry to attack, Hill overlooked the nearby U.S. II Corps and was unable to defeat the Federals in their strong positions. Long, *Day by Day*, p. 422; Boatner, *Dictionary*, p. 87.

Posey, wounded in the left leg by a ball from a larger shell, turned to his son, Stanhope, and said, "Well, son, they got me this time." Kitty Day Papers. p. 7;Winschel, "Posey's Brigade at Gettysburg, Part I," p. 8, ftn. 6.

5. *Quitman Guards*, p. 56.

6. Arnold Langham , private, Company F. Howell, *For Dixie Land*, Volume II, p. 1703.

7. Lightsey, *Veteran's Story*, p. 37.

8. Harris, *Movements*, p. 24.

9. Harry Thompson Hays (1820–1876), a Mississippi-born New Orleans lawyer and Mexican War veteran, was commissioned brigadier general in July, 1862 and commanded the Louisiana Brigade. He practiced law after the war and served as Orleans Parish Sheriff but was removed after only one year in office. Boatner, *Dictionary* p. 390.

Robert Frederick Hoke (1837–1912) of North Carolina graduated the Kentucky Military Institute and entered his family's manufacturing business. He was promoted to brigadier general in January, 1863 then to major general in April, 1864. He surrendered with Johnston in North Carolina. Boatner, *Dictionary*, pp. 404–5.

10. William M. Caldwell, private, sergeant, Company F. Howell, *For Dixie Land*, Volume I, p. 402.

11. Posey's wound from Bristoe Station was not initially thought to be serious, and he was moved to the home of his friend, Dr. J. Staige Davis, surgeon at the University of Virginia (Posey's alma mater), where he died on November 13, 1863. Kitty Day Papers, p. 7; Winschel, "Posey's Brigade at Gettysburg, Part I," p. 8, ftn. 6.

12. Possibly Private Cys Hoover of Company A. Howell, *For Dixie Land*, Volume II, p. 1441.

Bob Carpenter and Adams could not be identified.

13. Robert Hall Chilton (1816–1879) of Virginia graduated West Point in 1837, forty-eighth in a class of fifty. He served in the Mexican War and on the frontier, then resigned to accept a Confederate commission. From September 1862 until April 1864, he served as Chief-of-Staff for Lee, with the rank of brigadier general. He was in the manufacturing business in Georgia after the war. Boatner, *Dictionary*, p. 154.

14. At a meeting of the men, chaired by Colonel N. H. Harris, a committee was appointed to draft a resolution honoring Posey. The committee consisted of Major H. J. Hearsey; Sergeant P. A. Bottow and Sergeant-Major William O. Chapman of the Twelfth Mississippi; Captain S. M. Bain, Sergeant J. J. Kirkpatrick, P. R. Leatherman, of the Sixteenth; Captains R. W. Phipps, J. H. Duncan, and W. E. Dooly, of the Nineteenth; and Captains L. C. Moore, W. R. Stone, and James Elliot of the Forty-eighth. Kitty Day Papers, p. 8.

Chapter 15

1. *Quitman Guards*, pp. 59–60; Harris, *Movements*, p. 24; Martin F. Graham, *Mine Run: A Campaign of Lost Opportunities* (Lynchburg, VA: H. E. Howard, Inc., 1987), pp. 1–41; Boatner, *Dictionary*, p. 552; Lightsey, *Veteran's Story*, p. 38.

2. *Quitman Guards*, p. 60.

3. Ibid.

4. "T. O. D." is probably Tom O. Davis; see Yates's letter of December 16, 1863.

5. Charles H. Dobbs, Chaplain, Twelfth Mississippi. Howell, *For Dixie Land*, Volume I, p. 726.

6. The Mine Run Campaign took place between November 26 and December 1, 1863. Afterward, Meade retired his army across the Rapidan River and went into winter quarters. Mine Run was the last major operation in the Eastern Theater until Grant began the Wilderness Campaign in May 1864. Long, *Day by Day*, p. 441; Boatner, *Dictionary*, p. 552.

7. William Joseph Hardee (1815–1873) of Georgia graduated the U.S. Military Academy in 1838, twenty-sixth in a class of forty-five. After studying two years with the French cavalry, he fought in the Mexican War and then became commandant at West Point. He resigned when Georgia seceded and was appointed brigadier general in June, 1861; major general in October, 1861; and lieutenant general in October, 1862. In September, 1864, he was given command of the Department of South Carolina, Georgia, and Florida. Unable to stop Sherman's March to the Sea, in December, 1864, Hardee abandoned Savannah and later joined Johnston in North Carolina. Boatner, *Dictionary*, p. 374.

Chapter 16

1. Graham, *Mine Run*, p. 91; McPherson, *Atlas*, p. 141; Long, *Day by Day*, pp. 452, 459, 470; *Quitman Guards*, p. 61.

2. Hector Smith, private, Company F. Howell, *For Dixie Land*, Volume III, p. 2730.

3. Oris C. Jones, third lieutenant, Company F. Howell, *For Dixie Land*, Volume II, p. 1596; Works Progress Administration, Federal Writers Project, Source Records of Jasper County, Mississippi, Will Abstracts, 1855–1914, ed. Jean Strickland and Patricia Edwards (privately published, 1995), p. 111.

4. John S. Loper, private, Company F. Howell, *For Dixie Land*, Volume II, p. 1786.

5. Town Ball was the predecessor of baseball. Edmond Gosse, et al., *All There is to Know: Readings from the Illustrious Eleventh Edition of the Encyclopaedia Britannica*, ed. Alexander Coleman and Charles Simmons (New York: Simon & Shuster, 1994), pp. 95–6.

6. James T. Alford, private, Company C. Howell, *For Dixie Land*, Volume I, p. 28.

7. Sherman had just concluded his march to Meridian, Mississippi and returned the majority of his troops to Vicksburg. Long, *Day by Day*, p. 472. See also Margie Riddle Bearss, *Sherman's Forgotten Campaign: The Meridian Expedition* (Baltimore: The Gateway Press, 1987).

8. The reference is to the Kilpatrick-Dahlgreen Raid on Richmond, February 28-March 4, 1864. Colonel Ulric Dahlgreen, one of the raid's leaders, was actually the son of Admiral John Adolph Dahlgreen who commanded the South Atlantic Blockading Squadron. It was Dahlgreen's plan, according to papers allegedly found by a teenager, to burn Richmond, kill President Davis and his cabinet, and free Federal prisoners. The authenticity of the papers has never been resolved. Boatner, *Dictionary*, pp. 218, 460; Long, *Day by Day*, pp. 471–2.

9. Johnson's Island was a Union prison camp for Confederate officers in Lake Erie. Boatner, *Dictionary*, p. 439.

10. Winan S. Hoard, private, Company K. Howell, *For Dixie Land*, Volume II, p. 1403.

11. Also spelled "Litmyr"; Frank Litmyr, private, Company K. Howell, *For Dixie Land*, Volume II, p. 1764. Chapman may be John Chapman, private, Company K; captured April 29, 1863 near Fredericksburg and held in the Old Capitol Prison in Washington but was either paroled or escaped ten days later. Holt, *Mississippi Rebel*, ed. Cockrell and Ballard, pp. 135, 182; Howell, *For Dixie Land*, Volume I, p. 473.

12. Peter R. Leatherman, private, Company K. Howell, *For Dixie Land*, Volume II, p. 1724.

13. Alexander A. Lomax, chaplain, field-staff. Howell, *For Dixie Land*, Volume II, p. 1779; Holt, *Mississippi Rebel*, ed. Cockrell and Ballard, pp. 231–2; See also "Journal of Alexander A. Lomax, Sixteenth Mississippi Regiment,"MDAH.

14. George D. Nixon, private first lieutenant, Company A, Twelfth Mississippi. Howell, *For Dixie Land*, Volume III, p. 2231.

15. William T. Gray, sergeant, Company C. Howell, *For Dixie Land*, Volume II, p. 1184.

Chapter 17

1. *Quitman Guards*, p. 62; Gordon C. Rhea, *The Battle of the Wilderness, May 5–6, 1864* (Baton Rouge: Louisiana State University Press, 1997), pp. 8–9, 21, 47, 52; Gordon C. Rhea, *The Battles of the Wilderness and Spotsylvania* (Eastern National Park and Monument Association, Civil War Series, 1995), pp. 1–2; Grady McWhiney, *Battle in the Wilderness:Grant Meets Lee* (Fort Worth, Texas: Ryan Place Publishers, 1995), pp.

13, 136; Trudeau, *Bloody Roads South*, pp. 21, 41–132; Holt, *Mississippi Rebel*, ed. Cockrell and Ballard, p. 238.

2. Rhea, *Wilderness, May 5–6, 1864*, p. 468; *Quitman Guards*, p. 63.

3. Gordon C. Rhea, *The Battle for Spotsylvania Court House and the Road to Yellow Tavern, May 7–12, 1864* (Baton Rouge: Louisiana State University Press, 1997), pp. 232–307; Trudeau, *Bloody Roads South*, pp. 133–88; Holt, *Mississippi Rebel*, ed. Cockrell and Ballard, p. 238. See also William D. Matter, et al., *The Spotsylvania Campaign*, ed. Gary W. Gallagher (Chapel Hill, NC: The University of North Carolina Press, 1998).

4. Yeary, *Reminiscences*, pp. 147–8.

5. Lightsey, *Veteran's Story*, p. 38.

6. *Quitman Guards*, p. 64.

7. Ibid., pp. 64–5.

8. Yeary, *Reminiscences*, pp. 148–9.

9. Edward "Allegheny" Johnson (1816–1873) of Kentucky graduated the U. S. Military Academy in 1838, thirty- second in a class of forty-five. After serving in the Seminole War, Mexican War and on the frontier, Johnson resigned in June, 1861 to enlist in the Confederate army. Appointed brigadier general in December, 1861, in February, 1863, he was promoted to major general and commanded Jackson's old brigade at Gettysburg. After being captured at Spotsylvania, he was exchanged and led a division when Hood invaded Tennessee but was captured again at Nashville. He farmed following the war. Boatner, *Dictionary*, pp. 437–8. "Bloody Bend" is more commonly known as the "Bloody Angle" or "Mule Shoe."
Quitman Guards, p. 65.

10. Written from Vicksburg, Mississippi on August 24, 1871.
General Lee acted similarly at Spotsylvania Court House on May 12th with Gordon's Division. Being the second instance on the same day, this was obviously an inspirational tactic. N. H. Harris, "Lee to the Rear, The Incident With Harris' Mississippi Brigade" *Southern Historical Society Papers*, Volume 8 (January-December, 1880), pp.105–8. (*Southern Historical Society Papers* are hereinafter referred to as *SHSP*.) Compare this to James Johnson Kirkpatrick Diary May 6 entry.

11. Samuel McGowan (1819–1897) of South Carolina, graduated from South Carolina College, practiced law and sat in the state legislature. He fought in the Mexican War as a major general of South Carolina militia. After serving in the Confederate army as lieutenant colonel and colonel, he was appointed brigadier general in April, 1863. Wounded at the Bloody Angle, he remained in the army and surrendered at Appomattox. After the war, he again served as a state legislator and then on the South Carolina Supreme Court. Boatner, *Dictionary*, p. 533.
Alexander R. Mixon, private, Company E, waved the flag ". . . in the faces of the enemy and died on the breastworks." L. W. Conerly, *Pike County*, p. 188; Howell, *For Dixie Land*, Volume II, p. 2063. *Quitman Guards*, p. 66.

12. Stephen Dodson Ramseur (1837–1864) graduated West Point in 1860, fourteenth in a forty-one-man class. In April, 1861, he was commissioned a second lieutenant in the Confederate army and appointed brigadier in November, 1862. Wounded at the Bloody Angle, he returned to service and was promoted to major general in June, 1864. He learned of his first child's birth while at Cedar Creek on October 19, 1864. Wounded that same day, he died the next. Boatner, *Dictionary*, p. 677.

13. Asbury W. "Ap" Hancock, private, Company I, Nineteenth Mississippi. Han-

cock received the Confederate Medal of Honor for bravery at Spotsylvania. Howell, *For Dixie Land*, Volume II, p. 1260; Gregg S. Clemmer, *Valor in Gray:Recipients of the Confederate Medal of Honor* (Staunton: Virginia: The Hearthside Publishing Company, 1998), pp. 67–73.

Frank Dolan, private, Company A, Forty-eighth Mississippi. Howell, *For Dixie Land*, Volume I, p. 731. O.R., Series 1, Vol. 36, Part 1, Chapter XLVIII, pp. 1091–3.

14. *Quitman Guards*, p. 67.

15. No one named Archie Robertson could be located in the Sixteenth. Conerly probably meant Archibald P. Robinson, third corporal, Company F. Howell, *For Dixie Land*, Volume III, p. 2539.

16. Holden Pearson, private, Company E. Howell, *For Dixie Land*, Volume III, p. 2326. Yeary, *Reminiscences*, pp. 148–50.

17. J. D. H., "The Death Angle," *New Orleans Times-Democrat*, date unknown, pp.1–4; clipping on file in Record Group 9, Volume 132, Folder P at the MDAH has handwritten in the margin "by David E. Holt, 1900."

18. See Letters of John Berryman Crawford, MDAH. *Quitman Guards*, pp. 67–8.

19. O.R., Series 1, Vol. 36, Part 1, Chapter XLVIII, pp. 1091–3. Lee's losses during the battles of Spotsylvania Court House suggest as minimums: killed and wounded, 6,519; captured, 5,543; for a total of 12,062. Federal losses for the same period were: killed and wounded, 16,141; captured, 2,258; for a total of 18,399. After eight days of fighting, the armies were in virtually the same positions as when they began. Trudeau, *Bloody Roads South*, p. 213; Rhea, *Battle for Spotsylvania Court House*, p. 312.

20. Yeary, *Reminiscences*, pp. 148–50.

Chapter 18

1. John Cabell Breckinridge (1812–1875) of Kentucky served as a state legislator, Congressman and President Buchanan's vice-president. He ran against Lincoln then served in the U. S. Senate. To escape arrest in October, 1861, he fled Kentucky and was declared a traitor. In November that same year, he was appointed brigadier general in the Confederate army. Davis made him Secretary of War in February, 1865. After the war, he fled to Cuba, Europe and Canada, then returned to Kentucky and practiced law. Boatner, *Dictionary*, pp. 82–3.

Louis J. Baltz, III, *The Battle of Cold Harbor: May 28-June 13, 1864* (Lynchburg, Virginia: H. E. Howard, Inc., 1994), p. 2; Noah Andre Trudeau, *The Last Citadel: Petersburg, Virginia, June 1864-April 1865* (Boston: Little, Brown and Company, 1991), p.30; McPherson, *Atlas*, p. 158; Rowland, *Military History*, p. 492; Boatner, *Dictionary*, pp. 162–4; 597–8; 842–3; Long, *Day by Day*, pp. 514–15; *Quitman Guards*, p. 68; Ernest B. Furguson, *Murder Not War: Cold Harbor, 1864* (New York: Alfred A. Knopf, 2000), pp. 129, 146, 273.

2. *Quitman Guards*, p. 68.

3. Emory V. Lee, private, Company A, Twelfth Mississippi Infantry. Howell, *For Dixie Land*, Volume II, p. 1727. Samuel C. Baskin (also listed as Baskins), private, Company C. Howell, *For Dixie Land*, Volume I, p. 141. John Baskins could be John Stewart Baskin, corporal, Company E, Eighteenth Mississippi or J. A. Baskins, private, Company C, Twelfth Mississippi. Howell, *For Dixie Land*, Volume I, p. 141.

Layfayette T. Kelley, private, corporal, Company A, Twelfth Mississippi. Howell, *For Dixie Land* Volume II, p. 1623.

Probably William H. Gibbs, private, Company A, Twelfth Mississippi. Howell, *For Dixie Land*, Volume II, p.1116.

4. Lightsey, *Veteran's Story*, pp. 38–9.

5. *Quitman Guards*, p. 69.

6. Letter from General Nathaniel H. Harris to General William H. Mahone, August 2, 1866. MDAH.

7. James D. Stanford, private, Company E. Howell, *For Dixie Land*, Volume III, p. 2796. *Quitman Guards*, p. 69.

8. Howell, *For Dixie Land*, Volume III, p. 3317.

9. Yeary, *Reminiscences*, p.235.

10. Letter, Harris to Mahone, August 2, 1866, MDAH.

Chapter 19

1. Rowland, *Military History*, p. 492, Trudeau, *Last Citadel*, pp. xiii, 4, 6, 19, 22; McPherson, *Atlas*, pp. 160–1, 184; John Horn, *The Petersburg Campaign, June 1864-April 1865* (Conshohocken, PA: Combined Books, Inc., 1993), p. 11; Boatner, *Dictionary*, p. 646.

2. Letter, Harris to Mahone, August 2, 1866; *Quitman Guards*, p. 69.

3. Boatner, *Dictionary*, pp. 647–8. See Michael Cavanaugh and William Marvel, *The Battle of the Crater:"The Horrid Pit," June 25 -August 6, 1864* (Lynchburg, VA: H. E. Howard, Inc., 1989).

4. William Flake Perry (1823–1901) of Georgia was raised in Alabama. Self-educated, he taught school and became superintendent of education for Alabama, then president of the women's college at Tuskegee and was there when he enlisted as a Confederate private in 1862. He was soon elected major, then promoted to lieutenant colonel in September, 1862. After Antietam, he was promoted to colonel and in February, 1865, appointed brigadier general. He was a planter and educator in Kentucky after the war. Boatner, *Dictionary*, p. 642.

5. Letter, Harris to Mahone, August 2, 1866.

6. From June 22-July 1, 1864, General James Harrison Wilson led his cavalry in several successful raids around Weldon Railroad. Boatner, *Dictionary*, p. 931; Long, *Day by Day*, p. 528.

Joseph Finegan (1814–1885) of Florida was a lawyer appointed to command the state's military affairs in 1861. Appointed brigadier general in 1862, he commanded the Department of Middle and Eastern Florida. His brigade was transferred to Virginia in May, 1864, but returned to Florida in March of 1865. After the war, he returned to law practice. Boatner, *Dictionary*, p. 279.

7. Wilson's letter had Ewell making Early's Washington Raid, in which Confederates reached the outskirts of the capital on July 11, 1864. Boatner, *Dictionary*, pp. 255–6.

8. Mahone received an "on-the-spot" promotion from Lee for his actions at the Crater. Boatner, *Dictionary*, p. 502.

Lightsey, *Veteran's Story*, pp. 39–41.

9. Stephen Elliot, Jr. (1830–1866) of South Carolina was a wealthy planter and legislator when the war began. He was appointed brigadier general in May, 1864 and

was severely wounded at the Crater and later at Bentonville, South Carolina. Boatner, *Dictionary*, pp. 262–3.

Chapter 20

1. McPherson, *Atlas*, p. 184; Long, *Day by Day*, pp. 549, 564, 577; John Horn, *The Destruction of Weldon Railroad, Deep Bottom, Globe Tavern, and Reams Station, August 14–25, 1864* (Lynchburg, VA: H. E. Howard, Inc., 1991).

2. Michael Naul (also listed as Noll and Nall), private, Company C. Howell, *For Dixie Land*, Volume III, p. 2201.

3. Lightsey, *Veteran's Story*, p. 41.

4. Three soldiers named Cain (Hugh F., Thomas A., and William F.) were in Company F of the Sixteenth. Howell, *For Dixie Land*, Volume III, pp. 397–8.

5. Charles Williamson Fields (1828–1892) of Kentucky graduated West Point in 1849, twenty-seventh in a class of forty-three. He resigned as West Point's cavalry instructor to become a Confederate captain. Until March, 1862, he served under J. E.B. Stuart then was appointed brigadier general and given an infantry brigade and was later appointed major general. After the war, he was in business in Baltimore and Georgia and served as U. S. House of Representatives doorkeeper (1878–1881). Boatner, *Dictionary*, p. 279.

Harris wrote "Saunders" but obviously meant John Calhoun Sanders (1840–1864) of Alabama, who left the University of Alabama to captain the Eleventh Alabama. In May, 1864, he was appointed brigadier general. He was killed at Weldon Railroad on August 21, 1864. Boatner, *Dictionary*, p. 719.

Victor J. B. Girardey (?–1864) of Georgia was commissioned lieutenant in Confederate service in 1861 and adjutant general for General Ambrose Wright in January, 1862. Douglas Southall Freeman reported that while Girardey was serving as a captain, Robert E. Lee appointed him brigadier general on July 30, 1864 for his actions during the Battle of the Crater. If so, it was the only direct appointment of a captain to brigadier general that occurred in the war. Girardey was killed at Deep Bottom on August 16, 1864. Boatner, *Dictionary*, p. 344. Harris, *Movements*, p. 33.

6. Ibid.

7. After Finegan's Brigade was repulsed on the Weldon Railroad, Harris's Brigade charged the Union entrenched line. The Twelfth and Sixteenth reached the works and many were killed, wounded or captured. Colonel E. C. Councill later died at Washington, D. C. Reported as killed, wounded and missing were 254 out of 450 carried into action. The flag of the Sixteenth was taken by Corporal H. A. Ellis, of the Seventh Wisconsin. Rowland, *Military History*, p.466.

Quitman Guards, pp. 69–70.

8. The Bermuda Hundred is a thick neck of land between Richmond and Petersburg where the Appomattox and James Rivers converge. Cavanaugh and Marvel, *Battle of the Crater*, p. 1.

9. Harris, *Movements*, p. 34.

10. Located at the mouth of the Potomac River on Chesapeake Bay, Point Lookout was a Federal prison camp for enlisted men. Its 20,000 prisoners were housed in overcrowded tents, with water hauled in when the shallow wells became polluted. Boatner, *Dictionary*, p. 657; Long, *Day by Day*, p. 449.

11. James Dearing (1840–1865) of Virginia was scheduled to graduate the U. S.

Military Academy in 1862, but when the war broke out, he resigned. Appointed brigadier general in April, 1864, he was wounded April 6, 1865 at High Bridge, Virginia and died of his wounds April 23rd at Lynchburg, Virginia. Boatner, *Dictionary*, p. 228.

12. The Battle of Hatcher's Run (a/k/a Burgess Mill). After a period of relative quiet, the Federals moved to a point twelve miles southwest of Petersburg on Hatcher's Run. After gaining some ground on the enemy flanks, the Confederates lost it to counterattacks. Unable to reinforce or resupply themselves, the Federals withdrew. Long, *Day by Day*, p. 589; Boatner, *Dictionary*, pp. 384–5.

Harris, *Movements*, pp. 34–6.

13. *Quitman Guards*, pp. 69–70.

14. *Supp.* O.R.,Vol. 33, pp. 402, 405, 408, 412, 413, 419, 421, 423.

Chapter 21

1. Long, *Day by Day*, pp. 633, 661; Horn, *Weldon Railroad*, pp. 200, 217, 209–16, 217–40, 245; Noah Andre Trudeau, *The Siege of Petersburg* (Eastern National Park and Monument Association, Civil War Series, 1995), pp. 33, 40, 45; Noah Andre Trudeau, *The Campaign to Appomattox* (Eastern National Park and Monument Association, Civil War Series, 1995), p. 1; Rowland, *Military History*, p. 493; McPherson, *Atlas*, pp. 210–11; Ronald E. Bullock, "Last Ditch Rebel Stand at Petersburg," *America's Civil War*, Volume 10, Number 2 (May, 1997), p. 30. See also, Noah Andre Trudeau, *Out of the Storm: The End of the Civil War* (Boston: Little, Brown and Company, 1994).

2. O.R., Series 1, Vol. XLVI, Chapter LVIII, pp. 1144–5.

3. Harris, *Movements*, p.36.

4. See "Comrade's Tribute to General G. M. Sorrell," by C. W. Reynolds, *Atlanta Journal*, August 17, 1901.

5. John Gordon (1832–1904) of Georgia graduated from the University of Georgia, practiced law and was a coal mine superintendent in Alabama when the war began. Appointed brigadier general in November, 1862, he was named major general in May, 1864. His wife accompanied him on his campaigns, much to the chagrin of Early, who wished she would be captured. After the war, he served as U. S. Senator (Democrat), governor of Georgia and wrote *Reminiscences of the Civil War* in 1903. Boatner, *Dictionary*, p. 349.

6. Gilbert Maxey Sorrel (1838–1901) was appointed brigadier general in October, 1864 and commanded a Georgia brigade in Mahone's Division. At Hatcher's Run February 7, 1865, he was wounded in the chest. A merchant and businessman after the war, he authored *Recollections of a Confederate Staff Officer*. Boatner, *Dictionary*, p. 778. See also Reynolds, "Tribute to General G. M. Sorrell."

7. Harris, *Movements*, p. 37.

8. O. R., Series 1, Vol. XLVI, Part 1, p. 389.

9. Phillip Henry "Little Phil" Sheridan (1831–1888) of New York was appointed to the U.S. Military Academy from Ohio, graduating in 1853, thirty-fourth in a class of fifty-two. After a distinguished career in the Eastern Theater, Grant appointed him to command the Cavalry Corps of the Army of the Potomac in April, 1864. Voted "The Thanks of Congress" for his Shenandoah Valley Campaign which began August 7, 1864 and concluded with the decimation of Early's army at Waynesboro on March 2, 1865, Sheridan's actions were influential in bottling-up Lee at Appomattox. He remained in the army after the war and was promoted to full general in 1888. Sheridan

was described as five feet five inches tall with broad shoulders, squat, square head, and black hair. Boatner, *Dictionary*, pp. 747–8.

10. Harris, *Movements*, p. 38.

11. *Quitman Guards*, pp. 70–1.

12. Lieutenant Colonel James Henderson Duncan was thirty-five years of age when the battle of Fort Gregg was fought. L. W. Conerly, *Pike County*, p. 236. Harris, *Movements*, pp. 39–40.

13. General Nathaniel H. Harris, "The Defense of Battery Gregg," *Southern Historical Society Papers*, Volume VIII, (1880), p. 477. Conflicts appear in the various Fort Gregg reports; readers are left to draw their own conclusions as to which are the most accurate.

14. Harris, *Movements*, pp. 40–1.

15. For clarity, the fort next to Gregg is called "Whitworth" hereinafter.

16. John Gibbon (1827–1896) of Pennsylvania was appointed to the United States Military Academy from North Carolina, graduating in 1847, twentieth in a class of thirty-eight. He served in the Seminole War and then taught artillery at West Point. At Appomattox, he was one of the commissioners on the surrender. Three of his brothers fought for the South. After the war, he remained in the army and led the relief column at the Little Big Horn. In 1885, he retired with the rank of brigadier general and wrote *Personal Recollections of the Civil War* and *The Artillerist's Manual*. Boatner, *Dictionary*, pp. 340–1.

17. General Harris (who was in Fort Whitworth) in his "The Defense of Battery Gregg," *Southern Historical Society Papers*, Volume VIII, (1880), p. 477, disputes that bricks were thrown.

18. Buxton R. Conerly, "How Fort Gregg Was Defended," *Confederate Veteran*, Volume XV, Number 11, November, 1907) pp. 505–7.

19. Harris, "Defense of Battery Gregg, *SHSP*, Volume VIII, p. 478.

20. Thompson originally had "Twenty-ninth"; error is corrected here. Trudeau, *Out of the Storm*, p.64; Trudeau, *Last Citadel*, p. 383.

21. Martin G. Turner, corporal, Company F. Howell, *For Dixie Land*, Volume III, p. 2995. Another story about Turner is in Lightsey, *Veteran's Story*, pp. 15–16.

22. J. B. Thompson, "The Last Engagement of Lee's Army" as told to J. E. Gaskell, *Confederate Veteran*, Volume XXIX, Number 7 (July, 1921), pp. 261–2.

Thompson was born March 10, 1843 in Jasper County, Mississippi and enlisted in Company A of the Fortieth Mississippi in April, 1862. He later transferred to Company F, Sixteenth Mississippi. Yeary, *Reminiscences*, p. 746.

23. Lightsey originally wrote "Jayne"; error is corrected here. Lightsey, *Veteran's Story*, pp. 41–2.

Chapter 22

1. Boatner, *Dictionary*, pp. 22–23, 274–5, 723; McPherson, *Atlas*, pp. 211–12; Trudeau, *Appomattox Campaign* (Civil War Series), pp. 5–6, 14.

2. Harris, *Movements*, pp. 42–3.

3. Lightsey, *Veteran's Story*, p. 43.

4. Harris, *Movements*, p. 44.

5. William Tecumseh Sherman (1820–1891) of Ohio graduated the U. S. Military Academy in 1840, sixth in a class of forty-two. Sherman resigned the army during the

Mexican War to become a banker and practice law in California. Tired of civilian life, he re-applied for admission in the Army, but accepted superintendency of a military school in Alexandria, Louisiana upon the recommendation of friends in 1859. When Louisiana seceded, he resigned and re-enlisted in the U. S. Army, being appointed brigadier general in August, 1861 and major general in May, 1862. Later that same year, he convinced Grant not to resign after the latter had been repeatedly mistreated by General Halleck during the campaign against Corinth after the Battle of Shiloh. Sherman commanded the XV Corps during the last of the Vicksburg Campaign and succeeded Grant as commander of the Military District of the Mississippi, thus becoming director of military operations in the West. He is most remembered for his Atlanta Campaign and his "March to the Sea" through Georgia. After the war, Sherman was promoted to lieutenant general in July, 1866 and succeeded Grant as Commander in Chief of the Army in 1869, a position Sherman held until November 1, 1883. He retired from the army in 1884 and died February 14, 1891. Boatner, *Dictionary*, pp. 750–1.

The writer is most likely referring to George Henry Thomas (1816–1870). Thomas was born in Virginia and graduated twelfth in a class of forty-two in 1840 from the U. S. Military Academy. After teaching artillery and cavalry at West Point, he served as a major under Albert Sidney Johnston and Robert E. Lee in the Second U. S. Cavalry. Unlike Lee, Thomas remained in the U. S. Army when Virginia seceded and was appointed brigadier general in August, 1861 and promoted to major general of volunteers in April of 1862. At Chickamauga, he gained the nickname "Rock of Chickamauga" and was named brigadier in the regular U. S. Army in October, 1863, then major general in December, 1864. For his actions at Nashville and Franklin, Tennessee, he received the rare "Thanks of Congress." Boatner, *Dictionary*, p. 836.

Quitman Guards, p. 72.

6. Harris, *Movements*, p. 44.

7. Lightsey, *Veteran's Story*, p. 44.

8. Harris, *Movements*, pp. 44–5.

9. Lightsey, *Veteran's Story*, p. 44.

10. After the war, Thompson moved to Fort Worth, Texas. How he spent the remainder of his life and his date of death is not known. Yeary, *Reminiscences*, p. 746.

Thompson, *Confederate Veteran*, Volume 29, Number 7, p. 262.

Postscripts

1. Rowland, *Military History*, p. 465; Krick, *Lee's Colonels*, p. 43.

2. Conerly, "How Fort Gregg was Defended,"*Confederate Veteran*, p.506.

3. *Quitman Guards*, pp. XIII-XIV; L. W. Conerly, *Pike County*, pp. 111, 178.

4. Sheriff Tom R. Green, interview by editor, Jasper County Courthouse, Bay Springs, MS, March 6, 2000.

5. Karen Taylor to editor, April 13, 1999.

6. Boatner, *Dictionary*, p. 276; Roberts and Moneyhon, *Portraits*, p. 357; Rowland, *Mississippi*, Volume I, pp. 700–1.

7. Krick, *Lee's Colonels*, p. 137; Ott, "Diary Kirkpatrick," p. 19; Holt, *Mississippi Rebel*, ed. Cockrell and Ballard, p. 257.

8. Hardy, *No Compromise*, pp. 104–5, 206–18, 229–41, 244–50, 268–90, 306; Low-

ery Metts, "History: Hardy Endorsement—No Hardy County," *Meridian Star*, February 12, 1972, Section D, p. 3.

9. Roberts and Moneyhon, *Portraits*, p. 361

10. John W. Kirkpatrick to Dr. J. Evetts Haley, October 23, 1931, Center for American History, University of Texas at Austin.

11. John South Lewis to editor, April 9, 1999; "More on Oldest Continuous Business," *Mississippi History Newsletter*, June 1999, p. 2.

12. Rowland, Volume III: *Biographical Sketches*, p. 450; John South Lewis to editor, April 9, 1999; Norman Gillis, Jr. to editor, November 15, 1999.

13. Lewis Papers.

14. Davis, *Lightsey Family History*, pp. 66–8.

15. Winschel, "Posey's Gettysburg, Part I," p. 8, footnote 6; Kitty Day Papers.

16. Boatner, *Dictionary*, p. 849.

17. Fatherree, "Jasper Grays," p. 48.

18. Rowland, *Official Register 1912*, p. 198; "Obituary: The Late Jerome B. Yates," undated newspaper clipping, Yates Letters.

BIBLIOGRAPHY

PRIMARY SOURCES:

Mississippi Department of Archives and History

Crawford, John Berryman. Letters (Z/1774).
Harris, General Nathaniel H. Letter to General William H. Mahone, August 2, 1866.
Jones, Captain A. K. Letter.
King, Judge Bee. Unpublished notes.
Kirkland, Jesse Ruebel. Papers (Z/482).
Lomax, Chaplain Alexander A. Journal.
Powers, J. L. Scrapbook. "History of Mississippi Troops." (Z/742).
Records Group 9, Volume 132.
Wilson, J. J. Papers (Z/677).

University of North Carolina at Chapel Hill

Lewis, Harry. Papers (1222–Z), Southern Historical Collection.

Official Compilations

Records Group 109, "Letters Received by the Confederate Secretary of War," National Archives, Washington, D. C.
United States War Department, *The War of the Rebellion: A Compilation of the Official Records of the Union and Confederate Armies*, seventy volumes in 128 parts, Washington, DC: U. S. Government Printing Office, 1880–1901.

Private Collections

Day, Mrs. John W. (Kitty). Papers, "Carnot Posey, Brigadier-General, Anderson's Division, Hill's Corps, Army of Northern Virginia." Terrence J. Winschel Collection.
Dickson, Hugh Carroll. Letters. Mrs. Glenn (Karen B.) Taylor Collection.
Hardy, William Harris. Civil War Letters to Sallie Johnson Hardy. Hardy Family Collection and McCain Library and Archives, University of Southern Mississippi.

University of Texas at Austin

Kirkpatrick, James J. Civil War diary, Heartman Collection, Center for American History.

Yates, Jerome B. Letters, Eugene C. Barker Library.

Tulane University

"The Story of the Sixteenth Mississippi Regiment," Special Collections, Howard-Tilton Memorial Library.

BOOKS:

Allan, William. *History of the Campaign of General T. J.(Stonewall) Jackson in the Shenandoah Valley of Virginia from November 4, 1861 to June 17, 1862.* Philadelphia: J. B. Lippincott & Company, 1912. Reprint, Dayton, Ohio: Morningside House, Inc., 1991.

Constitution, By-Laws and Catalogue of Members of the Christian Philanthropic Society of Posey's Brigade, Anderson's Virginia, Composed of Mississippians, Organized March 28,1863. Richmond: MacFarlane & Fergusson, 1863. Photocopy (provided by Colonel William Frazier Furr).

Bailey, Ronald H. *The Bloodiest Day: The Battle of Antietam.* Alexandria, VA: Time-Life Books, 1984.

Baltz, Louis J. III. *The Battle of Cold Harbor: May 28–June 13, 1864.* Lynchburg, VA: H. E. Howard, Inc., 1994.

Bearss, Margie Riddle. *Sherman's Forgotten Campaign: The Meridian Expedition.* Baltimore: The Gateway Press, 1987.

Boatner, Mark Mayo III. *The Civil War Dictionary.* New York: Vintage Books, 1959.

Boykin, Alva Dairel. *Boykins: Limbs and Stems, Smith County, Mississippi Boykins.* Forest, MS: privately published, 1996.

Brieger, James F. *Hometown, Mississippi,* second edition. city unknown: privately published, 1980.

Calkins, Chris M. *The Battles of Appomattox Station and Appomattox Court House: April 8–9, 1865.* Lynchburg, VA: H. E. Howard, Inc., 1987.

————. *The Final Bivouac: The Surrender Parade at Appomattox and the Disbanding of the Armies, April 10–May 20, 1865.* Lynchburg, VA: H. E. Howard, Inc., 1988.

Catton, Bruce. *America Goes to War.* New York: MJF Books, 1958.

————. *The Army of the Potomac: Mr. Lincoln's Army.* Garden City, NY: Doubleday & Company, Inc., 1951.

————. *The Army of the Potomac: Glory Road.* Garden City, NY: Doubleday & Co., 1952.

————. *The Army of the Potomac: The Stillness at Appomattox.* Garden City, NY: Doubleday & Co., 1953.

Cavanaugh, Michael and William Marvel. *The Petersburg Campaign: The Battle of the Crater, "The Horrid Pit," June 25–August 6, 1864.* Lynchburg, VA: H. E. Howard, Inc., 1989.

Christ, Elwood W. *The Struggle for the Bliss Farm at Gettysburg, July 2 and 3, 1863.* Baltimore: Butternut and Blue, 1994.

Clemmer, Gregg S. *Valor in Gray: Recipients of the Confederate Medal of Honor.* Staunton, VA: The Hearthside Publishing Company, 1998.

Conerly, Luke Ward. *Resources of Pike/Walthall Counties, Mississippi, 1798–1910, Containing a Complete Reprint of the History of Pike County, Mississippi, 1798–1876.* Easley, SC: Southern Historical Press, 1978.

Davis, Burke. *To Appomattox: Nine April Days, 1865.* New York: Rinehart & Company, Inc., 1959.

Davis, Patricia Lightsey. *The Lightsey Family History.* Daleville, MS: privately published, 1990.

Dowdey, Clifford. *The Seven Days: The Emergence of Lee.* Lincoln, NE: University of Nebraska Press, 1964, 1993.

Evans, General Clement A. *Confederate Military History* (Volumes I–XII). Atlanta: Confederate Publishing Co., 1899.

Furguson, Ernest B. *Chancellorsville 1863: The Souls of the Brave.* New York: Vintage Books, 1992.

————. *Murder Not War: Cold Harbor, 1864.* New York: Alfred A. Knopf, 2000.

Foote, Shelby. *The Civil War: A Narrative* (Volumes I–III). New York: Random House, 1958.

Gallagher, Gary W. *The Battle of Chancellorsville.* Eastern National Park and Monument Association, Civil War Series, 1995.

————. editor. *The Spotsylvania Campaign.* Chapel Hill, NC: University of North Carolina Press, 1998.

Gosse, Edmond, et al. *All There is to Know: Readings from the Illustrious Eleventh Edition of the Encyclopaedia Britannica.* Edited by Alexander Coleman and Charles Simmons, New York: Simon & Shuster, 1994.

Graham, Martin F. and George F. Skoch. *Mine Run: A Campaign of Lost Opportunities.* Lynchburg, VA: H. E. Henderson, Inc., 1987.

Greene, A. Wilson. *The Second Battle of Manassas.* Eastern National Park and Monument Association, Civil War Series, 1996.

Grimsley, Mark and Brooks D. Simpson. *Gettysburg: A Battlefield Guide.* Lincoln, NE: University of Nebraska Press, 1999.

Hardy, William Harris and Toney A. *No Compromise With Principle.* New York: American Book-Stratford Press, Inc., 1946.

Harris, Nathaniel Harrison. *Movements of the Confederate Army in Virginia and the part taken by the Nineteenth Mississippi Regiment: From the Diary of General Nathaniel H. Harris.* Duncansby, MS: W. M. Harris, 1901. Photocopy (obtained from Texas Department of Archives and History).

Henderson, William D. *The Road to Bristoe Station: Campaigning With Lee and Meade, August 1–October 20, 1863.* Lynchburg, VA: H. E. Howard, Inc., 1987.

Hennessey, John J. *Return to Bull Run: The Campaign and Battle of Second Manassas.* New York: Touchstone (Simon & Schuster), 1993.

Historical Sketch of the Quitman Guards, Company E, Sixteenth Mississippi Regiment, Harris' Brigade, by One of the Quitman Guards, A. New Orleans: Isaac T. Hinton, Printer, 1888. Photocopy (obtained from Mississippi Department of Archives and History).

Holt, David E. *A Mississippi Rebel in the Army of Northern Virginia: The Civil War Memoirs of Private David Holt.* Edited by Thomas D. Cockrell and Michael B. Ballard. Baton Rouge: Louisiana State University Press, 1995.

Horn, John. *The Destruction of Weldon Railroad, Deep Bottom, Globe Tavern, and Reams Station, August 14–25, 1864*. Lynchburg, VA: H. E. Howard, Inc., 1991.

———. *The Petersburg Campaign: June 1864–April 1865*. Conshohocken, PA: Combined Books, Inc., 1993.

Howell, H. Grady, Jr. *For Dixie Land I'll Take My Stand! A Muster Listing of All Known Mississippi Confederate Soldiers, Sailors and Marines*(Volumes I–IV). Madison, MS: Chickasaw Bayou Press, 1998.

Jamison, Perry D. *Death in September: The Antietam Campaign*. Fort Worth, TX: Ryan Place Publishers, 1995.

Killian, Olivia Skaggs. *Boykins: Branches and Roots*. Tupelo, MS: Richardson Publishing Company, 1979.

Kinard, Jeff. *The Battle of the Crater*. Fort Worth, TX: Ryan Place Publishers, 1995.

Krick, Robert K. *Lee's Colonels: A Biographical Register of the Field Officers of the Army of Northern Virginia*, fourth edition, revised. Dayton, OH: Morningside House, Inc., 1992.

———. *Conquering the Valley: Stonewall Jackson at Port Republic*. New York: William Morrow and Company, Inc., 1996.

Lightsey, Ada Christine. *The Veteran's Story*. Meridian, MS: publisher unknown, 1899. Photocopy (obtained from Mississippi Department of Archives and History).

Long, E. B., with Barbara Long. *The Civil War Day by Day: An Almanac, 1861–1865*. New York: Da Capo Press, Inc., 1971.

McPherson, James M. *The Battle Cry of Freedom*. New York: Oxford University Press, 1988.

———. *Gettysburg*. Atlanta: Turner Publishing Company, 1993.

———. editor. *The Atlas of the Civil War*. New York: MacMillan, 1994.

———. *Drawn With The Sword: Reflections on the American Civil War*. New York: Oxford University Press, 1996.

———. *For Cause and Comrades: Why Men Fought in the Civil War*. New York: Oxford University Press, 1997.

McWhiney, Grady. *Battle in the Wilderness: Grant Meets Lee*. Fort Worth, TX: Ryan Place Publishers, 1995.

Martin, David G. *The Bull Run Campaign, July–August 1862*. Conshohocken, PA: Combined Books, Inc., 1997.

Marvel, William, and Donald Pfanz. *The Battle of Fredericksburg*. Eastern National Park and Monument Association, Civil War Series, 1993.

Matter, William D. *If It Takes All Summer: The Battle of Spotsylvania*. Chapel Hill, NC: University of North Carolina Press, 1988.

Miller, J. Michael. *The North Anna Campaign: "Even to Hell Itself": May 21–6, 1864*. Lynchburg, VA: H. E. Howard, Inc., 1989.

Miller, William J. *The Battles for Richmond, 1862*. Eastern National Park and Monument Association, Civil War Series, 1996.

O'Shea, Richard. *Battle Maps of the Civil War*. Tulsa, OK: Council Oaks Books, 1992.

Power, J. Tracy. *Lee's Miserables: Life in the Army of Northern Virginia from the Wilderness to Appomattox*. Chapel Hill, NC: University of North Carolina Press, 1998.

Priest, John Michael. *Antietam: The Soldier's Battle*. New York: Oxford University Press, 1989.

————. *Nowhere to Run: The Wilderness, May 4th and 5th, 1864.* Shippensburg, PA: White Mane Publishing Company, Inc., 1995.

————. *Victory Without Triumph: The Wilderness, May 6th and 7th, 1864.* Shippensburg, PA: White Mane Publishing Company, Inc., 1996.

Rhea, Gordon C. *The Battles of Wilderness and Spotsylvania.* Eastern National Park and Monument Association, Civil War Series, 1995.

————. *The Battle of the Wilderness, May 5–6, 1864.* Baton Rouge: Louisiana State University Press, 1997.

————. *The Battles for Spotsylvania Court House and the Road to Yellow Tavern, May 7–12, 1864.* Baton Rouge: Louisiana State University Press, 1997.

————.*To the North Anna River: Grant and Lee, May 13–25, 1864.* Baton Rouge: Louisiana State University Press, 2000.

Rhodes, James Ford, et al. *The Causes of the Civil War.* Edited by Kenneth M. Stampp. New York: Simon & Schuster, 1991.

Roberts, Bobby, and Carl Moneyhon. *Portraits of Conflict: A Photographic History of Mississippi in the Civil War.* Fayetteville, AR: University of Arkansas Press, 1993.

Robertson, James I. Jr. *Common Soldier.* Eastern National Park and Monument Association, Civil War Series, 1994.

Rowland, Dunbar. *Mississippi: Comprising Sketches of Counties, Towns, Events, Institutions, and Persons Arranged in Cyclopedic Form* (Volumes I–III). Atlanta: Southern Historical Publishing Association, 1907. Reprint, Spartanburg, SC: The Reprint Publishers, 1976.

————. *Mississippi Official and Statistical Register of Mississippi 1908 and Military History of Mississippi.* Nashville, Tennessee: Press of the Brandon Printing Company, 1908. Reprint, Salem Massachusetts: Higginston Book Company, 1984.

————. *Mississippi Official and Statistical Register of Mississippi 1912 and Military History of Mississippi.* Nashville, TN: Press of the Brandon Printing Company, 1912.

Sears, Stephen W. *The Landscape Turned Red: The Battle of Antietam.* New York: Ticknor & Fields, 1983.

————. *To the Gates of Richmond: The Peninsula Campaign.* New York: Ticknor & Fields, 1992.

————. *Chancellorsville.* Boston: Houghton Mifflin Company, 1996.

Smith, Carl. *Gettysburg, 1863: High Tide of the Confederacy.* London: Osprey Publishing, Ltd., 1998.

————. *Chancellorsville, 1863: Jackson's Lightning Strike.* London: Osprey Publishing, Ltd., 1998.

————. *Fredericksburg, 1862: "Clear the Way."* London: Osprey Publishing, Ltd., 1999.

Sommers, Richard J. *Richmond Redeemed: The Siege at Petersburg.* Garden City, NY: Doubleday & Company, 1981.

Stackpole, Edward J. *The Fredericksburg Campaign: Drama on the Rappahannock,* Second Edition. Harrisburg, PA: Stackpole Books, 1991.

Sutherland, Daniel E. *Fredericksburg and Chancellorsville: The Dare Mark Campaign.* Lincoln, NE: University of Nebraska Press, 1998.

Symonds, Craig L. *Gettysburg: A Battlefield Atlas.* Baltimore: The Nautical & Aviation Publishing Company of America, 1992.

Tanner, Robert G. *Stonewall in the Valley: Thomas J. "Stonewall" Jackson's Shenandoah Valley Campaign, Spring 1862.* Mechanicsburg, PA: Stackpole Books, 1996.

Thomas, Emory M. *The Confederate Nation: 1861–1865*. New York: Harper & Row, Publishers, 1979.

Tischler, Allan L. *The History of the Harpers Ferry Cavalry Expedition, September 14 & 15, 1862*. Winchester, VA: Five Cedars Press, 1993.

Trudeau, Noah Andre. *Bloody Roads South: The Wilderness to Cold Harbor, May–June 1864*, Boston: Little, Brown and Company, 1989.

———. *The Last Citadel: Petersburg, Virginia, June 1864–April 1865*. Boston: Little, Brown and Company, 1991.

———. *Out of the Storm: The End of the Civil War, April–June 1865*. Boston: Little, Brown, and Company, 1994.

———. *The Campaign to Appomattox*. Eastern National Park and Monument Association, Civil War Series, 1995.

———. *The Siege of Petersburg*. Eastern National Park and Monument Association, Civil War Series, 1995.

Varhola, Michael J. *Everyday Life in the Civil War*. Cincinnati: Writer's Digest Books, 1999.

Wiley, Bell Irvin. *The Life of Johnny Reb: The Common Soldier of the Confederacy*. Baton Rouge: Louisiana State University Press, 1943 (renewed 1978).

Woodhead, Henry. editor. *Echoes of Glory: Arms and Equipment of the Confederacy*. Alexandria, VA: Time-Life Books, 1996.

———. editor. *Soldier Life*. Time-Life Voices Series, Richmond: Time-Life Books, 1996.

Works Progress Administration, Federal Writers Project. *Mississippi: The WPA Guide to the Magnolia State*, 1938 Reprint, Jackson, MS: University Press of Mississippi, 1988.

———. *History of Smith County, Mississippi*, 1935.

———. *Source Records of Jasper County, Mississippi, Will Abstracts, 1855–1914*. Edited by Jean Strickland and Patricia N. Edwards, privately published, 1995.

Yeary, Miss Mamie. *Reminiscences of the Boys in Gray, 1861–1865*. McGregor, TX: publisher unknown, 1912. Reprint, Dayton, OH: Morningside Publishing, 1986.

PERIODICALS:

Allen, William. "Jackson's Valley Campaign." *Southern Historical Society Papers*, New Series, Number V, Volume XLIII (September 1920).

Anderson, R. H. "General R. H. Anderson's Report of the Battle of Gettysburg." *Southern Historical Society Papers*, Volume III, Number 1 (January 1877), pp. 49–54.

Bartlett, Napier. "Defense of Fort Gregg." *Southern Historical Society Papers*, Volume III, Number 2 (February 1877), pp. 82–6.

"Battle at Fort Gregg: Louisiana Survivors Tell the Story of the Fight, The." *Southern Historical Society Papers*, Volume XXVIII (1900), pp. 265–7.

Brown, Colonel Campbell. "Notes on Ewell's Division in the Campaign of 1862." *Southern Historical Society Papers*, Volume XI, Number 2 (February 1883), pp. 255–61.

Bullock, Ronald E. "Last Ditch Rebel Stand at Petersburg." *America's Civil War*, Volume 10, Number 2 (May 1997), p. 30.

Chamberlain, General J. L. "The Last Salute of the Army of Northern Virginia." *Southern Historical Society Papers*, Volume XXXII, Number XLII, pp. 355–63.

"Colonel Thomas Ringland Stockdale." *Confederate Veteran*, Volume VII, Number 4 (April 1899), pp. 176–7.

Conerly, Buxton, R. "How Fort Gregg Was Defended." *Confederate Veteran*, Volume XV, Number 11, pp. 505–7.

Day, Mrs. John W.(Kitty). "Brigadier General Carnot Posey." *The United Daughters of the Confederacy Magazine*, (August 1988), pp. 26–7.

"Down the Valley After Stonewall's Quartermaster." *Southern Historical Society Papers*, Volume XV, Number 11, pp. 505–7.

Elmore, Thomas L. "Torrid Heat and Blinding Rain: A Meteorological and Astronomical Chronology of the Gettysburg Campaign." *The Gettysburg Magazine*, Issue Number 13 (July 1995), pp. 7–21.

"Flag of the Sixteenth Mississippi Regiment," *Confederate Veteran*, Volume XXVI, Number 2 (February 1918), pp. 75–6 (reprint from *The Natchez Courier*, July 19, 1862).

Gambrell, Robert. "Fighting at Spotsylvania Court House." *Confederate Veteran*, Volume XVII, Number 5 (May 1909), p. 225.

Gaskell, J. E. "Last Engagement of Lee's Army" (as told by J. B. Thompson). *Confederate Veteran*, Volume XXIX, Number 7, pp. 261–2.

Gillespie, R. K. "Sixteenth Mississippi Regiment and General Lee." *Confederate Veteran*, Volume II, Number 11 (November 1903), p. 495.

Harris, General N. H. "Defense of Battery Gregg." *Southern Historical Society Papers*, Volume VIII, pp. 475–88.

———. "Report of General Harris Concerning an Incident at the Battle of the Wilderness." *Southern Historical Society Papers*, Volume VII, Number 3 (March 1879), p. 131.

———. "Lee to the Rear: The Incident with Harris' Mississippi Brigade." *Southern Historical Society Papers*, Volume VIII, Number 1 (January 1880), p. 105.

Hemingway, Al. "One Day at Chancellorsville." *America's Civil War*, February, 1996.

"Henry W. Evans." *Confederate Veteran*, Volume XXV, Number 5 (May 1912), p. 237.

"History of Quitman Rifles." *Southern Historical Society Papers*, Volume XXXIV (1906), pp. 239–42.

Irvine, Miss Mary A. "Letter From Miss Mary A. Levine." *Confederate Veteran*, Volume XXVI, Number 1 (January 1918), p. 16.

Jones, Captain A. K. "The Defense of Fort Gregg: One of the Bloodiest Battles of the War Between the States." Mississippi Department of Archives and History and *Southern Historical Society Papers*, Volume XXXI (1903), pp. 56–60.

Jones, J. William. "Reminiscences of the Army of Northern Virginia: Jackson's Valley Campaign, The Capture of Winchester and Rout of Banks' Army." *Southern Historical Society Papers*, Volume IX (May 1881), p. 185.

Kernan, Michael. "The Object at Hand." *Smithsonian Magazine*, Volume XX, Issue 2 (May 1989), pp. 24–7.

Lane, James H. "The Defense of Battery Gregg-General Lane's Reply to General Harris." *Southern Historical Society Papers*, Volume IX, Number 3 (March 1881), pp. 102–6.

———. "Defense of Fort Gregg-Brigadier-General Lane's Official Report." *Southern Historical Society Papers*, Volume III, Number 1 (January 1877), p. 19–28.

LeCand, Fred J. V. "An Eyewitness to Lee's Offer to Lead."*Confederate Veteran*, Volume II, Number 9 (September 1903), p. 393.

Lee, Robert E. "Battle of Chancellorsville-Report of General R. E. Lee." *Southern Historical Society Papers*, Volume III, Number 5 (May/June 1877), pp. 230–43.

McCabe, Captain W. Gordon. "Defense of Petersburg: Action of Twenty-Second of June." *Southern Historical Society Papers*, Volume II, Number 6 (December 1876), pp. 257–306.

McCaleb, Captain E. Howard. "Featherston-Posey-Harris Mississippi Brigade." *Southern Historical Society Papers*, Volume XXXII (1914), pp. 329–37.

McGowan, General Samuel. "McGowan's Report of the Wilderness and Spotsylvania Courthouse." *Southern Historical Society Papers*, Volume VI, Number 4 (October 1878), pp. 149–50.

McIntosh, Colonel David Gregg. "The Campaign of Chancellorsville." *Southern Historical Society Papers*, New Series, Number II, Volume XL (September 1915) , pp. 65–6.

Miller, Michael J. "Along the North Anna." *Civil War Times Illustrated* (November 1987), pp. 28–34, 45.

Minor, H. A. "Surrender of Mahone's Division."*Confederate Veteran*, Volume XXII, Number 7, (July 1914).

"Mississippi Troops Who Served in Virginia, 1861–1865." *Southern Historical Society Papers*, Volume XXXV, Number 5, pp. 58–9.

Old, William W. "Trees Whittled Down at Horseshoe." *Southern Historical Society Papers*, Volume XXXIII (1905), pp. 16–24.

Owen, Lieutenant Colonel William Miller. "The Artillery Defenders of Fort Gregg." *Southern Historical Society Papers*, Volume XX (1892), pp. 65–71.

———. "The Artillery Defenders of Fort Gregg-A Correction." *Southern Historical Society Papers*, Volume XX (1892), p. 33.

"Parolees of the Army of Northern Virginia-Harris's Brigade." *Southern Historical Society Papers*, Volume XV (1887), pp. 328–9.

Posey, General Carnot. "Report of Brigadier-General C. Posey." *Southern Historical Society Papers*, Volume VIII, Number 6 (June 1880), p. 322.

Ramseur, Stephen D. "From the Spotsylvania Courthouse-Ramseur's Brigade." *Southern Historical Society Papers*, Volume XIII (1885), pp. 236–40.

Raus, Ed. "Hell's Half Acre: The Fight for the Bloody Angle, May 12, 1864." *Blue & Gray Magazine* (June–July 1984), pp. 40–57.

"Reverend A. A. Lomax." *Confederate Veteran*, Volume XVIII, Number 2 (February 1910), p. 80.

Richards, George. "Fort Gregg Again-A Surgeon's Defense of the Garrison." *Southern Historical Society Papers*, Volume XXXI (1903), pp. 370–2.

Skoch, George. "The Last Ditch." *Civil War Times Illustrated* (January 1989), pp. 12–18.

Stedman, Charles. "Battle at Reams Station." *Southern Historical Society Papers*, Volume XIX (January 1891), pp. 296–303.

Swisher, James K. "From the Wilderness to Cold Harbor." *Confederate Veteran*, Volume 3 (1999), pp. 30–4.

Talcott, Colonel T. M. R. "From Petersburg to Appomattox: Bridges That Were Burned." *Southern Historical Society Papers*, Volume XXXII (1904), pp. 67–72.

Thetford, R. B. "Commands Holding Fort Gregg." *Confederate Veteran*, Volume XXIX, Number 9, pp. 335–6.

Trinque, Bruce A. "Hancock's Well-Conducted Fizzle." *America's Civil War* (January 1997), pp. 42–9.

Venable, Charles S. and General N. H. Harris. "The Incident with Harris' Mississippi Brigade." *Southern Historical Society Papers*, Volume VIII, Number 3 (March 1880), pp. 105–10.

Wickham, W. C. "Battle of Reams Station-Report of General W. C. Wickham." *Southern Historical Society Papers*, Volume IX, Number 3 (March 1891), pp. 107–8.

Wilcox, Major General C. M. "Defense of Batteries Gregg and Whitworth and the Evacuation of Petersburg." *Southern Historical Society Papers*, Volume III, Number 7, (July 1877), pp. 18–33.

———."Battery Gregg-Reply to General N. H. Harris." *Southern Historical Society Papers*, Volume IX (March 1881), pp. 168–78.

Winschel, Terrence J. "The Gettysburg Experience of James J. Kirkpatrick." *The Gettysburg Magazine*, Issue Number Eight (January 1993), pp. 111–19.

———. "Posey's Brigade at Gettysburg, Part I." *The Gettysburg Magazine*, Issue Number Four (January 1991), pp. 7–15.

———. "Posey's Brigade at Gettysburg, Part II." *The Gettysburg Magazine*, Issues Number Five (July 1991), pp. 89–101.

NEWSPAPER ARTICLES:

H., J. D. "The Death Angle: War at its Worst" (as told by David E. Holt) *New Orleans Times-Democrat*, 1900. Photocopy (obtained from Mississippi Department of Archives and History).

Metts, Lowery. "History: Hardy Endorsement-No Hardy County." *Meridian Star*, February 12, 1992, Section D, p. 3. Photocopy.

"More on the Oldest Continuous Business in Mississippi." *Mississippi History Newsletter*, June, 1999.

Reynolds, C. W. "Comrade's Tribute to General G. M. Sorrell." *Atlanta Journal*, August 17, 1901.

Watts, A. T. "The Bloody Acute Angle."*Galveston News*, July 15, 1893. (Quoted in *Rev. Henry Cohen, A Modern Maccabean, Baltimore*, Press of the Friendenwald Co., 1897. [Reprint of article by an unknown private in Company A, 16th Mississippi.])

UNPUBLISHED MATERIAL:

Boykin, Stennis L. J. *Boykin Family Military History*. Panama City, FL: year unknown.

Fatherree, Dr. Ben H. "John Wall Fatherree and the Jasper Grays, 1861–1865."Jackson, MS: year unknown.

Furr, William Frazier. "The 19th Mississippi Infantry Regiment in the Civil Warr (With Notes about Company E and Private William Meek Furr). Montgomery, AL: 1996.

Ott, Eugene M. *The Civil War Diary of James J. Kirkpatrick*. Master of Arts Thesis, Texas A & M University, 1984.

INDEX